THE CONTROL AND VALUATION OF INVENTORIES

NATIONAL ASSOCIATION OF
COST ACCOUNTANTS

385 MADISON AVENUE

NEW YORK

PRINTED IN THE UNITED STATES OF AMERICA
BY J. J. LITTLE & IVES COMPANY, NEW YORK

FOREWORD

THE demands of the defense emergency have accentuated the wide general interest in inventory control and valuation, stressing the urgent need for a comprehensive and practical treatment of the subject. Recognizing this need, the National Board of N.A.C.A. authorized the preparation of this volume in October 1940, and it has taken a year of deliberate care in selecting and editing the material to complete the task.

The book is basically a revised compilation of articles published separately in previous *Bulletins* and *Year Books* of the Association, with the addition of several specially written and previously unpublished papers, providing a well-balanced and concise presentation.

As a matter of policy throughout the twenty-one years of its existence, N.A.C.A. publications have dealt largely with case studies. Over fifteen hundred articles, covering a wide range of industrial accounting problems, have been published during that time. Many of these are out of print, and even where complete files are available it is not simple to locate specific information, although an excellent topical index is provided. These considerations point definitely to the value of an authoritative book dealing with this important subject. The material is essentially of the case-study type, drawn from diversified and important industries, presenting a variety of viewpoints, prepared by outstanding, practical, industrial accountants.

The book includes an adequate index and a useful bibliography; it will serve excellently as an advanced text and as a reference manual.

The Association is indebted to those whose original articles provide the substance of the book, and special acknowledgment is due Messrs. Samuel J. Broad of Peat, Marwick, Mitchell & Co. and Edward A. Kracke of Haskins & Sells for permission to include previously unpublished manuscripts on inventory valuation; and to Mr. George V. Fortune of The Reynolds Metals Co. for permission to include his previously unpublished article on uniform inventory instruction.

A special word of thanks goes to Professor Wyman P. Fiske of Massachusetts Institute of Technology, our National Director in charge of Publications, upon whose recommendation this project was undertaken, and under whose direction the book has been compiled. He has been assisted by Dr. Raymond P. Marple, Director of the Research and Technical Service Department, who has borne the brunt of the patient and meticulous editing which is inevitable in the preparation of such a publication.

VICTOR H. STEMPF
National President, 1940-41.

CONTRIBUTORS

Samuel J. Broad, Partner, Peat, Marwick, Mitchell & Co., New York, N. Y.

Russell F. Brockmiller, Cost Accountant, Fred Sanders, Detroit, Mich.

N. Madison Cartmell, Assistant to the President, General Cable Corporation, New York, N. Y.

Elson P. Dolliver, Industrial Engineer, R. Wallace & Sons Manufacturing Company, Wallingford, Conn.

William R. Donaldson, Partner, Miller, Donaldson & Co., New York, N. Y.

J. Ralph Fenton, Assistant Controller, Pennsylvania Liquor Control Board, Harrisburg, Pa.

Wyman P. Fiske, Professor of Accounting and Director, Sponsored Fellowship Program, Massachusetts Institute of Technology, Boston, Mass.

Stanley G. H. Fitch, Partner, Patterson, Teele & Dennis, Boston, Mass.

George V. Fortune, Supervisor of Accounting Systems and Methods, Reynolds Metals Company, Richmond, Va.

Earl W. Graham, General Auditor, Gulf Oil Corporation, Pittsburgh, Pa.

Frederic W. Kilduff, Assistant Professor of Accounting, School of Commerce, Accounts and Finance, New York University, New York, N. Y.

Edward A. Kracke, Partner, Haskins & Sells, New York, N. Y.

M. A. Lause, Assistant Factory Manager, Inland Manufacturing Division, General Motors Corporation, Dayton, Ohio

Sam A. Marsh, Assistant Professor of Accounting, Washington University, St. Louis, Mo.

George Nairn, Material Control Supervisor, Bridgeport Brass Company, Bridgeport, Conn.

Clarence B. Nickerson, Assistant Controller, Greenfield Tap and Die Corporation, Greenfield, Mass.

George W. Rood, Tabulating Machine Division, Remington Rand, Inc., Boston, Mass.

W. C. Skuce, Supervisor of Inventory Control, General Electric Company, Schenectady, N. Y.

H. T. Warshow, Vice President and Controller, National Lead Company, New York, N. Y.

C. J. Wibbelsman, Control Manager, United States Rubber Company, Eau Claire, Wis.

Clifford G. Wood, Staff, Lybrand, Ross Brothers & Montgomery, Rockford, Ill.

TABLE OF CONTENTS

INTRODUCTION

By Wyman P. Fiske

IT hardly seems necessary to defend the importance of inventories and inventory problems in modern business. Inventories have been called the "graveyard of American business" because they have so frequently been the prime cause of business failures. Either they have been allowed to grow to unwieldy and impossible size, with consequent loss of liquidity and impaired current position; they have contained an ill-assortment of poorly chosen or obsolete goods which have suffered tragic losses in value or are quite unsalable; or price speculations have been undertaken with disastrous results. In the typical industrial balance sheet, inventories of various kinds make up fifty per cent or more of the important current asset classification. Mercantile concerns frequently show over half of all their assets in this one form. Under conditions of style and design competition the risks attached to an investment in inventory is tremendous. Great judgment is required to manage such an investment wisely, and with profit rather than loss. There is little wonder that business managers and accountants have given great thought to the development of better inventory policies and control. Fortunately, with many minds at work upon the problem, progress has been made, both in the analysis of the problem and in the devising and operation of control plans.

The Inventory and Profit Determination

The effect and importance of inventory values in profit determination are elementary accounting concepts understood (though not always appreciated) by every accounting student. Every dollar added to or subtracted from the total value of the inventory is reflected in like amount in the profit and loss account. Indeed, the reality of the profit reported in the income account and reflected in surplus depends upon the validity of the inventory values shown in the balance sheet. Much of the industrial accountant's work has to

I

do with the determination of sound values for inventory items for use in determining profits. But the soundness of his routines and the values resulting therefrom depend upon the soundness of his policy decisions as to the bases for valuation. There is a wide range of choice for such bases, with marked variations in resulting value and profit depending upon the choice. His decisions go straight back to an understanding of the cost concept and to the necessity of different concepts for different analytical purposes. Not infrequently the values determined by his normal routines prove unsatisfactory for profit purposes and he is forced to give recognition to market conditions. In this area, too, much progress has been made in an understanding of the problems involved and in the development of procedures which will produce sound results.

Management versus Control

The idea of control implies regulation within predetermined limits. In business it is the function of management to set the direction and the limits within which it is the function of control to keep the business operating. This applies to inventories just as much as it does to sales, to labor or to finance. There must be an inventory policy set up by management if there is to be control. It is a total lack of such policy rather than merely a lack of control which explains many business failures attributed to inventories.

The management of inventories is a difficult and complex problem demanding the highest capacities of the managing group. Sound organization requires recognition of this and provision for responsibility for the determination of inventory policies. Because almost every division of the business is affected, the task is frequently assigned to an inventory committee which includes representation of the sales, production and controller's departments. Certain phases of the problems may even be decided by the board of directors, as in the case of companies using highly speculative raw materials. Details of the development of inventory policy can be left to responsible individuals in different divisions, but the broad outlines and limits are a top-management problem that cannot be delegated without great peril to the business.

The contrast between management and control of inventories is sharp but obvious. Management of the inventory is concerned with development of policy as to size and make-up. Both the total quantity and the assortment making up the total will change from time to time with changing conditions, as demand fluctuates or as economic or competitive risks change. Under some conditions raw materials may be built up; under others it may be desirable to reduce drastically one portion of the line while allowing the rest to increase equally. With all these things management of the inventory is concerned. Once the policy has been established, it becomes the problem of control to make certain that the desired inventory is maintained and that undue size or lack of balance do not arise. Management of the inventory is an administrative problem; control is an executive problem in which the industrial accountant must inevitably play an important part, for it is he who accumulates the data and makes the analyses which reveal conditions and trends. He does not control, for that is a line function. He does provide the factual basis for control, without which control is impossible in a complex situation.

Classification of Control Problems

To those whose approach to business has been through financial analysis, inventory control is a problem of the size of the inventory. Actually the problem of size is the simplest phase of inventory control. More difficult and perhaps of even greater importance is the problem of the make-up of the inventory. Industrial inventories are usually complex, being composed of thousands of items of primary raw materials, goods in process of manufacture, finished goods held for sale, and a wide variety of supplies used in various stages of manufacture and in the sales and administrative activities. Not all these items move in the same direction at the same time. Good management calls for increases in some while others are being liquidated.

Although inventory control concerns itself broadly with the size and make-up of the inventories, such a classification is an oversimplification of the problem. It is difficult to make a simple analysis of the several areas involved because of the inter-relations of the elements. One classification approaches the problem from the angle of the major sections of the inventory.

Raw materials
Goods in process
Finished goods
Supplies

Another attack cuts across these sections and considers the type of problem which can arise in each.

> Over-all size of inventory
> Make-up of inventory
>> Sections of inventory
>>> Raw material
>>> Goods in process
>>> Finished goods
>>> Supplies
>> Individual items
> Seasonal problems
> Problems arising from economic and other fluctuations
> Obsolescence and spoilage

Preliminaries to Control

In all these problems the approach to control is fundamentally the same, though the technique will vary widely according to conditions. Control presupposes the establishment of a policy and limits within which the inventory is to be kept. There must then be accumulated data showing actual conditions and trends, both related to the established policy. Responsibility for the various sections of the inventory must be established and the accumulation and analysis of data must be in terms of individual responsibilities in order that a finger may be pointed at the persons producing the result. Finally, the control reports must be sufficiently timely to make possible correction of undesirable trends before irreparable damage has been done. Later sections of this book will consider in detail problems relating to sections of the inventory in particular industries. These will reflect the many possible approaches to technique, but will also reveal upon analysis the common thread of a fundamentally similar control philosophy.

Inventory control is primarily concerned with quantities, whether the object of the control be the total inventory, some section or a single item. The quantity of any item (or of any section, or of the total) can be affected only through additions or subtractions. Subtractions from the total inventory are almost always in the form of sales. It is possible to put extra sales effort on items or parts of the inventory and so to affect the inventory quantity. This possibility is distinctly limited, however, for sales are closely related to economic conditions and can be increased only in relatively small proportion against the economic trend, and at high cost. It therefore follows that control efforts are largely directed to additions, which are purchases and manufacturing orders. Attack on sales (or substitute uses) is the only avenue open when the inventory of any item has become excessive, but the object of control is to prevent a condition of excessive quantity. Thus the usual attempt is to relate additions to expected or actual sales in such a way as to produce the desired inventory size. This is accomplished in one of four ways.

Four Methods of Controlling Inventory Additions

The first and most publicized method is the establishment of limits as to top quantity, minimum quantity and normal purchase (or manufacturing lot) quantity. With these set up, addition to the inventory becomes largely automatic. When the quantity reaches the low or order point an addition is initiated by the inventory clerk. Since an important problem is always the adjustment of the inventory size to the level of production, it is common to provide for a review of the requisition by a specified executive. It is intended, nevertheless, that the system shall operate largely automatically.

The second approach uses the popular budget concept. In the retail department store field a budgeted purchase allowance is established on the basis of expected sales, actual inventory quantities and budgeted end-of-period inventory. This open-to-buy usually applies to a department or section of the inventory. The buyer is left to his discretion as to purchases of individual items, but always with the limitation that he can buy nothing beyond his budget allowance until he has decreased his inventory to below the budgeted level, thereby creating a new open-to-buy. In the industrial field the plan presupposes a production budget for a given period. This budget must be in terms of specific items. The production budget is then analyzed to determine quantities of materials or parts required to make the established number of units of each item to be manufactured. The release of the production budget then serves as a release to the purchasing department to buy the definite quantities called for by the budget. Under this system, widely used in the automotive industry, the inventory becomes a bank or reserve to protect against failures in the purchasing routines or to make possible the use of economic purchase lots.

There is still a far larger volume of straight speculative purchasing than most business men would like to admit. Where the principal raw materials used are speculative and no hedge is available, there is little choice left to management. In such cases responsibility for purchasing these materials rests high up in the organization, even in some cases in the board of directors. Formal control is absent. Decision to buy or not to buy is based not only upon existing inventories and expected sales for the period ahead, but also upon market conditions over a longer period.

The final approach to control of additions has little application to inventories for it avoids any inventory. It is purchase to meet a definite sales or production order of an item not stocked. Most concerns find need for such purchases, either regularly as a matter of policy to avoid stocking slow-moving items or occasionally to meet a special unusual requirement.

Using one, and usually two or more, of these controls on purchases, different concerns have developed a variety of techniques and reports to meet the special needs of their organizations. Reports are prepared to cover key points in the particular inventory problem and are either submitted regularly to responsible and interested executives or are prepared and submitted when conditions seem to demand some action.

Determining the Amount of the Inventory

In order either to prepare a balance sheet or to determine profit or loss the dollar value of the inventory is an essential. This dollar value is the product of the number of individual items on hand multiplied by appropriate prices. Both of these elements involve problems and difficulties. Because of their individual importance the problems involved in the quantity of the inventory are set up as a separate section rather than included under the general head of valuation.

Most manufacturing concerns today place primary reliance upon a complete and detailed record of inventory transactions and continuous balances. Most department stores use the so-called retail method which maintains a running inventory balance at selling price but does not keep detail as to individual items. Many small merchants necessarily still rely on periodic physical inventory taking for the information essential to financial statements. Even department stores and manufacturers use the actual physical count as a check on the accuracy of their book records, and for more accurate information as to certain small items of supplies for which it is not economical or practical to keep detailed use records.

Book inventories require carefully planned and operated records of changes in inventory status. This means, in effect, adequate purchase and receiving records and detailed or summary recording of issue into production or use. These records may, and do, require many forms, each designed to the particular circumstances in which it is to be used. Information may be kept in quantities only (with periodic conversion into dollars), in dollars only, or in both dollars and units. The records and record keeping may be located in the actual storeroom, in an inventory section, or divided between the two with some duplication for the purpose of internal check.

Taking the Physical Inventory

The taking of a complete physical count of the inventories in a large and complex manufacturing enterprise or mercantile concern is a difficult problem, if it is to be well and accurately done. In the first place, time is usually of the essence. It is undesirable to disrupt operations for a longer period than is absolutely essential. A staff larger than is usually available in the accounting division is required. All this requires careful planning of each and every step in order that, once the actual count is started, everything may move expeditiously to a satisfactory conclusion.

Preliminary planning includes not only the organization and training of inventory crews but arrangement of the inventory to make sure that all items are counted, that there are no double counts, and that the counting is made as easy as possible. This means determining the required number of crews, with reserves, carefully training crew leaders, and providing them with adequate detailed instructions. Storerooms must be put in order, with all items brought into the open to avoid being overlooked, and arranged to facilitate accurate counting. Tally sheets must be made available and, in at least some cases, partially filled out. Attention must be given to the problem of goods received into the storeroom but not yet recorded in the financial records and of goods billed but still in transit. All these and other problems must be considered in advance and covered in the inventory instructions.

The most common approach to the actual inventory taking is by serially numbered inventory tags. Preliminary to the count, tags are attached to every inventory item. The count is then made and checked and the tags are taken up. When this procedure is completed, an examination and sorting of the tags by serial numbers will reveal the omission of any items from the inventory. Some companies use a divided tag, the first half of which is taken up by the counting crew. The second is used by the checkers to record their count as well as to make sure that no item is missed.

While many concerns using a continuous book inventory, as well as all those depending upon the periodic physical inventory, make the count all at one time at or very near to the end of the financial period, there is an increasing tendency to use the physical count merely as a test of the accuracy of the book inventory and to spread it throughout the entire period on a planned schedule. After experience with a book inventory this method can well approach an accuracy which has a smaller factor of error than is present in a complete physical inventory taken under pressure of limited time. Hence the use of a continuous physical check of the book inventory, taken under a regular routine, is accepted as producing a more reliable inventory than a simultaneous physical count where experience over a period of time shows adequate accuracy in the book inventory. A schedule is set up which will ensure covering every item in the inventory at least once (and preferably more often) during the financial period. Items are counted as they reach their low points and a comparison is made between the results and the book record. Necessary adjustments are made in the inventory records and financial accounts.

Valuation of Inventory

Determination of the quantity of the inventory leaves the problem of values still unanswered. Included under that problem is the question of the proper basis for pricing issues out of the inventory. A number of alternatives are available, each producing different final values. It is not always easy to choose the best basis, for a variety of factors are present and some are in conflict with others.

The importance of inventory values in the balance sheet and income statement is generally well understood today. Inventories constitute a significant item among industrial assets. The reality of net worth and earnings represented in surplus depends upon the validity of asset valuations. The current financial position of the concern in question is closely related to the cash which the inventory will ultimately produce when liquidated through sale. Viewed as a deduction from total cost of goods handled in determining cost of goods sold, it is obvious that every dollar added to or subtracted from the total inventory values is a dollar added to or subtracted from profits. Any change in the basis of valuation must be absorbed in the year's income and spoils comparability with reports of earlier years.

Written discussions of inventory valuation are frequently much over-simplified. Such generalizations as "cost" or "the lower of cost or market" are glibly made with little regard to the range of problems which these terms cover. Only a detailed consideration as is included in a later section can even outline the broad questions of policy involved. Long arguments have hinged on the choice, under the common heading of "cost," among first-in, first-out cost, average cost, and last-in, first-out cost. Market seldom connotes an immediate liquidation value. Rather it measures the replacement cost and is tied to liquidation only through sale in normal operations. Most authorities consider some one of the cost concepts as an ideal as far as income measurement is concerned, but recognize that balance sheet considerations and financial conservatism (which is fundamentally a recognition of the risk factor) require modification even at the expense of loss of comparability. Some cost definitions, such as last-in, first-out, if carried to their strict logical conclusions produce balance sheet figures which are entirely devoid of current significance. The choice is always a close decision among many factors and a mere change in emphasis as to the objective of the accounting may demand a shift in basis. There is no better illustration of this than the shift from a going concern basis to liquidation under receivership.

Among the many factors present, the tax problem deserves special consideration. Its importance largely accounts for the rapid popularization of the last-in, first-out method during the period of undistributed profits taxes. Under this tax many companies which could not distribute dividends based on inventory price gains would have been sadly penalized had not the law permitted a shift to a valuation basis which eliminated such profits. Tax regulations allow some bases and forbid others. While it is true that tax considerations should not be allowed to govern financial accounting, it is also obvious that taxes must be a governing factor and in many cases may well be the deciding factor.

Effect of Surrounding Conditions

It is difficult to study inventory problems independent of the surrounding conditions found in actual practice. Hence this introduction has had as its objective a mere outlining of the area and of the problems to be faced. The remainder of this book is given over to a detailed study of sections of the problem largely through the medium of case situations. By this device the light of special circumstance is brought to bear on the problem and its effect upon policies and procedures noted. For it is clear that both policies and procedures must reflect all factors and conditions. The nature of the industry, its risks, the type of company organization, the status of ownership, the size of the operation, its static or dynamic growth conditions, and the available personnel are all factors in accounting policy without knowledge of which a true understanding and judgment of the policy is impossible. Rather than emphasize a dogmatic statement of principle this volume chooses to point out the variety of approach possible. The need of fitting the policy and procedure to the situation is paramount.

PART I

INVENTORY CONTROL

ESSENTIALS OF INVENTORY CONTROL *

By Frederic W. Kilduff

THE important subject covered by this paper is inventory control. This term, broad in scope, adequately expresses what American business has been vainly attempting to secure for a long period of time. For a good many years I have followed this subject very closely. I have read many articles and I have listened to a number of so-called authorities or those professing to be authorities. But all that I have heard or read pertains not to the subject of inventory control—although such term has been employed as an introduction to the papers or discussions—but instead to detailed expositions of material accounting systems and methods. I maintain that there is a sharp distinction between system and control, although the former, if properly designed and executed, is of great help and in many cases a vital necessity to proper control. All of us have heard the following expressions at one time or another:

    A. Perpetual inventories
    B. Stores control system
    C. Material control system
    D. Stock control system
    E. Merchandise control system

The mention of any of these expressions generally brings to mind, first, some form generally known as a material or stores ledger on which appears a record of all transactions having to do with the past movements and present status of the various items of material; and second, the necessary paper and flow of such paper through the various channels of the organization. These titles mentioned above imply impersonal matters—forms, systems, procedures; they imply the tools for doing something, but not the actual doing. The very titles themselves set restrictive limits, and all because the personal element is relegated to a position of minor importance.

* From the *Bulletin* of February 15, 1939. Originally published under the title "Some Aspects of Inventory Control."

Evolution of Material Control Systems

Let us look for a moment at the evolution of what, for discussion purposes, we may call a material control system. Please observe that I am not using the expression "inventory control" at this point. The first record from which the present material ledger form (the pivotal point of any material record system) evolved was a bin tag. As material was placed in the bin and taken out, a record was presumably made on such tag for the purpose of showing the quantity in the bin still available for issue.

This record then developed into a bound day-book, which was kept in the office of the storekeeper and in which entries were made as materials were received and issued. This was a cumbersome and inelastic thing in itself, and the next move was toward the use of a simple card form, one card for each item of material in stock.

It was natural that if cards were acceptable, loose-leaf methods were acceptable and thus we see the adoption of the loose-leaf together with the card.

This is nothing new. We all know of this evolution. But the fact remains that the time came when someone discovered that these material ledger cards or sheets showed balances of material on hand which, in a great majority of instances, actually agreed with the quantity of physical material in the storerooms. The next move was to show, in addition to quantity balances, dollar balances. Accordingly, there evolved the idea that these records, properly employed, would make unnecessary the usual yearly or half-yearly physical inventory, and the term "perpetual inventory" was brought into the picture. A literal interpretation of this title would mean an inventory which goes on in perpetuity. The better name, of course, would have been "continuous inventory record" or "record of inventory."

Because of the entry of this country into mass production, there developed various kinds of material forms and procedures in connection with the use and flow of such forms, all having to do with material movement. And, of course, in such procedures it was necessary that all material paper should at some time in its course pass over the material ledgers for recording.

The result has been that there has now been developed in many concerns a record of material movement which is very accurate and in accordance with facts. All receipts are duly entered, all issues recorded, and the balance per the record (through periodic inspection and check) is in quantity agreement with the physical material itself. In other words, through gradual development many concerns have a material record which may be said to be a true picture of the status of each material in stock and an accurate history of all movements of these same materials.

To be sure, if the picture is to be an accurate one, the operations, procedures and routine necessary for creating that picture must be accurate and dependable also. Having secured these results, a very large number of business organizations in this country today have satisfied themselves that they have inventory control. Well, they may be satisfied, but they haven't inventory control. All they have is a *material record system*. They have very fine records but little, if any, control.

Control and Intelligence

If you look up the definition of the word "control" you will find that it means the act of controlling, the application of a restraining or directing influence, the act of regulating. An inanimate object cannot of itself exercise control, that is, in the final analysis. Control implies that some person is to perform the act of controlling, restraining, directing or regulating. Further, anyone capable of taking the proper action must have intelligence, and that is the ability to exercise the higher mental functions. Therefore, it boils down to this: Inventory control is a matter of intelligence and not a matter of any form, system or routine.

But this intelligence alone is not sufficient. It must be aided by means of the proper tools. A well planned, conceived and operated material record system is such a tool and can be made to be invaluable in helping such intelligence toward the solution of controlling inventory, which has for its object the following:

1. Placing the accountability for material with the proper person or persons and releasing such accountability only through the correct routine and channels.
2. Keeping the investment in inventories down to the lowest minimum point consistent with production and sales requirements.

3. Preventing interruptions to production schedules and sales programs as a result of shortages of materials and merchandise.

4. Preventing (if possible) and minimizing losses due to physical depreciation and obsolescence of materials and merchandise.

5. Keeping working capital in a more liquid condition.

A Case in Point

Recently I was asked to give my opinion with respect to a certain inventory situation. I first visited the storerooms and found them to be in very fine shape. Most of the material was neatly trayed and the trays were placed in steel bins and racks; all material was properly identified; the bins were numbered, the sections were numbered and the aisles were lettered. Many materials were "bagged" for easy issue. Access to materials was restricted to authorized and bonded employees only. All in all, it was a splendid example of good storekeeping.

I next looked at their material ledgers. They were well kept; the postings were up to date; everything seemed to be done in orderly fashion. At random I selected a few items of material, jotted down the quantity of each as shown on the ledgers, and returning to the storeroom found that the physical counts agreed with the respective book balances of the items selected for test. Apparently the material ledgers were a true picture of the quantities of the material on hand.

But I went a step further. Using average monthly consumption in dollars as the denominator and average inventory on hand as the numerator, I discovered the startling fact that there was an average of eight months' supply of material on hand. Inquiry brought out the fact that material known as standard could be obtained in quantities desired within a period of two to three weeks; and further, that in the instance of the comparatively small number of special materials carried, one month was the maximum time needed to replenish. Obviously, the inventory was excessive.

I went a step further by bringing the matter down to certain individual items. Some showed as much as a three-year supply on hand.

This particular concern was carrying about $2,000,000 in cash and their treasurer was getting a salary of $20,000 a year. The value of the inventory approximated $4,000,000 and the man responsible for that inventory (responsible as to its physical accountability only, for that was the only responsibility I could locate) was receiving a salary of $32.50 per week. Understand that the latter was meeting his responsibility in good shape, doing his work in an A-1 fashion; but the fact remains that from an *inventory control standpoint* there was no such thing.

Some Pertinent Questions

I answered the inquiry of one of the officials as to the reason for this condition with the following questions:

Have you one or more qualified employees in your organization constantly studying material movements:

a. To see if each item is getting a sufficient turnover.

b. To see what items are overstocked.

c. To see what items are understocked.

d. To locate slow movers.

e. To determine if material is over at one location and short at another.

f. To set proper minimum, maximum and ordering quantities and to change these respective quantities up or down as the occasion demands, because these factors are variables, not constants.

g. To determine whether the factor of safety in setting minimum limits is too high.

h. To determine whether the replenishing periods may be shortened, thus allowing minimum points to be lowered.

i. To determine what overstocked material, if any, may be substituted for proposed new products and to see to it that the engineering department is advised of the overstocked items.

j. To receive advance copies of proposed sales, production or maintenance schedules so that demands for material will be met on time and without delay.

k. Does this representative know at what periods inventories should be built up and at what periods they should be scaled down?

l. Have you placed at the disposal of this employee the type of equipment and material record best suited for *control* purposes?

In other words, have you someone in your employ equipped with all the necessary facts regarding the procuring, maintaining and disposal of inventory to permit him to regulate such inventory in accordance with present and future demands; and has he the necessary authority to take (and get) action when it is needed? His answers to the above questions were all in the negative. The particular organization mentioned here has an excellent stores department and a splendid material record system, but no semblance of inventory control. There is a difference and a big difference!

As with most concerns, they have been so busy making records and trying to keep them up to date that they have entirely overlooked the fact that such records are but a means to an end.

The recording of each and every transaction affecting the movement of material by itself will not bring about any corrective action in connection with controlling the inventory. Only by matching up such recording with certain standards, plus auxiliary and supplementary data, is it possible to determine whether or not corrective action is necessary. And whether or not any action is taken after such knowledge is made available is another matter.

As I see it, material control involves three processes:

1. Keeping of complete, accurate and up-to-date records of material movements.
2. Comparing such recorded information periodically with currently accepted standards and supplementary data.
3. As a result of such comparison, putting into operation immediately such corrective actions as will bring the inventory to the desired relationship with the standards set.

Comparison Between Receivables and Material Records

There is an analogy between the control of accounts receivable and inventory control. In any well operated collection department of an organization you will find employees whose duties are to review constantly the receivable ledger cards. These employees do no posting of various debits or credits to the accounts; they do no clerical work in connection with the balancing of these accounts. Their main function is to keep the accounts in a healthy condition and to convert these same accounts into cash as quickly as possible. The ledger sheet or card itself tells the story so far as the particular account is concerned. It is a picture of all transactions affecting such account over the period indicated on the account.

The collection man sees at a glance those accounts which need attention; whether or not the balance of an account is slowly working its way up to the credit limit; what collection letters have already gone forward and the result of such collection letters. By constantly reviewing an account and taking action when comparisons with standards and supplementary data show the account to be in need of correction, a good collection man should be able to keep such accounts in proper condition. As stated above, the purpose of the collection man is to turn receivables into cash, and if not eliminate, at least minimize, losses from bad accounts. Further, the collection man must keep his receivables in the proper relationship to charge sales.

Inventory control also has for its objective the keeping of the investment in inventory in a certain relationship with sales, the conversion of the inventory into cash as soon as possible and, if not the elimination, at least the minimizing of losses through obsolescence, depreciation and other cost factors resulting from an excessive inventory.

It is an unfortunate condition, however, with respect to inventory that practically all effort seems to be given to the accounting functions which have to do with the *recording* of material movements, whereas no noticeable effort is expended, separate and distinct from the work of recording, toward first reviewing the inventory for the purpose of originating corrective action, and subsequently, *keeping the inventory in normal relationship with maintenance, production and sales requirements*. If, in the case of accounts receivable, there is one group performing the clerical work of posting and a separate group functioning for the purpose of controlling such receivables, then certainly it would seem logical that there should be a like division of functions in connection with material records.

Hand-to-Mouth Buying

In my opinion one of the contributory factors to the present unsatisfactory business condition is that of hand-to-mouth buying. In most instances it has been an extremely crude attempt to keep inventories at a low level. It properly falls within what is known as the "hunch and hope" method. It is an unscientific method, one without a foundation of facts.

Hand-to-mouth buying has resulted in excessive manufacturing and distributing costs; it has resulted in incomplete lines with resultant losses of sales; it has given the customer little opportunity for proper selection and if the customer is in any way particular, a sale is lost; it has caused an increased expense in accounting. True, it has increased the number of turnovers; but after all, are we in business to create turnovers or to make profit? I mention hand-to-mouth buying for the simple reason that in the minds of a great many executives is the belief that through its adoption they have effected real control of inventories.

But unfortunately the craze for turnover has in many instances brought about results just the opposite to those intended. This is due to a misunderstanding that turnover is synonymous with volume. So much has been written on the subject of turnover that many business men are greatly confused. As a result many seem to be more interested in a percentage figure than in profits. A little thought and a few mathematical calculations, however, will demonstrate that a merchant may make ten turnovers a year and yet not make one-half as much profit as another who is turning his stock only five times. After all, profit depends primarily on volume. The merchant making a slow turnover may, however, be turning over a stock three or four times as large as the first merchant. Volume and inventories are the two determining factors of turnover. Turnover may be increased in three ways: (a) by leaving sales at present level and decreasing inventory carried, (b) by increasing sales and maintaining present inventory, or (c) by increasing sales and reducing inventory. In the first case, you increase turnover and increase profits slightly; in the second and third cases, you increase both turnover and profit. It all depends upon whether one is more interested in percentages or profits. At the same time, bear in mind that an inventory shaved down to too fine a point brings about lessening of profit through higher prices in fractional buying and loss of sales through incomplete stocks.

If space permitted, I could illustrate many concrete instances where the adoption and use of percentages has been proved a decided fallacy.

Selection of Personnel

As stated above, the real answer to the inventory control is *man-power* not *record-power;* the former is primary, the latter secondary. Results obtained from good tools in the hands of incompetent people cannot be expected to be the best; therefore, select the right man to control the inventory. Among other things, select a man with imagination, a man whose mind is capable of translating matters of static nature into a dynamic picture, a man with judgment.

Don't burden him with a lot of clerical details. Don't ask him to become a posting clerk. Don't let an inadequate salary be the governing factor in selecting the right man for the job. Don't use the office boy for the job and expect to get the results desired.

Selection of Record

The selection of the proper material record, its housing, the necessary operations in connection with its use, and determining whether or not posting to it should be a hand or machine job or a combination of the two, is not a matter for hasty decision. First, the speed of posting to such a record should not be the deciding factor in this selection. While an important factor, in my opinion it should be secondary. Speaking from experience, I find, unfortunately, that this factor *is* generally the deciding factor. While an important one, speed in posting should be subsidiary to the factor of control. Even the cost of posting, the cost of operating the ledgers, or the cost of the entire material system may be of secondary importance.

The matter of selection, as I see it, is a mathematical one. Add to the savings effected (through control) in reducing fixed and other charges arising from excessive inventory investment, the amount of reduction or elimination of inventory losses, and deduct the cost of operating the material system. It is quite obvious that a method operating at double the cost of another method may be the proper one to select and use if, through the employment of such a method, the savings to be effected not only pay for the difference in operating costs, but the balance of savings remaining exceeds the savings under the less expensive plan.

Select the method primarily from the angle of control and the savings that such control will bring about. Select that material record which will conserve the time of the inventory controller. Select the one that will flash the status of the material most rapidly. The good surgeon deserves the best instruments to perform the operation properly; the good golf player deserves the best clubs to play his best game; certainly also, the person who controls the inventory should be supplied with that equipment and method which will allow him to operate most effectively.

The Essentials

To bring about inventory control, then, I mention what I believe to be the absolute and necessary requirements thereof:

(a) A material, stores or merchandise ledger, or whatever you want to call it, complete, dependable, up-to-date—a record on which will be found entries having to do with all material movements and also, and vitally important, all data which is needed to round out the complete picture with reference to each item of material or merchandise in stock. Material records easy to handle; records which at a glance disclose favorable or unfavorable situations; records which may be said to flash particularly important information automatically; records so designed and operated that their use conserves the time of the user.

(b) Intelligent personnel—not for the purpose of posting entries to the material ledger or performing purely mechanical clerical duties, but for the purpose of continuously and carefully studying the material records—with the ability to grasp the picture quickly, to start instantly such action as will correct any situation which appears unfavorable. And further, such personnel should be given the authority which should necessarily go with the assumption of such responsibility.

The happy combination of the *right* material records with intelligent personnel possessing full authority to assume the specific duty of controlling, will, in my opinion, bring about what most companies in our country today contend they have but which, if facts are not brushed wilfully aside, they have not. That is *Inventory Control*.

THE VALUE OF A MATERIAL CONTROL SYSTEM *

By George Nairn

THE subject of excessive inventory costs is one which the writer believes receives much less attention and consideration than various other items from which the results obtained are not comparable with what can be accomplished through the setting up of a material control system.

The large automobile companies and those engaged in mass production have in the past few years gone into this subject carefully, realizing that high inventories are no longer a sign of good management, but, on the contrary, indicate the lack of it. Often an excessive inventory and the high costs involved in maintaining such an inventory have proved to be the factors most seriously affecting the very existence of the company.

This item is of such vital importance to all types of business, both manufacturing and otherwise, regardless of size, that a material control system of a nature that will adequately control the amount of the inventory is an absolute necessity in any modern business today. The savings that will be accomplished with this in effect are far reaching and can only be appreciated by a concern that has established such a policy.

In this article the writer will endeavor to show the value of a material control system by: (1) listing the elements of cost in high and excessive inventories; and (2) describing some actual experiences in the reduction of inventories.

Costs Involved in Excessive Inventories

(a) Market Depreciation

The experience of recent years has made every concern appreciate the danger of carrying excessive inventories because of the heavy inventory adjustments made necessary by a drop in market price. The losses sustained have in many instances wiped out concerns that paid little attention to the control of their inventories.

* From the *Bulletin* of July 15, 1934.

23

(b) Taxes

Another heavy burden of costs is reflected in the taxes paid for high or excessive inventories. These costs can only be reduced by the cutting of inventories. We must appreciate that taxes in the future will not decrease to any great extent and that the only way they can be kept to a minimum is through this procedure.

(c) Interest Costs

Interest costs savings are realized through a reduction in the inventory account, a reduction of $50,000 representing a saving of $3,000 in this respect.

(d) Obsolescence

The losses that come under this heading are usually very heavy if a thorough check is not kept on the excess or over-runs of articles that are not standard items. Therefore every effort should be made to get the customer to accept any such items before they go out of the picture.

These losses are usually buried in the inventory adjustment at the end of the year and would go a long way toward paying for the cost of a proper control of inventories.

(e) Equipment

The tie-up of equipment such as tote boxes, skids, bins, etc., makes it necessary to purchase additional equipment of this kind to take care of the active materials flowing through the plant. This is an expense that can be reduced considerably by the reduction of inventory.

(f) Soiled Material

Extra labor costs become necessary on materials that remain in stock for a long period of time, since the materials accumulate dirt and dust that must be removed before processing; otherwise tool trouble will develop or the materials will contain scratches and marks after processing.

(g) Loss of Space

Extra labor costs are considerable when there is an excessive inventory, especially in a plant where space is limited, since the slow-moving materials must be moved continuously to make room for the active materials.

This expense is reduced to a minimum when the materials are alive and active.

A Specific Case

The facts to be presented are those secured from the operation of a system set up in a manufacturing plant whose products are varied in nature and where the cost and production problems are much more complex than those in a concern where one day's work is a repetition of that of the day previous. The inventory in this concern had been steadily increasing over a period of time when the task of reducing and controlling it was placed under the accounting division.

There followed several discussions with reference to the proper procedure to be followed in connection with the reduction of the inventory. These discussions resulted in the decision to start with the raw material, for it was believed that immediate progress could be made at this stage and that whatever results were accomplished there might also be reflected in the work-in-process and finished-stock inventories.

Causes of High Inventory

An inventory of raw material was taken and from that point on a perpetual card inventory record showing the size, class of material, weight, location, the name of the article and the order number for which the material was received, was used. Upon completion of this inventory, which totaled approximately 1,750,000 pounds, the various items were checked with the orders for which the materials were purchased. This was done for the purpose of finding the factors responsible for such a high inventory. They were as follows:

(a) Materials which had been received on orders that had been cancelled or held up by customers had continued to accumulate, no effort ever having been made to use these materials on new orders.

(b) The sources of material supply had shipped materials in excess of what was ordered, the excess in some cases being of a considerable amount.

(c) The production department had placed order after order for materials of a more or less standard size. This had been considered bank stock (material carried to give quick service to customers), but the quantity on hand had been far beyond what could be used over a period of months.

(d) Materials had been ordered from the source of supply for immediate shipment when the actual processing of the materials was not to start until three to four weeks after receipt.

(e) Materials had been received for new items, but the blanks had not been cut because the customer had made a change in specifications.

(f) Materials had been ordered in advance of receiving actual orders from customers; the orders in some cases never materialized.

(g) An over-optimistic viewpoint had existed in the sales department regarding sales of standard items of manufacture.

(h) Materials had been ordered for the entire quantity of a customer's order, when customer specifications for delivery of finished product were spread over a period of months.

Rules Adopted

After ascertaining these causes, a plan was developed whereby all material orders were first approved by the material control division before being put into effect. Definite rules governing the methods to be followed in the ordering of materials were adopted, as follows:

(a) Materials were ordered in quantities sufficient to take care of the immediate specifications of the customer or for an economical run in the factory.

(b) The sources of material supply were notified that over-shipment on orders would be limited to 5 per cent of the amount ordered.

(c) The policy of ordering materials in advance of receiving orders from customers was discontinued.

(d) The ordering of materials for bank stock was discontinued and the vendor requested to stock such materials for which there was a regular demand on our part.

(e) A more conservative policy of ordering materials for standard items of manufacture was adopted.

(f) All materials on hand for which there were no customers' orders were applied against new orders, either by a slight change in the size or by taking a scrap loss by using materials of a size larger than was necessary.

(g) A more accurate follow-up on materials held up by customers was instituted.

The expected results materialized soon after these methods were put into operation. The inventory began to decrease almost immediately, the percentage of decrease amounting to approximately 50 per cent or 900,000 pounds in a period of six months. It continued to decrease thereafter until the total reached a figure of 25 per cent of what it had been originally.

Application to Finished Goods

When it became apparent that the methods adopted for the reduction and control of the raw material had been productive of results, plans were laid for finished stock control. A finished goods inventory was taken and transferred to perpetual inventory cards set up to carry the necessary information to keep this inventory at a minimum.

The reasons for an excessive inventory of finished stock were somewhat similar to those given above, i.e.:

(a) Production overruns on customers' orders.
(b) Banks of finished products carried for customers.
(c) Materials processed in advance of customers' specifications.
(d) Materials held up by customers.
(e) An excess of standard items of manufacture.

The methods by which this inventory was reduced and controlled were as follows:

(a) Production overruns were controlled on practically all new orders by holding the vendor to a 5 per cent excess on raw material, there being no better point at which to control this item than at the source of material supply.

(b) Standard items of manufacture were held to a minimum amount sufficient to give good service to a customer, but in no case was a larger stock permitted than was necessary to meet demand for the period of time needed to manufacture additional quantities.

(c) All new customers' orders received were checked first against the perpetual inventory records and if there was on hand any material similar to that ordered, the run in the factory on the new order was reduced accordingly.

(d) Banks of finished goods were reduced, the only amount carried being that which the customer gave definite instructions to carry with the agreement that it would be taken within a reasonable length of time.

(e) Materials were not processed months in advance of specifications by customer.

(f) A monthly inventory report showing the value and the number of pieces of all items in finished stock was made up, copies of which were forwarded to the company executives, the sales department and production department. This report, in addition to showing the number of pieces of any article in stock, was classified according to commodity, and showed the name of the customer for each article and the period of months that the material had been in stock.

(g) In addition to the monthly report, the material control division furnished the sales department, on a new form set up for the purpose, the individual items which had not moved within a period of 30 days. This form gave the name of the article, the amount on hand, the name of the customer and whether the material was on order or an excess lot.

(h) Upon receipt of these reports, the sales department would request the customer to accept the material which was an overrun on a previous order and request immediate release on material which had been held up by the customer an unreasonable length of time. These reports proved their worth, for the action taken by the sales department in the disposition of this material was the means of reducing this inventory considerably, and no doubt they effected real savings in disposing of those items which were of such a nature that obsolescence would become effective in a short period of time.

The reduction in the finished stock inventory through the procedure outlined was of a very high percentage, and this reduction together with the reduction of raw material increased the turnover in the plant considerably and effected real savings.

RECOMMENDATIONS FOR THE CO-ORDINATION OF PURCHASING POLICIES FOR MATERIAL CONTROL *

By Sam A. Marsh

THE following recommendations will, I believe, enable the purchasing function to contribute the maximum to the control of material costs:

1. Establish Budgetary Control

Establish a system of budgetary control for keeping expenditures within limits and within proper channels. I wish to emphasize the importance of a budget in controlling the purchase of material, and I feel that the time has come for its universal adoption by all concerns. If this is too theoretical, make the most of it. I suggest that a purchasing budget be prepared from the master budget, expressed not in terms of dollars and cents, but in terms of commodities desired. A commodity classification can then be prepared, divided into items, sizes, descriptions, quantities, prices, etc. From this an ordering schedule can be prepared (with reference to the production schedule), specifications can be adopted, bids requested, contracts executed, and orders (either blanket, special or specific) issued.

2. Develop Control Accounting

Develop an accounting system to provide the management with the necessary control information.

3. Give Purchasing Proper Place in Organization

Set up a purchasing department which functionally ranks with production, selling, accounting and finance, properly organized, not only for the procurement of supplies, materials, equipment, etc., but also for inspecting, storing and distributing.

* From the 1937 Year Book. Originally published under the title "Co-ordinating Purchasing Policies for Material Control."

4. Select Proper Purchasing Agent

Select a purchasing agent equipped with the necessary ability, training, education and experience, and with sufficient authority to act with the assurance that he will be supported by the management.

5. Establish Centralized Purchasing

Establish a centralized purchasing system for the following reasons:

a. Responsibility can be established through setting up officials, specialists in their line, properly equipped through training and experience with sufficient authority and ability to function so that all the possible gains of a purchasing budget will materialize. This can only result through dealing with one responsible head.

b. Buyers, specialists in a given field or commodity line, can be employed, thereby delegating responsibility to individuals properly trained and in this way answering one of the main objections to centralization, namely, that the user knows more about the article than the buyer. The buyers become thoroughly acquainted with the sources of supply, the quality required by the different divisions, and the fluctuation of prices within the market.

c. Uniform standards, representing quality, grade, size and price best adapted for uses can be established in co-operation with the production, inspection and research departments and the advantages of bulk purchasing can be obtained. Through consolidating requirements and setting standards for inventories of materials and supplies, economy is promoted which results in savings through reduced inventories.

d. It facilitates the preparation of detailed specifications which probably will result in the attainment of the requirements and at a much better price.

e. Centralization permits quantity purchases and therefore reduces to a minimum the paper work involved. By pooling the requirements the advantage of quantity discounts, lower prices and savings on delivery costs result. Through proper planning current requirements can be anticipated in advance, and the orders marked "rush" can be eliminated or reduced to a minimum. Contracts, blanket orders and staggered orders can be executed, assuming a continuous supply to be shipped when required, thus reducing to a minimum the storage space and the storage and handling expenses. In many instances it eliminates the necessity of a central storeroom and permits the delivery of the material desired to the point of usage.

f. A small staff working full time can handle the work since the number of orders is reduced. The increased efficiency facilitates the execution of procedure, records and routine, and also expedites the inspection and approval of materials.

g. Centralization frees the individual from useless routine and encourages the individual to use the time to greater advantage. It encourages market analysis of price trends and an analysis of the vendor's production cost, with the result that purchases are made under the most favorable conditions. It encourages a study of substitutes which may be the proper antidote for those who are brand conscious or unconscious.

h. Centralized purchasing assures a centralized supervision over deliveries as well as uniform inspection by trained inspectors so as to be assured that the goods were actually received and were the kind ordered.

i. Centralized purchasing facilitates closer accounting or budgetary control over expenditures, regulates buying through an effective control of purchases, an adequate knowledge of purchase requirements, and the formulation of a purchasing program fixing the responsibility for putting the program into effect and setting standards for measuring results. Assuming the proper cooperation between the purchasing and accounting officers, excess expenditure of appropriations can be avoided, invoices can be more speedily and accurately checked, and payments can be made promptly so that invoices can be discounted within the proper period. This increases the possibility of gauging the cash position more accurately and enforcing the master budget.

j. Cost of purchasing material and also the cost of handling material is minimized. These costs include: (1) administrative costs, (2) storage and warehouse expenses, including storekeeper expenses, interest, deterioration, obsolescence, spoilage, waste and carelessness, (3) losses from errors, delays, improper records, etc. The accumulated savings resulting from a purchasing policy are reflected in low material costs and should naturally mean low costs of finished goods which should afford a favorable differential in competitive markets.

k. Since most questions at present are being weighed from the point of view of their social and economic significance, why not join the intelligentsia by pointing out that a proper purchasing policy encourages efficient dependable suppliers and discourages the other kind; and too, it effects savings resulting from adjusting our purchases to our requirements, thereby eliminating waste and too many misdirected efforts.

6. *Establish Scope of Purchasing Agent's Authority*

The scope of the purchasing agent's activities, as well as his authority, should be definitely understood. I do not mean that he should be surrounded by a strait-jacket with all of his duties specified, but that his activity should not be abridged by regulations or annoying exceptions. The way to develop responsibility is by giving a more or less free rein, by being interested in accomplishments and not details. What will this include? The purchase of:

a. Materials and supplies only?
b. Equipment?
c. Machinery?
d. New construction?
e. Advertising?

Whatever limits are established, the purchasing agent should be given free rein to exercise those functions which are peculiarly his. If any modification of this idea is necessary, then the solution is probably a new purchasing agent and not interference with his duties or responsibilities.

7. *Formulate a Purchasing Policy*

The most important function of the purchasing agent is the selection of the supplier. Are there to be any restrictions? If so, when? And by whom? Is the purchasing agent to be given free rein, or should a broad policy be established, particularly about certain controversial questions?

There are so many factors which must be considered: quality, service, price, the assurance of a sufficient supply, the development of friendly relationship with a vendor so that emergencies can be met, flexible adjustments in requirements, etc. Relationship of this sort can be established only after years of pleasant contacts, and connections of this sort should not be destroyed by the establishment of some narrow restrictions or pressure from some outside source. The selection of the right sort of vendor can contribute much towards the happy solution of many problems.

The problem of reciprocity, if established as a policy, may be very helpful and, on the other hand, extremely annoying. The purchasing department may not be able to function, at least it cannot be held responsible for its failures, if its vendors are selected by the sales department or the real estate division.

"Buy at Home" is probably the most abused kind of false propaganda. If that is the only sales argument a firm has, then it probably offers the very reason why one should not buy at home.

Just how significant or important commercial bribery is in selecting the vendor depends entirely on the organization and the purchasing agent. The development of a purchasing budget and a purchasing policy can curb this definitely and it succeeds in transferring to the firm concessions in the form of price and services rather than to the purchasing agent or buyers in the form of gratuities.

All things being equal, price, quality and service are probably the most decisive factors. I assume that you realize that price may or may not indicate quality and service; that if service is not considered, it may affect the ultimate cost. By quality we do not necessarily mean the finest, but that quality which is best adapted to our needs.

How can we be assured of attaining the right material? Purchasing according to brands, market grades, samples or specifications? It is difficult to generalize since each type of industry has its peculiarities. I do wish to suggest the last method as the objective, since it offers such an opportunity to study, analyze and standardize requirements, and eliminates the objections associated with brands.

The price factor is an all-embracing one and oftentimes is the main objective rather than a means to an end. Is this to be a ruthless policy, exercising the whip hand at every opportunity to force prices down, or to obtain concessions, taking advantage of a distressed market and helping to pull out the pegs? Just how much has a purchasing policy of that sort contributed to a continuation of the depression?

The purchasing department should consider all factors which affect price, familiarize themselves with the possible price trends, study costs so as to know whether the price submitted is reasonable, and arrange contracts which protect the firm against a rising or falling market. A careful selection of bidders and a study of the bids received in the light of what has just been said should indicate whether there has been collusion or whether the price is too high or too low. Shall the bids received be final, assuming of course the permission to correct obvious mistakes? Should the demands of the bidder to revise the guess be permitted, or shall one raise the ethics of playing the low bidder against the higher, etc.? Cash discounts, trade discounts, quality discounts and cumulative discounts play a part in the decision and affect materially the cost of the product.

One further question which is of extreme significance and which is settled by a budgetary procedure is speculative vs. controlled purchasing. Recently I viewed a half-million dollar pile of scrap iron accumulated as a result of a favorable price and the possibility of an increase in price. Any objection? By speculation I do not include hedging-purchasing cotton futures. The main objection is that often it is carried on without realizing that it is being done and may involve either quantity purchasing or hand-to-mouth buying. I feel that it should never be done without authorization, without realizing the possible consequences, and recognizing the fact that other means might be used to assure a supply at the right price without assuming all the risks and consequences involved.

8. Develop Purchasing Procedure and Personnel

The development of a purchasing procedure and personnel to carry it out involves the development of forms, reports, procedure, routing (not with the W.P.A. idea of keeping a lot of people busy, but with the thought of furnishing maximum information), facts, internal checks and control, with a minimum of effort; with the understanding that no policy or procedure is sacred, but that it is subject to constant revision; with the thought in mind of eliminating useless red tape and freeing the personnel from the deadly effects of mechanical repetition. In selecting the personnel or developing the procedure, one should not overlook the value of "horse-sense" which, so far as value goes, has not been affected by the gold decision.

9. Establish Relation to Other Departments

Establish definitely the relation between the purchasing department and (1) stores, including materials and supplies inventories, (2) receiving department, (3) testing and inspection, (4) research, and (5) traffic. If we are to have budgetary procedure, I believe we all agree that purchasing should not be a function under the stores department, but we may not be in agreement as to whether the stores should be under the purchasing department or under production. The same questions apply to inspection. I will not list the arguments pro and con, and there are many. Whatever the decision is, so long as it is made on its merits and with the realization that there exists the necessity of complete co-operation on everyone's part, no objection will be raised from the point of view of budgetary control.

10. Formulate Procedure for Auditing Invoices

Formulate proper accounting procedure for auditing invoices for vouchering. In reaching a decision as to the policy which should be adopted three things should be considered: (1) provide the proper internal check and assurance that certification means something; (2) eliminate all duplicate work wherever possible; and (3) facilitate the auditing of invoices for vouchering in payment. I suggest the following arrangement:

1. Purchasing department certifies the quality, quantity, price, extensions, discounts, back order credits.
2. Receiving department certifies the quantity and condition of goods received.
3. Traffic department checks freight claims, handling the problem of demurrage, drayage, and other delivery costs.
4. Testing and inspection department test both the quality and use.
5. Accounting department checks invoices, extensions, prepares the vouchers, distributes the charges to the stores' cards and the control accounts.

6. Stores department symbolizes the material, prices, stores, issues, inventories.
7. Cost department maintains stores card and prices requisitions, and collects costs.

In conclusion, I ask you to look at this question with an open mind, to visualize the opportunities and possibilities, to consider the maximum benefits which will result through adopting the proper purchasing policy and to realize that the only limitations to achieving this results from our inability or unwillingness to adjust ourselves to a new point of view.

CO-ORDINATING PRODUCTION AND INVENTORY CONTROL *

By Elson P. Dolliver

Why Control Inventory?

MONEY is one really basic reason why inventory should be controlled. Not money in the sense of so many dollars in the bank, for if it were, much more attention would undoubtedly be given to it. Rather it is merchandise—so many cases of shoes, dozens of shirts, watches, yards of cloth or whatever the manufactured product may be. Money was spent for the labor, material and overhead necessary to make the finished product. Why, then, is it not logical to expect the maximum return from the money invested in such an inventory of merchandise?

Cost of Carrying Excessive Inventories

In past years it was possible in many industries to obtain a profit which was satisfactory to management and stockholders alike because a sufficient profit margin covered the various costs of carrying excessive inventories of both finished and in-process goods. Competition has steadily forced these profit margins down. To get them back to somewhere near a satisfactory point it is essential that the lowest possible costs be secured. Manufacturing processes have been carefully scrutinized and efforts to reduce costs have, in many instances, borne fruitful results. Salaries and wages have been reduced to this end. Yet in all this cost reduction program the possibilities through the control of inventory have very often been overlooked.

Take for example a concern doing an annual volume of $2,000,000 and carrying an average inventory of $750,000. Assuming that these figures are based on cost prices, there should be a turnover of

---

* Consisting of portions of the following two articles by Mr. Dolliver: "Co-ordinating Production and Inventory Control," published in the *Bulletin* for September 15, 1936; and "Finished Goods Inventory Control," published in the *Bulletin* for February 15, 1939.

approximately 2.67 times. If this turnover could be increased one-third, there would be a resulting average inventory of $562,500, or a saving of $187,500 in inventory investment. It has been estimated that the cost of carrying an inventory, including interest on investment, insurance, taxes, obsolescence loss and other causes, is in excess of 10 per cent per annum, depending on the business under consideration. At 10 per cent, therefore, there would be a saving of $18,750 annually. Inventory control installations have in many cases demonstrated that substantial improvement in turnover is possible.

Obsolescence Costs

Another point in connection with the need for inventory control is evidenced by the radical changes which have taken place during the last few years in the buying habits of the nation. Style, design, color, utility and price play increasingly important parts in today's market drama. Inventory control offers a means whereby the substantial obsolescence losses brought about by this ever-changing demand may be minimized. To cope with these trends in present-day conditions, the manufacturer is faced with two major considerations. In the first place, he must maintain an adequate stock of the right kinds of merchandise at the right time if he is to give his customer service, yet at the same time avoid excessive stocks which take their toll in heavy obsolescence losses and excessive carrying charges. Secondly, he must, particularly if he is in a type of business where the demand is seasonal, plan his production program so that there is as nearly as possible an even flow throughout the year in order to obtain maximum benefits of plant, equipment and labor utilization.

The accomplishment of these ends demands control mediums which effectively co-ordinate sales and production activities within the enterprise. Predetermined objectives must be set up, based upon careful and conservative studies of trends, market conditions, production capacities, financial requirements, capital expenditures, etc. The attainment of these objectives must represent the co-operative efforts of, and be accepted by, the major functions of the business organization.

The Sales Forecast

Obviously, the first step in the plan is to determine in a general way where you are headed. The carefully prepared sales forecast or budget is designed to serve this end. Inasmuch as this forecast is to be the starting point for all executive programs and policies, it is of fundamental importance that every care and thought be used in its preparation. It must be realized at the outset that this sales forecast is only an estimate, although surprisingly close actual results have been experienced by concerns who have given careful thought to its preparation. A sales projection of some sort is necessary, for, even if imperfect, it is better than going along from month to month without a definite plan. Invariably it will be found that somebody, somewhere along the line, does make such estimates. Informal and disorganized estimates lose any benefits which are to be had through the efforts of the entire organization directed toward a carefully thought out master program. For this reason, if none other, the preparation of the sales forecast should be made a formal procedure and employ all available thought and facts during its preparation.

The sales forecast need not and should not be a rigid program; it should be sufficiently flexible so that it may be readily adjusted to changing conditions that were not foreseen at its inception.

Sales forecasts should be prepared covering dollar-sales expectancy in each of the major commodity groups manufactured. These are broken down into months according to seasonal variation data. The various commodity sales schedules are then compiled into a master sales schedule which is a basis for determining overall sales, manufacturing, purchasing and financial programs.

Points to Consider in Sales Forecasting

In arriving at the figures to be used in the sales forecast, some of the points which should be considered are:

1. General plans and policies of the company.
2. Judgment of the sales department.
3. Judgment of the sales branches.
4. Past performance, sales analysis.
5. Trade and business conditions.
6. Cost of sales and estimated gross profits.
7. Plant capacity.
8. Amount of low-margin, overhead-carrying business which is desirable.

9. Financial requirements of proposed programs.
10. Advertising and sales promotions plans.
11. Such statistical information as is available for industry through trade associations, etc.
12. Market analysis.

It is evident from the foregoing that the compilation of data necessary for preparing the sales forecast involves the entire organization: executive, sales, manufacturing, control, production, etc. A common objective is the result towards which the activities of all departments are directed.

The Production Program

The next progressive step in the plan is selecting the best route on which to proceed toward the destination set up by the sales forecast. This step involves the translation of the sales forecast into a productive program. In planning the production program the following factors are considered:

1. Nature of business; type of product; etc.
2. Manufacturing limitations and plant capacity.
3. Seasonal sales variation, i.e., rate of demand during sales period.
4. Inventory position desired during period.
5. Labor conditions; stability of employment.

The carefully prepared sales forecast solves many of the questions which arise in the preparation of the production program concerning the commodity groups to be concentrated upon; the volume which might reasonably be expected; etc. Here again, we recognize that although the production program is an estimate it represents a carefully planned approach to the attainment of the sales forecast as set up and that, as flexibility was observed in setting the sales forecast, so it must be a factor in preparing the production program.

Master Production Schedules

The master schedule or forecast of production to meet sales requirements is the road map which guides us to the attainment of the goals of inventory control, which are better customer service, better turnover and a more uniform month-to-month production curve.

The mechanics of setting up a master schedule are relatively simple. A sales estimate is secured from the sales department for each commodity line or group in units. The total of the units estimated for the various groups extended by the sales value for the items should check with the total dollar sales volume anticipated. These estimates are broken down further into monthly forecasts for each commodity group. Through a study of previous sales trends for each of the commodity groups, it is possible to determine fairly accurately the relation that the sales of any one month bear to the sales of other months. This study will disclose the seasonal demand for each of the commodity classifications and provide the basis for the production forecast. In setting the production to meet the sales requirements, it is desirable from a manufacturing standpoint to divide the unit sales expectancy into twelve equal portions and manufacture one of those portions each month. From a turnover standpoint, it is desirable to manufacture just as near to the consuming season as possible.

Some industries are fortunate in having commodity lines that have sales peaks occurring in different seasons of the year. Others, less fortunate in this respect, must arrange to manufacture their more staple items as a fill-in to their hazardous style and novelty items which should be manufactured just as near to the consuming season as possible.

For purposes of illustration, we will assume that a concern manufactures three commodity lines:

        Line A—sales forecast   30,000 dozens
        Line B— "   "   125,000   "
        Line C— "   "   50,000   "

A study of the monthly sales trends of these lines for the previous five years shows that the average monthly variation is:

	LINE A	LINE B	LINE C
	Per Cent of Total Year		
Jan.	5	0	8
Feb.	5	2	8
Mar.	6	3	9
1st Qtr.	(16)	(5)	(25)
Apr.	7	10	9
May	7	20	9
June	8	25	8
2nd Qtr.	(22)	(55)	(26)
6 Mos.	(38)	(60)	(51)

	Line A	Line B	Line C
	Per Cent of Total Year		
July	5	20	8
Aug.	15	15	8
Sept.	15	5	8
3rd Qtr.	(35)	(40)	(24)
9 Mos.	(73)	(100)	(75)
Oct.	10	0	10
Nov.	10	0	8
Dec.	7	0	7
4th Qtr.	(27)	(0)	(25)
Year	(100)	(100)	(100)

The monthly variation percentages applied to the sales forecasts would give us the following information:

	Line A	Line B	Line C	Total
	Unit—Dozens			
Jan.	1,500	....	4,000	5,500
Feb.	1,500	2,500	4,000	8,000
Mar.	1,800	3,750	4,500	10,050
Apr.	2,100	12,500	4,500	19,100
May	2,100	25,000	4,500	31,600
June	2,400	31,250	4,000	37,650
July	1,500	25,000	4,000	30,500
Aug.	4,500	18,750	4,000	27,250
Sept.	4,500	6,250	4,000	14,750
Oct.	3,000	0	5,000	8,000
Nov.	3,000	0	4,000	7,000
Dec.	2,100	0	3,500	5,600
Total	30,000	125,000	50,000	205,000

From this breakdown it is apparent that Line B has a highly concentrated sales demand, 75 per cent of the sales occurring in four months. A line of this nature is often one which is composed of style or novelty items to a large extent, and an expression of consumer demand is necessary to determine just which items in the line are "going over." It is imperative, therefore, that this line be manufactured during or just as near to the consuming season as possible. Line A peaks up moderately in the third quarter and line C is reasonably stable. With this information at hand, the production forecast can be set up. We will assume that our starting inventories are:

Line A	10,000 dozens
Line B	25,000 dozens
Line C	15,000 dozens
Total	50,000 dozens

It is assumed that we will aim for an end-of-year inventory of 40,000 dozens, which would mean that our production forecast will be 10,000 dozen less than our sales forecast, or 195,000 dozen. In order to keep a uniform load in the plant, it will be assumed that we will manufacture 16,250 dozen per month. Combining this with our total sales forecast into the master schedule will give us the following:

	PRODUCTION	SALES	END OF MONTH INVENTORY
	Unit—Dozens		*50,000*
Jan.	16,250	5,500	60,750
Feb.	16,250	8,000	69,000
Mar.	16,250	10,050	75,200
Apr.	16,250	19,100	72,350
May	16,250	31,600	57,000
June	16,250	37,650	35,600
July	16,250	30,500	21,350
Aug.	16,250	27,250	10,350
Sept.	16,250	14,750	11,850
Oct.	16,250	8,000	20,100
Nov.	16,250	7,000	29,350
Dec.	16,250	5,600	40,000
Total	195,000	205,000	....

From the total unit master schedule the individual schedules for each line are built up.

PRODUCTION

	LINE A	LINE B	LINE C	TOTAL
	Dozens			
Jan.	250	14,000	2,000	16,250
Feb.	1,000	13,250	2,000	16,250
Mar., etc.	1,000	13,250	2,000	16,250

SALES

	LINE A	LINE B	LINE C	TOTAL
	Dozens			
Jan.	1,500	....	4,000	5,500
Feb.	1,500	2,500	4,000	8,000
Mar., etc.	1,800	3,750	4,500	10,050

INVENTORY END OF MONTH

	LINE A	LINE B	LINE C	TOTAL
	Dozens			
Dec.	10,000	25,000	15,000	50,000
Jan.	8,750	39,000	13,000	60,750
Feb.	8,250	49,750	11,000	69,000
Mar.	7,450	59,250	8,500	75,200

Usually it is not possible to work out in practice a uniform production forecast that will fit the inventory requirements necessary to service sales without charting a hazardous course. In practice, a happy medium is struck between the ideal uniform production curve and one which gives the best turnover ratio, bearing in mind that it is far safer to manufacture staple merchandise far in advance of its actual consumption than it is to pursue this policy with style or novelty merchandise. Many manufacturers find it advantageous to refuse to manufacture novelty lines after a certain date, knowing full well that before the goods can be manufactured and gotten into the market, the consumer demand for them will have ceased. It is sometimes better to pass up some business than to have a carry-over of merchandise that will necessitate a heavy markdown to liquidate it.

An Illustrated Master Schedule

The detailed master schedule for a commodity group is shown on page 45 as Exhibit 1.

The production portion of the master schedule shows:

1. Month.
2. Days worked per month.
3. Daily rate.
4. Total production estimated for month.

The sales portion shows:

1. Monthly estimated sales (shipments) through each of the major distribution channels.
2. Total sales for all distribution channels.
3. Per cent of month to total year: used for comparison with index of seasonal variation, based on a five-year average.
4. Bookings—Total of orders booked by months. This figure is useful as a guide to making production plans, particularly on a commodity which has a highly seasonal demand. Difference between bookings (orders) and sales (shipments) over a period of a year shows "firmness" of orders.

The inventory portion shows:

1. Total end-of-month inventory in units, adjusted with physical inventory at each inventory period.

XYZ CORPORATION
MASTER PROGRAM

March, 1936, Actual
April 15, 1936

Commodity Group #8

	Days Worked	Production Daily Rate	Total	Sales Retail	Dept. Store	Chain	Distributors	Total	Unit—Dozens % Year	Bookings	Total E.O.M.	Inventory Service Position [1]	Excess	Turn-over [3]
1932	200	25.0	5,000	565	1,174	1,685	1,275	4,699		5,010	1,085			4.32
1933	209	26.5	5,539	876	1,589	1,801	1,222	5,488		5,895	1,136			4.83
1934	230	27.8	6,394	895	1,738	2,152	1,475	6,260		6,701	1,270			4.93
1935 Actual Jan.	22	33.0	726	12	23	28	20	83	1.1	343	1,913	1,219	694	
" Feb.	20	33.0	660	73	141	176	120	510	6.8	858	2,063	1,740	323	
" Mar.	22	28.1	618	203	393	487	334	1,417	18.9	899	1,264	851	413	
" Apr.	22	30.9	680	92	179	222	152	645	8.6	728	1,299	537	762	
" May	21	31.0	650	59	115	142	97	413	5.5	531	1,536	356	1,180	
" June	22	34.1	750	35	69	85	58	247	3.3	164	2,039	803	1,236	
" July[4]	17	35.3	600	31	60	75	52	218	2.9	417	2,421	1,916	505	
" Aug.	22	33.0	726	167	324	403	276	1,170	15.6	1,619	1,977	1,876	101	
" Sept.	20	26.0	520	213	413	513	353	1,492	19.9	1,561	1,005	960	45	
" Oct.	23	26.1	600	108	213	263	181	765	10.2	425	840	465	375	
" Nov.	20	20.0	400	56	108	134	92	390	5.2	434	850	216	634	
" Dec.	15	20.0	300	21	42	52	35	150	2.0	196	1,000	349	651	
Total	246	29.4	7,230	1,070	2,080	2,580	770	7,500	100.0%	8,175	1,525 Av. 4.93 To.	938 Av. 8.0 To.		Av. 4.93
1936 Actual Jan.	22	30.9	680	18	38	45	31	132	1.7	352	1,548	1,181	367	5.04 [2]
" Feb.	20	34.0	680	62	120	149	103	434	5.6	879	1,794	1,840	46 [2]	5.07
" Mar.	22	33.9	746	213	413	513	356	1,495	19.3	921	1,045	911	134	5.22
Budget Apr.	22	31.9	702	98	191	237	164	690	8.9	745	1,057	570	487	5.32
" May	21	33.5	703	63	122	152	105	442	5.7	544	1,318	365	953	5.45
" June	22	36.3	798	36	71	88	61	256	3.3	167	1,860	824	1,036	5.53
" July[4]	17	36.2	615	31	60	74	52	214	2.8	427	2,258	1,979	279 [2]	5.60
" Aug.	22	32.9	724	172	336	417	289	1,214	15.6	1,657	1,768	1,925	157 [2]	5.72
" Sept.	20	27.0	540	217	425	525	363	1,530	19.8	1,599	778	987	209 [2]	5.84
" Oct.	23	24.9	572	112	222	271	185	790	10.2	435	560	472	88	5.95
" Nov.	20	21.0	420	56	109	136	94	395	5.1	444	585	221	364	6.06
" Dec.	15	21.3	320	22	43	53	37	155	2.0	201	750	349	401	
Total	246	30.5	7,500	1,100	2,150	2,660	1,840	7,750	100.0%	8,371	1,278 Av. 6.06 To.	970 Av. 8.0 To.		

[1] Service Position—6 weeks.
[2] These figures indicate shortages.
[3] Computed on Moving Annual Total Basis.
[4] Annual Summer Shutdown.

EXHIBIT 1

2. Service inventory—That number of units required to service a certain period of sales. This is perhaps more of a theoretical figure than a practical one, inasmuch as it is based on the assumption that the right quantities, of the right sizes, colors, designs, etc., of merchandise are on hand at the right places to service sales. Its chief usefulness to management is as a guide in planning production programs.
3. Excess inventory—The difference between total inventory and service inventory.
4. Turnover—The rate of turnover of inventory calculated on the basis of total moving sales divided by average, end-of-month moving inventory.

The master schedule's chief function is to present to management a composite picture of what the plans are and the ultimate result if the plans are successfully carried out. As the actual results of each month's performance become available, they are posted to the master schedule and noted as actual. If conditions warrant, revisions should be made on any of the forward projections.

Preparation of Detailed Manufacturing Schedules

From the master schedules, the approximate total quantity of each commodity group to be manufactured can be ascertained. The preparation of the detailed monthly manufacturing schedule showing what items, colors, sizes, etc., are to be made and how many of each, involves further consideration. The items comprising the commodity class are classified in detail as to estimated sales volume, whether of a novelty, specialty or staple character, and as to cost, hazard of obsolescence, manufacturing limitations, availability of supplies and materials, etc. Each industry has its own problems in these respects. For example, a concern manufacturing clothing should seriously consider, in the preparation of a detailed production schedule for a month early in the producing season, the desirability of producing at that time the more staple items in the commodity group, holding off style and specialty items until as close to the selling season as possible. The anticipation of this type demand should be delayed as long as is possible and production started only when the demand is made evident through advance orders.

Too much consideration and care cannot be given to the preparation of the detailed manufacturing schedule for herein lies the degree of success or failure of the inventory control plan. As previously outlined, the aim of an inventory control plan is to provide for the proper quantities of the right kinds of merchandise in the right places at the right time, and that is truly a large order. It is felt that the detailed schedule should be set up for a month at a time with tentative schedules for one or two months ahead of the one to be actually produced. This will furnish the purchasing, sales and production departments a basis upon which to plan their needs and determine their courses of proposed action.

Co-ordination Through a Standing Committee

The detailed production schedule should be prepared by the member of the organization in charge of inventory control, working in close harmony with the sales department. The completed schedule should be reviewed by the sales and production departments and adjustments, if any, made prior to final approval of the schedule for actual manufacture. At this point it is taken in hand by the production control department and scheduled to the various manufacturing operations for production.

As outlined in a preceding paragraph, it is of particular importance that all functions of management co-ordinate their thoughts, ideas and information into the preparation of the program. It is equally important that they review the results of their planning periodically. A standing committee comprised of members of sales, sales promotion, inventory control, production, purchasing and executive functions should meet periodically to discuss actual results and revise future plans where necessary.

The Order and Stock Available Report

In addition to the master schedule, which is brought up to date each month with actual results substituted for estimated figures, there is one other current report that should be reviewed and discussed at these committee meetings—the Order and Stock Available Report, Exhibit 2.

INVENTORY CONTROL

Issued April 25, 1936
ORDER AND STOCK AVAILABLE REPORT
COMMODITY No. 8
Two-Week Period Ending April 18, 1936

Stock No.	Orders Rec'd Period	Yr. to Date	Customer Shipments Yr. to Date	Available Stock Fac.	Consigned to Distributions	Total	Prod. Sche.
CLASS 1							
5,526	144	695	465	409	226	635	400
5,527	25	315	208	300	190	490	150
5,530	1,098	5,219	4,819	2,109	2,086	4,195	2,500
B5,546*	165	400	....	(289)	(111)	(400)	650
ACTUAL 1936	1,432	6,629	5,492	2,529	2,391	4,920	3,700

* New item—introduced Feb. 15, 1936, for shipment June 1, 1936

1936 ESTIMATE		7,680	6,100				4,500
1935							
To DATE	1,969	7,500	5,940	2,897	3,069	5,966	

CLASS 2
Total
All Classes
Copies to Gen. Mgr.
Sales Mgr.
Production Mgr.
Factory Supt.
File

EXHIBIT 2

The order and stock available report is a summary of the orders received, orders shipped, stock available and the planned production schedule. This information, to be presented for each item in the active lines manufactured and sold, is arranged according to group classification to facilitate its use. Typical group classifications for a footwear plant might be: novelty oxfords sport shoes, sandals, etc. A review of the group classifications quickly shows those groups which need attention and the individual items which comprise a group can be readily isolated and concentrated upon. Sales estimates for this year, comparative sales for last year, etc., together with the periodically unfolding of actual accomplishment for the current year, make this a valuable report worthy of management's consideration.

The order and stock available report is prepared weekly, semimonthly or monthly as the needs of the particular commodity dictate.

The figures for it are taken from the regular stock control records (balance-of-stores type).

The Stock Ledger

A complete, well arranged and well kept stock ledger is a valuable part of an inventory control program. The basis of much of the data used in the control of inventories originates in the stock ledger. A well ordered stock ledger should provide for such information as bookings, shipments, balance of stock, stock on order, also ordering point, economic batch size, estimated sales for year, cost value of unit, sales of past four or five years, returns, cancellations, etc.

Stock ledger operation should not be made too automatic. When items reach the ordering point, it is well to include on the reorder such information as bookings for year-to-date, stock on hand, stock on order or in process, sales estimate for the year and economic batch size. This information should be carefully reviewed by the executive who approves the stock order. The executive who passes on stock should be thoroughly conversant with plans of the sales department. He should know what items are on their way out, which are really going over, etc., for the economic quantity to manufacture at one time depends largely on the quantity to be sold during a year, and the adherence to stock book "ordering quantities," without this constant review, is very often responsible for building inventories inconsistent with actual needs.

Economic Batch Sizes

The economic batch size is frequently given insufficient consideration in placing manufacturing orders. Guesswork rather than scientific methods have too often been employed to determine the manufacturing quantities.

There are many economic batch size formulas in use and a fairly complete treatise on this subject may be found in an article entitled "Inventory Control" by H. P. Dutton, which appeared in the Plant Operation Library of *Factory Management and Maintenance,* August 1935.

Department Responsible

There is another point in connection with inventory control which seems worthy of consideration, namely, "Who shall be responsible for the inventory?" Former practice tended to place the responsibility for inventory upon the manufacturing department. The modern trend shifts this to the sales department. There are several good reasons for this:

1. There is a greater tendency on the part of the sales department to concentrate on the current line and do a real selling job, since it is their duty to turn in a profit from a line of merchandise turned over to them at manufacturing cost.
2. The sales department is in the best position to know the market for the merchandise, to know what types are required, and to sense changes in trend. They are less likely to use this pertinent information adequately if someone else is responsible for the inventory.
3. Estimates given by the sales department are apt to mean more than just words, as is often the case when the responsibility is not theirs. The master sales forecast schedule acts, too, as an overall guide to keep the estimating within due bounds. Too often the laurels have been heaped on the sales manager's desk for a record volume of sales and in the same breath severe criticism has been directed against the manufacturing department for excessive inventories and low profits.

Inventory control is but another procedure or system. It is a tool which, if properly and expertly used, may well direct a business enterprise into a more satisfactory and profitable position. Effective management demands eternal vigilance from its highest salaried executive down, without which no system ever devised will function properly, if at all.

With the interest and enthusiasm of management behind it, an inventory control plan will pave the way to renewed profits and improved position.

INVENTORY AND PRODUCTION CONTROL FOR THE CORSET INDUSTRY *

By George W. Rood

MANY lines of business producing style goods are confronted with a serious problem of inventory and production control. Inventories of finished stock and work in process must be kept at a minimum to avoid frozen capital and losses from obsolescence. This is particularly true of the corset industry where it is not unusual to find a company manufacturing several hundred styles of garments with each style made in fifteen to twenty sizes.

New garments are constantly designed and certain seasons of the year bring forth a flood of new styles. Each new style may or may not affect the manufacture of one or more of the old styles. Minimum manufacturing quantities must be maintained for each style and size to keep costs in line.

Although sales in a particular style may run uniformly, the sales in the sizes of that style may fluctuate rapidly from week to week and month to month. Yet a balanced inventory in sizes is the only means of filling customers' orders quickly and completely. Delay in filling orders or incomplete shipments cause cancelled orders and loss of customers.

Information Needed

The information necessary for a satisfactory control of inventory and production in the corset industry may be classified as follows:
1. Control of raw materials.
2. Control of cutting orders issued.
3. Control of work in process by production centers.
4. Control of customers' orders, filled and unfilled.
5. Control of available stock.
6. Sales statistics.

To one part of each of the above, add a dash of sales and designing forecast, several parts of good judgment and one part of pure gamble. The results will be very satisfactory.

* From the *Bulletin* of May 15, 1935.

Since the variety of information necessary for control is usually scattered at several points, the first step is to centralize the information at one point. The procedure described in the following pages makes use of hand methods, punched cards and punched card accounting machines, visible index records and charts.

Customers' orders are checked for credit, name and address, special shipping and billing instructions, and each style is checked for the correct range of sizes, priced and coded for the production center in which it is manufactured. A sample order is shown in Exhibit 1.

Procedure

The orders then go to the punch card accounting machine operator who has arranged in a semi-circle on a desk before her, a series of files. Each file represents a production center and contains a series of guide cards for each style and each size manufactured. On the desk in front of the files are stacks of prepunched cards. These prepunched cards are prepared on the punching machine at the rate of 100 cards per minute. Each stack of cards is punched for one quantity and there is a stack for each quantity up to one dozen pairs.

The first style on the order is No. 950, production center No. 6. It calls for three pairs of size 34 and four pairs of size 36. The operator picks up one 3 card and one 4 card, reaches to file No. 6 guide No. 950 and drops the 3 card behind the size 34 guide and the 4 card behind the 36 guide.

Copies of cutting orders issued, reports of cutting, deliveries to stock, returned goods and cancellations are sent to the operator who punches a card for each style and size affected. The quantity is punched into the card to make the additions and deductions to or from the proper controls. The cards are tabulated by groups to obtain control totals for cutting orders, cutting, work in process, deliveries to stock, returned goods and cancellations. All the cards are then sorted by style and size and filed behind their guide cards in the previously mentioned card files.

The card files therefore contain at all times additions to and deductions from the various inventory controls. Last minute information regarding any style can be furnished at a moment's notice.

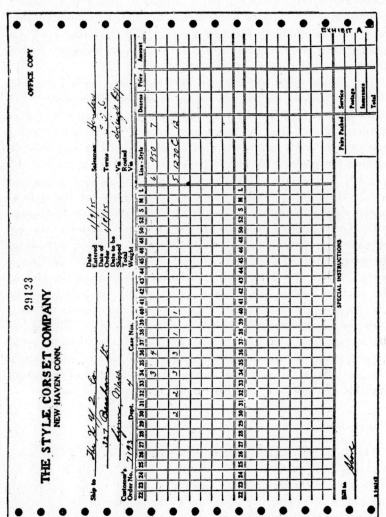

EXHIBIT 1

Sample of punched card is shown in Exhibit 2.

Each day the filed cards for one or more production centers are passed through the tabulator and a tabulation, similar to Exhibit 3, is automatically obtained. This report is printed in duplicate, one copy for the production center foreman and the other copy for posting to the visible index records for use by the inventory control manager.

The visible index records are portable books, each containing 70 visible pockets, indexed by styles in numerical sequence. The styles are arranged in the books by lines (types of garments manufactured) rather than by production centers. Each visible pocket contains two cards and a chart which are exposed to full view on opening the pocket. A sample pocket is illustrated in Exhibit 4A and 4B.

A clerk posts to the lower card the grand total for the style as shown on the tabulation. She checks "Total Available Inventory" with "Quantity Ordered for Month to Date," obtaining the approximate number of weeks of available stock on hand, and moves the progressive signal at the bottom of the pocket to the proper point. When she receives the tabulation taken off at the end of the calendar month, she not only posts as just described but she also posts to the card in the upper part of the pocket, the total sales for the month for the style and for each size. She figures the average size sold and the cost price of that particular size as the cost price used for costing the sales of that style for that month. She also charts the sales for the month and the end-of-the-month available inventory on the chart at the bottom of the pocket.

Use of Records for Control

The inventory control manager makes use of both the visible index record and the tabulation. He considers, first, the style as a whole. If he places a cutting order, he posts it in red ink to the card record and moves the progressive signal out to the number of weeks' supply of available stock he will then have. To properly allocate the total quantity for the style to the sizes, he refers to the tabulation, which gives the complete information for each size as well as each style as a whole.

The foreman of each production center is held responsible for the early delivery to stock of all styles and sizes appearing as back

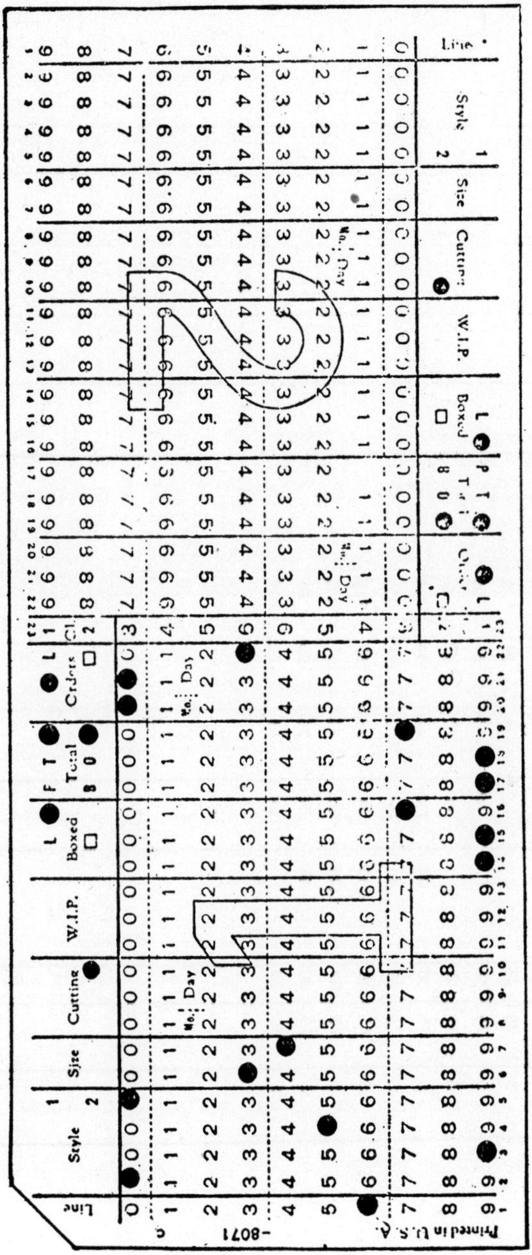
Line
Style
Size
Cutting
W.I.P.
Boxed
Total
Orders
Printed in U.S.A.

EXHIBIT 2

INVENTORY CONTROL TABULATION   AS OF 1/1/35

Exhibit C

LINE	STYLE	SIZE	CUTTING ORDERS	WORK IN PROCESS	AVAILABLE BOXED	TOTAL AVAILABLE	ORDERS FOR MONTH	TOTALS BY STYLES				
								CUTTING	W. I. P.	BOXED	TOTAL AVA.	ORDERS
5	75	34			8	8	3					
5	75	33			24	24	2					
5	75	32		48	14–	34	38					
5	75	31		60	20–	40	52					
5	75	30	24	132	42–	114	119					
5	75	29	48	144	33–	159	135					
5	75	28	116	76	55–	137	158					
5	75	27	116	136	71–	181	155					
5	75	26	44	76	25–	95	89					
5	75	25		24	1	25	14					
								348	696	227–	817	765

Exhibit 3

MO	TOTAL QUANTITY	N⁄32	31	32	33	34	35	36	37	38	39	40
Dec.	292	36		32	18	30	27	62	29	54	16	24
Jan.	330	36		40	22	40	24	67	28	61	22	26
Feb	422	36		38	30	54	35	82	40	77	24	42
Mar.	231	36		24	17	26	21	48	21	46	17	31
Apr	208	36		22	16	24	16	45	17	38	18	32
May	253							etc				
Jun.	288											
Jul.	194											
Aug.	157											
Sep.	196											
Oct.	294											
Nov.	436											
Year Total	1934 427											
Dec.												
Jan.												
Feb.												
Mar.												
Apr.												
May												
Jun.												
Jul.												
Aug.												
Sep.												
Oct.												
Nov.												
Year Total												

LINE STYLE DESCRIPTION

SALES – POSTED MONTHLY FROM TABULATION

EXHIBIT 4A

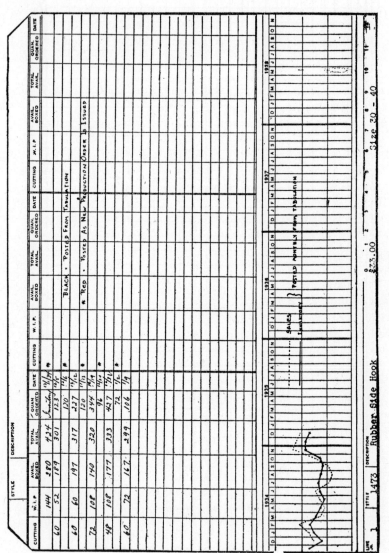

EXHIBIT 4B

orders on the tabulation copy which he receives. There must be a logical explanation for putting through production on styles and sizes which are already well stocked when the tabulation plainly shows that other styles and sizes are needed to fill customers' orders.

The company executives make frequent use of the visible index records where they can spot at a glance over- and under-stocked conditions. The condensed information is useful in making decisions for dropping or adding styles and in planning new sales and merchandising policies. Summary charts of each line and of all lines keep the executives informed daily as to the exact progress of the business.

Actual operation of the above procedure has furnished very satisfactory control over inventory and production. With an increase in business, the total inventory has been substantially reduced. Through a better balance of inventory by sizes, earlier and more complete filling of customers' orders has been accomplished in spite of increased volume and decreased inventory. Furthermore, the degree of accuracy has proven to be far greater than by former hand methods.

Perhaps it will not be amiss, however, to sound a note of warning based upon experience. Hand methods alone do not produce the desired results. Punched cards and punched card accounting machines are not the answer when used alone. Likewise, visible index records or other fast posting media are incomplete when used alone. The combination of all three, plus control and scheduling of paper work, makes the procedure no more expensive to operate and furnishes complete control.

INVENTORY CONTROL UNDER FLUCTUATING PRODUCTION *

By Wyman P. Fiske

THE LAST ten years have produced almost unbelievably large variations in business volumes and have included other economic characteristics which have made successful management of inventories extremely difficult. In spite of its importance, the problem of inventory control and management under conditions of fluctuating volume has received comparatively little attention in published sources. It appears particularly timely at the moment to consider the factors involved and some of the possible approaches to a solution of the problem.

The discussion will be divided into three sections. It will be concerned first with the business significance of the problem. This will be followed by a summary report on actual practices by which the control is being sought in a group of companies which have co-operated in an investigation on which this paper is substantially based. The final section will consist of conclusions drawn from the investigation, as to the important elements and the best approaches to a solution.

Significance of the Problem

Many actual companies could be cited as witnesses to prove the losses resulting from unsuccessful inventory control under conditions of varying volumes. Most companies have, at one time or another, lost some business because of failure to provide adequate inventories. Many have suffered inventory losses when declining volumes found them with excessive inventories. The sheriff has made many a call which is directly traceable to inventory losses.

Most of the difficulty arises from excessive inventories. There are, however, isolated cases where substantial losses are experienced because of an undue worship of turnover. The investigation disclosed one or two such cases. These were the exceptions, how-

* From the *Bulletin* of July 15, 1938.

ever. The general rule is excessive inventories when business turns down. Four sources of loss were found—three definite and tangible, one less apparent but nevertheless important. Price losses are the most spectacular, particularly in the case of inventories of basic raw material. Style obsolescence follows closely in importance. Annual models raise that problem in some cases, and the whims of public demand produce it in others.

Deterioration and spoilage are a third cause of loss, potentially great in industries where freshness is important or where perishability is a product characteristic. The fourth source is financial in nature. Capital is tied up and charges are incurred to carry excessive inventories. The capital cost is intangible unless funds are borrowed. It is, nevertheless, real. Carrying charges, other than interest, are tangible and directly reduce total profits by the amount of the outlay. For inventories of high value or requiring expensive storage conditions, these costs can be substantial. More than one case of financial difficulties has been traced to such an unprofitable freezing of capital in inventories which can be liquidated only at great loss.

Types of Volume Fluctuations

One further point requires consideration before commencing the report of actual practices. The sources of volume fluctuations are significant. There are three, usually referred to as seasonal, cyclical, and random. Each presents its own problems and demands its own approach. Success varies widely, from usually good results as to the seasonal problem to poor results and even to failure in other phases. Seasonal fluctuations in volume are traceable to fairly predictable weather characteristics. On the other hand, even the economists do not agree as to the causes of the broader movements which they call cyclical. There is far less regularity in these curves than in seasonal variations, and cyclical characteristics include price movements which are potentially disastrous to those who manage badly or not at all. Random fluctuations are what the term implies— changes entirely irregular and attributable to chance or unusual conditions. The N. R. A. boom of 1933 is an example. The problem raised by random movements is made difficult because both the intensity and the extent of the force must be predicted if success is to be attained. Thus, in the binder twine industry, random

weather conditions are an important factor since all sales are concentrated in short selling seasons and unusual weather conditions
prior to harvest may upset carefully laid plans.

Results of the Investigation

This paper and the investigation on which it is based were undertaken upon the initiation of the Bridgeport Chapter. It was felt
that a study and report on actual practices might constitute some
contribution to the topic. Accordingly, an assigned investigator [1]
visited and interviewed various executives in sixteen different companies representing almost as many different industries. We contacted by mail about two dozen other companies. Half of the
companies visited are in the Bridgeport area; all are represented in
the National Association of Cost Accountants. Industries covered
in Bridgeport and other places included silverware, plumbing, rope,
soap, leather, drugs, paper goods, textiles, rubber, cutlery, brass,
electrical, office supplies, roofing, machinery, and miscellaneous spe-
cialties. While the total number is obviously too small to constitute
a real statistical sample, the range of industries and of the possible
phases of the problem appear satisfactory. Co-operation was very
gratifying and a tribute to the interest of our members in the work
of the Association.

The investigation sought to discover as to each company the
importance of the problem, the parts of the inventory affected, the
reaction of the industry to cyclical conditions, the extent and success
of forecasting business conditions, the methods followed and success
attained in inventory control, and the general attitude toward the
whole inventory problem. The volume of material collected was
so great that only a bare summary of important points will be
possible here.

General Attitude Toward the Inventory Problem

It seems logical to report first on the general attitude toward the
whole inventory problem, since that attitude is the spring whence
flow the details of method. The range was from an acceptance of

---

[1] The investigation was carried out by Mr. Donald G. Robbins, Jr., a gradu-
ate student in the Department of Business and Engineering Administration at
Massachusetts Institute of Technology.

inventories as a necessary evil to inclusion of inventories as an integral element in broad administrative policy. Some emphasized purely production aspects, others, financial phases, and a few refused to allow any point of view to dominate. Five objectives of inventory control were advanced: service to customers, service to production, improved industrial relations and personnel management, speculative profit and financial strength. The companies which look upon inventories merely as a necessary evil seek a turnover as high as is consistent with satisfactory service to customers, or use the inventory for price speculation. Others balance turnover, financial considerations, service and personnel considerations against each other, seeking, to the extent consistent with the financial risks involved, a reduction in productive activity fluctuations, a lowering of labor turnover and continuous jobs for a constant force.

Raw Materials Problem Most Severe

Control of inventories in relation to changing activity is, of course, but one aspect of the broader problem of inventory management. Its importance varies from industry to industry and in different sections of the inventory. We found that the most likely source of difficulty is the raw materials inventory. This is due to several facts. Many raw materials are characterized by violently fluctuating prices, that show no correlation to movements of prices of the finished goods of which they are the most important part. Speculative positions are frequently unavoidable, such as where commitments must be made at time of harvest. Then again, the time lag between purchase and sale is at a maximum in the case of raw materials, allowing maximum time for market changes. In many cases raw material costs are a substantial or even predominant part of the cost of the finished product. This condition, found in such industries as textiles, tanneries, hatters, rope and soap, makes raw material inventory management a critical problem in every case.

Finished goods inventories run a close second to raw materials, but for different reasons. Obsolescence is an ever-present risk. Style is important. Sudden changes in demand are fairly common. The problem is frequently accentuated by long manufacturing cycles and short selling seasons, both of which necessitate rather long-range forecasts and the taking of important speculative positions on the basis of such forecasts. Industries which experience the finished goods problem include silverware, pipes and valves, novelties, clothing and radios.

Three Aspects of Problem

The practices followed in attempting a solution appear to have three aspects. There is a recognized requirement for information as to actual conditions, a similar need for information (forecasted) as to what business is to be in the near and distant future, and a problem of reflecting in purchasing and production the inventory policy adopted. We found general satisfaction and success as to the first phase. All of the companies visited had a material control system that provided, more or less accurately and quite regularly, detailed and summary information regarding the size, distribution and location of the inventory. The frequency and detail varied directly with the acuteness of the inventory problem and with the difficulty of control. Almost all the companies used a card system with a card for each item or each class of items, showing generally: the activity and movement of the item over a period of time, often as long as five years; the amount currently in stock; the location of the inventory; its use in the finished product; stock limits; and segregations on account of orders not yet in production.

As to the second element in the problem, that of information as to the future course of business, the situation was definitely less satisfactory. Performance varied widely and for several reasons. Some companies have given the problem little or no attention. Some face a real dearth of statistical background. A few are subject to a complication of random factors which make forecasting extremely difficult, if not impossible.

The obvious advantages of eliminating seasonal fluctuations from production and the relative simplicity of this phase of forecasting account for fairly general success in this particular area. Use of the inventory to permit the leveling of production from one season to another is also common and is generally recognized as a legitimate management device where the nature of the product permits.

Forecasting Cyclical Movements

It is in the other two areas of forecasting that conditions are generally less satisfactory. These are forecasting prices and cyclical movements. Relative success seems to depend upon having one man devote all or most of his time to the problem. In the companies that do a large amount of price speculation in raw materials (such as textiles, tanning, etc.), there is usually one man, either the buyer, treasurer, or president, whose job it is to watch the market and forecast prices. The man who has this responsibility is usually an older, experienced man with high analytical judgment, courage, and what amounts to a sixth sense. Smaller companies which cannot afford a full-time man on this function are under a handicap and must depend heavily upon other methods.

We found many approaches to forecasting cyclical movements. Some companies base their forecast on sales estimates by the sales force. Some use a multitude of general economic statistics. Others merely project their own present apparent trends, a method which has obvious limitations. Some depend upon economic services. A few use a lag or lead relationship to published series. Still others base their conclusions on executive judgment derived largely from general reading. Perhaps the most successful companies have combined almost all of these methods, giving each proper weight and synthesizing a forecast, not of what will certainly come, but of what is the most probable thing to come. The really surprising fact was that only a few of the companies made any attempt at cyclical forecasting *per se*.

Control Devices Used

With a varying background of facts and forecasts, the companies use different control devices to accomplish their different objectives. The two points of attack seem to be purchasing policy and routines, and production authorizations. Thus, in the case of raw materials, control of authorization to commit for purchases and of production programs require attention; for goods-in-process, it is new orders started through and the program for finishing up orders in process; in the case of finished goods, sales can be controlled only to a minor degree, but the amount of goods finished is subject to manipulation. Two elements are common to control of all parts of the inventory: purchase and production authorization.

The location of authority to commit for purchases or to issue production orders appeared to depend upon the number of items that must be started into process, the value of each, both absolute and in relation to total product cost, and the cost to the company if a mistake were made. Most companies had stock limits on at least a part of their inventory. Maxima-minima control is the simplest system; under proper instructions it can be largely operated by clerks. Wherever there are a large number of items to be controlled, many of which are standard and most of which are of low value, the source of the authorization is an order point set by an executive, often minor, and a purchase requisition for a standard quantity by a stock clerk. Maximum and minimum limits and order points are fairly generally subject to review by the inventory manager. Usually, the requisitions cross his desk as a matter of routine, in order to permit at least a casual check. Where this executive has good judgment and is informed as to objectives and expected conditions, this procedure provides for desirable flexibility in control. In some instances, the stock limits are used to bring an item to the attention of an executive who decides not only whether the item shall be ordered, but also what quantity should be ordered.

In a few cases, the budget is being used as the source of both the purchase and production authorization. Its use to authorize production schedules is the more frequent. Both are limited to larger companies which have been working with the budget for an extended period. Usually, stock limits are used in addition as a check on the budget, and serve to bring an item up for review whenever quantities exceed the limits in either direction.

In job order plants, the production authorization is usually a copy of the sales order. We found a few cases where the sales department also directly controls the purchase authorization, although it is much more common for the production department to authorize purchases of materials after its own analysis of the sales order. The placing of responsibility for production authorization in the sales department was also exemplified in industries making highly styled merchandise. Here the merchandise manager was considered to represent a proper balance between the sales and production points of view. The plan seems to have worked well where we found it.

Top executives are a direct source of the authorization for certain types of purchases. Usually the more difficult the decision and the greater the cost of a bad decision, the higher in the executive scale the authorization starts. Top executive responsibility is particularly characteristic where speculation in the raw materials is a matter of policy. In textiles, for instance, the treasurer or president decides

when and how much to buy. High executives indirectly initiate purchase or production authorizations in other cases. For instance, if
the inventory policy is changed to permit accumulation by increasing
the stock limits all along the line, a flock of production and purchase requisitions will be started in response to the change.

Price and Demand Speculation

We were particularly interested in the extent of conscious speculation. All companies speculate to some degree, either as to prices
or potential demand. Where there is a long manufacturing process,
it is unavoidable. The degree of speculation varies widely as between companies, running all the way from the use of speculation
as the primary source of profit to cases in which there is no conscious
speculation and even a conscious avoidance of it. One company goes
so far as to have its day's requirements of its principal raw material
delivered at its plant each morning; no reserve is carried. At the
other extreme many tanneries and textile companies look to price
speculation as the primary source of profit or loss. In general it
appears that speculative activities have been only moderately successful. This has been due, at least in part, to a failure to recognize
all phases of speculative possibility and to develop a policy based
on this knowledge. Perhaps those companies have been most successful which have been able to stay in the middle ground, avoiding
price speculation rather completely, but carrying on a moderate
amount of demand speculation and using speculation to protect
profits rather than to make them.

Conclusions Suggested by Study

So much for our report on conditions as we found them. There
remains only a more subjective summary of what appear to us to be
the significant conclusions. Eight points appear worthy of emphasis:

**First: The approach to the inventory problem must be an
administrative approach and not merely departmental in its
point of view.** If there is any one thing that is clear as a result
of our study, it is that inventory policy has its implications in every
division of the business. Maximum turnover can be obtained only

at the cost of production delays, loss of orders, sharp fluctuations in productive activity and high labor turnover. Constant production involves fluctuating inventories with financial problems and great risk of spoilage, obsolescence or price loss. Inventory policy in each individual case must be founded upon a compromise between conflicting interests and aimed toward administrative balance. It is a major administrative problem. We were interested to note how far ahead some companies were looking in their inventory policy and how near-sighted and opportunistic others were. The far-sighted companies tried in every way to use the inventory for the best advantage of the enterprise—as an aid in industrial relations, for occasional speculation to protect profits, and for various kinds of service.

Second: Control must rest upon knowledge as to present facts and forecasts as to future conditions. Control implies a conscious direction of something. Inventory control presupposes information as to present facts and a conclusion as to the desired direction of change, if any. An intelligent decision as to the desired direction of change is inconceivable without some assumption as to future conditions. A plan of action is similarly impossible without like assumptions. Specifically, this means that forecasting is unavoidable. Since so much policy depends upon forecasting, it demands serious attention. Lack of information on the part of management as to the normal seasonal characteristics of any business is almost inexcusable. Cyclical forecasting is more difficult. That great precision is impossible of attainment is, however, no reason to avoid the attempt. It is particularly important that cyclical trends be sharply differentiated from seasonal trends. The two cannot successfully be treated together in forecasting.

Third: Speculation is unavoidable. There is considerable misunderstanding as to this point. Any commitment in inventories is a speculation. Increasing production in anticipation of increased sales is just as much a speculation as price speculation, even though the latter may be more spectacular. There are times when a price speculation may be less risky than a demand or style speculation. The important point is again that recognition of the problem is a prerequisite to solution. Denial of the speculative element is an ostrich approach. Inventory control policy must be based upon a realization that speculation is not only a risk but a tool to be considered in deciding upon inventory policy.

Fourth: A do-nothing attitude will make net inventory losses inevitable. Too few realize that ordinary control routines operated mechanically are certain to result in inventory losses which are greater than any possible profits. Inventory losses tend to be concentrated in the crisis phase of the business cycle; inventory gains appear in the recovery phase on the basis of increasing volumes and stiffening prices. Anything approaching a constant turnover will result in maximum inventory quantities at the peak of the business cycle and minimum quantities in the depression trough. Thus losses will be taken on maximum quantities while profits will be possible only on minimum units. Some companies in the peak of prosperity consciously drag their inventory below the point where they can give adequate service because they realize that some orders will be cancelled and that a reduction in inventory quantities may avoid more loss than the profit they might make on a few more orders. Speculation to protect profits is to be distinguished from speculation to make profit. Certainly companies in which inventory losses are important may well consider devices to keep inventories down as business reaches the peak and may well accept as desirable a much lower turnover when business is poor. Demand speculation as carried out by most business, is a more subtle but equally dangerous form as compared with price speculation. It serves to build up a basis on which, in case of bad forecasting, large price, spoilage or obsolescence losses may be taken when business turns for the worse. With avoidance impossible, intelligent use of the right kinds and proper timing of speculation demands judgment and courage.

Fifth: Different types and degrees of control are called for by different parts of the inventory; the same is true for different industries and different parts of the cycle. This principle needs little discussion as to types of inventory and industry. Goods-in-process inventory presents relatively minor control problems as far as cyclical conditions are concerned, for it is, from this point of view, primarily a link between raw material and finished goods, the two important speculative points. Certain industries face an acute problem because of unsettled price conditions or style factors. In all industries the inventory problem becomes more important as business approaches the peak of the cycle. The particular characteristics of each industry require consideration in policy making.

Sixth: There are a series of devices useful in the problem of control under varying activity conditions; all are directed at controlling purchase commitments and production authorizations. These devices have already been indicated in the previous discussion. They are repeated here for clarity and summary.

(a) Maxima and minima points may be varied at different stages in the cycle. This will affect the total size of the inventory.
(b) Control may be exercised through turnover, leaving the responsibility for the make-up of the inventory to an inventory manager. This is analogous to the open-to-buy concept used in department stores.
(c) The budget may be used as a basis for production and purchase authorizations. Planning should, of course, include definition of the desired size of the inventories.
(d) The problem may be left entirely to the judgment of one or more high officials. This is a type of approach used where the speculation is an important element.

In the usual situation at least two of these devices will be found and can be justified for different parts of the inventory. A maxima-minima control may work for supplies, while top executive control is demanded for a few basic raw materials.

Seventh: Flexibility is an essential element. This principle cannot be better illustrated than by reference to the common maxima-minima basis for inventory control and purchase authorization. If minima and order quantities are large enough for high activity levels, they are too high for low levels. If they are low enough for poor business, there will be production delays and lost sales when business is good. To meet changing conditions there must be flexibility.

Eighth: There is no mechanical substitute for human judgment. Changes in business activity are the result of an interplay of complex economic forces in which different elements have differing weights from time to time. Under such conditions keen judgment is necessary, for no mechanical system can be devised to meet these complexities. There must be judgment in forecasting, judgment in decision as to proper policy, and judgment in execution. Responsibility must be placed with due regard for the degree of judgment required and for the cost of mistakes. There can never be a sound program based on an assumption that the problem can be reduced to mere routines. There is no mechanical substitute for brains and judgment.

In conclusion: At the moment business men are inventory conscious. Inventories are generally recognized as an important problem. It is to be hoped that this attitude will promote a more generally constructive approach. Inventories should be a tool of management, managed throughout the cycle for the greatest good to the business. This broader attack requires a frank recognition of all the elements of the problem, use of the best technical methods available and, above all, sound judgment and great courage.

INCREASED PROFITS THROUGH INVENTORY CONTROL *

By W. C. Skuce

THE purpose of inventory control is to assure the provision of proper material, finished parts, work-in-process and finished stock at the right time, in the right amount, for the requirements of the immediate future. When correctly administered, inventory control results in low cost, high turnover of working capital and good service to customers. This paper deals with the control of factory inventory, with particular emphasis on the control of material as a cost element.

The function of inventory control may be subdivided as follows:

1. Selection of material and parts.
2. Determining the required inventory investment.
3. Establishing proper manufacturing time or time required to replenish stock.
4. Determining how much to order.
5. Ordering materials.
6. Handling and storing materials.
7. Controlling the generation and disposition of obsolete inventory.
8. Material utilization.
9. Control of losses.
10. The physical inventory.

These functions represent a large portion of the manufacturing job, and improvement of these functions has a decided effect on costs, services and profits.

Selection of Material and Parts

One of the outstanding problems in manufacturing is the control of material as a cost element because material is a very large percentage of the cost of products manufactured. Material used by a manufacturing concern may be defined briefly as the purchased part of the product on which no work has been performed by the pur-

* Consisting of the major portions of an article in the 1938 Year Book, entitled, "Control of Material as a Cost Element," and a talk, entitled "Increased Profits Through Inventory Control," presented by Mr. Skuce before several N.A.C.A. chapters during 1939 and 1940.

chaser. Consequently, material may be basic raw material or it may be the finished product of some other manufacturing division or vendor. Since each progressive step in processing material might result in a finished product, which in turn could become the material element of cost in another manufacturing division or plant, the control of material should be of constant concern to the manufacturer from design application to shipment to the customer as a finished product.

It has been stated that the objective of inventory control is low ultimate cost and high turnover. If this is to be accomplished, good judgment must be exercised in the selection of materials so that designs will call for the minimum amount of material of the correct grade in a standard size.

Industry has been giving much more attention to materials in the last few years than at any period in the last sixty years of industrial progress, as competition has become keener and cost reduction necessary to continued success. It has been found that even with the use of the most modern methods of manufacture and with good control of expenses, costs could not be reduced sufficiently because of the large material element of cost. Subsequent action has found that proper consideration of material, grade and size had not been given in the original selection of design. *Many times materials or sizes of materials have been selected for availability rather than desirability.* Because there are so many kinds of materials, and so many sources of information, the *best* materials have not always been selected. Many times, too much material has been specified. Wrong sizes have been specified. Very expensive materials, or less expensive materials requiring excessive machining have been called for. Relatively little effort has been expended in analyzing the various "extra costs" (such as quantity extras, finish extras, etc.) on materials, even though industry has for years been analyzing "extra costs" of labor and waste. Too often there has been the false conclusion that material offered very little opportunity for cost reduction. The real fact is that there is a big opportunity to reduce material costs.

Since material is so important and is such a large element of cost, *we must not be complacent about materials but must realize that proper selection of materials offers the opportunity of making substantial cost reductions.*

The responsibility of material selection rests primarily with the engineer. The engineer must select from the available materials those which will most adequately meet the requirements of quality and performance in the product being designed and, at the same time, give minimum over-all cost. To do this job well, the engineer must have a *thorough knowledge of materials* embracing:

> (a) Physical properties of materials
> (b) Availability of materials
> (c) Tolerances on material sizes
> (d) Cost of materials

Engineers and designers must be constantly on the alert to incorporate the materials and products of industry in their designs. Every day new materials are developed, or old materials are modified to improve their properties. Chemists, metallurgists, and laboratories develop these materials with one thought in mind—to produce new materials which will be better and less costly than those already in existence. It is essential that industry keep in close touch with these sources in order to take full advantage of any new developments as quickly as possible.

In order that everyone who selects materials may be able to do so intelligently, it is necessary that the information regarding materials be collected, arranged and published in a form that is handy to use, and a routine be established to keep this information up to date.

All of these items (physical properties, availability, vendors' tolerances and costs) must be considered in relation to each other in order to attain low-cost designs. As already stated, the best place to make cost reductions is on the original drawing, which means that the engineers and the designers should be supplied with the necessary data on *all four* of these properties in as brief and concise a form as possible, so that they can locate the required information easily and quickly, especially for jobs of low production or small value. If, as is sometimes the case, the designer must refer to one source of information for physical properties, to another for availability, and to a third for costs, he cannot design rapidly and will, if pressed for time, particularly on jobs of low production or small value, have a tendency to overlook some of the factors. Also, if information is scattered in this way, it is difficult to visualize all of the factors in proper relation to each other and to evaluate them correctly.

Cost and stock sheets, similar to Exhibit 1, have been developed by the General Electric Company to give the engineer a convenient source of information. These sheets provide in one source all of the information that used to be contained in material cost books, stock lists, and vendors' schedules of extras and tolerances. Therefore, cost and stock sheets are used not only by engineers and designers but also by order clerks, stock clerks, cost clerks, planners and others interested in materials and parts. The preface on each sheet also gives specific information about the material, its application, and reference to similar materials with slightly different characteristics. If complete information on chemical and physical properties is required, reference must be made to the company's properties books or laboratories.

Preferred Numbers

Preferred numbers have been selected as sizes to be stocked. They are now available as American Standards and their use should be of vital interest to anyone concerned with the general subject of material control.

"Preferred Numbers" are a geometric series of numbers selected by convention to permit and assist in establishing logical ranges of sizes or capacities that can be used universally where interchangeability is desirable. Being a geometric series, each succeeding number is approximately a fixed percentage greater than the preceding number, as, for example, 10, 16, 25, 40, 63, 100. Each of these numbers is approximately 60 per cent greater than the preceding number as contrasted with the constant arithmetic difference in a series such as 10, 20, 30, 40, etc. Preferred numbers are established in relation to the number 10 and the series agreed to by convention are on the basis of the number of steps between 10 and 100. The 5, 10, 20, 40 and 80 series of numbers indicate, respectively, the number of steps in the series between 10 and 100; higher or lower numbers are obtained by multiplying or dividing by 10, 100, etc. The specific numbers that have been approved as American Standards are contained in the American Standards publications Z17.1-1936. In addition to the basic decimal series, fractional preferred numbers are included for linear dimensions that are commonly expressed in inches and fractions.

| WORKS
ISSUED BY
DATE | STANDARD MATERIAL
COST AND STOCK ROUND, SQUARE, HEXAGON
HOT ROLLED MACHINE STEEL BAR | B4A2A

PAGE 1 |

B4A2A is low-carbon hot-rolled machine steel. This is the most common grade and should be used wherever possible. For special conditions use: B4A2C, for parts requiring accurate size and good finish without machining; B4H1, for better machinability; B4B1, for screw machine; B4C1 or B6B1, for high strength.

COST PER 100 LB: (Wt. 0.283 lb/cu in.)

Round and Square				Hexagon	
Dia, Inches	Cost	Dia, Inches	Cost	Dia, Inches	Cost
3/16		2 1/8 to 2 1/2		1/4	
1/4		2 9/16 to 3 1/16		5/16	
5/16		3 1/8 to 4 9/16		3/8	
3/8		4 5/8 to 5 1/16		7/16	
7/16		5 1/8 to 5 9/16		1/2 to 9/16	
1/2		5 5/8 to 6 1/16		5/8 to 11/16	
9/16		6 1/8 to 6 9/16		3/4 to 1 9/16	
5/8 to 11/16		6 5/8 to 7 1/2		1 5/8 to 3 1/16	
3/4 to 1 1/2		7 9/16 to 7 3/4		3 1/8 to 3 3/16	
1 9/16 to 2 1/16		7 13/16 to 8			

For B4A2A3 (pickled & oil finish) add $.25 per 100 lb to above prices.

ORDER DATA - NOT FOR USE IN BILLING
 Specific Length Extra: (All machine cutting - consult Order & Stores Dept.)
  5 ft and longer - no charge.
  Under 5 ft - Consult Order & Stores Dept.
 Straightening Extra:
  Bars ordered within a variation from a straight line of not more than 1/8 in. for each
  5 ft of length will incur an extra charge - Consult Order & Stores Dept.
 Quantity Extras: Calculated on single item basis

Quantity (lb)	Under 1000	1000-1999	2000-3999	4000-5999	6000-49999	50000 & over
Extra (¢ / lb)	+1.5	+1.0	+.25	+.10	0	See O&S Dept.

STANDARD TOLERANCES: VARIATIONS IN SIZE, INCHES

Round and Square				Hexagon			
Dia, Inches		Over & Under	Out of Rd & Sq	Dia, Inches		Over & Under	Diff in 3 Meas.
Over	Incl			Over	Incl		
-	5/16	±.007	.010	-	1/2	±.007	.011
5/16	7/16	±.007	.011	1/2	1	±.010	.015
7/16	5/8	±.008	.012	1	1 1/2	+.021 -.013	.025
5/8	7/8	±.009	.014				
7/8	1	±.010	.015	1 1/2	2	+1/32 -1/64	1/32
1	1 1/8	±.012	.016				
1 1/8	1 1/4	±.014	.018	2	2 1/2	+3/64 -1/64	3/64
1 1/4	1 3/8	±.016	.022				
1 3/8	1 1/2	±.018	.026	2 1/2	3 1/2	+1/16 -1/64	1/16
1 1/2	2	±.022	.030				
2	2 1/2	+1/16	1/32				
2 1/2	3 1/2	+3/64	3/64				
3 1/2	4 1/2	+3/32	1/16				
4 1/2	5 1/2	+7/64	5/64				
5 1/2	8	+1/8	3/32				

EXHIBIT 1 (FACE)

B4A2A
ROUND, SQUARE, HEXAGON   **STANDARD MATERIAL COST AND STOCK**
PAGE 2   HOT ROLLED MACHINE STEEL BAR

WORKS
ISSUED BY
DATE

PREFERRED SIZES (★ or ◆)   STOCK SIZES ( )

Dia	Round	Square	Hex.	Dia	Round	Square	Hex.
3/16	◆	◆		1 1/2	★	★	★
1/4	★	★	★	1 3/4	◆	◆	◆
5/16	◆	◆	◆	2	◆	★	◆
3/8	★	★	★	2 1/4	◆		
7/16	◆			2 1/2	★	★	★
1/2	★	◆	◆	2 3/4	◆		
9/16	◆			3	★	◆	◆
5/8	★	★	★	3 1/2	◆		
11/16	◆			4	★	◆	
3/4	★	◆	◆	4 1/2	◆		
7/8	◆			5	★	◆	
1	★	★	★	5 1/2	◆		
1 1/8	◆			6	★	◆	
1 1/4	★	◆	◆	7	◆		
1 3/8	◆			8	★		

★ or ◆ Preferred sizes; give preference to sizes marked with ★.
Code:

SPECIAL WORKS STOCK
Do not use on designs repetitively ordered.

Dia	Round	Square	Hex.	Dia	Round	Square	Hex.

EXHIBIT 1 (REVERSE)

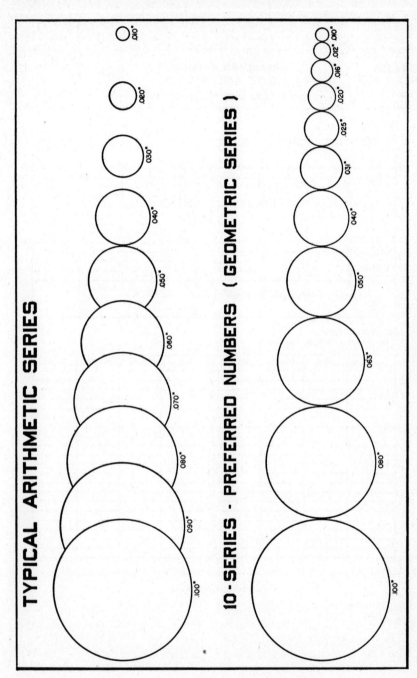

Exhibit 2

Because they are a logical system of numbers (Exhibit 2), preferred numbers permit the use of a minimum number of sizes to adequately cover a given range for ordinary requirements. Obviously, if everyone uses the preferred numbers in standardizing material sizes, additional economies will accrue both to the manufacturer and to the user because of the greater demand for the same (as well as fewer) sizes that will ordinarily be manufactured, stocked and ordered. Immediate prospective economies in fewer sizes stocked, reduced inventories, interchangeability of stock and greater quantities per purchase order make the use of preferred numbers by the General Electric Company attractive even in advance of general acceptance by industry as a whole. General acceptance will result in further advantages and economies such as increased availability of material in the common sizes, elimination of dissimilar gauge sizes and, hence, interchangeability of materials heretofore dimensioned and priced in accordance with those gauges, etc.

In introducing preferred numbers, it is expected that the sizes shown initially will not adequately cover present requirements; hence numerous special sizes will be continued for some period of time. However, new designs should call for preferred number sizes, and on the basis of demand, the recommended size shown on these sheets may be revised to more accurately reflect requirements. To concentrate the demand on the fewest number of sizes, the coarsest series possible should be used. The five series preferred number range gives about 60 per cent difference between sizes. The ten series gives 25 per cent, the twenty series 12 per cent, and the forty series gives 6 per cent difference between sizes. It is felt that the forty series can be avoided in practically all cases.

It is planned to use these cost and stock sheets to take further advantage of large quantity purchases and to eliminate small quantity direct purchases when stocks of such materials are available in another location within the company. It will also be possible to purchase carload lots of some materials by combining two or more plants' requirements in order to take advantage of quantity lot prices through the use of stopover freight car deliveries.

Determining the Required Inventory Investment

In order to determine the required inventory for a department or plant, an inventory control chart is prepared. This chart (Exhibit

3) shows the estimated output at various rates of capacity for a given department or plant. Based on the length of time required to produce the average product in this department or plant, or in other words, the production cycle, the turnover at capacity output can be determined. The fact that working inventory should be

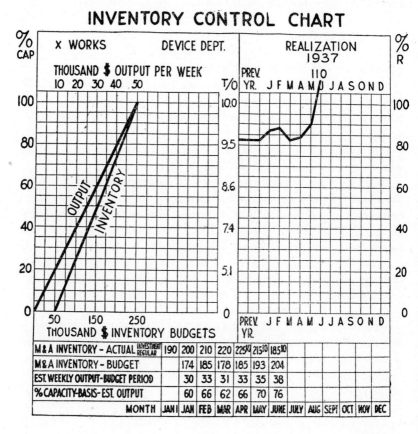

INVENTORY CONTROL CHART

M & A INVENTORY – ACTUAL INVESTMENT REGULAR	190	200	210	220	225¼	215¹⁰	185¹⁰						
M & A INVENTORY – BUDGET		174	185	178	185	193	204						
EST. WEEKLY OUTPUT-BUDGET PERIOD		30	33	31	33	35	38						
% CAPACITY-BASIS-EST. OUTPUT		60	66	62	66	70	76						
MONTH	JAN I	JAN	FEB	MAR	APR	MAY	JUNE	JULY	AUG	SEPT	OCT	NOV	DEC

A-88052

Exhibit 3

proportional to the rate of output based on capacity turnover is recognized. At zero capacity, however, a certain amount of inventory is necessary in many lines of manufacture so that adequate service to customers may be maintained. This available inventory is called a minimum or standby inventory. Having established the minimum inventory, it is added to the working inventory. As the rate of production increases, the need for this minimum or standby inventory diminishes, so that at capacity none is needed. Using this as a basis, a budgeted inventory is set up for any rate of production based on a given turnover at 100 per cent capacity. Consequently, a bogey turnover is established for all rates of production. It will be noted on this chart that the measurement of the actual inventory against the budgeted inventory gives a percentage realization which indicates the effectiveness of inventory control and which is not distorted by fluctuating rates of production.

The control chart, therefore, is a barometer because it looks into the future and indicates whether or not the inventory of today is adequate for the output of the coming period. It also indicates the probable load, shows trend of business activity, indicates discrepancies in billing costs, and presents other vital departmental statistics in a compact and concise manner.

The foremen and other members of a manufacturing organization are equally responsible for the realization of the inventory budget because greater industrial efficiency shortens production cycles and shorter production cycles result in increased turnover and a greater return on capital investment.

Establishing Proper Manufacturing Time or Time Required to Replenish Stock

The turnover that is possible on any material or apparatus is largely dependent on the time required to secure materials and manufacture apparatus. If it takes ten weeks to secure material, replenishing orders must be placed for stock material when a minimum of ten weeks' stock is on hand. This would result in an average investment of five weeks' stock in inventory. Similarly, on internally manufactured parts the manufacturing time has a decided effect on turnover and average inventory investment.

A great deal of effort has been and is being made to determine accurate time allowances to establish labor piece prices. However, the same attention has not been given to manufacturing time, including the preparation of paper, the waiting time due to load or key machines and transportation time between operations. These elements represent a high percentage of the total manufacturing cycle. This phase of the manufacturing job is very important from a turnover viewpoint. It is also essential for good scheduling, elimination of production follow-up and conservation of manufacturing floor space.

It is hard for the average person to realize that some small part with very low labor content should take several weeks to secure. The first reaction is naturally "Why should it take five weeks to produce 1,000 parts that only contain $1.00 labor?" If there is a rush demand for these parts so that delivery is required in less than five weeks, the tendency is to force the factory to upset its schedule and produce the parts desired ahead of their scheduled date. This, of course, upsets the normal schedule, extending deliveries on other orders. To secure parts ahead of schedule also requires special production follow-up and added expense. *Too often there is a tendency to work on "cases" instead of "conditions."* If a five-weeks' schedule is too long, analysis should be made of the steps in manufacturing time to reduce the normal manufacturing time, as that is the only way in which consistent short deliveries can be made with low inventory investment and low production expense.

Determining How Much to Order

Materials, parts and apparatus are ordered by the production department for actual customers' orders and in anticipation of customers' orders. Special materials, parts and apparatus are ordered to meet the requirement date of the manufacturing schedule, in the amount that is required for the customers' orders. Any material, parts, or apparatus ordered in anticipation of customers' orders must be authorized for stock. Authorization for materials and parts must have the approval of the engineering and production departments. Finished apparatus is authorized by the commercial department.

It is extremely difficult to forecast accurately production requirements as far in advance as a year, or even for six months. Experience has proved that effective inventory control should be based on short-period forecasts of business, for example, on a ten-week period revised monthly. By using a relatively short period as a basis for producing stocks of materials, parts or finished products, safer and more flexible inventories are the result.

One of the most difficult tasks in the control of inventory is that of determining the quantity of authorized stock material or component parts to order, so that high turnover with low ultimate costs will be the result. In the discussion of manufacturing time or time required to replenish stock, it was pointed out that the minimum replenishing order was the quantity that would be consumed in the period required to replenish stock. If, however, starting costs are high, as is the case on automatic machines or punch presses, very unsatisfactory costs might result if the minimum quantity was manufactured. In addition, automatic machines and punch presses should be run for a reasonable period to assure satisfactory machine tool utilization. Vendors of raw materials now recognize these factors and consequently charge extras for small quantities.

On the other hand, there are physical or practical limitations on the maximum order quantity of any type of purchased or manufactured material or part. Some of these limitations are caused by dies becoming dull, requiring a setup to be broken to sharpen a die. In other cases it is necessary to sharpen tools, etc. If the quantity that can be made without such interruption is much in excess of normal requirements, the maximum quantity should be limited to three or six months' requirements, depending on the line of product.

To summarize, the basic information necessary to properly determine order quantities are:

1. The expected weekly usage.
2. The design status.
3. The time required to replenish stock.
4. The minimum quantity that can be produced on a machine tool without seriously affecting its operating time.
5. The maximum quantity based on physical or practical limitations.
6. The base quantity price or the material and labor cost excluding setup.
7. The setup cost or the quantity extra charge.

The analysis of this information results in the expression of two conclusions—the cost in the minimum and maximum order quantities. If the saving that can be made by ordering more than the minimum order quantity is sufficient, the order quantity may be set as the maximum or an intermediate quantity.

Because the hazard varies on each item ordered, and because

the problem of storage, handling, obsolescence and deterioration is different in each case, the judgment of the head order clerk in determining the proper order quantity is essential. As a guide, however, a 10 per cent return on investment in raw material and 25 per cent on finished parts is recommended before six months' stock of an item of good design is ordered for stock. Lower percentages should be furnished for shorter periods of coverage.

Half of all items in a physical inventory are generally stock items and a large proportion of the materials and parts are purchased in anticipation of customers' orders. It is, therefore, very essential that a proper method of determining order quantities be used, if ultimate costs are to be low and turnover high.

To control the volume of input, it is recommended that a record of commitments be kept. This is best accomplished by figuring commitments on material and labor separately. The material commitments are best accumulated through the orders placed on vendors. The labor commitments may be accumulated from labor load charts, from required labor for scheduled production, etc. Actual material charges are usually received several weeks after commitments are placed. A current control of commitments permits advance knowledge about whether input will be of the proper magnitude to support the planned output.

Ordering Materials

It is the function of the purchasing department to make favorable contracts for materials. However, the factory must provide the purchasing department with the estimated quantities required for the contract period. In the preparation of these raw material estimates the factory must give proper consideration to design status, so that the material contracted for will be used without loss.

When contractual agreements have been made, ordering direction cards are distributed to the factory. These cards indicate upon whom orders should be placed, the terms of the contract, the quantity contracted for, etc. Special items not on contract must be referred to the central purchasing department for ordering directions.

As a guide to the factory, the purchasing agent and inventory control supervisor advise the factory monthly on the number of weeks' protective stock that should be carried on materials and also indicate the probable delivery time during unsettled periods caused by violent changes in volume of business.

Upon receipt of requests for raw material purchases, the order and stores department in each works should determine whether the material can be secured from another plant in order to eliminate quantity extras or to use up material that is obsolete in another plant. If the material must be ordered from an outside vendor, requisitions are placed in accordance with the ordering direction card from the purchasing department.

Handling and Storing Materials

Handling and storing of materials is a major problem in the control of inventories, because much of the effort of manufacturing is in receiving, storing and moving materials. This problem has been discussed to some extent under manufacturing time. It should also be considered from the following points of view:

1. Reduction of expense in unloading and handling materials to put them in storage, through requesting proper packaging by vendors and proper loading of cars to facilitate unloading by means of fork trucks, cranes, etc.
2. Crane facilities in storage areas for heavy materials.
3. Reduction of expense in dispensing stock and keeping inventory records by unit quantity packages.
4. Conservation of storage space by proper packaging, and the use of fork trucks or stocking devices.
5. Reduction of expense in taking physical inventories by unit quantity packages properly stacked.
6. Conveyorized setup in manufacturing departments and between departments.
7. Trucking facilities between buildings and storage.
8. Proper stock bins in convenient locations.

Material handling expense is primarily indirect labor, although handling at work stations is often a part of the direct labor operations. We should be constantly on the alert to make reductions in handling expense, because such reductions may also shorten our manufacturing time.

Controlling the Generation and Disposition of Obsolete Inventory

Obsolete inventory is defined as items of superseded design on which there is over six months' supply on hand.

In order to maintain a leading position in an industry, it is essential that new and improved designs be introduced. This brings with it many problems, such as the control of production during the transition period, so that all the parts on the old design will be utilized before the new design is placed on the market. In order to accomplish this, a transition committee composed of an engineer, a commercial representative, a production man, a cost man and a factory superintendent must work in close co-operation. Trial balances of present stocks compared with proposed transition date should be prepared as a guide to determine the proper date of change to the new design.

Many changes involve only integral parts of a piece of apparatus, rather than a complete new product. An effective system to take care of these alterations or changes is essential in order to distinguish between current losses caused by engineering changes and obsolescence losses due to inability to use inventory provided for future production. It is also important that items of current design on which excessive stocks exist be reviewed currently because *these excessive stocks may become obsolete inventory.* It is likewise important that overruns of parts and materials to be used expressly on a given requisition be controlled so that the factory floor will not be cluttered up with so-called "surplus goods," and so that conditions causing overruns can be corrected and such materials disposed of to the best advantage.

In order to know the condition of the inventory, it should be classified as active, inactive or obsolete. This classification enables the manufacturer to know the amount of inventory which is obsolete, and also that part which is inactive and, therefore, in some danger of becoming obsolete. The disposition of obsolete inventory is best accomplished by having lists of such material prepared and analyzed by a group composed of representatives of the engineering, manufacturing, cost and planning departments. Monthly progress reports are prepared from the totals derived from these lists. The better-known methods of disposing of obsolete material are by direct application on current orders, by substitution for other items on current orders, by reworking in order to apply on current orders, by sale to an affiliated company or another works or department which has a use therefor, by returning to the vendor for credit (since vendors often have better outlets for materials than the consumer), or by scrapping and obtaining whatever salvage value is possible if no other alternative can be found.

Material Utilization

Material utilization which prevents waste is primarily a problem of careful planning to use the minimum amount of gross material to manufacture a given unit. In general, waste losses amount to almost as much in dollars as manufacturing losses (spoilage and extra costs). The co-operation of the foreman and material handlers is needed to assure the success of the planned procedure. The function of material utilization to prevent waste may be broken down as follows:

I. PLANNING

1. Make designs which require minimum theoretical waste.

While quite some thought has been given to theoretical waste in designing products, the effect of physical waste has often misguided material selection. A minimum number of preferred sizes should be used as a working objective, so that the lowest ultimate costs may be obtained.

There are many recognized methods of designing for minimum waste, and the manufacturer should be critical of all designs which necessitate:

(a) Excess turning because of one large fit, if the large diameter of the piece can be welded on or otherwise assembled to a smaller dimensional piece.

(b) Excess machining, if a casting or forging or molded part can be substituted.

(c) Excess waste, due to corner edge and center losses on punch-press parts.

(d) Screw-machine work instead of header manufacture.

(e) Over-all machining when a finished surface can be purchased at less cost.

2. Make tool layouts to minimize material waste.

This is very important to punch press work to eliminate corner, edge and center losses. In general, from a physical viewpoint planners have been very waste conscious but unfortunately have overlooked a very important factor. To illustrate what has happened, let us assume that a steel punching had a finished dimension of .060″ x 1″ x 5″. The tool for this punching might be made to accommodate a 5 3/32″ strip, leaving a skeleton of only 3/64″ on each side of the punched strip. If the quantity of punchings normally made on a setup was 1,000 pieces and this size strip was only used to make one particular punching, then the quantity of material purchased to make these punchings would be only 89 pounds of a special width. The saving made in edge waste over using a preferred stock width of, say, 5¼″ would be 1/32″ or .6 per cent. On the other hand, the special purchase of 89 pounds of special steel would cost a minimum of 60 per cent more than the preferred stock width purchased in larger quantities. If you have no widths purchased in large quantities, it may be due to the large variety of widths stocked. If these can be reduced, the purchase quantities may be correspondingly increased to more than offset the edge waste. By designing to these widths, the engineer may be able to also eliminate the edge waste that first occurs.

The following opportunities for waste elimination in tool planning are typical of the kind of cost reduction planners should look for:

(a) If a disc and four other pieces are required for a product, and the piece can be made from the corners of the sheet, they should be included in the disc die.

(b) If a circular stator punching die is being made, a compound die should be made to produce the rotor punching from the stator center.

(c) Punchings can often be nested to eliminate waste.

II. EXECUTION OF PLANNING

1. The factory must use the material specified or report the excess as an extra cost.

Planning can only be as effective as its execution. Failures to follow planned procedure should be reported so that improvement in planning can be made or so that correction in facilities can be made to permit the proper functioning of the plan.

2. Careful control of expensive materials, such as silver solder (which may not be totally controlled by drawings, specifications, or planning), must be exercised.

III. SALVAGING WASTE MATERIALS

There is a continual need for proper segregation and collection of scrap materials to assure the best realization from such material.

Control of Losses

Fundamentally, the key to the control of losses lies in five points:

1. **A thorough analysis of the losses and their causes.** The analysis of losses is most important. We have our reports showing the loss for each department in relation to its direct labor load. Against this we have a bogey which was established by the head of that department. Thus we have a standard of performance by which the management can judge the departments that are out of line. But it is not enough to know the dollar value. We must know what the principal items are and their cause.

We must pick out the largest items and attack them first in a systematic manner. We must present a simple day-by-day picture of losses to those who are in a position to control them. In the General Electric Company we have a small organization whose duty it is to analyze waste and spoilage losses, to point out the high spots and to stimulate the line organization to take action.

2. **Proper training of workers, both factory and office.** Proper training of employees has an important bearing on the reduction of spoilage. During periods of increasing business, losses caused by new help are an important item. To minimize this we must first select the best type of employee available, using mental and physical aptitude tests where practical. We must then give special attention to the training of the new employees, using competent instructors who are skilled in teaching rather than using the best workmen. In some places we have separate training rooms in which the employee spends

a few days before being placed in the production line. We must see that every worker, both factory and office, knows the best way to do his job.

3. Proper tools and equipment to do the job, and proper maintenance of that equipment. Much spoilage can be eliminated by having the proper tools and equipment and seeing that they are properly maintained. All new tools must be checked carefully before they are placed in production and after that it is the responsibility of the foreman and the inspector to quickly detect and correct faulty equipment. A maintenance program is recommended to keep equipment in operation at a high standard of accuracy.

4. Careful planning. It is impossible to do any job well without first doing a careful planning job. This applies to the control of waste and spoilage. When an original design is made up, co-operation between the engineer, factory methods man, tool man and factory supervisor is of the utmost importance in developing designs and methods for low cost and low hazard. We should plan our inspection to detect poor quality as soon as possible. We must keep in mind that inspectors are not merely rejectors but can be of great assistance in the control of spoilage. Proper scheduling reduces extra setups and extra costs due to the use of less efficient machines. The prepricing of rework operations may substantially reduce the cost of such rework. Waste may be controlled almost completely when the job is planned by the design of dies and tools and by the size of stock order.

5. Active interest by every member of the organization in reducing waste and spoilage. Behind the first four points must be an active interest by every member of the organization in reducing losses. We must impress the importance of good work on the workman by establishing pride in the finished product, by acquainting him with the cost of defective work and by setting up competition between groups of workers. I do not think that any workman wants to do poor work but many times he is careless or indifferent. It is the responsibility of the management to stimulate his interest in doing a good job. Foremen and supervisors should visit the salvage department to observe at firsthand the tremendous magnitude of scrap from any plant. This will be more eloquent than any figures in convincing them that a better job can be done.

The Physical Inventory

We take a physical inventory each year and run a perpetual inventory system throughout the year. Besides the regular accounting and tax purposes the physical inventory is taken to correct stock records and to classify the inventory by stock class and utility.

The physical inventory consists of counting, writing inventory cards, verifying stock records, classifying, costing, extending, summarizing, and preparing final statements.

The expense of taking a physical inventory is subject to continual reduction through careful planning and active interest. Furthermore, *the physical inventory can be taken in one day,* eliminating costly shut-downs. The people engaged in inventory control work should plan daily for the taking of physical inventory. The benefits that accrue from a well planned physical inventory will well repay us for the out-of-pocket expense incurred.

A manual of inventory procedure should be prepared, giving in detail recommended procedures to be followed for all steps of a physical inventory. This will result in a better classification of inventories, substantial economy in the cost of taking an inventory, and equal or greater accuracy in the results.

Conclusion

To summarize, inventory control, if properly administered, should:

1. Reduce manufacturing time, resulting in lower inventory investment, lower production expense, better service to customers and lower costs.
2. Reduce quantity extra charges or high unit setup costs through establishment of proper material sizes and ordering quantities.
3. Reduce the hazard of obsolescence and the losses that accrue from obsolescence.
4. Reduce handling costs.
5. Minimize waste losses.
6. Reduce the manufacturing space required by excess inventories.
7. Reduce the cost of taking physical inventories.

All of these benefits should accrue from good inventory control. The opportunity confronts all of us, and the responsibility for effective administration rests on all of our shoulders.

The cost of our product may be affected by almost every step of the manufacturing process from the moment a design or formula is conceived until the finished product is shipped.

If we are to realize the greatest profits from our investment in inventory, we must *select inventory correctly, control it properly, and use it carefully.*

MATERIAL CONTROL FOR A CHAIN OF CONFECTIONERY STORES *

By Russell F. Brockmiller

THIS paper has to do principally with the control of raw materials and the distribution of their costs to the various stores and manufacturing departments of the company with which I am connected. I will also comment on some of the results which we obtain from our system and tell how we use these results.

The Company

In 1875, Fred Sanders, after a disastrous encounter with the Chicago fire, moved to Detroit, and on a borrowed barrel of sugar from the Edgar Sugar House and a lot of economic foresight, or just plain luck, established the first Sanders Store. From that borrowed barrel of sugar the business has grown until today it consists of a chain of twenty-one stores all located in Metropolitan Detroit, serving approximately twelve million people a year at its fountains.

Some idea of its size is best obtained from the quantities of raw materials used each year, of which I will cite a few examples: We use in our combined manufacturing departments 326,000 pounds of butter, 375,000 gallons of cream, 165,000 gallons of milk, 4,000,000 pounds of sugar, 580,000 dozen eggs, 20,000 barrels of flour and 750,000 pounds of shortening per year.

Controlling Accounts

Our stock ledger is divided into four principal divisions or accounts. We call them:

1. RAW MATERIALS

   Raw materials are items that go into the candy, bakery goods or ice cream.

* From the *Bulletin* of June 15, 1940.

2. SUPPLIES

   Supplies are items that go along with the sale of candy,
   bakery goods or ice cream, such as boxes, ribbons, wraps, etc.

3. ACCESSORIES

   Accessories are items that are used over and over again. Outstanding examples of these are dishes and silverware.

4. EXPENSE

   Expense items are what most of you men in your metal
   working factories would call factory supplies.

These four groups comprise some 6,000 different items and it is
the job of our stock control system to record the orders, receipts and
disbursements of these items, and to balance at the end of the year.
I might mention at this point that we are dealing with highly nego-
tiable merchandise and we feel that this merchandise should be safe-
guarded to the fullest extent.

We use a ledger card for recording the history of each item. The
receipts and disbursements are posted daily on a bookkeeping machine, posting today's work tomorrow. Our distribution by accounts
is made once a month. We usually give the figures to the accounting
department not later than the 7th of the following month.

Order and Receiving Records

The first step in this system is our order form. We have an
ordinary four-part form, the first copy of which is sent to the vendor.
The second copy is retained in the purchasing office. The third is
sent to the receiving room, and the fourth copy goes to the cost department for posting. This copy is posted to our ledger card showing the date of order, the quantity on order, the price and the vendor's
name.

Upon receipt of merchandise a three-part receiving record is
prepared. The first copy remains with the merchandise until completely verified as to count and condition, and is usually delivered
along with freight and cartage bill to the cost department late in the
afternoon of the day it is received. The second copy is sent immediately to the cost department, and there filed by vendor's name. It
is used as a check to insure the receipt of the first copy, and remains

on file under the vendor's name to assist in locating any discrepancy that might occur through loss of the original copy. The third copy is retained in the receiving room.

The work in the cost department on the receiving record proceeds as follows: We check the original copy against the second copy. Then we stamp the back of the original receiving record with a rubber stamp, thereby providing headings and space for figuring the information necessary for posting. We pick up from our ledger card the balance, both in quantity and value, and add to it the quantity and value plus any freight or cartage on the merchandise received. We then divide the new quantity into the new value and obtain a new average if there has been any change in price. This new average is then posted to the top of ledger card by pencil and the receiving sheet is filed in front of the ledger card ready for posting on the machine. The posting of these receiving sheets is very similar in detail to the posting of our requisition which I will explain a little later.

So far, as you will have no doubt noticed, there is nothing exceptional in our handling of our orders or our receipts, but I think you will agree with me, as we proceed with this discussion, that the handling of our disbursements is somewhat unique.

The Stock Room Order

We have what we call our stock room order. This is a four-part form. If this order is written in one of the stores, the first two copies are sent to the stock room to be filled. The third copy is retained in the store, and the fourth copy is mailed directly to the cost department as a notification that such an order has been written, and serves as a check in the event of loss of the original.

The stock room fills the order showing the quantity delivered, also signifying that it has been checked and that the account is accurate. The first copy goes with the goods back to the store where it is rechecked and initialed, brought back by the drivers and given to the cost department.

This stock room order has space for thirteen items, which is just about enough for one store's daily orders of such perishable goods as butter, eggs, coffee, etc. It is an ideal arrangement for the person ordering the merchandise, but not very good as a unit requisition suitable for posting.

This was one of the hardest hurdles to get over. The stores and manufacturing departments wouldn't listen to the suggestion that they should write one item on a requisition, so that the cost department could sort them to like items and reduce the inventory daily. It was necessary for us to find some other way of doing this. With proper cataloging of all items carried on our inventory, we were able to design a Keysort card to accommodate several items on each card.

The Unit Card

The Keysort card, which most of you have seen or heard about, is a card punched all around the edges with each hole marked with a number or with a descriptive title according to the use for which it is designed. We provided spaces on our card to accommodate fifteen items and also code numbers, page numbers, stock numbers, account numbers and factory departments. In addition, there is a space at the bottom of the card for quantity and amount which is extended and not punched.

Our next task was to group these aforesaid 6,000 items of ours into classifications such as flour, dairy products, colors, flavors, ribbons, wraps, china, silverware, etc., arrange them under these classifications, alphabetically or by size, and then assign descriptive code numbers. We use numbers beginning with 1,000 for raw materials, 2,000 for supplies, 3,000 for accessories and 8,000 for expense. We then put these items on the Keysort card, approximately ten items to a card, allowing room for the addition of an item here and there and assigned page numbers.

Now at this point you will notice that we have a problem of stenciling these cards. These items are subject to change without notice, and we had to have a degree of flexibility that would not be permitted if these items were set on a plate and printed.

Preparing the Cards

The device that we use is one that reproduces those crude drawings on penny postal cards which practically all of you have received from cleaners and dyers and insurance firms advertising almost anything. We buy small oil paper stencils which we rule, and type in the items that we want to print on our unit card, put them in this machine and run them off at the rate of 500 in less than fifteen minutes. This stencil also provides an easy means of erasing an item from our card or adding an item. We usually do not run more than a hundred cards of any page at one time.

The cards are then slotted by page number with the gang punch provided for this purpose. This takes only a fraction of a minute,

CODE NO.	DESCRIPTION	QUAN
1070	Bourbon	
1071	Caracas Liquor	
1072		
1073	F.S.Vanilla	
1074	Hershey & Merkins Milk	
1075	Broc. Milk Choc.	2500
1076	Choc. Rice Milk	
1077	Lexin	
1078		
1079	Choc. Rice Dark	
1080	Cocoa Powder	
1081		
1082		
1083		
1084		

GROUP NO — COATINGS   PAGE NO — 5

	QUANTITY	AMOUNT	
	2500	62500	

EXHIBIT 1

after which they are put in a file very similar to that used for sorting mail, the divisions being smaller, of course.

The cards are now ready for pulling. The stock room orders are sorted by stores and departments and paired off with the fourth copies which had been mailed in previously by the stores. Then a unit card is pulled from the rack for each item appearing on a stock room order. We might have on our stock room order two or more items appearing on the same card. However, a card is pulled for each item. The quantity delivered is then marked on the card opposite the item ordered. (See Exhibit 1.)

At this point, before the cards are separated from the stock room orders, which you will remember are in store or department order, they are again slotted to store, department or account number. We then date the back of the card by hand with an ordinary rubber dater. We find this an aid in locating any errors which may crop up later on. At this point the cards can be separated from the stock room orders because we now have all the information necessary to trace a transaction from the card back to the order again.

So far all the slotting of information on this card has been done on the gang punch where you can slot anywhere from ten to one hundred cards with one stroke of the grooving knife.

Punching Code Numbers

The next step is to punch the code number which enables us to conveniently sort these cards in code number order, or the same order as our ledger is arranged. This is done on an individual card punch that looks something like a small adding machine. The card is inserted in the back and the key depressed for whatever number is desired, the handle is then pressed, and the card is slotted. One hole is all that is necessary to be slotted per card, because the page number previously slotted in combination with the one hole slotted on the side of the card is all that is necessary to have this card sorted out in the desired sequence. Our operator averages 2,400 per hour on this slotting operation.

The sorting of these cards is done by means of a tumbler. When you insert the tumbler through these holes and raise the cards from the table the slotted cards drop out. My description of this sorting is in no way comparable to the results obtained by this method of sorting. However, I know we can take a month's collection of 26,000 cards and sort them in a few hours by store number, department in the store, and account number ready for distribution.

Posting

After our daily cards have been slotted on this individual card keypunch, they are then sorted by code number ready for posting. The girl doing the posting glances at the unit card, pulls the corresponding ledger card from the file, and lines it up in the bookkeeping machine in front of a carbonized journal sheet on which the entire day's postings will be recorded. The ledger sheet is then in position so the operator can see the last average price at the top of the sheet.

At the opposite end of the carriage we have a double roll of adding machine tape, the back of the first sheet being carbonized. We place the unit card in front of this tape, set up the price in the machine and multiply by the quantity as shown on the card. The result prints on the card both in quantity and value, and also on the second part of the adding machine tape.

There may be as high as twenty-five cards for this same item. Each card is extended as the first one was, and the total quantity disbursed is carried over by the machine and posted in the issued column. This amount is automatically deducted from the quantity on hand, and the new balance in quantity only is set up. This new quantity is multiplied by the same price at the top of the ledger sheet that was used to extend the unit cards and the new value set up. The carriage is spaced so that the next transaction appears on the journal sheet and the new balance is subtracted from the previous balance. The carriage then returns and the difference is printed and accumulated on the left hand side of the adding machine tape. If the sum of these two columns on the tape agree, there has been no error made in extending the unit cards, reducing our inventory, or figuring the new balance on the ledger card. This gives us a definite proof of the accuracy of our posting. These totals are then posted to the various controls for materials, supplies, accessories and expense, showing the total amount of disbursements to date.

The cards are now filed away until the end of the month. They are then all grouped together and sorted by store number, department in the store, manufacturing department, or account number, and added. The totals are balanced with the totals appearing on our stock ledger controls. Our record of these disbursements is given to the accounting department for entry into their respective accounts.

ANALYSIS OF FINISHED GOODS INVENTORY FOR BETTER CONTROL *

By Elson P. Dolliver

Analysis of Inventory and Simplification of Line

One of the first jobs to be done in properly controlling a finished goods inventory is to make a complete analysis of the sales and inventory on each unit which goes into the make-up of the line. As an illustrative example, a line of cutlery will be subjected to this analysis.

A complete listing of the inventory is made by units, showing the quantities sold for preceding periods, the number of orders in the

ANALYSIS OF INVENTORY

As of January 1, 1938

Description	Dozens Sold 1935	1936	1937	Frequency of Orders 1937	Dozens Inventory E.O.Y.	Active	Slow Moving	Obsolete
19356 Dessert Knife ...	194	443	778	12	508	508	...	...
19357 Dessert Knife ...	135	373	285	2	311	...	311	...
19358 Grill Knife	...	13	...	0	60	...	...	60
19401 Medium Knife ..	5	15	5	1	25	...	...	25
19402 Medium Knife ..	620	364	185	18	192	192	...	...
19403 Child's Knife ...	113	217	53	4	106	...	106	...
19404 Infant's Knife ...	27	0	27	1	35	...	...	35
19406 Breakfast Knife .	34	28	3	1	178	...	...	178
19408 Steak Knife	282	91	95	13	65	...	65	...
19409 Steak Fork	290	100	99	15	63	...	63	...
19410 Lge. Carv. Knife.	25	31	53	12	31	...	31	...
19411 Lge. Carv. Fork.	28	27	55	12	35	...	35	...
19412 Lge. Carv. Steels	17	11	27	2	40	...	40	...
20025 Medium Knife ..	4,963	4,386	5,942	30	300	300	...	...
20026 Dessert Knife ...	4,513	1,798	3,362	30	298	298	...	...
20027 Breakfast Knife..	181	121	113	6	95	95	...	...
20028 Grill Knife	955	1,095	850	12	306	306	...	...
32001 Dessert Knife ...	931	743	200	2	75	...	...	75
33001 Medium Knife ..	2,992	2,270	957	6	768	...	...	768
35001 Medium Knife ..	1,450	912	5,960	24	412	412	...	...
35002 Grill Knife	10	200	1,834	12	300	300	...	...
35003 Child Knife	150	300	1,640	12	220	220	...	...
						2,631	651	1,141
						59.4%	14.9%	25.7%

* A portion of an article from the *Bulletin* of September 15, 1936.

course of the year and the end-of-year inventory. This inventory is further broken down into active, slow moving and obsolete classifications. In cases where there is a wide difference in costs between items in the group being analyzed, it is desirable to cost the units and carry the analysis on a dollar as well as a unit basis.

The tabulation on page 100 shows that 59.4 per cent of the inventory is active, 14.9 per cent is slow moving and 25.7 per cent is obsolete. Obviously the first indication of this analysis is that action must be taken on the 25.7 per cent of the inventory that is obsolete. One very satisfactory way of handling this is to prepare a sales schedule in conjunction with the sales department and set up a monthly report to management showing the progress that has been made toward its disposal. The following is an example of this report:

SALES PROGRESS REPORT OF OBSOLETE MERCHANDISE
FEBRUARY 1 TO FEBRUARY 28 INCL.
CLASSIFICATION—CUTLERY

Item	Total Inventory 1/1/37 (Dozens)	Forecast Sales to Date (Dozens)	Period Sales	Year to Date Sales
19358 Grill Knife	60	10	2	6
19401 Medium Knife	25	10	3	5
19404 Infant's Knife	35	12	1	1
19406 Breakfast Knife	178	45	0	20
32001 Dessert Knife	75	5	15	15
33001 Medium Knife	768	100	40	68
	182	61	115

Attention is now directed to the active and slow-moving items with a view toward simplification of the line and determination of a stock carrying policy. The sales department viewpoint is essential to this part of the program. The line must be reviewed item by item. A few of the conclusions which might result are as follows:

19356 Dessert Knife—active seller—listed in current price lists—requires 6 weeks to manufacture—is a staple likely to be in the line for some time—inventory appears too high for volume of sales—suggest placing minimum stock limit of 100 dozen, maximum of 300 dozen as two important accounts require 150 to 200 dozen per order—other orders are small.

19357 Dessert Knife—essentially a special item for two accounts —one purchase made by each in March and second in October or November—customers will accept part shipment and usually place order five to six weeks in advance of needs. This item placed on a make-to-order basis plus a minimum inventory of 50 dozen at all times.

19402 Medium Knife—a moderately active pattern with relatively small sales volume—item 20025 was put into line to replace 19402 eventually—apparently some accounts were never shifted over—decided to continue item for balance of year inasmuch as it was listed in the current price lists, but manufacture no further quantities and plan to drop from line at the end of the year.

19403 Child's Knife—listed in price list but apparently overlooked by salesmen in displaying their lines—should be an active seller—sales department to endeavor to stimulate sales activity—item to be watched closely and to be either placed in active group or discontinued at the end of the year.

19408 Steak Knife—listed as an active item although sales volume small—must be included to round out the line—set stock limit minimum at 10 dozen—remake in 35 dozen batches which is the economic batch size for this item.

These are some of the points which may come up in reviewing the line. A careful review of the entire line at least once, and preferably twice, a year will disclose many points which need attention. In this respect an inventory is like a machine—it needs systematic and periodic inspection to insure maximum operating efficiency.

Simplification of the line is an extremely important consideration. It is very easy to keep adding items to a line without too much thought as to how they will ultimately affect the line. Very frequently it has been found that the addition of a fourth item to three already in a line group only results in splitting the sales four ways instead of three with no total increase in sales but a decided increase in inventory. If the new item is needed it should replace one already in the particular line group, with plans formulated to systematically reduce the stock on the item closed out as quickly as possible before the words "job lot" or "close-out" make it a target for "price chiselling." Once a simplification program is established and the number of items in each commodity or line group determined, it is relatively easy to control inventories for good customer service and reasonable turnover.

Periodic Sales and Inventory Report for Executives

Management has been accustomed to thinking of sales in terms of total dollars and by dollars for various commodity classifications. It is true that dollars do give a measure of activity and it is a language universally understood, but sales dollars are not usually coupled with the inventory value of the commodity group from which the sales were made. The fact that 80 per cent of the sales may have been made on 50 per cent of the inventory usually does not come to light until much later, if ever. It seems desirable, therefore, to call periodically to the attention of management, principally executives and sales divisions heads, just what the sales-to-inventory situation really is. From stock records it is relatively easy to obtain this data in units and a report can be drawn up that will command the attention of those in management who are in a position to prescribe the corrective action necessary to obtain the most satisfactory results. A typical report on sales and inventory is shown below:

SALES—INVENTORY REPORT
MONTH AND PERIOD ENDING FEBRUARY, 1938
COMMODITY—CUTLERY

Item	Sales Last Year	Estimate This Year	Sales This Month	Sales Year to Date	Inventory Finished Goods	In Process
19356 Dessert Knife	778	800	50	75	433	0
19357 Dessert Knife	285	285	0	0	311	0
Total 19000 Line	1,063	1,085	50	75	744	0
20025 Medium Knife	5,942	6,500	460	1,050	195	500
20026 Dessert Knife	3,365	3,500	200	475	100	250
Total 20000 Line	9,307	10,000	660	1,525	295	750
etc.						

In conjunction with this report, the inventory control department usually indicates in a letter of transmittal those items which are not moving in accordance with sales estimates, pointing out those items on which the sales are slowing down and making specific recommendations to management. The inevitable result of this procedure is that timely action is taken on the slow movers or erratic items before excessive markdowns are necessary to move the stocks. Also, in those organizations where the sales department places the manufacturing orders, there is reason to feel that a tabular report of this nature is conducive to a more concentrated sales effort on the items which appear to be overstocked and there is less inclination to place a large manufacturing order on an item which is not selling at the particular time.

On lines where the style factor is of paramount importance and the consuming season relatively short, such as sport clothing, bathing shoes, etc., a report of sales and inventory is compiled each week. In organizations where it has been used, this has resulted in ending the year with practically no carry-over, whereas without this information in previous years it was customary to have a considerable carry-over which would not return 50 cents on the dollar when finally closed out.

When this report is used it has been found that the sales department does a better selling job on the entire line than on a few selected items in the line, for the report shows up those items on which the sales are not commensurate with the amount of inventory carried on them. A few queries of "why" to the sales manager by the executives who receive this report usually result in stimulating the desired action.

Experience in many industries has shown that the sales-inventory report plays an important part in an inventory control program. It sets down in a clear-cut, understandable manner what is happening with respect to both sales and inventory. At the same time, it focuses attention on those items which need corrective action. While it is frequently difficult to get sales executives started in the use of this report, it is not very long before it is one of the accepted tools of their trade. They really like it and use it effectively.

There is no one cut and dried procedure applicable to each and every problem. However, a technique for each problem can be developed using the fundamentals outlined herein as a basis. The costs of operating an inventory control plan are not excessive; often a concern pays for inventory control but does not get it because the trouble has never been taken to make the proper presentation from records and data already being compiled in the company.

Proper inventory control does have a direct bearing on costs, for it helps to protect the cost advantages that have been built up through labor, material and overhead controls in common use in most plants.

ACCOUNTING FOR CONTROL OF FINISHED GOODS *

By C. J. Wibbelsman

IN PREPARING this paper it has seemed advisable to take up each phase in clearly defined steps, in order to show the relationship existing between each of such steps, and consequently to permit a more readily assimilated understanding of the means by which, in my opinion, finished goods can be effectively controlled and valued. First of all let us consider the question of control.

Two Phases of Control

There are two separate and distinct phases of control, namely that which deals with the physical control of finished goods for purely accounting purposes, and that which deals with control from the investment and merchandising viewpoint.

Since a good system of recording finished goods transactions is absolutely essential for good accounting control, I believe it goes without saying that the most practical and efficient method of recording such transactions, for investment and merchandising purposes, is to provide stock control records that serve both purposes simultaneously, and that without conflict or delay to either interest.

In this connection, we are sometimes confronted with opposition from management to the cost of such record keeping. This, I believe, is due to a more or less common tendency on the part of operating management to accept inventory adjustments at the end of any accounting period as a natural phenomenon, particularly if similar adjustments in percentage and in amount have been the history of prior years' operations. By the same token the same management would never countenance similar adjustments of cash funds; but is not merchandise as important and as valuable as cash?

Perpetual Inventory System Essential

Recognizing the value and importance of controlling finished goods in the same manner as we do with respect to cash, I think we will all

* Part of an article from the *Bulletin* of September 15, 1936.

agree to the statement just made—that a good system of recording finished goods transactions is absolutely essential to obtain proper accounting control. Furthermore, I think we will also agree that a perpetual inventory record system maintained primarily with respect to units, but combining related money values whenever and wherever practicable, is generally accepted as the most effective and economical means of such recording of finished goods transactions.

These perpetual inventory records depend for their accuracy and effectiveness on the following:

1—Correct starting inventory.
2—Adequate and accurate internal control of receipts.
3—Adequate and accurate control of deliveries from finished goods stocks.
4—Periodical selective checks of physical inventories.

Let us consider each of the points just mentioned at greater length.

Securing a Correct Starting Inventory

Good internal control, as a general rule, provides that inventories be taken under the supervision of the accounting department. It therefore becomes our own responsibility and prerogative to secure a complete and accurate starting inventory.

Adequate and Accurate Control of Merchandise Receipts

For the manufacturer merchandise receipts represent the deliveries from the last processing department or operation into the custody of the finished goods warehouse storekeeper. As such deliveries are made, the manufacturing division should secure a form of receipt, certified by signature of the storekeeper as to count and description, which is then turned over to the accounting department to be used as the basis of the original entries which are necessary to record relief of in-process accounts and additions to finished goods accounts.

In our own business, which is the manufacture of rubber tires and tubes, this step is effectively controlled since our count of finished goods produced is determined as such merchandise passes physically from the last manufacturing operation to the finished goods warehouse. The receiving record obtained at this point is turned over to the stock control division where it serves as the basis of entries recording additions to stock, and from there to the cost department for accumulation and monthly recapitulation for cost of production entry purposes. Prior to the entry recording cost of production, the cost department's summaries are verified with a recapitulation drawn off the stock control records to insure, insofar as possible, the accuracy of both records. As a point of interest, I might mention that this same receiving record serves payroll purposes also, being used as the means of verifying the production reported by operators on their individual or group daily time and production cards.

Control of Deliveries from Finished Goods Stocks

I believe you will all agree with me that no orders calling for shipments to customers should be turned over to the finished goods warehouse for packing and shipping without, *first,* the approval of the customer's credit, the reason for which is obvious, and *secondly,* without a copy of the order being retained by the controller's or treasurer's department to provide a positive means of securing the original order after shipment. Thus quantities actually shipped and other incidental shipping data are secured so that proper invoices can be originated.

With a procedure as just outlined in effect, the next step is to provide sufficient copies of invoices, so that a means is available of systematically providing the stock control division with the necessary data to support entries relieving the finished goods stock records of the merchandise shipped out, as indicated on such invoice copies.

Again citing our own practice, relief entries to the finished goods stock records are made from customers' original orders before they are rewritten on our shipping order form, thus enabling us to determine immediately our stock position with respect to giving preference to certain orders or customers, to determine the necessity of back-ordering any quantities and to make it possible to so advise our customers without delay. Under this procedure, the stock control division's copy of the invoice becomes the medium of checking the original relief entry and of noting any differences between actual shipments and the quantities ordered as entered originally.

In this same connection let us not overlook the necessity of following essentially the same procedure in delivering merchandise to internal divisions for testing, inspection, display or any other purpose for which merchandise is required. Failure to secure proper records of such movements of stock gives rise to a common source of petty inventory differences, not to mention the consequent failure to secure the necessary data for proper charges to expense accounts.

Periodic Selective Check of Physical Inventories

Selective checks can only be made effectively when stock records are divided into as many minor control groups as experience indicates is necessary to localize and ferret out inventory differences. Naturally, stock records must at all times be kept posted currently, and we must guard against improperly reconciling unrendered invoices and goods-in-transit items, particularly when complete inventories are taken at the end of definite accounting periods. In this latter connection, it might be well to mention that accurately maintained perpetual inventory records, together with an effective procedure for selective checking inventories, often preclude the necessity of shutting down operations and the extra costs involved in the taking of inventories for purposes of substantiating inventory quantities and related values for annual financial statements.

Control of Investment Through Perpetual Inventories

In introducing this subject, we stated that the most practical and economical method of controlling inventories from the physical or accounting, as well as the investment standpoint, was to provide stock records serving both purposes simultaneously. We then proceeded to point out that a perpetual stock record was generally accepted as the most accurate and effective means of obtaining the desired control.

In order to avoid a lengthy discussion of the advantages or disadvantages of several systems for controlling investments in finished goods, since many of such systems are highly specialized and scientific in their very nature, I believe I can best illustrate the use of a perpetual stock record system for obtaining the investment control considered desirable by referring again to the company which I represent for material, and by outlining their procedures in this connection.

Estimating Sales Requirements

In the first place, we have learned through quite a few years of experience that to be in a position to properly service customers at all times, we require an inventory approximately equivalent to thirty days' sales requirements. Such sales requirement figures are based on sales estimates, which in turn are based on:

(1) Past experience.
(2) The outlook in our own industry.
(3) The outlook in allied or related industries.

Of course, we take into consideration estimated changes in relative size and style popularity and seasonal demand fluctuations. While these estimates are not posted to the stock records in our case, due to the intimate knowledge of our inventory position possessed by the individual in charge of that work, in most cases I would consider it advisable to enter such estimates on the stock record, with suitable space for noting successive revisions in those estimates.

Use of Perpetual Inventory Records

In addition to posting production and shipment figures to our stock records and determining daily balances, as mentioned in the earlier part of our discussion, we also enter all future delivery orders received in a special "On Order" column, which is deducted from the "On Hand" figures to determine the quantities available for immediate shipment.

With the information as outlined available, we then proceed to review all stock records shortly after the first of each month to determine a reasonably definite production program for the following month and a tentative production program for the two succeeding months. These production schedules are used as the basis for purchasing the required raw materials. The actual production schedules are prepared weekly and are based directly on the exposure position indicated in the perpetual stock records. In the preparation of these firm weekly schedules, full consideration is given sales estimates, unfilled orders and stock available, and seasonal demands, and also to a factor that for us has a direct bearing on costs, namely, the minimum quantities which can be put through our manufacturing processes economically. In recognizing this latter factor, we get into "long" and "short" inventory positions on certain items, but these are usually the less popular and slower moving sizes and, being in smaller quantities, do not represent a substantial investment.

MULTIPLE STORE INVENTORY CONTROL AS APPLIED BY A LIQUOR STORE SYSTEM *

By J. Ralph Fenton

THE STATE store system of monopolistic control of the liquor traffic presents an interesting and unique problem of accounting control such as is seldom encountered in other lines of business. Primarily, the fact that the average unit value of the merchandise handled in such a store system is relatively high in comparison with other retail chain stores, makes it feasible and desirable to control inventories by unit rather than by value alone. Secondly, the operation lends itself admirably to an adaptation of the "Retail Method" of costing sales and inventory.

In a large organization, such as that in operation in Pennsylvania, the problem of inventory control is naturally quite intricate and involved. The requirements are commensurate with other large retail businesses which enjoy sales of from fifty to seventy-five millions of dollars annually. In addition to basic accounting requirements, there is a vast amount of statistical information required similar to that needed by other large chain store organizations where a systematic method of merchandising is in operation.

In order that the reader may obtain a definite picture of the problem, the writer will attempt to briefly outline the organization in operation in Pennsylvania. With varying differences such organizations are in operation in many other states, although most are considerably smaller. The Liquor Control Board has over five hundred stores throughout the state. Many are operated by one man, while some have as many as fourteen people comprising their personnel. The line of merchandise consists of over twelve hundred items of various kinds of liquor and wine in containers of different sizes from half pints to two gallons. Four large regional warehouses situated in the four divisions in which the state is divided care for restocking requirements of the stores. Each division is subdivided into districts in which are located sub-warehouses. These sub-warehouses are concentration points for slow-moving merchandise which is shipped to stores in less than case lots.

* From the *Bulletin* of February 1, 1937.

This paper is not intended to describe the accounting system which is in operation in any state liquor control board or commission. It is rather a brief outline of the writer's theory as to the ideal system of inventory control for such a setup. The plan which will be discussed is one which must be adapted to accounting machines. Although the writer is of the opinion that it may be operated best with the punched card method of machine accounting, this paper should not be construed to definitely limit the application of the system to this type of machine.

Central Control of Billing

The ideal system, as will be outlined in the following paragraphs, is predicated, as far as stocking the stores is concerned, upon central control of stock and pre-billing of all orders. The first problem in this connection is control of warehouse inventories so that availability of every item is at the finger tips of the supply division. This is accomplished by a file of pre-punched tabulating cards. There will be a file for each warehouse, and as warehouse receipts are received, a card will be placed in that file for each case of merchandise placed in warehouse stock. This card will be punched with all basic information such as number of bottles in the case, retail value and cost of the case. These cards are numbered serially as they are placed in the file. As a result of this procedure the file of cards represents the "available" inventory in the warehouse at any given time. This file is for billing purposes only and is not to be confused with the true warehouse inventory which is maintained in a different manner.

Recording Receipts

At this point we are considering charges to warehouse inventory and this entry is made by means of a punched card for each item on the warehouse receipt. This card will carry all the information which has been punched on the detail case cards except that one card represents the total number of cases received and, of course, the total retail value and total cost. The receipt number and the purchase order number are also punched on this "debit" card for the purpose of reference. We now have a debit card for the total amount of the receipt which will be used in the preparation of our warehouse inventory record, and we have detail case cards representing the same number of cases in the warehouse file to be used for billing purposes.

Recording Shipments

We will now assume that the supply division has prepared orders for the stores and we wish to set machinery in motion so that such orders will be shipped to the designated stores. First, it should be explained that every store must be placed on a definite delivery schedule. The warehouse will make deliveries to stores every day according to that schedule. Thus shipping orders must be given to the warehouse in sufficient time so that orders may be selected and delivered on the scheduled day. A two-day margin of time is usually sufficient, and since deliveries are seldom made on Saturday, this means that the shipping orders for the week are completed by Wednesday, thus enabling us to close the warehouse records and balance the inventory by the end of the week.

Now to prepare the shipping order, which is also an invoice of merchandise to be shipped to the store. The order is taken from the supply division and cards are pulled from the warehouse file to correspond to the number of cases of each item desired. Cards are pulled from the low serial numbers in accordance with the "first-in, first-out" method. These cards are then run through an electric billing machine which tabulates them in such a way as to indicate the total number of cases, total number of bottles, total retail value and total cost of each item to be shipped. This information is printed automatically on the "Shipping Order and Store Invoice," which is prepared in quadruplicate. The cards are then gang-punched with the store number and delivery date and filed to be used later in crediting the warehouse inventory and debiting the store inventory. Two copies of the shipping order are sent to the warehouse. One copy is mailed to the store as an advance notice of shipment and as notification that this merchandise has been charged to its account. A fourth copy is retained in the Central Office to be matched up later with a signed receipt from the store.

After all invoices have been prepared for the week, the detail cards which were used in the preparation thereof are sorted in code or item order and summarized by item so as to provide total cards which will be used to credit the warehouse inventory. After these summary cards are obtained, the detail cards are resorted by store

and filed in individual store files to be used in charging the stores
for receipts from warehouse. A total card is punched from each
invoice which is used in preparation of store controls and as a
means for providing controls so that total shipments from the warehouse may be proven against the total receipts in the stores. The following chart illustrates the entire operation and shows the control
provided:

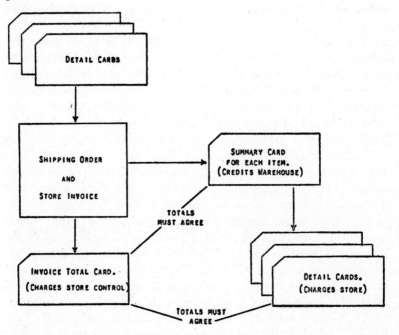

Supplementary registers are made of these various sets of cards
so as to provide a complete record of the transactions involved.
The following are suggested:

1. Register of shipments by code, showing complete detail of
   stores to which each code was shipped. This should be a listing
   of all the detail cards at the time they were being summarized.
2. Register of invoice totals. These should be listed in store
   order and also in invoice number order.

These registers will be of value, not only as support for credits
to the warehouse inventory record but also in auditing warehouse
invoices for storage and for transportation.

Warehouse Inventory Record

The only step now remaining as far as the warehouse accounting is concerned is the preparation of the warehouse inventory record. This is accomplished by sorting all of the receipt cards together with the shipment summary cards and the balance cards of the previous week. They are then tabulated and printed so as to calculate and show the following information: opening balance, debits, credits, closing balance. This record is tabulated by code and each amount shown thereon is supported by a register of the detail thereof. The record should be maintained so as to reflect number of cases, retail value and cost value of each item. Similar records will be made for each warehouse.

Recording Sales

We will next consider our problem from the sales angle. We will assume that the merchandise has been delivered to the stores and that sales have been made. The store reports of sales should consist of a daily report of sales value and a weekly report of item sales. All merchandise is charged to the store at retail value. They should be held accountable for units and value. Sales discounts, if properly reported, will be allowed in accounting for a portion of the retail value of sales. The balance must be accounted for by a transmittal of cash or check.

When the daily report of sales value is received by the Central Office it must be audited for addition and subtraction of all items. The detail of all discount sales must be verified to prove the accuracy of calculation and it must be proven that amounts have been carried forward to the summary properly. The only manual verification necessary is that of proving the discounts. The report is then given to a key-punch operator who punches a card for each store's report, showing thereon all information noted on the report. At the end of the week these cards may be sorted by store and tabulated to obtain store totals. Two registers are prepared as follows:

1. Sales Audit Report: Showing total retail value of sales and the distribution thereof to the different classes of sales and to discount allowed.

2. Cash Transmittal Report: Showing net value of sales reported and distribution thereof to cash transmitted and over or short.

In this operation the addition and subtraction on every report is automatically proven and verified, corrections being made where necessary and notification sent to the affected stores.

At the end of the week, the stores must submit a report of item sales for the week. That is, they must report the total number of units of each item sold together with the retail value of same. This report must be audited in order to prove that the correct retail price has been charged and that the total retail value of the report agrees with the total of the daily reports submitted. This audit is made by means of pulling pre-punched tabulating cards from files for every item reported sold. These cards have all basic information punched thereon, such as: number of bottles, retail value, unit price, case equivalent, vendor code, type of liquor, etc. Some of this information is for accounting use and the rest for statistical purposes, as will be explained later. Reservoir files are maintained with quantities of cards for each item in various denominations. Thus, if a store reports the sale of 123 bottles of a certain item it is necessary to pull one card representing 100 bottles, two for 10 bottles each, and one for 3 bottles. The denomination cards vary according to sales activity, the usual selection being cards representing 1, 3, 5, 10, 25, 50, 100, 200, 300 and possibly 500 units.

In this manner, cards are pulled for every store and reports are audited. The detail sales cards of each store are summarized by code in order to provide credit cards for the store inventory reports which will be described later. The detail cards are then returned to the reservoir files and may be used over and over again.

We now have the basis for any type of sales analysis which could be desired. Among the many reports which may be demanded, the following are of particular value to the purchasing, merchandising or operating departments:

1. Sales by code for each supervisory district.
2. Sales by code for each major division.
3. Sales by code for the state.
   (All of the above reports may be in bottles and cases.)
4. Sales by type of liquor.
5. Sales of liquor in price groups.
6. Sales of liquor by vendor.

Store Inventory Reports

The next major step in the system is the preparation of the store inventory reports. These are prepared weekly in the following manner: balance cards, obtained from the previous week's reports, are sorted with the detail shipment cards and the sales summary cards previously described. They are sorted in code order for each store and then tabulated on an electrical accounting machine which calculates new balances for each code and prints the results on a regular report. The report shows the balance at beginning of the week plus receipts of merchandise minus sales, which gives the balance at end of week. The balance is shown in both units and retail value. Retail value of sales is also shown so as to provide a check against a similar figure shown on the weekly Sales Audit Report which, as previously explained, is obtained from a summary of values reported daily by the stores.

The new balance cards obtained in this operation also provide a medium for the preparation of many types of analytical reports, such as:

1. Inventory by code for each district, division or state.
2. Sales activity (compared to inventory) of each code.
3. Inventory by type, etc.

Controls and Sub-Controls

All of the previous discussion has dealt only with detail records. Provision must be made for control accounts which tie in with the general ledger accounts. The general ledger inventory account is charged with receipts of merchandise and credited with sales, whereas the detail records and the sub-controls must record all subsidiary transactions dealing with movement of merchandise within the system, such as shipments from warehouse to store, transfers from one store to another, transfers from one warehouse to another, and transfers from store to warehouse.

These sub-controls are merely summaries of the detail cards used in the preparation of the detail records. For instance, the card punched for the total value of an invoice covering shipment to a store provides the means of charging the sub-control for that store.

A card punched for the total retail value of sales for the week is the basis for crediting the sub-control for the store. Similarly, every transaction is summarized and the resultant summary card used in the preparation of these sub-controls. All charges to a store are recorded at both retail value and cost, whereas credits are recorded only at retail value. This is the basis for the "Retail Method" of costing inventories and sales.

The sub-controls are prepared monthly by sorting all control cards together for each store and tabulating them on an electric accounting machine which calculates and prints the total of the opening balance and all charges for the month at both retail value and cost; the total credits for the month at retail value; and the closing inventory balance at retail value. This statement, which may be called "Store Cost of Sales and Inventory Statement," is then checked with the "Store Inventory Report" in order to see that the closing inventory figure is the same on both statements. We are then ready to calculate the cost of sales and the cost value of the closing inventory. As stated above, the total of all charges to the store inventory is shown at both retail and cost. We obtain the ratio of cost to retail by dividing the total cost value by the total retail value. The percentage figure thus obtained is then applied against the retail value of sales shown on the statement and we obtain the cost of sales. Cost of sales is then deducted from the total cost of charges to the store and we obtain the cost value of the closing inventory, which will be carried forward to the next month's statement.

Adjustments

Up to this point nothing has been said about adjustments. In an operation as large as this there will certainly be many adjustments and these must be made in detail by code in order to comply with the system of unit control. A detailed discussion of adjustments could well take up many more pages than have been devoted to the foregoing paragraphs. It must suffice to say that the handling of adjustments is similar to the routine described for the regular transactions described heretofore. They would be key-punched in detail from original papers and run through the detail inventory records as debits or credits as the case might be. They would be summarized by transaction and run through the sub-controls at the end of the month. Debit adjustments would be made at both retail value and cost, and coded to appear "above the line" or with "other charges" in the cost of sales statement. Credit adjustments would be made at retail value only and appear "below the line" on that statement. Cost would be determined by the same method as described for costing sales.

It has been the writer's desire in the foregoing paragraphs to give a word picture of the ideal method of inventory control for a liquor store system. It is thought that the reader may see the picture a little more clearly if the words are supplemented by a few actual examples of the various records described. The forms are illustrated below and on the following page.

	MONTHLY COST OF SALES AND INVENTORY ACCOUNT	Store Number 1 Month Ending:			
		BOTTLES	RETAIL	%	COST
11	Opening Inventory				
12-1	Receipt from Warehouse				
12-1	Receipt from Warehouse				
12-1	Receipt from Warehouse				
12-1	Receipt from Warehouse				
13	Retail Price Changes				
14	Adjustments to Receipts				
17	Returns to Warehouse				
19	Transfers to Other Stores				
	Total Charges to Store				
21	Sales				
23	Inventory Over or Short				
24	Operating Breakage				
25	Claim Breakage				
26	Short Packs				
28	Miscellaneous Claims				
	Total Credits to Store				
	Closing Inventory				

			WEEKLY WAREHOUSE INVENTORY REPORT		Warehouse Number 1 Week Ending	
CODE	OPENING BALANCE	DEBITS	CREDITS	CLOSING BALANCE	RETAIL VALUE	COST

			WEEKLY SALES AUDIT REPORT		Week Ending	
STORE	DATE	RETAIL VALUE OF SALES	TOTAL DISCOUNT	TOTAL NET SALES	RETAIL SALES	WHOLESALE SALES

		WEEKLY STORE INVENTORY REPORT		Store Number 1 Week Ending	
OPENING BALANCE	RECEIPTS	SALES	RETAIL VALUE OF SALES	CLOSING BALANCE	RETAIL VALUE OF INVENTORY

THE CONTROL OF INVENTORY INVESTMENTS *

By N. M. Cartmell

I T IS a unique industrial corporation that does not have inventory problems. Probably every corporation has one, two or all of the three principal types of problems:

1. Excessive inventories: Perhaps they are also badly out of balance and in part non-salable. Probably at least half of you realize that you have this problem now. Many of you always have it without knowing it. Comparatively few managements can recognize it during normal times because they know of no measuring stick, except previous experience, of what their inventories should be.

2. Inadequate accounting for materials: Many of you who recognize this problem, know how the accounting should be done, but your superiors will not approve the methods which you recommend.

3. Excessive manufacturing costs of products because of the materials: You may be accounting adequately for the materials used and the recognized wastes, but you believe that there must be unnecessary costs and wastes because competitors consistently underprice you or earn more profits. Probably you can see some of these wastes but cannot reflect them as such in your accounting data because those who are responsible claim that they cannot be avoided and must be included in the manufacturing cost standard. On the other hand, these costs may be too high because more costly materials are used than necessary, or the kinds of materials and parts may require higher manufacturing labor costs than necessary. Management faced with this type of problem is often unable to recognize existing conditions because they have had no experience to compare with present practice.

Let us frankly acknowledge the important reason why such problems arise or continue. The detection of faulty conditions within a business is usually dependent upon the management's experience, and the time devoted to the critical analysis and the improvement of internal affairs. Correction can be initiated only if the conditions are recognized, and this usually occurs when they are acute. I hope the

* From the 1938 Year Book.

day will arrive when the heads of businesses, who periodically go to their doctors for physical examinations to prevent or correct physical problems, will be as energetic in examining their business organizations to prevent or correct faults. Both types of organizations— the body and the business—are subject to the same ills—high or low blood pressure, anemia, and even cancer—and too frequently the materials of diet or of manufacture are at fault.

In each industry, only one manufacturer is the most efficient and has the lowest costs. All others have higher costs than the one most effective unit; some are very ineffective with high costs in serious need of control. Furthermore, all too frequently, the high cost producers are those who are complaining about "low" prices in the industry, although their complaints and their problems could be solved by an adequate control of their operating costs.

Inventories are accumulated for five reasons:

1. In order that materials will be on hand for production to proceed in an orderly manner and that shipments may be made to customers on short notice.

2. As a result of purchasing or processing materials in quantities sufficient to attain the optimum costs.

3. As the result of definite long-term policies and plans for such reasons as increasing the output per production unit or dollar of investment in fixed assets, decreasing labor turnover, and increasing the continuity of employment.

4. In anticipation of periods of difficulty in obtaining materials, as occur when there are strikes in suppliers' plants or when war is threatened. This is a service reason.

5. In anticipation of higher prices or costs because of expected increases in labor rates or raw material prices. This may be pure speculation or it may be insurance against loss from higher costs without accompanying higher selling prices.

All of these reasons for accumulating inventories are legitimate and logical and, when used with discretion, are sound, but the limitations governing good judgment must be recognized.

Practically all inventory and other business problems are the results of human errors or mistakes in judgment. For example, no business ever planned deliberately and intentionally to build up an excessive inventory of either raw materials or finished products. When the materials in an excessive inventory were ordered, there was no expectation that the inventory would become excessive or out of balance; it becomes so only in the course of time and in the light of conditions of the future. Errors of judgment as applied to inventories result from:

1. Unsound forecasts of future business conditions, particularly of commodity prices. These errors are especially serious when they result in disastrous losses of large sums from large purchases of basic raw materials, regardless of whether they are bought for service, insurance or speculative reasons.

2. Reliance upon insufficient and unco-ordinated data. These errors are large in number and frequently result in huge losses. They usually result from inadequate procedures, which cause is also a contributing factor to the first group of errors which arise from unsound forecasts.

We are here because we are interested in ways and means to minimize these errors in the future so that we can reduce the losses and improve the general effectiveness of our operations.

There are three obvious methods of accomplishing this:

1. By establishing sound policies.

2. By installing adequate procedures so as to provide a sound basis for executing policies and exercising judgments.

3. By teaching those who exercise judgment the dividing line between sound practice and speculation.

Four Vital Controls

No policies or procedures are more difficult to establish or require more technical knowledge and deliberation than those pertaining to inventories. Furthermore, inventory control is handled less effectively in most corporations than any other activity and management is just as adverse to this criticism as to any other. Inventory control cannot be established as an isolated function. It must be co-ordinated with budgetary control, sales control and production control. The position of inventory control will be clarified if we define these related functions:

1. The primary purpose of *budgetary control* is to plan all operations so as to secure the maximum profit from the minimum investment in working and fixed capital.

2. The primary purpose of *sales control* is to plan the sales activities so as to exploit the potentials of selling the maximum quantity of the most profitable products at the lowest possible selling cost.

3. The primary purpose of *production control* is to secure the maximum production of products of the standard quality at the lowest cost and at the right time.

4. The primary purpose of *inventory control* is to maintain minimum inventories consistent with sales requirements, manufacturing programs and the policies of the company, to assure a proper balance of parts and raw material inventories with respect to assembly and parts manufacturing requirements, and to serve as the basis for sound purchasing.

When these four controls are adequate, the inventories will conform with the general policies of the company, and will permit prompt service to customers, orderly production at a reasonable cost and the minimum losses from material and labor variances and from obsolescence.

Initial Steps to Establishing Inventory Control

In establishing adequate control, we must study our organization, personnel, policies and procedures, all of which are involved. Without attempting to define the problem in terms of only one of these considerations, and basing our discussion upon an established manufacturing enterprise, I suggest the following initial steps as essential:

1. The standardization of materials, which frequently is the key to successful control. While standardization begins with and is based upon the finished products, it cannot be divorced from considerations of raw materials and component parts, and of manufacturing operations and processes. The aim is to secure the greatest flexibility possible in the inventories and the optimum approach to mass production of all parts and to mass sale of all products. Practically every enterprise has much to do in the way of standardization.

2. The establishment of records which list the standard quantities and kinds of raw materials, component parts and sub-assembly requirements, as well as labor and equipment requirements for manufacturing each finished product. They should also record the standard allowances for scrap or other wastage and other factors, such as standard manufacturing lot sizes and minimum economic ordering quantities. These records are of vital importance to the production control activities and in co-ordinating procurement orders and inventories with demands for finished products. Revisions should be made as soon as any change is authorized in the design of a product

or in the method of manufacture. Some concerns do not have such records, but most do have them, although they are not always complete, up-to-date or distributed as widely as desirable.

3. The establishment of adequate physical handling and storage facilities. Of all the essential steps in the adequate control of inventories, this one is recognized most universally, although many plants are deficient and large losses result from deterioration, damage and even theft. On the other hand, many plants are incurring unnecessary storage and handling costs because their methods are too elaborate. Any arrangement is adequate that recognizes convenience of location and reasonable protection against any kind of loss.

There are no by-passes to these steps, although some methods are much simpler than others.

Essential Control Procedures

Having outlined the basic initial steps for establishing our control of inventories, and assuming that adequate procedures will be established for continuing them, we now consider the steps essential in maintaining the day-to-day controls. These steps are discussed in terms of procedures, but with references to the appropriate organization, personnel and policies. Procedures must be established for:

1. Forecasting the long-term sales demand for finished products.

2. Planning the long-term production program based upon the long-term sales forecast.

3. Forecasting the short-term demand for specific products.

4. Originating and scheduling procurement orders for finished products and their related parts and raw materials.

5. Recording quantitatively and financially all transactions affecting materials so as to determine:

    (a) The value of inventories for balance sheets.

    (b) The cost of sales and other expenses for profit and loss statements.

    (c) The variances between standard and actual costs of and for materials.

These inventory control procedures could be included in a discussion of the related essential controls because of their close relationship, and because each will reflect financial, sales, engineering, purchasing, personnel and manufacturing policies.

Forecasts Are Basic Needs

Every business does *some* forecasting of both the long-term and short-term types, but usually it is neither orderly nor sufficiently comprehensive to effect satisfactory results. Furthermore, the forecasters usually fail to record their data in writing. All businesses, even those manufacturing special or style products, can be planned at least in terms of total business to be done. Planning for the manufacture of standardized products is quite simple, although many such manufacturers still question the advisability of careful quantitative forecasting and planning. Although it has been years, even decades, since we began discussing budgetary control and standard costs, in many cases managements still regard them as applicable only to someone else's business.

The long-term sales and production forecasts are the *first* elements of day-to-day control of inventory investments. Upon them will be based most of our manufacturing, sales and financial policies. Furthermore, success in earning profits is largely dependent upon long-term planning. The period to be forecast will vary according to the business and the industry, and perhaps a year will be the average. The forecasts should be expressed in terms of quantities of a denominator common to all products, such as dozens, pounds or man-hours. The use of dollars as a denominator is to be avoided when forecasting for control purposes, but afterwards when the quantities are translated into dollars, accurate figures will be obtained for the budgets.

Long-Term Sales Forecast

For simplicity, these forecasts are illustrated in terms of the manufacture of shirts, but the exhibits which follow are not exactly like those used in the industry because they have been modified in order to serve as general illustrations. Furthermore, *no short cuts are shown.* Contrary to what you may guess, the forecasting or planning of shirt manufacture is not simple, but the manufacturers could not exist without detailed forecasts. While shirts are quite standardized as to styles, and to some extent as to patterns and colors, sales from season to season vary greatly as to patterns and even as to styles. For example, a short time ago, French cuffs on shirts to be worn

EXHIBIT 1

LONG-TERM SALES FORECAST FOR STATE OF NEW YORK

Period—July 1, 1938, to June 30, 1939

(Shipments in dozens)

Class	Shipments during preceding 12 months		Forecast for next 12 months		Forecast of Shipments by Months											
	Dozens	Dollars	Dozens	Dollars	July	Aug.	Sept.	Oct.	Nov.	Dec.	Jan.	Feb.	Mar.	Apr.	May	June
BY CLASSES OF CUSTOMERS																
Dept. Stores	8,000	$ 96,000	7,500	$ 90,000	375	425	600	750	900	750	450	480	900	820	600	450
Chain Stores	2,750	33,000	2,500	30,000	125	145	200	250	300	250	150	160	300	270	200	150
Ind. Retailers	11,000	143,000	10,000	130,000	500	580	800	1,000	1,200	1,000	600	640	1,200	1,080	800	600
TOTAL	21,750	$272,000	20,000	$250,000	1,000	1,150	1,600	2,000	2,400	2,000	1,200	1,280	2,400	2,170	1,600	1,200
BY CLASSES OF SHIRTS																
Whites	4,000	$ 48,000	3,800	$ 45,600	190	219	304	380	456	380	228	243	456	412	304	228
Blues	6,000	72,000	5,500	66,000	275	316	440	550	660	550	330	352	660	597	440	330
Fancies	11,000	137,500	10,000	125,000	520	565	781	970	1,134	945	612	635	1,234	1,141	836	627
Dress	750	14,500	700	13,400	15	50	75	100	150	125	30	50	50	20	20	15
TOTAL	21,750	$272,000	20,000	$250,000	1,000	1,150	1,600	2,000	2,400	2,000	1,200	1,280	2,400	2,170	1,600	1,200

with separate stiff white collars were the predominant style. Try to buy a shirt today with French cuffs and note the meager selection of patterns displayed. Furthermore, practically all of you are wearing shirts with attached or soft collars, and very few stiff white collars are visible.

Exhibit 1 is a long-term sales forecast for a period of one year. It should be revised at least quarterly, when an additional quarter should be included if each forecast is to cover one year. The revision should take cognizance of happenings since the last revision, as well as current prospects for the coming period. The exhibit is for one state, the geographical basis being the best for determining the sales potentials and supplying the base for the sales control in each area. The first tabulation is for shipments by classes of customers. To the right are the forecasts for individual months which, like the annual figures, should be translated into dollars for the budgets. The second tabulation is by classes of shirts and the total equals the first total. Additional tabulations on other bases, such as grades or price ranges, would also be useful and assist in accuracy.

The data used in compiling the forecast are of many kinds, each of which requires individual consideration. For example, the trend in economic conditions is important, as well as the status of stocks on dealers' shelves and in consumers' hands, the latter being of paramount importance because dealers do not move their stocks when the consumers have built up their supplies. Too much reliance must not be placed upon the quantities sold in previous years. Style trends are very important, such as the shift from the stiff collar which quickly wore holes in our shirts and increased the number we bought annually.

Responsibility for Long-Term Sales Forecast

Such a forecast should be compiled by the sales manager personally, assisted by the production control manager in order that the forecast may be practical from the manufacturing standpoint, and by the controller who should be watching the general business outlook in order that the production and sales requirements will produce the optimum profits without straining the financial resources. Of course, the forecast must receive the final approval of the president and the general manager.

The sales manager should have the primary responsibility because:

1. He will have difficulty in explaining any failure to meet a forecast for which he is responsible.

2. To forecast, he must analyze the sales potentials for each class of product in each sales territory. Thus he will obtain personal knowledge of such possibilities, and can plan the sales activity in definite terms of individual cities, prospective customers, and so on.

3. He will learn and appreciate the effect upon the business of the relative profitableness of the various classes of products in time to stress or put pressure behind the sales of the profitable products.

Note that I assign the primary responsibility to the sales manager. Many accountants and others believe that a sales manager is incapable of making a sound forecast. At a recent meeting of accounting executives, it was found that over half of those operating budgetary control have two budgets, one for the sales manager based upon his forecast, and a second official budget, just as though the sales manager did not belong to the same organization. Of course, salesmen's quotas for various reasons may total more than the sales budget total, but that should not affect the budget. I have seen many ridiculously optimistic sales forecasts by sales managers, but they have served only to strengthen my conviction of the need for the training of sales managers in the understanding of control work. I have never seen a really bad forecast based upon the detailed analysis just suggested, nor have I seen many sales managers do a sound sales control job without that analysis. Few sales managers, as yet, believe in such an analysis and are willing to give their time to it, but I believe that if we do our part the sales managers, like the factory managers, will seek our assistance.

Long-Term Production Forecast

When the long-term sales forecast has been approved by the management it should be resolved into a long-term production forecast as the basis for all important inventory and production policies. The production manager should be responsible for preparing this forecast, which should be developed for each class of products individually and in the following manner, as illustrated by Exhibit 2:

1. Translate the sales forecast of monthly shipments, as shown on Exhibit 1, into terms of the months in which the products must be manufactured in order to meet shipping requirements. Usually the forecast of shipments is merely advanced by the manufacturing time

interval plus some factor of safety. For example, if one month were
required normally to produce shirts, exclusive of the time for obtaining materials and completing clerical work, the forecast of work to
be started during June will be the shipping forecast for July.

2. Endeavor to plan the rate of production so as to secure as level
or even a rate as possible. If production were planned exactly in

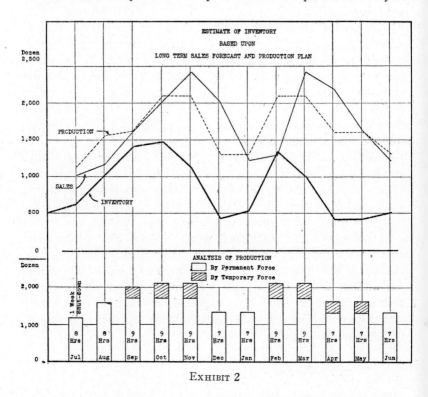

ExHIBIT 2

accordance with the shipping requirements, all peaks and valleys of
the sales curve would be reflected. While in some businesses production may be leveled arbitrarily almost to a straight line, it is usually
neither desirable nor possible. However, it can be leveled moderately and on a very desirable basis by such measures as concentrating
factory vacations within the dull season, working the minimum number of hours during the dull season and the maximum number during
the busy season, and refraining from replacing members of the working force who resign unless necessary.

3. This modified production program should then be reviewed in the light of the present inventory of products and any other pertinent factors. For example, further leveling of production might be attained at times by permitting the inventory to become very low.

Exhibit 2 illustrates such a development for the control of the inventory investment in finished products. The light solid line represents the forecast of monthly shipments as developed in Exhibit 1. The broken line represents the long-term leveled production program, determined as just described. The resulting inventory balances are shown by the heavy solid line. The leveled production program is also represented by the bar chart at the bottom of the exhibit. The bars indicate the production by the permanent force and by the temporary force. While there is considerable curve in this leveled production program, note the practical considerations and limitations established for this example:

1. While the permanent force is constant in number, its production is varied considerably by varying the hours per week. The total hours for the year average forty per week, the maximum possible under a union contract which also established nine hours as the maximum per day.

2. While a larger permanent force would eliminate the temporary force and thus permit further leveling of the total production curve, it is not practical because the inventory would peak earlier, causing financial difficulties, and because the manufacturer minimizes inventory close-outs at the end of the selling season by keeping production as close as practicable to orders. Furthermore, an adequate supply of satisfactory workers is available for recruiting the temporary force, and the production facilities exist to accommodate them.

Thus a definite sales, production and inventory program has been established which is the optimum for the control of inventory investment and all other considerations.

Production control and inventory control now begin. For instance, the quantities of products to be manufactured in each month can be translated through formulae into quantities of important raw materials and appropriate purchase contracts placed for future delivery. Furthermore, additional accurate budget figures are now available by translating the quantities to be produced and the resulting inventory balances into dollars.

Short-Term Sales Forecast

The primary purpose of the short-term sales forecast is the orderly initiation of sound production orders for manufacturing specific products. The production control manager should have the primary responsibility, assisted by the sales manager and controller. The sales manager must advise upon sales trends for individual products, and upon plans to discontinue certain styles or numbers and to create new styles and numbers. The controller's function is to check the effects upon the financial program.

The procedure for forecasting is comparatively simple, and is based upon the long-term production forecast. Each class of shirts (the second tabulation in Exhibit 1) is comprised of many individual styles and patterns. Short-term forecasts are made for each of those products. For convenience, the appropriate details should be recorded on the stock records for the products.

A stock record illustrating this procedure is shown in Exhibit 3. Note that this form provides for "cumulative" and not "balance" quantities. While this type of record is usually the best for all stock record purposes, it is essential for this control procedure.

The heading contains a few of the essential reference data. The most important are sales class, yardage of material required per dozen shirts, the manufacturing time and the "minimum economic ordering quantity." This term is defined as the smallest quantity which can be manufactured (or purchased) without an important sacrifice in cost or price. It corresponds roughly with the old term "maximum," but it is worded to imply that any larger amount may be ordered that is not excessive, considering such factors as the time that the shirts may remain in inventory and the possibilities of their becoming obsolete. It is subject to revision at any time with changes in conditions, such as a decrease in demand which would result in an excessive inventory.

For simplicity, a new number in the line is illustrated and initially no orders or inventory are on hand. The entries for quantities produced and shipped are similar to those on any stock record and will receive no further reference. The other entries can be traced in sequence by the small key letters in the quantity columns, each letter denoting the entries made simultaneously. We do not have time to trace all entries, but the high spots are:

A—A reserve quantity of 25 dozen is provided as deliberate protection against actual sales exceeding forecast sales. It represents the maximum quantity we desire to have in inventory for *that* reason.

PRODUCT-- Shirts CLASS--Fancy STYLE NO.--Y1531

PIECE GOODS PER DOZEN--29 Yards MINIMUM ECONOMIC ORDERING QUANTITY-- 50

S'T'D HOURS PER DOZEN--11 ORDERING POINT--50

UNITS-- Dozen S'T'D CUTTING SCALE--BX TIME REQUIRED TO MAKE -- 2 Weeks

SHORT-TERM FORECAST			SHIPPING ORDERS				PRODUCTION ORDERED				PRODUCED				SHIPPED			
Date	Month	Quan.	Total	Date	Month	Quan.	Total	Date	Order No.	Date Wanted	Quan.	Total	Date	Order No.	Quan.	Total	Date	Refer. No.	Quan.	Total
Reserve		25a	25	Reserve		25a	25	6/25	1234	7/25	80c		7/23	1234	25					
6/25	July	55b	80	7/10	July	26d	51	"	"	8/10	70c	150	7/24	"	55	80				
7/25	"	65f	90	7/25	"	27e	78										7/24	162	25	
7/31	"	62i	87	7/31	"	9i	87										7/26	171	37	62
6/25	Aug.	-60b	+40	7/10	Aug.	31d	82	7/25	1345	8/25	60g	200	8/4	1234	20	100	8/10		60	122
7/25	"	90f	147	7/25	"	22e	131						8/5	"	50	150	8/25		10	132
7/31	"	±	177	8/10	"	16f	156						8/22	1345	50	200				
8/25	"	80l	167	8/25	"	8k	164													
6/25	Sept.	134	228	7/10	Sept.	16d	98	7/25	1345	9/10	100g	300								
7/25	"	100f	280	7/25	"	110	158	7/25	1445	9/25	200m	85								
7/31	"	-6	-277	8/10	"	15f	198	8/25			100m	400								
8/25	"	90l	257	8/25	"	21k	227													
6/25	Oct.	400b	328	8/25	Oct.	43k	240	8/25	1445	10/15	100m	500								
7/25	"	±	380																	
7/31	"	-6	377																	
8/25	"	90l	347																	
6/25	Nov.	4326	440	8/25	Nov.	9k	449													
7/25	"	±	515																	
7/31	"	-5	509																	
8/25	"	1	479																	
6/25	Dec.	-650	525																	
7/25	"	±	577																	
7/31	"	-5	571																	
8/25	"	1	544																	

EXHIBIT 3

We would not need to provide this reserve if we could forecast with mathematical accuracy, or if we were unwilling to speculate to that extent on this new number. The reserve will be included in all considerations until it is cancelled.

B—The initial short term forecast. The usual minimum period

would be the manufacturing period (not less than one month) plus an additional month for clerical work, the securing of material and similar work. These forecasts should be made and revised just before the first of each month, though in peak seasons it may be advisable to do so more frequently.

In this example, the period forecast is the period that the shirt (a fancy item) is expected to remain in the line. On June 25, forecasts are made for each of the succeeding six months: 55 dozen for July delivery, a cumulative total of 80 including the reserve quantity; 60 dozen for August delivery, a cumulative total of 140; and so on with a final cumulative total of 525 dozen (shown opposite the June 25 entry for December delivery).

C—The "Production Ordered" column shows order #1234, initiated to cover the first two months' requirements, 80 dozen for July 25 delivery to stock and 70 dozen for August 10 delivery to stock— a total of 150 dozen or three even lots of 50 dozen each. Note that production is split as to delivery date in observance of the principle that manufacture should be delayed as long as practical. The cumulative total of the production ordered column exceeds the "forecast" total as of the same date by 10 dozen which is a small additional speculation but probably safe in view of the later sales expectations.

This routine is followed for each shirt in that class, namely, the fancies. Then the quantities on the resulting orders are added in terms of the common denominator, dozens, and compared with that month's long-term production forecast for *that one* class, which should be based upon the sales forecast shown in Exhibit 1 and developed upon the plan of Exhibit 2. The total of the production orders will not equal the long-term production forecast. The next step is to balance them. If the ordered total is the higher, as is usual during busy seasons, the individual orders are reviewed and the quantities decreased to the extent necessary. Of course, adjustments are made first upon the orders for patterns which have the least sales possibilities, and hence are most likely to be slow moving and become obsolete.

If the orders total less than the long-term production forecast, individual orders are increased, the largest adjustments being made upon the orders for shirts most likely to sell. Of course, adjusting entries would be made in the production ordered column of the appropriate stock records. By this step we have insured that production will be balanced and co-ordinated with expected needs.

Notice that the order total is adjusted to the long-term forecast, because the latter governs the amount to be produced. Furthermore, it is usually the more accurate, although occasionally during the intervals between revision a change in trend will be shown by the short-term forecasts. Of course, if there is any doubt about the accuracy at that date of either forecast, it can be checked very quickly for taking corrective and appropriate action immediately, if necessary.

D—Shipping orders, as received, are entered individually or accumulated for periodic entry in the shipping orders column according to delivery months as shown. Cumulative totals are maintained.

F—After the shipping order entries of July 25 (E), the forecasts are revised to reflect the orders received and the current sales outlook for this pattern and style. In this illustration, sales look good and the forecasts for July, August and September are increased, all cumulative totals being changed accordingly and the previous entries and totals cancelled by drawing a line through them so that no confusion will exist later as to which is the most recent total.

G—On July 25, a production order for 150 dozen is written for split deliveries on two dates. A second order for 200 dozen for September 25 delivery is also written. Thus the total quantity has been ordered which is expected to be sold before this number is discontinued. This optimism regarding the popularity of the number is not sound, as seen later.

When all of the fancy numbers have been reviewed, the previously described step is taken for balancing orders against long-term forecasts.

Notice that the first delivery on order #1345 was scheduled for August, one month after the order was written, instead of two months. In spite of careful planning, such rush deliveries often will be required. To maintain the balance between production plans and schedules (unless our production plan is to be changed) we must delay the production on some order written in June for August delivery in a quantity equal to the rush order. Sometimes the reverse is desirable, as illustrated by entry (M) postponing part of the September delivery to October. In that case, a compensating quantity of an order for October delivery would be rescheduled to September. Of course, all such changes are handled as totals rather than by matching the quantity of one order with another.

There is time for only a few more references to the entries.

I—On July 31, the final entry is made of shipping orders for July delivery and the forecast for July is adjusted to the actual sales.

L—Note that forecasts as of August 25 for August, September, and October shipments have been decreased because the optimism of the previous forecast was not justified. For this reason, production of 100 dozen on order #1445 was postponed to October 15 (entry M).

Under this plan we can be quite certain that the quantities produced will be adequate and will be produced to meet shipping requirements without being excessive. In fact, if we could forecast with mathematical accuracy, finished product inventories at the end of each month would be exactly equal to the production authorized in excess of the short-term forecasts. Of course, such accuracy is impossible, but the maximum month-end inventory should not be more than the quantity resulting from providing reserve stocks, leveling production, or ordering the minimum economic ordering quantities, all of which will have resulted from *deliberate* judgment.

Scheduling Procurement Orders

The dates on which the production orders were scheduled for completion were based upon attaining an adequate stock just prior to shipping requirements. This step alone, however, is not sufficient to insure delivery on time. Each production order should also be scheduled as to the date to start, and co-ordinated with the inventories and procurement orders for component parts and raw materials, particularly because, through the standardization program, the application of each material (and part) to a number of products has been increased to the optimum. For example, the same pattern of piece goods might be used for six styles of shirts, and our total requirements must be known in order to procure all at one time. The tools for this purpose are the stock records for the materials which are similar to the finished product record in Exhibit 3, but with these changes in the columnar headings:

HEADINGS OF STOCK RECORDS FOR

FINISHED PRODUCTS	MATERIALS AND PARTS
Short-Term Forecast	Short-Term Forecast
Shipping Orders	Product Production Orders
Production Orders	Purchase Orders
Produced	Received
Shipped	Issued

First, each production order should be matched with the previously described bills of materials for the specified product, and computations should be made of the required quantity of materials, including standard allowances for waste, etc. The quantities needed are entered in the second group of columns of the appropriate records with notations as to dates when the orders are to be started. When all entries are made, our accumulated needs are compared with the cumulative total of the purchase order column, and purchase orders are written for the deficiencies, preferably for the minimum economic ordering quantities. Deliveries are scheduled so that the material will be available when needed for production. If the quantity ordered is in excess of the actual requirements, it is important that the excess be reasonable and be scheduled for delivery on dates which will minimize the carrying costs.

Sometimes it is worth while to translate the short-term forecasts for shipments into terms of materials for placing blanket contracts. For example, the first short-term forecasts on Exhibit 3 were made by months for six months. These might be translated into yardage of.materials needed for the six months.

By this complete procedure, we have assembled all of our requirements for materials (or parts) in order that we may handle the minimum number of procurement orders and purchase or manufacture in the largest practical quantities, and that production may proceed in the most orderly manner possible. Moreover, this control will discourage buying in excess of needs that are directly co-ordinated with the sales and service requirements, and will discourage the burdensome costs of carrying inventories in excess of those built up as a result of co-ordination, deliberation and judgment.

It will be interesting to each of you:

1. To calculate the necessary increase in production of raw materials if there should be a 25 per cent increase in consumption of the products you produce, and if your own inventory policy were to be followed by each unit in the chain from the raw material producers to the retail distributor. Many supposedly sound plans require an increase in raw material production equal to several times the rate of increase in the finished product consumption.

2. To make a similar calculation based upon the policies and procedures which I have just presented.

Problems of Advance Buying

The installation of adequate control procedures and sound interpretation of the data determined by the procedures is not sufficient, however, to keep the inventory investment under control. We still must cope with deliberate advance buying which too often is greatly in excess of immediate requirements and is encouraged by external conditions. I have stated that such buying may logically occur: first, as insurance that adequate stocks of materials of the right qualities will be available to maintain service to customers; and second, as insurance against product costs rising faster than selling prices. Buying in excess of those quantities is usually dangerous and may produce serious financial and other problems.

CONTROL OF SPOILAGE AND MATERIAL USAGE *

By M. A. Lause

A S YOU perhaps know, we are engaged in the manufacture of automotive accessories, steering wheels, running boards, motor mountings and other rubber insulating and cushioning products. In addition to the automotive accessories, we make a complete line of rubber ice-cube trays for the electric refrigeration industry. Our problems of control, therefore, are as varied as those of the average plant, and I am of the opinion that any points of merit in our method of controlling scrap and material usage might be applied to the average plant with like results.

Preparation for Control Work

It might be well at the outset to explain the method we used to prepare a foundation for the control work we planned. From the very outset, reports of scrap and reoperations, as well as reports of other costs, had been prepared by the cost department for the use of the various divisions and department heads. These reports were complete—showing not only the costs, but also a narrative of the causes of these costs—but little improvement resulted from the reports for the reason that they were not properly used. They were not properly used because not enough preparation had been made to have them understood and interpreted by the department heads.

Since the major portion of the expenses which we wished to control occurred in the making departments, a department known as the standards department was organized within the manufacturing division, reporting to the factory manager, its function being the interpretation of cost data and control of costs within the manufacturing section itself.

The attitude of the shop toward costs began to change almost immediately. Where the factory manager had looked upon the cost reports as criticisms of his division by another division, he now recognized the interpretation of these reports and the control of

* From the 1935 Year Book.

costs through their use as his job, since the supervisor of the standards department was a member of the factory manager's staff. He
became interested in having his department heads understand the
various reports more clearly and a program was begun of training
each department foreman to feel that he was the manager of his
department and should, therefore, be conversant with the cost of its
operation. This training program has been carried on to the point
where we feel that our department heads are more "cost conscious"
than the average.

I have dealt with this preparatory work at some length for the
reason that I feel it is of vital importance to any cost control method
in any plant.

Control of Spoilage

As we began to interpret more clearly in the manufacturing division the cost data submitted by the cost department, the report that
struck us most forcibly was that which concerned our high scrap
and reoperation cost, and we took that item up first for correction.
We decided that we would set standards of scrap and reoperation
costs for each division and department of the plant, determine the
responsibility for scrap and reoperations by departments and keep
up a record, in figures and graphically as well, of each department's
performance in relation to its predetermined standard, and hold meetings at regular intervals to review the performance. Our methods
of accumulating the information as well as our methods of presentation have been changed here and there during the five years we have
operated the control, but I will attempt to explain in detail just how
this work is now done and tell you something of the results we have
had.

Setting the Standards

Our scrap is measured in terms of its relation to the direct labor
dollar. Scrap costs are charged, not to the department in which they
occur, but to the department responsible for the spoilage. Each
productive department's scrap is measured against its own direct
labor, while the scrap made or caused by service or burden departments is measured in terms of the direct labor of the entire plant.

The first requisite, then, for fair and adequate scrap standards is the development of efficient direct labor standards. We will not dwell on the method of building these labor standards, but mention only, in passing, that the labor control section of the standards department reviews each job in its detail operations and forecasts the unit direct labor cost of each operation on each product and the time at which this cost will be attained. The unit direct labor standards are broken down by departments and multiplied by the forecasted production of each product for the coming year. The result is the forecasted standard departmental and plant direct labor for the year on each product and in total.

In a similar way the scrap control section reviews each product of our manufacture and develops a unit standard scrap cost. This unit scrap standard is built up in two ways:

1. Percentage of quantity of scrapped product to quantity of O. K. product.

2. Unit cost of scrap to be added to the cost of O. K. product.

In the case of products which we are continuing to manufacture from one year to another, the standard is based on experience; not on the best performance we have had, nor on the worst, but on the best performance we have maintained for a reasonable length of time. Abnormal conditions are left out of consideration. Then, too, we provide in the standard for some improvement in the department.

In the case of products which are new at the time of setting the scrap standards, comparisons are made with similar products or classes of products and differences of design and specification are allowed to influence the standard upward or downward, as the case may indicate.

This part of the work of preparing the standards is described in a few words, but in reality it is a very painstaking job requiring at least several weeks.

After the standards on each product are developed by departments in terms of percentages of scrapped to O. K. product and in terms of unit scrap costs, the foreman of each department is called in and these standards are reviewed with him so that he has an opportunity to familiarize himself with what will be expected of him when the standard becomes effective. He may question this or that provision we have made and if he does, we go into the case with him so that when the review is finished, the foreman has agreed that he should and will operate within the percentage standard and unit cost stand-

Form 5 Revised I. D.—100M Sets—3-35
STANDARDS DEPT. COPY

5795

SCRAP TICKET

Part No.	Part Name	
751790	Westinghouse Motor Mounting	
Dept. Responsible	**Last Oper. No.**	**Last Oper. Name**
12	15	Assemble
Quan. Rejected	**Date**	DO NOT PAY GROUP 12-8
40	4-26-35	Foreman's Initials W. P.

CAUSE OF SCRAP

Wrong Insert Assembled.

Stamp here when salvage

Insp. **A. H.**

Foreman **W. Protsman**

RESPONSIBILITY BY STDS. DEPT.

Stock Preparation - Protsman.

COST EXTENSION

	Quan.	Unit Cost	Amount	
Material	40	.02013		81
Labor		.01609		64
Burden		.02111		84
TOTAL			2	29

TRU-PAK The Egry Register Co Dayton Ohio

EXHIBIT 1

ard set. As in the case of the direct labor, the unit scrap standards, broken down by departments, are multiplied by the forecasted production of each product for the coming year and the result is the forecasted standard departmental and total plant scrap for the year on each product and in total.

The forecasted scrap cost for each department is now divided by its forecasted direct labor cost, and we have the percentage of scrap cost to direct labor cost, or in other words, the standard cost of scrap per standard dollar of direct labor. For instance, a department with a forecasted direct labor of $50,000 and a forecasted scrap cost of $5,000 will have a scrap standard of $.10 per dollar of direct labor cost. Similarly, a service department expected to make or cause $1,500 scrap would have a standard of $.001 per direct labor dollar on a forecasted plant direct labor volume of $1,500,000. The standard for each division and for the plant as a whole is computed in the same manner.

Why did we choose the productive labor dollar as a basis of measurement? We might have selected the cost dollar or the sales dollar, or have measured actual scrap with standard purely on a quantitative or percentage basis. As a matter of fact, direct labor was the measuring stick most available. After all, the payroll has to be computed and paid, in our case weekly, and since we wanted to hold weekly sessions to review performance, direct labor lent itself most readily to our plan. Then, too, we think direct labor is the best gauge for this purpose. I think you will agree that the average foreman is more familiar with the labor in his department than with any other factor of cost, and we felt our selection would appeal to him and be more easily understood by him. So much for our scrap standards.

Gathering the Information—The Scrap Ticket

Information concerning the actual scrap occurring in the plant from day to day is reported daily on the scrap ticket illustrated in Exhibit 1, made out by the inspection department. The ticket is made up in sets of five copies. For economy and speed in the writing of the tickets as well as to insure legible copies, we are using a standard type of register order machines. The form provides space for the inspector to show the part number, part name, department responsible in his opinion, the number and name of the last operation performed, the quantity rejected, the date, and his statement of the cause of rejection. Separate scrap tickets are made up for each part, and if scrap occurs for several different causes on the same part or product, a scrap ticket is made out for each cause. Then, too, if rejections occur on the same product for the same cause, but the rejections take place after different operations, separate scrap tickets are made out due to the difference of last operation performed and the resultant difference in cost.

The writing and distribution of the scrap tickets for each day's scrap is completed by ten o'clock on the morning of the following day. The five copies are used as follows:

The original, standards department copy, is delivered by the inspection department to the cost department, where the cost of the scrap described on the ticket is entered in the space provided. The ticket is then delivered to the standards department whose job it is to determine the responsibility for the scrap.

The second, payroll department copy, accompanies the original until the responsibility is determined. When the responsibility has been fixed, the foreman, if he knows that the operators carelessly caused the scrap, marks this copy, "Do not pay group no. so-and-so," in the space provided. This second copy then goes to the payroll department for adjustment of its records with regard to group payment.

The third, foreman's copy, is delivered by the inspection department to the foreman whose department, in the inspector's opinion, is responsible. Received, as it is, before noon of the following day, it gives the foreman a daily report of his performance early enough to assist him in making decisions with regard to the correction of his operators, equipment or methods to the elimination of the cause of such spoilage in the future. All of our foremen use this copy. They have become accustomed to figuring daily the percentage of scrapped pieces to O. K. production in their department, at least on major volume jobs, and in this way keep themselves conversant with their performance from day to day.

The fourth copy is delivered to production control department and then to materials control department for adjustment of their process inventory records.

The fifth copy is attached by the inspector to the parts or products rejected.

The Salvage Ticket

Information concerning material, parts or product salvaged is written up and distributed in exactly the same manner as the information concerning scrap. In fact, the same scrap ticket form is used, but on each copy is stamped in large red letters the word "Salvaged."

Physical Disposition of Scrap

Each day, after the scrap tickets for the previous day have been issued, the inspectors attach the fifth copy of the scrap tickets to the rejected parts, which are then removed to a designated location just outside the department foreman's office. Here each day the foreman and his assistants examine the rejected product. The scrap is not disposed of until the department responsible for it has had an opportunity to look at the defect that occasions the charge to this department. Obviously, the familiarity with the cause of scrap which results from this physical examination makes it easier for the scrap control section to affix responsibility; the operators are more careful because their mistakes will be seen by their boss; and the inspector is more critical of his own work, since the foreman accused checks the inspector's work.

In the case of a dispute as to whether or not this or that part should be scrapped, the final decision is made by the chief inspector.

Pricing Scrap Tickets

As mentioned before, the original copies of the scrap ticket are delivered to the cost department. Here the unit direct material, labor and burden cost are set on the tickets in the spaces provided and each ticket is extended for the quantity it covers. The previous month's costs are used in pricing the tickets. Salvage tickets are priced and extended in the same way and all tickets for the day are then delivered to the scrap control section.

Daily Reports

The first use of the tickets by the scrap control section is in the preparation of daily reports on major volume products and on those products currently in difficulty. The tickets are sorted first by classes of product, steering wheels, running boards, motor mounts, etc., and under these classes are sorted by products and parts. Reports are then made showing the quantities scrapped, the quantities produced O. K. and the percentage of scrap to O. K. production. An analysis of the scrap by causes without regard to responsibility is then prepared for each product on which a report is filed. Daily reports of products on which performance is bad are sent to foremen and supervisors concerned, with copies to the general management.

We make it a point to discontinue daily reports on any product just as soon as its actual performance day after day comes into line with its standard. We feel that to the foreman as well as to the management, a daily report soon becomes monotonous and loses its value. Reports of this nature are valuable only so long as they make an impression, and they cease to make an impression when they monotonously report a sameness of condition, whether good or bad.

Determining Responsibility

Just as soon as any necessary daily reports are completed, the scrap control section begins the work of affixing on each ticket the name of the department and foreman responsible and securing the signature of the foreman admitting this responsibility. On sixty to eighty per cent of the tickets this or that division head or foreman has admitted his responsibility by signing the ticket at the time it was presented to him by the inspector. In these cases, it is only necessary to stamp the department name in the space on the ticket provided for responsibility, together with the name of that group of products in which the scrap is to be classified.

In the case of tickets received unsigned, it is necessary to contact the foreman who passed the ticket without signing it to learn his reason for withholding signature. His explanation may involve another department and that foreman is then contacted. In some cases several departments are involved, and where this occurs a meeting is called by the scrap control section, the case is reviewed and the responsibility determined. Sometimes a compromise results and the responsibility is split. Should the meeting result in a deadlock, the case is then reviewed and decided by the supervisor, a member of the factory manager's staff, in charge of the particular group of products or operations on which the spoilage occurred.

We have had a few cases where it was impossible definitely to determine responsibility before the close of the period. We sometimes run tests to determine the effect of an error said to be the cause of the scrap. In such cases, the cost is carried for the week in a "Responsibility Undetermined" account in the control record. This account, however, is not allowed to become the proverbial "dump." We insist on the clearing of the account during the succeeding week and the final definite allocation of the charge.

The department to be credited with salvage is determined in the following manner: Before the scrap tickets charge the scrap clear through the control department, a record is made of the quantities charged to each department on those parts or products where something is usually saved. Distribution of the quantities salvaged is made in exact ratio to the distribution of the quantities scrapped as shown by this record.

When all tickets have been marked with the name of the responsible department and the product class to which the scrap belongs, the tickets are checked back against a numerical record of tickets issued to insure accounting for all the tickets. We seldom have a missing ticket, and when we do, we trace it through the inspector to whom it was issued and in practically all cases we locate it.

The tickets for the week are completed as to responsibility fixing, signing and checking, and are delivered to the cost department by the following Wednesday evening.

The Weekly Scrap Report

A weekly report of scrap cost by responsibility is prepared by the cost department. We have seen that each scrap ticket is priced and extended daily before its delivery to the scrap control section, so that upon the return of the tickets to the cost department, it is only necessary to sort the tickets according to departments responsible and run totals for each department. The total scrap for each department for the week is now divided by the department's direct labor for the same period and the result is the scrap cost per direct labor dollar for each department.

The scrap per direct labor dollar for each division and for the plant as a whole is computed in the same manner.

If you will refer to Exhibit 2, you will see that the weekly report shows the name of the responsible department, its direct labor,

Exhibit 2

SCRAP COSTS BY RESPONSIBILITY—WEEK ENDING APRIL 27, 1935

Responsibility	Direct Labor	Scrap Cost	Unit Scrap Cost Per Direct Labor Dollar	Std. Unit Scrap Cost Per Direct Labor Dollar	Gain or Loss (—) From Std.	Cumulative Gain or Loss (—) From Std.	Scrap Cost Cumulative 3/31—4/27/35
Manufacturing Division							
Compound and Rubber Mill	$ 3,083.55	$ 66.68	$.02162	$.02500	$ 10.41	$ 90.96	$ 201.42
Stock Preparation	2,114.58	41.67	.01971	.04000	42.91	186.19	149.93
Uncured Trimmings							
Wheels	165.40	99.34	.60060	.70000	16.44	9.80	385.18
Running Boards	873.03	4.98	.00570	.01500	8.12	32.72	16.40
Miscellaneous Parts	1,909.18	138.76	.07269	.12000	90.34	221.05	714.83
Running Boards	5,439.97	82.70	.01520	.02400	47.86	— 74.45	590.04
Miscellaneous Vulcanize							
Rubber Metal	1,503.08	100.89	.06713	.09500	41.90	214.09	360.68
Soft Rubber	535.05	60.69	.11344	.10000	— 7.18	20.71	209.24
Ice Trays	971.65	134.51	.13843	.19000	50.10	232.80	475.75
Miscellaneous Finish	2,980.24	8.51	.00285	.01100	24.27	58.35	64.79
Rubber Wheel	4,480.11	3.65	.00081	.00400	14.27	16.46	50.63
Machine	3,104.45	38.90	.01253	.02300	32.50	72.13	202.97
Running Board Insert	1,465.32	2.78	.00190	.00500	4.55	24.26	9.15
Plating	781.87	86.81	.11102	.11000	— .80	383.69	54.77
C. V. Strip Vulcanize	419.30	43.17	.10296	.14000	15.53	26.00	185.82
Windshield Strip	978.99	50.49	.05157	.30000	243.21	559.74	484.86
Control Laboratory	29,508.89	63.15	.00214	.00600	113.90	460.84	227.95
Miscellaneous Manufacturing	29,508.89	28.49	.00097	.00300	60.04	210.74	333.68
TOTAL MANUFACTURING DIVISION....	$29,508.89	$1,056.17	$.03579	$.06700	$920.92	$3,083.14	$4,608.55
Material Division	$29,508.89	$ 140.37	$.00476	$.00900	$125.21	$ 344.16	$ 689.05
Engineering Division	29,508.89	32.38	.00110	.00180	20.74	131.99	74.66
Sales Division	29,508.89	277.39	.00940	.00620	— 94.44	44.28	667.49
TOTAL PLANT	$29,508.89	$1,506.31	$.05105	$.08400	$972.43	$ 520.43	$1,431.20
CUMULATIVE PLANT (MONTH)	$114,801.52	$6,039.75	$.05261	$.08400		$3,603.57	$6,039.75

F. A. BOETTGER,
Factory Accountant.

the cost of the scrap for which it is responsible, the actual scrap cost per direct labor dollar, the standard scrap cost per direct labor dollar, the amount of gain or loss from standard for the week, the amount of gain or loss accumulative for the month and the total amount of scrap for the month to date. You will note that totals are shown for each division and for the plant as a whole.

The Monthly Scrap Report

At the end of each month the cost department prepares a report of the scrap cost of each product without regard to responsibility. This report is divided by classes of product and under these classes each product is shown with its scrap cost for the month, the number of O. K. pieces produced, the unit scrap cost, the standard unit scrap cost and the amount of variance. This monthly report is reviewed by the scrap control section and the products showing unfavorable variances are analyzed and reviewed with the department heads causing the variance.

Control Records and Charts

The weekly report of scrap by responsibility is delivered to the scrap control section on Monday evening so that an average of from one week to ten days elapses between the actual spoilage and the review of the case. All copies of the report are delivered to the control section, which in turn sends them to the various foremen and division heads with a note specifying the time of the reviewing meeting. Each department head, therefore, has an opportunity, by analyzing his performance as shown in the report, to prepare himself for the discussion of his performance at the meeting.

The scrap control section posts from the weekly report to its cumulative control record for each department the following information as shown on Exhibit 3: the weekly and cumulative direct labor, the weekly and cumulative actual scrap cost, the weekly and cumulative scrap cost per direct labor dollar, the standard scrap cost per dollar of direct labor, the standard scrap cost in total, and the weekly and cumulative variance from standard. This record will show, therefore, the story of the department's performance for any period of the year. It serves not only the purpose of ready reference, but

Stock Preparation Dept.—Mr. Protsman

Exhibit 3

SCRAP RECORD 1935

Date Week Ending	Direct Labor Week	Direct Labor Cum.	Actual Scrap Cost Week	Actual Scrap Cost Cum.	Scrap Per Direct Labor Dollar Week	Scrap Per Direct Labor Dollar Cum.	Standard Scrap Per Direct Labor Dollar	Standard Scrap Cost Week	Standard Scrap Cost Cum.	Variance Week =Loss	Variance Cum. =Loss
January 5	$1,792.94		$49.18		$.027		$.04	$71.68		$22.50	
12	2,200.49	$ 3,993.43	76.58	$125.76	.035	$.031	.04	88.00	$ 159.68	11.42	$ 33.92
19	2,151.37	6,144.80	114.53	240.29	.053	.039	.04	86.04	245.72	—28.49	5.43
26	2,380.55	8,525.35	96.56	336.85	.041	.039	.04	95.20	340.92	— 1.36	4.07
February 2	2,229.64	10,754.99	82.39	419.24	.037	.039	.04	89.16	430.08	6.77	10.84
9	2,249.51	13,004.50	11.81	431.05	.005	.033	.04	89.96	520.04	78.15	88.99
16	2,192.79	15,197.29	69.12	500.17	.032	.033	.04	87.68	607.72	18.56	107.55
23	2,185.87	17,383.16	36.78	536.95	.017	.031	.04	87.40	695.12	50.62	158.17
March 2	2,093.46	19,476.62	37.39	574.34	.018	.029	.04	83.72	778.84	46.33	204.50
9	2,354.66	21,831.28	39.39	613.73	.017	.028	.04	94.16	873.00	54.77	259.27
16	2,397.14	24,228.42	57.86	671.59	.024	.028	.04	95.88	968.88	38.02	297.29
23	2,287.94	26,516.36	65.25	736.84	.029	.028	.04	91.48	1,060.36	26.23	323.52
30	2,065.83	28,582.19	38.17	775.01	.018	.027	.04	82.60	1,142.96	44.43	367.95
April 6	1,914.39	30,496.58	39.73	814.74	.021	.027	.04	76.56	1,219.52	36.83	404.78
13	2,179.35	32,675.93	27.87	842.61	.013	.026	.04	87.16	1,306.68	59.29	464.07
20	2,195.03	34,870.96	40.66	883.27	.019	.025	.04	87.80	1,394.48	47.14	511.21
27	2,114.58	36,985.54	41.67	924.94	.020	.025	.04	84.56	1,479.04	42.91	554.12

at the end of the year affords valuable information for use in the setting of new standards.

From the control record sheets a chart is kept up for each department. In some cases several charts are required if the products in the department fall into several classes requiring separate standards.

Exhibit 4 shows what happened in our stock preparation department for the first four months of this year. Whether or not this type of chart will survive the critical eyes of the graphic presentation experts present, I do not know. We do feel, however, that the chart can at least lay claim to completeness of information. That is what we are after and we know we have had results.

You will note that the standard or dotted line carries through the four-month period at the same level of four cents per direct labor dollar. As a matter of fact, standards are not changed during the year except for very grave reasons. In the margin at the extreme left is the chart scale of scrap cost per dollar of direct labor. The second column shows the average performance of the department for the previous year. In the preparation of the chart for the succeeding four months, this column will be changed from the 1934 average to the average for the first four months of 1935. The actual performance from week to week is shown as a solid line and the average for each month, representing the trend, is shown as a broken line.

In actual practice, we use a color scheme, red for the standard line, black for the weekly actual and blue for the monthly average.

The items listed under the chart give the foreman, we think, all of the information he would want. His direct labor is shown for the week and for the year to date, as is his actual scrap cost, his standard scrap cost and his variance from standard. The weekly and cumulative scrap cost per direct labor dollar, represented by the solid and broken lines in the chart, are also shown in figures at the bottom of the sheet.

The examination of this chart has probably led you to the opinion that this department's standard must have been set rather loosely, since the department has been able to beat the standard consistently during the last three months, having operated at an average for the four months of two and a half cents on a standard of four cents, or at sixty-three per cent of standard. Perhaps the standard did not forecast sufficient improvement and was, therefore, loose. It is worthy of note, however, that this same department operated at four and nine-tenths cents in 1934 on practically the same products. The

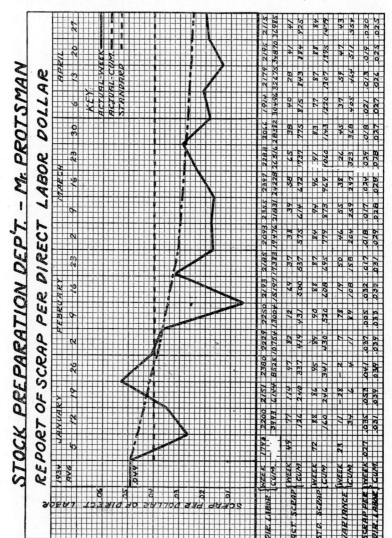

EXHIBIT 4

standard, therefore, provided for improvement of almost twenty per cent. The actual performance is an improvement of almost fifty per cent.

The Reviewing Meeting

Each week, on Tuesday morning, a meeting is held to review the scrap performance. This meeting is presided over by the factory manager or by the assistant factory manager and is attended by all general foremen, staffmen, the chief inspector, the production control head, and representatives of the scrap control section and cost departments.

The performance of the plant in relation to the standard is first reviewed, then that of the manufacturing division. If the performance of the division as a whole is good, we usually approach the individual department review in a spirit of commendation of those who have contributed to the division's favorable variance from standard. If the actual performance of the division results in an unfavorable variance from the standard, the departmental review is one of criticism of those who have caused the "fall down." In any case, the chart for each department is put up before the group and analyzed. If the performance is good, the foreman is commended. If the contrary is true, the foreman must explain what product or products were responsible and what the causes were, together with a story of the subsequent performance in the week just passed— the scrap report being reviewed is for the preceding week, you will remember—and he must forecast his future performance to the group. Obviously, this puts the foreman who has lost out to his standard "on the spot" before his fellows, and since he does not like to be put in this position, he tries to avoid it by improving the scrap cost in his department, which is exactly the purpose of the whole control plan.

The foreman is his own defense counsel and is permitted, of course, to state his case. In fact, any problems relating to the elimination or reduction of spoilage are discussed at the meeting and notes are made of the suggestions offered. Staffmen are assigned to the tryout of suggested methods of improvement. The staffman, by the way, has a very marked incentive for helping the foreman with his problems. If the staffman does not co-operate and the foreman is criticized, he may implicate the supervisor assigned to the tryout of improvement methods in his department; thus, to avoid being put on the same spot with the foreman, the staffman usually acts on his assignment promptly.

At the close of the meeting each department head is given his chart attached to a backing prepared for the purpose, and the chart is put on display in the foreman's office. If he has been "in the rough" at the meeting, the foreman will most certainly have a session with his assistant foremen, job foremen and group leaders and put the case squarely up to them. They, in turn, contact the operators. In some cases, if the performance continues out of line, special reports by shifts are prepared, and a spirit of competition between shifts promoted. If this does not correct the condition, the record of each operator is kept; good work is commended and poor work criticized and penalized until better conditions are brought about.

Reoperation Costs

The control of rework or reoperation costs follows almost identically the method of controlling scrap. We do not, however, use a ticket for the reoperations as we do for the scrap. Our rework costs on any product are due in the great majority of cases to the same cause. The reoperation is done and paid for on the basis of the operation sequence and predetermined standard labor cost as outlined on standard labor routings, and the responsibility is shown by the scrap control section by marking the name of the department responsible on a list of reoperation costs by products, prepared by the cost department. From this point on the report by responsibility is made, the control records and charts are kept and reviewing meetings held, just as in the case of the scrap control.

Results of Control

Our plant, of course, is not a Utopia where everything always moves along exactly as planned and forecasted. We have our share of trouble and sometimes we are faced with problems of spoilage that are not readily solved. We have had one department this year making a new type of windshield glass channel which has given us a lot of trouble. That department is not operating within its scrap and reoperation standard, but we feel certain that its operation is considerably better than would be the case if we had no control plan in operation.

Reference to Exhibit 5 will explain our position with regard to scrap and reoperation cost before and after our control plan was applied to these costs.

In 1930, the year before the control plan was started, we spent $206,800 for scrap and reoperation on a direct labor of $395,000, or $.524 per dollar of direct labor. In the succeeding four years and five months under the control plan, we have spent $355,000 for scrap and reoperation on a direct labor of $2,800,000, or at $.127 average scrap and reoperation cost per dollar of direct labor, a reduction of 75.8 per cent. The saving in scrap and reoperation during this four and one-half year period amounts to approximately a million dollars under the 1930 performance, an annual saving of about $220,000.

As shown by the chart, our standard in the first year of control, 1931, provided for a fifty per cent reduction. The standard was beaten, the actual cost being only $.188 on the standard of $.25. In 1932, the standard provided for another drop of fifty per cent from the previous year's actual, the new standard being set at $.09, which we did not reach. Our best performance was in 1933 when the actual amounted to $.106 on a standard of $.10. Since 1932, we have never quite reached our goal. Our 1935 standard is $.10, and so far we have operated at $.114. Fifteen of twenty-one departments are operating within their standards; six are not.

It is worthy of note that these cost reductions occurred in a period in which our product became more difficult to manufacture because of the addition of cushioning motor mountings requiring high-grade adhesions between rubber and metal. At present, our scrap and rework costs are at an average of approximately two and a half cents per dollar of total factory cost.

Cost of Control Operation

To my mind, the surprising part of the control plan is its low cost of operation. A scrap record of some kind would have to be made out in any case, and the slightly more detailed method of reporting the information requires no more than about four hours

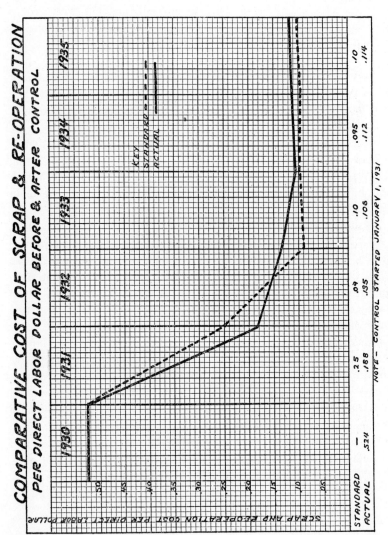

COMPARATIVE COST OF SCRAP & RE-OPERATION
PER DIRECT LABOR DOLLAR BEFORE & AFTER CONTROL

	1930	1931	1932	1933	1934	1935
STANDARD	—	.25	.09	.10	.095	.10
ACTUAL	.524	.188	.135	.106	.112	.114

NOTE — CONTROL STARTED JANUARY 1, 1931

Exhibit 5

additional per day for the inspection department clerk. One man in the cost department does all the ticket pricing and the making of the weekly report. Approximately one day per week will cover the additional time spent by a comptometer operator and typist. Two men are employed in the standards department on this work of responsibility fixing and the making of reports and charts. The entire clerical cost of the control will not exceed approximately $7,500 annually, which is only three and a half per cent of the resultant saving.

Control of Material Usage

In the limited time we have left at our disposal, I should like to spend a few minutes discussing with you our method of measuring and controlling usage of materials within the plant.

Unquestionably expense materials and supplies control will be covered under "Expense Control" this afternoon, and I will, therefore, confine myself to our method of controlling direct material consumption.

We had always put plenty of emphasis on the control of direct labor element of cost and had always "borne down," at least "in the pinches," on overhead expense. Our direct materials, however, were, frankly, not very closely controlled. As in the case of scrap, reports were made regularly by the accounting section, but they did not accomplish all they should have, because, as in the case of scrap, no one made proper use of them.

As the result in savings brought about through scrap and rework control, direct labor control and expense control began to impress us, we began to take stock of ourselves with regard to materials. Materials, we found, represented about two and a half times as much of our production cost dollar as direct labor, and from twenty to twenty-five times as much as the controlled scrap. Logically, then, we ought to be able to make some saving in the direct material element of cost. Varying material costs due to varying prices, we said, are problems of the purchasing division, but usage is the shop's problem and we will do something about that.

Approximately one-half of our material costs are in purchased parts, stampings, etc., and we decided that as a start we would confine our control activities to the rubber compounds, which make up the other half of our direct material costs. This program of intensive control was begun only recently, and we have not as yet extended it to all classes of products. Our running board production was treated first and will, I believe, afford a fair example of the results obtainable through a method of control such as we are using.

Setting the Temporary Standards of Usage

In order to begin the program at once without waiting for the development of accurately studied and measured standards of usage, we started in by reducing to terms of weight the mean specifications as established by our control laboratory, and called that our standard. We selected an industrial engineer from our standards department and put him in charge of the work. He made studies of the various processes through which the material must pass in its fabrication preparatory to molding and set up limits to which these various processes could be held. Having thus satisfied ourselves that the specifications and limits of length, width and gauge as set by our control laboratory were possible of attainment by the several departments concerned, we set our temporary standard on the weight computed from the mean specification on each running board of our manufacture.

A meeting of all foremen and department heads concerned was called and they were informed that control of their usage of material was starting *now* and that they would be held to account for their performance in relation to the standard. The method of establishing the standard was explained, as well as the methods we proposed to use to gather the information. A man was assigned by the cost department to accumulate the information and to furnish to the standards department reports of performance to assist in the administration of the control.

Gathering the Information

For the purpose of payment of our calender and preparation operators, we secure the amount calendered by weighing out to the calender crews a number of skids or trucks of the compound for this or that running board. After the run, the uncalendered stock that remains is weighed back and the difference, of course, is the weight calendered. The number of preparations for each type of board are counted and recorded by the production control department, and the division of the total weight calendered by the number of preparations received by production control is the average weight of each preparation for any type of running board product. We, therefore, know the number and average weight of the prepared material as it is delivered to the molding department and are thus in position to measure the performance of the milling and preparation departments who supply this material.

The number of O. K. boards delivered by the molding department, plus the number of boards scrapped, plus the number of preparations returned, must equal the number of preparations delivered to the molding foreman, and we have him rather tightly "bottled up" on usage.

The total net weight used divided by the number of boards produced gives us the usage per board.

Reports

A daily report is furnished by the cost department to the foremen concerned, showing them only those items on which the weight used is in excess of standard. In the case of the calendering process, these reports reflect the performance of each shift and crew. The foreman, therefore, has at his disposal each day information from which he can control the operators in his department.

A report for each week is made by Wednesday of the week following, showing performance in relation to standard. This report lists for each model of running board the total number produced during the week, the total weight of material used, the unit actual weight, the standard weight, the variance and the cost of the variance, red or black, on each product for the week and accumulative to date.

A second weekly report is made by the cost department comparing the present usage with the average usage before the inauguration of the control. This report shows the quantity and value of the material saved for the week and accumulative since the starting of the control. The former and present usage are priced at the same figure, so that the report will reflect only the difference in consumption and not include variables in prices of raw materials.

Presentation

As in the case of scrap and reoperation control, a weekly meeting is held, with either the factory manager or his assistant presiding.

The weekly reports are reviewed and foremen are commended or criticized as the case may require.

As a matter of fact, there has been little cause for criticism. As shown by the last chart, Exhibit 6, from January 26 to May 25, our actual consumption of rubber compounds for running boards was 99.9 per cent of the standard usage set, our actual cost being $291,719 against the standard of $291,918—a difference of approximately $200.

The cost of the material usage for this same volume before control would have been $313,295, so we have had a saving of $21,576 on this one class of product in four months. You can bet we are extending material usage control into other product lines just as rapidly as we can.

Here again the cost of operation of the control is slight when compared to the return. One man was added in the standards department and one in the cost department. The control of material usage on running boards has become a routine job requiring no more than about one-fourth of their time. They are working up methods and standards on other jobs during the major portion of their time.

Perhaps exception may be taken to our practice of having foremen sit in on several cost meetings each week. Is it not a foreman's job to spend his time in his department pushing production and familiarizing himself with conditions that way? Yes, it certainly is necessary for him to be thoroughly conversant with his production problems, his schedule, his equipment and his men. But we have found him a better foreman for this cost training. We give him all the cost data we can. We think we have made him not only a better foreman in the old sense of the term, but a department manager who is beginning at least to take a pride not only in the fact that his department is putting out the schedule, but putting that schedule out economically and profitably. He thinks so, and he likes it. He feels himself of more importance in the organization, and in a sense he is now pushing us for cost information that we could not sell him a short time ago.

I have attempted to recount for you our methods of controlling

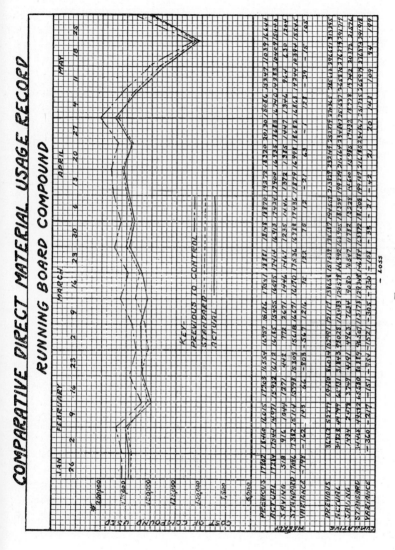

Exhibit 6

spoilage and material usage. I think you will agree from the figures given that our scrap and reoperation control has made very worthwhile cost reductions. In this control of materials we have only just scratched the surface, but we are down deep enough to have found out that there are big dividends in this control, and we are going further.

Our method, briefly stated, compares actual performance with a predetermined standard, fixing the responsibility for failures and securing the department heads' signatures admitting this responsibility, and then through regular reviewing meetings keeps before the department head the fact that his work is being watched. All of us try at least a little more, we feel, if we know our work is being checked.

There are two theories we have followed in building up this control work:

1. That it is better to start crudely than not at all, or to wait until a finished method is developed. Start now and get some results while the finished plan is being developed.
2. That in a plan such as ours, where the product is likely to be different from year to year due to the frequent change of design in the automotive industry, the highest rate of return is achieved if the control plan, on any element of cost, is designed to glean from all products those reductions which are most easily obtained, rather than to spend the entire effort in refining methods to get the ultimate saving in any one or in only a few cases.

Someone, another economic prophet perhaps, has said that business will always be good for those who can "take it" and that only those who can take it will get it. It seems to me that it is the duty of the industrial accountant to see that his plant is in proper condition to "take it." Adequate and informative reports, of course, are necessary, but the accountant's responsibility does not end there. He has to assure himself that his reports are properly understood and interpreted, and above all, that they are used, even if he himself has to design the method and lead the way in their use. Only then is he doing his job.

PART II

INVENTORY VALUATION

VALUATION OF INVENTORIES *

By Edward A. Kracke

"COST or market, whichever is lower": There is perhaps no term in modern accountancy which has greater need of clarification, possibly even reform, than this—unless it be that perennial reprobate, "Capital Surplus." That convenient measuring rod of inventories has been with us these many years, with its votaries as votive, its critics as critical, and its tolerators as tolerant, as ever.

I have sometimes felt that the term itself (and the same thought extends to its companion, "the lower of cost or market") is just a little bit unfortunate. The words sound somewhat as if one were to say: "Here are two possible yardsticks. You can have your choice, provided you choose the shorter."

As a matter of fact, it is cost which is the initial consideration, cost which would be the logical, the simple rule, if we were not harassed by that evil spirit of our present-day economy, "price level changes." I have sometimes felt our terminology might have been an improved one if we had started in with some terser form such as "cost, or market, if lower." But enough of mere word quibbling.

Confusion of Thought on Cost Versus Cost or Market

There is encountered not altogether infrequently a confusion of thought with regard to the two bases of inventory valuation; that is, cost, on the one hand, and the lower of cost or market, on the other. Perhaps our income tax regulations are in part responsible for it. Mention of our income tax laws and regulations in this connection (as well as further reference thereto) are not to be taken as an indication that it is an income tax disquisition which I am making, for it is not that at all; but such mention is almost inevitable in any accounting discussion because the influence of tax laws and regulations upon accounting has been great, though not always, unfortunately, in the role of a preceptor of what to do.

This occasional confusion of thought consists in regarding these

* A previously unpublished address which Mr. Kracke delivered before the New York Chapter in December, 1938.

two bases as being a matter of a free choice between them, as if one were to say, "I elect cost alone as my basis, notwithstanding the fact that others in my line use the lower of cost or market." Such an individual or concern might not, for instance, find the S.E.C. concurring in that thought if it were a registration statement that brought the matter to issue. These two are not alternatives in any such sense. The use of cost alone is, in the present state of accounting practice, attributable to some particular reason. That reason may be the lack of meaning of any market valuation, the difficulty or impracticability of determining what market is, the ineptitude of market value from the point of view of either the balance sheet or the income statement, or the settled usage of certain "trades or businesses."

A Few Examples

Let me illustrate with a few examples. The "average cost" method of the tobacco industry, which excludes any specific market devaluation, does not, however, make any such exclusion a matter of defying the idea of market revaluation. With huge selected stocks of tobacco from prior crop years required to be kept on hand in process of maturing, the thought of giving any expression to such a thing as a replacement cost based on current prices is rather visionary. Another consideration which I shall discuss is the relative absence of influence of any conjecturable market changes on the sales price of the product.

As another illustration, I may mention the last-in, first-out method as adopted by the American Petroleum Institute for its industry, in which the thought is that by reason of the adoption of the method at a time of a low price range in the economic cycle, the company using the method should normally escape situations where its inventory values exceed market.

Then there are those industries like the public utilities, where (except in such instances as merchandise for resale) the basis of cost, with the lessened value of obsolescent stock, however, being duly reckoned with, is the one generally used. Aside from the difficulty of a fair market revaluation, there is the further meaninglessness of it. On the balance sheet the working capital in the case of a utility possesses in no wise the significance which attaches to the current position of a merchandising or manufacturing concern, and the revenue of the utility would be only remotely influenced by any reasoned-out market differential in the general run of its operating materials and supplies.

The concept that cost alone (as a recognized basis for inventory valuation in the present state of accounting practice) is not thus recognized as something in defiance of the need for any recognition of a decline in value away from cost, should be evident from the fact that even on this basis, adjustments are in order for decline in value of damaged or imperfect or obsolete goods; and every such adjustment is a departure from the idea of cost alone as the theoretical value which adheres to its related article until that article disappears as sold and its cost shadow disappears into the past with it as an undiminished whole. The retail method, too, may be instanced as an illustration of this view—assuming that there will be agreement upon that method being included in the broad category of "cost only"—for here the adjustments for markdowns reckon with the same need for a scaling down from theoretical cost.

Separate Reporting of Market Decline Data

The foregoing may seem to be stepping on the toes of those to whom I referred at the opening of my remarks as the critics of cost or market, whichever is lower. But let us see if we cannot reach a mutual and complete understanding of viewpoints. In a great many cases there is real merit in the objection to a hybrid item called "cost of goods sold," which contains the cost of *some* goods sold, something less than the original cost of *other* goods sold, together with a loss taken on goods not yet sold at all. If it were practicable in all cases to resolve this hybrid into its components, namely, the original cost of the goods sold, on the one hand, and the previous market write-down at the beginning of the period together with the market adjustment of the closing inventory, on the other, it could not fail to be more informative to the reader of the income statement.

The degree of helpfulness of such information would vary, in some cases materially, according to a variety of factors such as severity, irregularity or constancy of price changes, and the relative importance of the item thus affected as a part of the entire aggregate of the related goods. Viewed in this light, I have the feeling that in a number of cases the gain resulting from deriving this additional information would be a doubtful one in the light of the effort and cost involved in securing it. But on the other hand, there is no doubt that there are cases where this fuller information would be of great significance in avoiding a distorted presentation of operating results.

The particular form in which such segregated "market decline" information should be shown, it seems to me, is of less importance than the fact of its being shown in *some* way. I would personally not be averse to its continuing, as a separately distinguishable item, to be a part of the "cost of goods sold"; and if it were shown as an income charge as a matter of regular treatment in certain industries, that also would be acceptable. The best answer to the question of the form and place of the item would be to let the particular conditions in the industry decide.

Criticisms of Cost or Market Considered

One sometimes hears, where the cost or market formula is undergoing criticism, reference to the duality of the balance sheet and the income statement as two separate reports, as if the relations between the two were slightly strained. Admitting their essential functional difference—the one as at a time, static, and the other for a time, kinetic—they are nevertheless so closely knit together that one can hardly speak of divergent viewpoints in the case of one or the other. Where the market decline from cost in the case of the goods on hand is more than merely an ostensible condition (which is the real point), where it constitutes a significant factor to be considered in regard to the current position, it is naturally an equal factor for the income account.

We hear, in criticism of cost or market, that it distorts results between periods, that the ensuing period is artificially benefited by reason of a loss with which the preceding period is likewise artificially burdened . This objection, as I see it, while invalid in many cases, is a real objection in others. There is, however, still so little material at hand for judgment—requisite information which will require analysis and research beyond that made thus far—that we can as yet do little more than generalize. The point is in the real relationship between the prices of the present inventory and the prices of its future disposal.

Exception to Market Devaluation Where Price Hedge Exists

We already have a partial recognition of this point in the exception to the operation of the rule for market devaluation where an effective price hedge exists. One such hedge is firm sales contracts, concerning which the income tax regulations, which here agree with recognized accounting principles, provide that the market write-down does not extend to "goods on hand or in process of manufacture for delivery upon firm sales contracts (i.e., those not legally subject to cancellation by either party) at fixed prices entered into before the date of the inventory, which goods must be inventoried at cost." Another such hedge concerns commodity futures for cotton and grain. Again to quote from the income tax regulations (or rather, rulings thereunder) which here, too, properly mirror accepted accounting practice, such futures, where they are not speculative, are "a form of insurance necessary to conservative business operation— compensating for fluctuations in the market price—adversely affecting the selling price." But the cotton textile manufacturer and the grain miller are a conspicuous and small coterie, in the possession of this device, as against the broad field of industry.

But do these hedges go far enough—do they cover the whole field of exemption from market devaluation? I should like to read the answer to that query out of the words of the income tax ruling just quoted, which mentions "fluctuations in the market price—adversely affecting the selling price." Those words will furnish a convenient text for elaborating the point.

Responsiveness of Selling Price to Market Price of Raw Material

In February, 1938, the National Industrial Conference Board published the results of a questionnaire study of the inventory valuation practices of manufacturing companies. In all, 826 replies were received covering a diversified classification of industries. Question number 4 asked:

Which carries the most weight in pricing product—
A. Replacement or market cost?
B. Actual or average cost?

Of the 747 replies received to this question 51 per cent responded to A, and 49 per cent to B.

I imagine that each of these groups in turn would reveal various degrees of price responsiveness: that is to say, at one end a pronounced responsiveness of its product prices to the related determinant in that group, with a tapering or shading off at the other end to the point of junction with the other group. But even without definite knowledge, at present, on this point, the results shown are interesting and definitely instructive—in fact so much so that we can profitably reflect upon them before further analysis determines just what gradations there are in each group. Assuming, however, for the purposes of discussion, that in each group the members are all alike, it would seem that the quotation given from the Internal Revenue Bureau's ruling in regard to commodity futures ("fluctuations in the market price adversely affecting the selling price") would fairly describe the situation as to Group A, in which replacement or market cost carries the most weight in pricing product.

How Group A can possibly settle the problem of its profits without dealing somehow with the question of market valuation of inventories, is nothing short of enigmatical. Market, that is to say, replacement cost, is the magnet which draws the product selling prices up or down, and the accounting procedure of Group A cannot possibly overlook that magnet if rational operating results are to be achieved.

Within that group there will, of course, be a variety of different operating conditions to be reckoned with as between one industry and another. The speed of responsiveness of product sales price to the changing replacement cost, we have already mentioned. In some industries this influence will make itself felt almost instantaneously; in others, there will be lags of varying degrees extending to fairly protracted delays. And the severity and suddenness of the price changes of the underlying material need to be considered.

Inventory Turnover and Relative Investment in Inventories

But in addition to all this there are these two inventory attributes in any industry which will have a decided effect upon profits in this connection: the rapidity or sluggishness of the inventory turnover, and the relative proportion of the investment in inventories to the total assets of the business.

An industry with a high degree of price responsiveness between material and product, which has a very slow turnover and a very large percentage of its total assets tied up in its inventories, is very much at the mercy of the price magnet. ; On a basis of first-in, first-out cost, without making any inventory market write-down, the period of rising prices will show exceedingly gratifying profits. When the economic cycle enters its price decline phase, those profits, if there are any at all, will be exceedingly ungratifying.

Another industry in this group which has a rapid turnover but follows the same cost procedure (without market devaluation), will likewise enjoy prosperity on the price upswing and not do nearly so well on the price downswing. However, as compared with the slow turnover industry, its upswing prosperity will not be so great, and compensatingly, its downswing adversity will be less extreme.

Moreover, as between two industries in this group with approximately similar rates of turnover, the industry with the greater proportionate investment in inventories will experience a greater spread between the upgrade and downgrade movements of the economic cycle than will the industry with the lesser inventory investment.

As will be readily appreciated, the effect of any cost averaging procedure in any of these industries will temper these extremes at both ends, as compared with cost on a first-in, first-out basis.

What about cost or market, whichever is lower, in these situations? Theoretically, the magnification of profits in the upward phase of the economic cycle is not affected one way or the other. On the turn of the cycle, however, the market devaluation tends to temper the results by anticipating price shrinkages. To that extent, at any rate, one might even view it theoretically as a somewhat belatedly applied brake on the accumulation of profits in the inventories.

Comparison of Two Types of Industries

But now let us refer to Group B, where are gathered the industries whose product pricing is largely influenced by actual or average cost. Perhaps a comparative example between Groups A and B will not be amiss.

Company A (which is in Group A) has a product costing $10, on which it normally would expect a final profit margin of $2; but the market has declined to $9, at which figure Company A inventories the article. It sells this article in the next year for $11—not $12, since the resale price dropped with the "content" market price—and so in that next year achieves its margin of $2 profit.

Company B (which is in Group B) has a product also costing $10, on which it also normally would expect a final profit margin of $2; the "content" market price of that product also dropped to $9, but when it sold the product the next year, it got $12 for it, its profit margin being $2 over its cost. What reason should there be for it to make an inventory market write-down to $9? If it does, the resulting $1 charge-off, which is fully recouped in the next year along with the normal profit margin, will only be a fictitious loss in the old year, resulting in an artificially swollen profit in the new.

Company B is, one might say, "hedged by nature." Market values have a different meaning from what they have for Group A. As a matter of fact, Group B undoubtedly includes—among others—such concerns as those instanced in the earlier part of this discussion as "cost alone" companies. The query comes to mind—and of necessity it must remain unanswered until future research provides the answer —what about those others? It may well be that such research will show that some companies now following "cost or market, whichever is lower" really may not have a very strong basic justification for thus following it, may in fact be following it largely because it is the fashion.

The problem is by no means as simple as my examples might seem to indicate. I am well aware that in this day of complex currents, clear-cut cases are not the rule. But it is only by thinking our thoughts through with the aid of simplifying examples that we can hope to attain fundamental reasoning.

"Cost, or Market, if Lower, Where Necessary"

I fear by now I may seem to have maneuvered myself into the corner where are gathered the supporters (I shall not indicate as between votaries and tolerators) of cost or market; but you must let me add, after "market, if lower," the important words "where necessary," in other words (to continue the phraseology of my previous word quibbling), "cost, or market, if lower, where necessary." For my part I can accept such a formula as covering, in a broad sense, the field of inventory valuation. If you speak of first-in, first-out, or of average costs, or of last-in, first-out, or even of "base stock," you are referring to simple variants of the cost part of the formula—variants made necessary in this complex day and age of inevitably and inextricably intermingled goods, an age when the simple situation of identical and identifiable costs has largely gone the way of other phenomena of the horse and buggy era. Moreover, under such a formula, I can also marshal other variants as well— even the retail method which, after all, is nothing more than doing the most feasible job of approximating costs, with a little market thrown in, when you have to deal with merchandising needles in an industrial haystack. And as for "market, if lower, where necessary," that will simply indicate that the market factor, in so far as the particular industrial conditions require its being considered, has not been overlooked. In the course of this discussion we shall consider it again for a moment.

Reported Earnings and Inventory Values

We are today in an accounting transition period where we are no longer smugly satisfied with the solutions once given to some of our accounting problems. Aside from new problems arising from new conditions, some of our older ones are being re-examined, and inventory valuation is certainly one of these.

The year 1929 and its economic aftermath partly gave rise to this introspection, and the political exigencies of the tax-gatherer gave further impetus to it. In the months and years following our economic debacle, business did much pondering upon the phantasmagoria of the once proudly hailed "new era," whose orgy of fantastic profits resulted in the headache of the "new deal." In that pondering it wondered what was wrong with those profits which men multiplied by an indeterminate and increasing "x" times in order to ascertain the intrinsic value of stocks. And that pondering produced much food for thought; for when one takes the earnings of a very prosperous quarter, multiplies them by four, calls the results "current annual earnings," and then capitalizes those "earnings" by multiplying them by ten, or even fifteen, as was done, it is risky not to be sure about what those earnings mean. Too often they did include an element of so-called profit tucked away in an inventory valued at peak prices, a profit that never was realized, a profit that was later cancelled out by that bugbear of business—an "inventory loss."

Of course, not all businesses were affected alike. In the nature of things it would be the Group A of our previous discussion which would suffer most because of the vulnerable nature of its price structure. And within that group the two factors already mentioned—the relative amount of total assets invested in inventories and the rate of inventory turnover—would play a role.

Influence of Taxation

But before we proceed to a brief discussion of Group A and what some of its members have done about their problems, I must mention some other factors which made it a matter of vital importance to undertake a reconsideration of our ideas about profits in relation to inventory valuation. It never rains but it pours; and so our business perplexities in times of depression are almost always aggravated by the additional bedevilments which the tax-gatherer inflicts upon us. Of course, in such times the tax-gatherer has his troubles too. The government needs revenue, and income taxes computed on red-ink incomes are not nourishing. So devices are resorted to in order to manufacture "taxable income." Let me mention three which have influenced business men to reconsider their profits, to see if they really are bona-fide profits. Of these tax-producing devices, two took place in 1934—the abolition of consolidated returns and the abolition of the allowance for prior year's operating loss carried forward. On top of these, in 1936 came the undistributed profits tax. All these taxation expedients contributed to putting business "on the spot," to questioning the substance, character and soundness of its profits, particularly profits locked up in the inventories.

Before these happenings, it did not matter quite so much if the profits out of which taxes were paid were not on a basis of close figuring. Business could afford to be a bit big-hearted in the knowledge that a possible degree of liberality of profit determination, due to the particular method of inventory valuation which was being used, could not, except for incidental changes in the basic tax rate, work a harm that was to be regarded as irreparable; in the long run, it would all be evened out.

With these tax-producing devices, however, the situation was changed. Each year was a thing apart from all others, just as each company also from then on stood on its own legs. An attitude of condoning a profit determination which did not conform to the traits of the trade or business might become tantamount to inviting the sheriff to come around.

Last-In, First-Out Emerges

Before these tax considerations became additional reasons for a serious re-examination of our "inventory versus profits" problem, but while the lesson of 1929 and after was being learned, the American Petroleum Institute began to examine the problem. To studiously minded officials in that industry it became clear that something should be done when the accounting department continually showed the profit (or loss) results to be something irreconcilably at variance with that margin over current crude oil costs and refining and marketing expenses which the operating officials recognized as the measure of operating results.

From their studies it became clear that, in an industry whose product sales prices were guided upward or downward by the price movement of the raw material (crude oil in their case) and where, further, that sympathy of price movement was a matter of quick responsiveness, the real operating results were more faithfully portrayed by co-ordinating the revenue with the costs which were directly causative of the prices which produced that revenue. In other words, in an industry where those operating conditions prevail, the really understandable, the truly meaningful operating results could be attained in the accounts only on a basis whereby the cost of sales reflected the current replacement costs of the goods sold.

As a matter of fact, in so far as one can speak at all of identical costs being really identifiable in this day of preponderantly inter-mingled goods, the concerns in that industry could point to a large measure of goods which were in fact physically "last-in" as entering into those "first-out," with large reserve stocks remaining substantially undisturbed. Accordingly, there was evolved the accounting procedure of associating the goods last-in with those first-out, thereby attaining a charge for cost of goods sold approximately representing the replacement cost of such goods.

Other industries of the Group A type have also adopted this method—the non-ferrous metals and the leather tanners—industries which likewise possess inventory attributes of relatively slow turn-over and substantial percentage of investment, along with a pronounced degree of price responsiveness between material and product. Indeed, the accounting concept of correlating sales with the

reproductive cost thereof in order to cope with these conditions is by
no means new in one of these industries.

Adjustment to Market under Last-In, First-Out

And now, how about "market if lower" in these cases? Market
influences their prices. What does it do to their inventories? Theoretically, market is supposed to have been robbed of its terrors as to
inventories because of the inauguration of the method at a time
when the economic cycle had only just got under way. Under normal circumstances, therefore, no situation should develop where the
residual inventory valuation would be in excess of market until
the cycle was well on the wane. But where the point at which the
method is adopted happens to be considerably on the rising curve of
the cycle, with a goodly measure of price appreciation already experienced, there will come a time, or times, in the downward range of
prices when inventory devaluation to market inevitably will require
consideration. This would be in the nature of a necessary corrective
whose effect, lasting beyond the immediate period and extending into
the future beyond, would be to get the residual inventory valuation
down to a basis where regularly recurring market fluctuations would
not thereafter need attention.

This "extraordinary adjustment" kind of market revaluation might
also happen, by way of exception, in the case of Group B, even
though the trade conditions in that group do not ordinarily inject the
effect of market fluctuations into the sales prices of that group. Such
things as price upheavals do happen and need to be reckoned with.
Since the established or seasoned "last-in" practitioner of Group A
(who has discounted ordinary market fluctuations by his accounting
procedure under that method) and those of Group B (where trade
conditions with regard to sales prices discount ordinary market
fluctuations) both will regard a market revaluation adjustment of
inventories as something altogether out of the ordinary, that adjustment certainly should be separated from the ordinary cost of goods
sold item in the income statement.

Adjustments in Other Cases

The Group A chronic invalid sufferer from the serious ailments of
sluggish inventory turnover, high inventory investment and rapid

price responsiveness can get his profit and loss account functioning normally by undergoing the major operation of the "last-in, first-out" cure. The Group B patient is ordinarily in good health and only occasionally needs a market write-down alternative. We still have the case of the more lightly afflicted patient of Group A to consider. He has good metabolism through a fast turnover, a relatively low inventory investment, and is not over-allergic to price responsiveness. He doesn't need a major operation, but he has some conditions to correct; a tonic will do for him. If he is in a line where he can get the "hedge" treatment—the commodity futures in such adequate markets as grain and cotton—he can take care of himself by resorting thereto. Otherwise he has to take the medicine of market revaluations—a medicine which, in view of the relative lightness of the ills which affect him, should not ordinarily be a bitter one. But some mild medicine is necessary to counteract his indulgence in "first-in, first-out"; where he has been relatively abstemious by using average costs, he may perhaps do without medicine. So much for metaphor, and now to cases.

Application of Losses as Between Years

Let us take two years, 1937 and 1938, for purposes of an illustrative example: 1937 as the year whose closing inventory we are discussing, and 1938 the year whose sales liquidated that inventory. Was it not 1937 which actually experienced the price shrinkage reflected by the write-down of the closing inventory? Was not that a loss attributable to 1937—I am not saying a loss finally realized in 1937, but a loss which had its true origin in 1937? And, though actual realization as such was deferred to 1938, when the goods were sold, was it not nevertheless a real loss, as distinct from a recoverable loss, for those in an industry whose product sales prices responded to the market trend of the contents of that product? To me that controlling attribute in such an industry would definitely, in our example, fasten upon 1937, the year of the price decline, the responsibility for a loss which 1938 inherited from 1937.

Whether, in considering it, you think of the balance sheet and of just exactly what the current position on that balance sheet should mean, or you think of the income account and of just what the results of operations should mean, in the case of an industry like the one we have been discussing, can you think of leaving out of the reckoning a prospective operating loss, not protected by any hedge and not recoverable in the normal course of events in that industry—a loss "prospective" only in that its exact dollars and cents have not yet been computed?

Application of the "Going Concern Concept"

We speak, often rather vaguely, of a "going concern" and "going concern value." Too frequently it has been used in connection with writing something intangible into the balance sheet, with enlarging the picture. It is a good concept, that of a "going concern," but it works both ways; it also imposes obligations. The balance sheet on a real "going concern" basis should portray a status enabling the concern to enter the new fiscal year with normal operating prospects, or at least as near to normal as lies within the power of those responsible for that balance sheet. If that which some fearsomely view as a procedure whereby a loss is incurred in one year for the sake of making a profit the next, is in reality the inevitable procedure to set a going concern normally on its way, should one not hesitate in this day to advocate otherwise?

Let us pause a brief moment to clarify the thought by considering two companies in the same industry, with everything else throughout being equal except the specific variances mentioned. Company No. 1 has been in business a long time, accumulating good-will and much experience, developing an outstanding seasoned organization—in short, everything attaching to the concept of "going concern value." Company No. 2, on the other hand, has just been formed, and so has none of these intangible attributes. Company No. 1 possesses an inventory, at the date under consideration, of 10,000 units, having cost $50,000, with, however, a current replacement cost or market value of only $40,000. Company No. 2 possesses an inventory quantitatively and qualitatively identical with that of Company No. 1 in every way, but since that inventory was just acquired, it has a cost of only $40,000.

On any fair follow-through of the "going concern value" concept —that value which No. 1 claims to enjoy and which its balance sheet might reasonably be expected not to contradict, an advantage which No. 2, not enjoying, cannot represent—would it be in accordance with sound accounting to permit No. 1 to overstate its inventory by $10,000 as compared with No. 2—an overstatement which, under the conditions of the trade or business which both companies are in, will mean that in the ensuing year (again with everything else being equal) No. 1, the "going concern" will wind up with $10,000 less profit than No. 2? That view of the meaning of "going concern," I am afraid, verges too perilously close to the auctioneer's connotation of "going" as a condition precedent to "gone." I submit that in no wise is it logical to say, on the basis of the conditions assumed to exist in that industry, that No. 1, by writing its inventory down from $50,000 to $40,000, has doctored its profits for the next year by taking an artificial loss in this year.

If, to put the example the other way about, the market had risen and No. 1 had an inventory costing $40,000, now worth $50,000 on the market, whereas No. 2 with a new inventory, had a cost of $50,000, the "going concern" advantage of No. 1 is automatically taken care of.

Just a concluding thought about the equity and merit of recognizing a market write-down in the days of the price slump, instead of kidding yourself about its being not yet a realized loss, when, according to the conditions, it is not in the category of things recoverable. A friend of mine who had disposed of an investment in a common stock, bought before 1929, which suffered grievously in that year and its immediate successor years, and which enjoyed only a comparatively little subsequent recovery in value, remarked, "That closes the chapter of 1929 for me." His words indicated that he had not the slightest illusion about what was the year of unkindness to him.

Results of Questionnaire Study

Before we leave finally the subject of curative treatment of our accounting procedures in respect of cost or market, there are three or four matters I should like to touch upon. The American Institute of Accountants' Special Committee on Inventories, of which I happen to be Chairman, undertook to "sound out" opinion on these several points in a questionnaire, with rather interesting results, the most important being the disposition evinced to review, reconsider and reshape some of our concepts.

On the question as to whether market includes the idea of reproductive cost, the preponderance of opinion was that market should be so construed. Unless it is, the meaningfulness of the operating results of our Group A is not served.

Then came the question of whether the market devaluation might be attained through an adjustable reserve. While the consensus was that, in practice, the reserve method was decidedly the exception, a majority viewpoint of those taking sides inclined to the reserve method from the viewpoint of sound theory. The trend of such philosophizing about cost or market as this paper has indulged in would definitely support this position—a viewpoint, incidentally advanced many years ago, when practice was not as crystallized as it is today, by my late friend and partner, one of the charter members of N.A.C.A., John Wildman.

Should the market decline be regarded as something "gross" or "net"? was the next question; "gross" meaning aggregate market declines, disregarding market rises in other articles, and "net" meaning the gross loss as diminished by such rises in the other articles. The majority viewpoint supported the contention that it was the gross decline which properly should be effectuated. "There was, however, a minority expression of opinion," the committee's report states, "favoring the use of the 'net' measure in given instances. Such instances were related by the repliers either to the existing practice in certain industries or to a proper consideration of an effectively 'hedged' position in the case of two or more important items of inventory." I believe I can hardly escape, after the before-mentioned philosophizing on the real meaning of cost or market which I have perpetrated in this paper, from being compelled to line up with the minority viewpoint just expressed.

The fourth matter related to the inclusion of indirect materials and supplies in inventories as current assets, thus making them subject to the considerations of "cost or market, whichever is lower." This would concern a wide range of supplies including repair parts for machinery and equipment. On this point the replies were somewhat in conflict. For my part, I cannot bring myself to make any valuation distinction on this basis between the direct and the indirect materials, when they will all come together anyway in ultimate dollars and cents in the valuation of the completed product, the only difference being that one came by the overhead route instead of the prime material cost route.

Inventory Reserves

Upon the subject of endeavoring, gropingly, to accomplish the objective of valuation correction by some manner of general reserve, instead of the more drastic change of basic method, I shall add a word or two. Over the years conservative management has sought to moderate profits which have been regarded as uncertain of ultimate realization for one reason or another by the use of inventory reserves—reserves for possible obsolescence, for price changes and contingencies of one sort or another. However commendable the motivating conservatism in the making of such reserves may be, they are often unsatisfactory in that there is no adequate way to independently check the judgment of those determining the amounts thereof. However conscientiously that judgment may have been exercised, the practice, as an instrumentality of accounting, is open to the objection that it may be abused, with no really effective means to prove or to disprove the abuse. As an accounting expedient, it is probably best classified in the category of necessary evils.

But to the extent that this evil can be done away with through the substitution therefor of an available means that will attain the objective of a proper conservatism, but attain it in full compliance with procedures that are systematic, that will insure consistency of method as between one fiscal period and another—to that extent the evil can hardly be condoned as a necessary one.

Present-Day Practice

As a concluding topic of this paper, may I say something about the present status of the cost or market procedure in actual practice. For some years past, we have been making annual compilations in our office of an extended variety of accounting practices and terms as revealed in the annual reports of some five hundred corporations. Over these years, these compilations have been made for the same corporations except only as changes through mergers and the like may have made changes unavoidable—this in the interest of having a truly comparable body of matter.

I have made a condensed summary of certain of those compilations relating to the matter of inventory valuation practices. I should like to present this summary for whatever interest it may have, both with regard to the present status of such practices and the changes therein during the past five years.

I must explain in advance that this standard "five hundred" of ours includes certain concerns, such as investment trusts, which, since they have no inventories, are excluded from this summary. On the other hand, this summary accounts for an aggregate of over five hundred examples, an anomaly due to the fact that in a number of concerns where inventories have been shown in subdivided form with differentiated explanations, each such different presentation is necessarily represented in the total.

NUMBER OF INSTANCES

	1933	1937	Increase *Decrease
1. At the lower of cost or market............	229	265	36
2. On a comparable basis but with variant terminology, such as at cost and below or not exceeding market, at cost which is approximately market, with also, in instances, reserves deducted..............	50	47	*3
3. Total on a lower of cost or market basis...	279	312	33
4. At cost or less, or at cost less reserve......	45	59	14
5. Total on a basis of cost but with modification in respect of market or otherwise...	324	371	47
6. On a straight cost basis..................	67	87	20
7. On a market basis, or with a reduction therefrom (including packing houses)...	17	19	2
8. Basis not indicated (or stated only as "book value")	100	58	*42
9. Total........................	508	535	27

Comments on Practice

These numbers disclose several very interesting bits of information, but first let me say that while we have generally been careful to treat matters uniformly so as not to vitiate comparisons, there is one exception to be noted in the earlier years when no particular trouble was taken to include certain relatively minor inventory items where separately classified, whereas later on none such were left out. It is this which substantially accounts for and explains the increase of 27 in the amount of the aggregate totals. Moreover, it is that increase of 27 which, to a not inconsiderable extent, accounts for the increase of 20 in the sixth item, "On a straight cost basis." Much the greater part of the decrease in the eighth item, "Basis not indicated," is reflected in the increase of 47 in the fifth item, "On a basis of cost, but with modification in respect of market or otherwise."

The latter two changes are to me the significant factors in this summary. The decline from 100 in 1933 to 58 in 1937 of cases of "Basis not indicated" very definitely exemplifies the trend towards presenting more information in published financial statements. The increasing use, or at any rate increased disclosure of the use, of a valuation basis of cost but with departure from cost for market decline or for other valuation shrinkages has resulted, in the 1937 figure, in a total of 371 as against a straight cost basis numbering 87—81 per cent against 19 per cent.

When I examine these figures, two questions loom up in my mind. One is: "How many of the 81 per centers, upon further consideration of their peculiar trade conditions, might join the 19 per centers?" The other is: "How many of the 19 per centers, after likewise further considering their conditions, might go over to the 81 per centers?" And there is the further question which perhaps both the 81 per centers and the 19 per centers might also ask themselves: "Under the conditions existing in my trade or business, should I regard the cost of the goods sold as something to be correlated with the goods first-in, or the goods last-in, or an average of the two?"

I venture to believe that the answers would all be such that they could be placed in a broad category labeled "The basis is cost, though market, however, if that be lower, but only where necessary." And for those who must have a more succinct phrase, I should like to shrink it into "Cost, or market, if lower, where necessary."

THOUGHTS ON INVENTORY VALUATION *

By Samuel J. Broad

PRACTICALLY all methods of determining the amount of an inventory for accounting purposes are based on cost or on market or on the lower of the two. The trend in accounting thought over the last several years has been moving strongly in the direction of favoring historical cost as the primary, and perhaps the sole, underlying basis for stating the balance sheet. However, some concern has been expressed at the apparent inconsistency with the historical cost basis of applying the formula of the lower of cost or market to the inventory. One writer has suggested that the inventory basis might be described as "cost, but market if lower where necessary," but this would still be a departure from cost under conditions in which it is necessary to use "market if lower."

Cost Only for Income Determination

Especially in relation to the income account, arguments have been advanced to the effect that profit on the sale of merchandise should be determined by reference to the original cost of the articles sold. For example, assume that a pair of shoes were purchased for $3 in the summer of 1937 with the expectation that they would be sold for $4, but that due to a decline in leather prices, and also a cut in retail prices forced by competition in a period of poor business, the selling price was reduced to $3.50 and the shoes were sold for this price early in 1938. Proponents of the original cost basis only for the income account would say that the profit made in 1938 was the difference between original cost and selling price ($3.50 less $3.00), or 50¢, and that the fact that the inventory may have been written down to replacement market of, say, $2.75 at December 31, 1937 does not affect the fact that selling price was 50¢ above original cost. They consider that price adjustments in the inventory to

---

* A part of an address by Mr. Broad delivered before the New York Chapter in 1940. The balance of Mr. Broad's address will be found in the section on Inventory Taking, starting on page 305.

reflect replacement market merely have the effect of switching part of the profits, in this case 25¢, from one year to another.

The difficulty with this point of view is that so long as goods on which there has been a decline in price remain in the inventory, there is, in effect, a mortgage on future earnings in that expectations of normal profits must be reduced until the decline in price is realized by sale. This is not the psychology under which inventory write-downs are taken. It is good merchandising to reduce prices and recognize shrinkages when they occur and to be done with them. This is good business policy and, in my opinion, the income account in particular should be a fair reflection of the policies adopted.

Again, with a view to applying the cost principle so far as practicable to the inventory, it has been suggested that the basis should be cost and that the valuation should only be reduced below cost to the extent that the cost may not be realizable upon sale; in other words, that the cost used should not exceed the expected net selling price after providing for costs of selling. This might be described as the basis of "cost to the extent realizable." I shall make further reference to this later.

Appraisal Valuation

Terms indicating an appraisal or valuation have also been used in reference to inventories, but appraisals or valuations can be made on many different bases. If it is meant solely that the inventory has been valued without relation to cost and presumably on the basis of the market in which the inventory could be purchased (rather than sold), the question immediately arises whether the valuation is or is not above cost. To the extent that some items may be below cost, the valuation represents the application of the lower of cost or market formula to those items. To the extent that some items may be valued above cost, however, unrealized profit is included in the inventory and presumably in the income reported, a result which is contrary to one of the canons of accounting principle. Thus, any valuation which gives effect to market prices without reference to cost if lower is not suitable for income purposes, although it might have its place as supplementary information in connection with the statement of the inventory on the balance sheet.

Valuation at Net Selling Prices

In some industries it is trade practice to state the inventory at net selling prices, regardless of cost. There should be justification for the practice, I think, to warrant its being considered acceptable and this justification is sometimes found. For example, sugar producing companies (I refer to raw sugar, not refined) are really in an agricultural business and largely use a natural business year. To show the results of a crop, it is necessary to apply the costs of producing the crop against the proceeds and this can only be done if the sugar unsold at the end of the fiscal year is stated at estimated net realizable value. The use of cost for the sugar inventory would result in mixing up the results of one crop with those of the next and be less informative. Justification for using net realization value doubtless exists in other industries too.

What Market?

In applying the cost or market formula to inventories it is necessary first to decide what is cost and what is market in order to determine the lower of the two. Let us deal with market first.

There is considerable difference of opinion, some of it on fundamental questions, as to what is or should be meant by the term as so used. Thus, any views which I may express should be considered as my own personal opinions and not those of any organization with which I may be connected.

The first question, to which I have referred above, is whether the selling market or the replacement market is meant. In my opinion, market for a merchant should be regarded as a price at which he could buy the relative quantities from sources to which he has access and from which he customarily can, and does, buy; in other words, the cost of replacement. Generally speaking, cost of replacement could also be used by a manufacturer as the measure of market, though in the case of work in process and finished goods, certain variations are involved. For example, due to increases in labor rates, the cost of reproduction may be higher for labor, but this may be offset by a decline in the market price of the raw materials involved. Obviously, it would not be proper to provide for the decline in raw material prices but to exclude the increased labor costs.

Again, reduced selling prices do not always follow immediately upon declines in raw material prices, especially where the process of manufacture covers an extended period. To reduce work in process and finished goods immediately to the cost of reproduction at lower raw material prices when there is no anticipated reduction in selling prices may thus result in showing an abnormally high profit in the immediately succeeding period and be subject to criticism as, in effect, switching profits from the current year into the next. Particularly is this the case where there are firm sales commitments, though discretion should be exercised so as not to consider as firm sales commitments what are in reality little more than buyers' options, exercisable only if the prices do not decline. These are further instances of the extent to which accounting policy should reflect the conditions and policies under which the business operates.

Use of Net Realizable Values

On the other hand, cost of replacement or reproduction value for a manufacturer may not only be below cost but also above the amount which he can realize. There are occasionally cases where this results from business policy, in order to carry a complete line. As a rule, however, such a condition will arise as a result of low volume and the adoption of actual (rather than normal) overhead. It would seem that net realization price (i.e., selling price less costs of selling) should ordinarily be the maximum extent to which replacement cost should be included in the inventory. If net realization price is lower than normal cost, I do not think it is necessary in a manufacturing enterprise to go below it and provide in addition for a margin of profit in the ensuing period, though this in effect may sometimes be the result under the "retail method" used in many retail enterprises.

I have already referred to one suggestion which has been made, that inventories should be reduced below cost only to the extent that a loss upon realization is expected after deduction of costs of selling but without allowance for any margin of profit; or, in other words, that market should be related to the net realization price so defined and should ignore replacement cost. The suggestion arises, I believe, primarily from a desire to adopt a uniform historical cost basis for the balance sheet, so far as practicable, and from a desire to depart from cost only if cost cannot be expected to be realized. I do not think, however, that it is necessary to depart so far from current business practice and business psychology in order to maintain the cost principle. A manufacturer who has copper on hand which cost him 10¢ a pound believes that something has happened if copper declines to 9¢ a pound and the decline is reflected in the selling prices. In his mind a shrinkage of 1¢ a pound occurred when the price declined, and it is not deferred until he finally delivers the goods and makes 1¢ a pound less profit than he would otherwise have realized.

I think that the reflection in inventory prices of declines in the purchase market can be reconciled with the theory of the historical cost basis. Generally speaking and with occasional minor exceptions, the purpose of purchasing or producing goods in trade and manufacture is to sell them at a profit. If the market has declined to a point where the goods cannot be sold at the customary net profit, part of the cost value has disappeared as a result of the market decline and this loss of part of the cost value should be recognized, even under the historical cost basis.

Application of Rule to Aggregate Inventory or Each Inventory Item

Another question which arises in applying the formula of the lower of cost or market to an inventory is whether it should be applied to each inventory item, to the totals of each major division of the inventory, or to the aggregate of the entire inventory. There might be a case, for example, where sheets and blankets were included in the same inventory and the replacement cost of sheets had declined but had been offset by an increase in the replacement cost of blankets. A tentative statement issued recently by the Research Department of the American Institute of Accountants suggests that "The application of the rule to the totals of each major division of the inventory would seem to be all that is called for, and its application by individual items, though specified in the Treasury Regulations, represents an unnecessary measure of conservatism."

There will undoubtedly be further discussions of this point before a final statement is issued. Some accountants would agree with the Treasury Department while others would go to the other extreme and apply the over-all comparison. I must confess to a personal preference for the application to individual items, but perhaps the support for both extremes indicates that the middle course is the best one.

Cost Formulas

There are various methods or formulas for determining cost. Cost may be determined on the theory that the first goods to be received are the first goods to be sold or that the last goods to be received are the first goods to be sold. An intermediate basis is that which is called "average cost," under which cost is determined by the average of the cost of goods acquired or produced during a period, usually taking into the computation the average cost, similarly determined, of goods which were on hand at the beginning of the period selected.

The "retail method" is primarily a convenient method for determining the cost of a large number of assorted articles, though it also reflects, in addition, declines in market price and obsolescence, to the relative extent to which these have been reflected in selling prices.

Specific identification of cost against particular merchandise consumed or sold is approved practice in certain cases such as the leaf tobacco business where the quality of the tobacco between different crops and different lots may vary so greatly that an averaging of the costs would not be conducive to accurate operating results. Specific identification, however, would not be an approved method, I think, in cases where conditions did not justify or necessitate its use.

The hedging basis of determining costs is frequently used by cotton and grain dealers where commitments, hedging, etc. may be as important, if not more important an element in determining costs as the cost of the actual inventory on hand. Here again, business conditions warrant, and necessitate, the adoption of a variation in practice.

Methods of Computing Cost Will Vary

The point I would like to make, and I think it is fundamental, is that the policies, methods and conditions under which a business is operated have an important bearing in determining what method of computing cost should be adopted in a particular case. Such policies, methods and conditions should be reflected, so far as possible, in the income statement, and thus in the determination of the amount of the inventory. Accountants have frequently been criticized because there is a lack of uniformity in accounting practices and especially as to the inventory. Such lack of uniformity is necessary and essential to the presentation of financial data which indicate fairly the position and results of operations. It is necessary and essential because the policies, methods and conditions under which business operates vary greatly and these variations and their effect on operations are an important factor in the operating results.

To carry my point a little further, a grocery merchant who has a quick turnover may have on his shelves approximately one month's purchases. His selling prices reflect very rapidly changes in his purchase costs and his purchase costs are probably very close to current replacement market at the close of the period. The merchant would hardly be justified in considering that the cost to him of a sack of flour, for example, was the average cost of all the sacks of similar flour which he had purchased during the year. For a business with a quick turnover it would seem that the first-in, first-out method of determining cost would be appropriate.

The Last-In, First-Out Method

We come now to the last-in, first-out method of determining cost. This method has been subjected to considerable criticism on the grounds that it is not realistic; that it tends to flatten out the peaks and valleys of earnings and show a stability which does not exist; that it subordinates the balance sheet to the statement of operations; and that it is primarily designed for the purpose of minimizing income tax payments. Space does not permit me either to deal fully with these criticisms, or to do justice to the arguments favoring the method and, accordingly, I shall merely touch upon some of the questions involved.

The fact that many important companies had adopted the method before they were permitted to use it for tax purposes indicates that, in some cases at least, benefits other than those arising from income tax reasons were responsible for its adoption. On the other hand, substantial tax savings, or at least the deferring of taxes, on profits which have not been realized (or, if realized, are tied up in higher inventory costs) may result if the last-in, first-out method is adopted at the proper time.

The criticism that the use of this method tends to flatten out the peaks and valleys of earnings and show a stability which does not exist is usually supplemented by examples showing the effect of the method under specified circumstances. Again, I will come back to the proposition that any method of pricing should be applied only under conditions to which it is suited and in which it reflects methods and conditions of doing business. Proponents of the last-in, first-out method have consistently maintained that the method was not applicable in all cases, but only under specified conditions. According to a memorandum submitted by the Committee on Federal Taxation of the American Institute of Accountants to the United States Treasury Department on September 1, 1938:

"The last-in, first-out or similar inventory methods would appear to be appropriate when:

1. The inventory is of relatively greater importance than in other industries as evidenced by the large ratio to other assets and by the fact that it consists of basic or homogeneous goods which form a substantial part of the cost of the products sold.
2. Inventory turnover is slow either because of length of process or conditions of merchandising.
3. Raw material prices and finished goods prices tend to run parallel.
4. The cost of raw material is such an important factor in the conduct of the business that fluctuations in raw material prices cannot be absorbed in the ordinary operations of business, making it necessary, so far as possible, to match purchases and sales (or sales and purchases) in a manner similar to that in which hedging operations in an available futures market may be used."

An Illustration

Let me endeavor to show how these conditions apply or fail to apply in certain circumstances. Some time ago I was consulted as to the adoption of this method in an integrated enterprise which carried on all the processes of manufacturing and selling a product; buying the raw material, manufacturing it, and eventually selling it in a chain of retail outlets. To avoid identification I shall illustrate by reference to the hosiery business where somewhat similar conditions apply, though the enterprise involved was not in the hosiery business.

The company purchased raw silk in the market and manufactured hosiery to sell in a limited number of price lines, retailing at 69¢, 89¢ and $1.35, and sold practically all of its output through a chain of retail stores in which hosiery sales predominated. From year to year the inventory of hosiery at the retail stores did not vary greatly, although there might have been peak inventory periods at seasonal dates during the year. At the close of the year, the inventory at the stores was substantially at a minimum. The question was raised whether the retail stocks of inventory were not, in the aggregate, very much in the nature of a fixed or permanent asset, although the identity of individual pairs of hose was, of course, changing day by day. In other words, was not a pair of hose manufactured and sold at a standard retail price of 89¢, and which had to be kept in stock in order to continue in business, of substantially identical value for accounting purposes at, say, December 31, 1939 as it was at December 31, 1935? If this was the case, would it not be desirable for the company to establish a more or less uniform price for inventory purposes by adopting the last-in, first-out method of inventory valuation, particularly as to the cost of silk, instead of the average cost method which had heretofore been used? Profits increased in times of good business but, as the cost of raw silk tended to increase too, part of the profits were tied up in higher inventory costs. Such increases would be minimized, as would also declines in profits at times of a declining raw silk market when inventory losses had to be taken.

The situation was studied with a view to seeing what would have been the effect had the last-in, first-out method been applied during the last five years. The surprising result was that instead of showing a straightening out of the peaks and valleys of earnings as between years, these peaks and valleys were changed in their position and were accentuated.

The next step in the study was to determine how this came about, and the answer soon became apparent. By using the last-in, first-out method the cost of sales used was being reduced immediately to reflect the reduced cost of raw materials. However, the business was such that retail selling prices did not respond for some time to declines in price of raw materials, so that as a result of applying lower costs to unchanged selling prices an increased profit per pair of hose sold was immediately reflected. This increased and somewhat fictitious profit continued to be shown until such time as retail prices were reduced or a higher grade of hose was produced for the same price, sometimes weeks or even months later. Further, these greater profits were shown in periods of declining prices and poorer business and this was not felt to be realistic. The idea was abandoned as a consequence.

It will be seen that in this particular instance the business involved did not meet the conditions specified in (3) above that raw materials prices and finished goods prices tend to run parallel.

Another Example

In the case of another business in which I was consulted with regard to the adoption of the method, raw material prices are reflected promptly—in fact almost daily—in the price of the product. Sales made are immediately covered by purchase commitments so that the difference between the cost price of raw material and the selling price, which represented the cost of manufacture plus a margin of profit, was immediately fixed. However, in this case the strict adoption of the last-in, first-out method would have meant that the cost of goods shipped on a particular day would be determined by the price of raw material most recently received, and this might have no relation to the cost at which the raw material was purchased for the particular order at the time the order was received. In that case it was decided that the sales should be costed at the price of the identical raw material purchased to cover. This decision meant that commitments had to be taken into account in the determination of the amount of the inventory and that basis was adopted by the company as reflecting most accurately the policies, methods and conditions under which it conducted its business. It is interesting to add that the method was adopted before the Commissioner's regulations regarding the application of the last-in, first-out method for tax purposes were issued, and without any assurance that the method would be permissible for tax purposes or that the regulations would permit consideration to be given to commitments.

The adoption of the last-in, first-out method of determining cost for inventory purposes does not necessarily mean a departure from the general formula of the lower of cost or market. It is merely a method of determining one-half of the formula, namely cost. If market should be less than cost as so determined, market would still govern, at least for balance sheet purposes, though it might be deemed desirable to reflect the reduction to market by setting up a reserve rather than by applying market directly to each individual item in the inventory.

Difficulty in Connection with Interim Statements

A difficulty which has sometimes been encountered in the application of the last-in, first-out method is in connection with interim statements, especially in the case of an inventory in which the quantities may during the year be temporarily less than at the opening date. If the inventory at June 30, for example, should be lower than it was at the beginning of the fiscal year, say January 1, should the cost of the goods theoretically sold out of the opening inventory be based upon the opening inventory prices? In that event a substantial variation in the gross profit margin might be reflected in the month of June for the sole reason that the opening inventory price might be based on prices which were two or three years old. Should this method be adopted regardless of the fact that the reduction of the inventory is considered to be seasonal and temporary only and is expected to be made up before the end of the fiscal year? If so, the result might be that any excessive profit which might be reflected during the month of June would have to be taken out again in a later month. This could involve substantial fluctuations in monthly profits, which have no basis in reality and distort the interim figures. Such a situation only arises when the aggregate sales quantities exceed the purchase quantities. Regarding the situation as a whole, I think it is preferable to cost the excess quantities sold at current costs, representing substantially the costs at which they may be expected to be replaced before the end of the year.

COST OR MARKET, WHICHEVER IS LOWER*

By William R. Donaldson

WHEN the close of the fiscal year comes rolling along we get out our forms of inventory tags and tickets and summary sheets, distribute them to designated employees out in the factory and in the office, issue instructions on what should be counted and tallied and how it should be done, and then proceed with the bustle of taking and recording the physical inventory. From the tags and tickets turned in, sorted by product groupings, the data may then be carried on to summary tabulations. Check-up is made to insure that everything has been covered and all forms issued are accounted for, and then we launch into applying the proper prices and extending the value of the inventory.

"Cost or market, whichever is lower," we are told, is to be the basis for this pricing and valuing, so we must ascertain the "cost" and the "market" prices of the various items included in our inventory and put them down alongside of the respective items. And now we face the important problem of deciding: What is cost? What is market?

Variations in Practice

In the writer's fourteen years of practice as a public accountant he has reviewed hundreds of inventories in many and varied industries and has found that the concepts of "cost" and of "market" actually employed are widely diverse—so much so, that thousands, even millions of dollars, higher or lower, would result in using one concept as against another. Practices followed in one enterprise in an industry are quite dissimilar to those of another enterprise in the same industry. Each contends that its concept of pricing is correct and the other wrong. Some companies are decidedly conservative and keep values as low as they dare, deducting reserves against inventory for all sorts of contingencies; others lean toward liberal, almost inflated, valuations. Yet both companies can with logic defend

* From the *Bulletin* of October 15, 1933.

their prices as representing "cost" and "market." Public accountants
have become used to this situation and recognize that a wide zone
exists in which prices used may swing and still be acceptable as
proper in stating that inventories are "at cost or market, whichever
is lower."

Method of Obtaining Data

In his desire to secure for inclusion in this article a succinct cross-
section of opinion as to the practices generally recognized as proper
and acceptable, the author prepared and caused to be distributed at
meetings of the New York and the Brooklyn Chapters of the
N. A. C. A. a form of questionnaire containing 58 statements of
practices he has found followed in various companies and requested
the members and guests present to indicate their views as to those
practices they approved, those they deemed optional but less desirable
and those they did not approve. It was also requested that responses
indicate which practices were used in their companies. This questionnaire appears here in full as an Appendix, but in the spaces
designated for response there have been inserted reference numbers
which will be mentioned in discussing the subject comprehended by
the particular statements and the responses received thereto.

While fewer questionnaires were returned than had been hoped
for, still they were sufficient in number to give a fair view of opinion
and to check the writer's observations. In one respect they were
disappointing; they did not show generally the extent to which the
views were used or followed in the respondents' companies.

To keep this article concise and to avoid repetitious cross-refer-
ences, the suggestion is made that at the conclusion of this paragraph the reader turn to the Appendix and read carefully the 58
statements which will be found grouped by classes and kinds of
inventory. Within the compass of these statements is practically
every consideration apt to arise in most industries in determining
the "cost" and the "market" prices of the items of inventory to be
priced. The introduction to the questionnaire explains the viewpoint with which it was conceived and the angle of approach to the
responses which was sought. Having read the Appendix, the reader
can follow more clearly the discussion which follows:

Raw Materials (1 to 15)

Both the "average" price and the "first-in, first-out" bases were reported as acceptable, with the "average" slightly favored. Those preferring the "average" almost unanimously indicated the other method as optional, while those approving the latter method were not inclined to consider the "average" method as proper. "Price of last purchase" was generally rejected as wrong, but several indicated approval and a few, optional. Rebates in the form of quantity discounts not receivable until the subsequent year must be applied to reduce price was the consensus, yet a substantial number indicated this was not necessary and a scattered few that it was optional. As to pricing under a system of standard costs, the weight of opinion is that the use of standard costs is proper, that debit price variations may be added back into price if desired and that credit variations should be given effect to reduce price. Opinion seems nearly evenly divided on the question of whether standard cost without adjustment for credit variations should be used; the majority say "no," but if there is added to those approving those who say it is optional, the total about equals those who oppose. A substantial series of negative replies to all these statements on standard costs points out, from the angle of inventory pricing at least, that there are still many opponents of standard costs.

As to market price, the verdict is overwhelming that year-end market quotations should be used and not the latest purchase price. A bare majority say that a lesser market price announced to be effective the first day of the new year need not be recognized, but while about half that number state it should be considered, an equal number state it is optional. Practically all responses favor writing down to market only in instances where free market and quotations exist and require that specially made material be adjusted to current lower quotations, where obtainable. Quite a number indicate, however, that market reduction is required of materials other than those freely marketed and quoted. Likewise, several state it is optional or unnecessary to reduce specially made material to the basis of a year-end replacement quotation. Opinion is evenly divided as to whether prospective loss on purchase commitments based on year-end market price should be taken in current year's profit and loss or footnoted on the balance sheet as a contingent loss. Including the "optional" responses as indicating acceptability, 70 per cent is the score for the footnote practice.

Factory Supplies (16 to 18)

It is somewhat difficult to draw exact conclusions from the manner in which these three questions were answered, but the thought appears to be that it is not essential to reduce special supplies, repair parts, etc., to current quotations from suppliers. On the other hand, bulk and general supplies with free markets such as coal, fuel oil, etc., should be reduced to current market quotations.

Work in Process—Labor (19 to 27)

For the first three statements (19 to 21) comes approval that labor in inventory as shown by work-in-process account is the correct practice, with a substantial number responding that this base or the replacement wage rate base is optional. Nevertheless, a large number insist that labor in inventory should be reduced to current replacement wage. The vast majority state that price should not be reduced to wage scale announced effective in the succeeding fiscal year; several indicate this adjustment as optional. As for standard costs (23 to 27), responses vary widely and seem to bear no relationship to one another in consistency of treatment. This again evidences that while a standard cost system may be in operation, just how resulting costs should be treated for financial statement purposes is still a matter of general indecision, if not dispute. This much seems clear: that while a fair number state that inventory may be priced at standard disregarding debit and credit variations, a far greater number believe that prices at standard should be reduced if large credit variations occurred. If debit variations occurred, several state that price should be increased and a greater number specify this action as optional. Reducing inventory to a new and lower standard set for the succeeding year draws about equal division of opinion, but increasing to a higher standard meets decided disapproval.

Material in Process (28 to 34)

Whether materials in process should be regarded for market pricing purposes from the angle of the raw material constituents therein or from the angle of the finished product which they will compose, is a moot question. While the majority incline toward the raw material view and specify pricing should be on the same basis as raw material, they signify quite strongly that if resulting finished product shows a profit above cost it is not necessary to reduce material in process to raw materials market. Such an attitude, when combined with the ideas of those who lean toward the finished product angle, leaves the question a bit confused. The writer is inclined to think that this supports his own observation that in those industries where basic raw material constitutes the largest part of finished goods cost, market price of finished goods moving somewhat in relation to raw material prices, the materials in process are priced on the raw material base (for example— woolen and cotton yarns and piece-goods, castings, pipings, strip steel and brass, copper wire, etc.). In other industries where raw material cost is low and labor and overhead represent the principal manufacturing costs, market price is viewed from finished goods price base. As for standard costs (32 to 34), again the responses show the same inconsistency in accepting the prices developed by the cost system. About half say adjustment is not necessary for price or usage variations and the other half say adjustment should be made. Pricing at new standard evoked the same division of opinion, with tendency toward disapproval.

Factory Burden—Overhead (35 to 43)

Most of the responses approved the use of burden prices developed by the normal functioning of the cost system; adjustment to closing month's actual rate of burden met with disapproval; predetermined rate set at the beginning of the year received 50 per cent approval; and new rate based on review of year's operations drew the same degree of acceptance. As for the latter two methods, those indicating "optional" about equaled the approvals. This would tend to indicate that no fixed rule for pricing the burden element is recognized and that any reasonable basis is looked upon as acceptable. That cost of carrying wholly idle buildings, etc., is not a proper part of burden pricing was agreed upon with only a straggling contra and "optional" vote. Cost of unused time of only part-time departments, etc., may properly be included in burden pricing, according to about one-third of the responses; one-third say it is optional, while the remaining third disapprove. As for standard costs (41 to 43), another series of inconsistent replies appear. The conclusion drawn is that standard prices are generally satisfactory, but adjustment upward or downward ought to be made to weigh in the effect of variations.

Market Price of Work in Process (44 to 46)

It was agreed by a substantial preponderance, if cost appears to be above equivalent finished goods market, that reduction should be made. Views are not as strongly expressed on the percentage deduction referred to in 45, a substantial vote for "no" and "optional" being tallied. However, the view prevails that, in addition, future loss on uncompleted work should be provided for.

Finished Goods (47 to 56)

Pricing of finished goods on basis of "average" and of "first-in, first-out" receives about equal approval, somewhat more favorably toward the first method but with many marking "optional" as to both methods. Last lot produced and current month's (replacement) cost methods do not register approval, some few, however, indicating "optional." As to stating finished goods prices on basis of anticipated costs (51), most responses are not in favor of this practice, but those approving and saying "optional" almost total those disapproving. As to market prices (52 to 56), the fair average price offered to the trade, though lower prices may be extended to a favored few, is approved by a large majority. That quantity year-end rebates and discounts should be considered in determining proper market price is favored, but not by any great weight of opinion. Whether selling price must be reduced by an allowance for selling expenses, etc., to arrive at "market price" for inventory purposes is a question on which opinion is almost equally divided, with the tally inclined toward approval, but if the "optional" votes are included with the negative that viewpoint would register a majority. That further reduction should be made to allow for administration expenses evoked a negative majority with a heavy contra opinion recorded.

"Cost or market, whichever is lower," as defined in 57, wins approval "hands down"; as defined in 58, it loses heavily but strangely draws a substantial "optional" following.

Conclusions to Be Drawn

Thus, having learned how New York and Brooklyn men look at the problems and practices involved in pricing inventories, what conclusion can be drawn? Only this—that hard and fast rules do not exist; that the field is wide open for the person who has a passion for standardization and the formulation of definite rules. Perhaps our own N. A. C. A. might like to undertake the task of settling this open question and announcing its stand. The United States Government in its income tax regulations and rulings touches only lightly some of the disputed points.

It is interesting to read what the Committee on Co-operation with Stock Exchanges of the American Institute of Accountants has to say on this subject in the recent pamphlet "Corporate Accounts and Reports," which has been sponsored by the New York Stock Exchange and distributed by it to corporations whose securities are listed on that Exchange. On page 6 is found:

> Again, the most commonly accepted method of stating inventories is at cost or market, whichever is lower; but within this rule widely different results may be derived, according to the detailed methods of its application. For instance, at times like the present, cost of finished goods may be deemed to be the actual cost as increased by subnormal operation, or a normal cost computed on the basis of a normal scale of operations. It may or may not include interest during the period of production, or various kinds of overhead expenses. Market value may be either gross or net, after deducting direct selling expenses. The choice between cost or market may be made in respect of each separate item or classes of items, or of the inventory as a whole. Frequently, whether a profit or a loss for the year is shown depends on the precise way in which the rule is applied. And since the conventions which are to be observed must, to possess value, be based on a combination of theoretical and practical considerations, there are few, if any, which can fairly be claimed to be so inherently superior in merit to possible alternatives that they alone should be regarded as acceptable.

On page 8:

> Again, it is not a matter of great importance to investors whether the cost or market rule for stating inventories is applied to individual items or to the inventory as a whole, but it is very important to the investor that he should be advised if the test is applied to individual items at the beginning of the year and to the inventory as a whole at the close thereof.

The Institute's Committee has recommended (not yet required by the Exchange) that each listed corporation cause to be adopted, made available to its stockholders and filed with the Exchange, a statement of the methods of accounting and reporting employed by it which is to be binding on its accounting department. The pamphlet states, on page 15, as to the contents of this statement:

> (b) In respect of inventories: The statement should show in fairly considerable detail the basis of valuation of the inventory. The statement under this head would be substantially a summary in general terms of the instructions issued by the company to those charged with the duty of preparing the actual inventories. It would not be sufficient to say that the inventory was taken on the basis of cost or market, whichever is lower. The precise significance attached to these terms should be disclosed, for the reasons set forth on page 3 of the letter.
>
> The statement should include a specific description of the way in which any intercompany profit on goods included in the inventory is dealt with. It should show under this head, or in relation to income or surplus account, exactly how reductions from cost to market value are treated in the accounts and how the inventories so reduced are treated in the succeeding period. It is, for instance, a matter of first importance to investors if inventories have been reduced to cost or market at the end of the year by a charge to surplus account, and the income for the succeeding year determined on the basis of the reduced valuation of the inventory thus arrived at. Obviously, under such a procedure the aggregate income shown for a series of years is not the true income for the period.

The movement toward full and proper disclosure of corporate accounts, initiated by the New York Stock Exchange as to its listed corporations and now receiving impetus from many quarters, is resulting in the crystallizing of thought on mooted accounting treatments. The Exchange has already announced its views (almost rules) on the proper classification and reflection in financial statements of such things as treasury stock owned, dividends received on treasury stock, capital and earned surpluses, income derived from retirement of own bonds and stocks at less than par, etc. Should the Exchange proceed to adopt further the suggestions of the American Institute, the day may come when we shall have some sort of official or semi-official pronouncement covering the inventory pricing practices discussed in this article.

APPENDIX

COST OR MARKET, WHICHEVER IS LOWER

Most of us these days have been struggling with the proper pricing and valuing of inventories. Raw material prices constantly decreasing, wage rates reduced several times within the year, plants operating at a fraction of capacity—all these conditions make the problem of proper pricing difficult. And then the question, "What is market?" It is generally recognized that there is a wide zone within which prices may swing and still be acceptable. Some enterprises are conservative, even ultra-conservative, and follow the policy of slashing year-end inventory valuations to the bone; others, more liberal in viewpoint, follow the policy of setting valuations at as high a figure as it is possible to do without drawing criticism from their auditors.

The questionnaire below requests your views on the statements therein. Please bear in mind that the intention is to find the consensus of the chapter members on these important points in pricing and treating inventories. Do not view the statements in relation to what is the best method of determining costs for management control or for cost system purposes, or what is the most conservative treatment, but leaning toward liberalism in valuation, what are the proper and acceptable practices which could not be criticized in presenting a balance sheet with the inventories stated to be "at cost or market, whichever is lower."

Please indicate your answers with letters. A = approve; O = optional but less desirable; No = wrong and not approved. Please also indicate, if known, whether the company with which you are connected follows the practice by writing U = use. (For example, A U = approve and use; No U = do not approve but company uses.) Statements should not be signed so that your views and the practices of your company will be kept confidential. Statements will be collected before the speaker of the evening commences his talk. You will then be given another form for your information and upon which you may enter the tally when announced. It is the intention to tabulate these statements and announce the results.

A = (Approve)   O = (Optional but less desirable)
No = (Wrong and not approved)   U = (Used by Company)

Statements to Be Checked

Raw Materials

As to Cost

1. Cost is the average price from stores cards determined by averaging purchases.
2. It is that shown by stores cards on "first-in, first-out" basis.

3. It is the price of the last purchase.

4. Rebates in the form of quantity discounts accrued but not receivable until succeeding year should be applied to reduce cost.

As to Standard Cost

5. Cost is the standard predetermined cost.

6. Where debit variations in standard material costs were reflected during year, part of "price variation account" may be apportioned back to inventory to adjust upward to actual cost.

7. Where credit variations occurred (carried to profit and loss) part of "price variation account" should be apportioned back to inventory to adjust downward to actual cost.

8. Such credit variations may be entirely disregarded and standard price used without adjustment.

As to Market Price

9. It is the latest purchase price.

10. It is the market quotation at the close of fiscal year.

11. If a price reduction is announced effective the first day or early in the succeeding year, price must be stated at the announced change even though not effective until succeeding year.

12. Inventory price must be reduced to market only where basic standard raw materials and a free market and quotations exist.

13. Price must be reduced on raw materials specially made where lower current market quotations from suppliers can be secured.

14. As to all raw material commitments (not yet received and therefore not in inventory), where market price is less than contract price the reduction to market should be charged off to profit and loss in the current year.

15. Such reduction need not be charged off; it is sufficient to show as footnote on balance sheet as a contingent loss.

Factory Supplies

16. These must be priced at cost or market on exactly the same basis as raw materials.

17. These must be reduced to market only on basic products with free market, such as coal, fuel oil, paints, etc.

18. It is not necessary to reduce to market special supplies such as electrical fixtures, hardware, machinery and motor parts, etc., where a vast number of current quotations from individual manufacturers must be obtained.

Work in Process

Labor in Process

19. Labor cost should be stated at actual as represented by work in process on hand at close of the year, even though labor rates were reduced toward the close of the year.

20. Labor cost in inventory should be stated at reduced wage rates in effect at close of year to adjust inventory to current replacement cost.

21. Labor cost should be stated at average wage rates in effect during period inventory on hand was built up.

22. Where wage scale is announced to be reduced effective early in the succeeding year, labor in inventory should be reduced to new scale.

Standard Cost

23. Labor cost should be stated at standard even though substantial debit or credit variations occurred during the year were carried to profit and loss.

24. Inventory should be adjusted to reduce standard labor content where large credit variations (all taken in profit and loss) occurred during period inventory was accumulated.

25. Inventory should be adjusted to increase standard labor content where large debit variations (all taken in profit and loss) occurred during the period inventory was accumulated.

26. Where lower standard labor cost is set for succeeding year, labor in inventory should be reduced to new standard.

27. If new higher standard is set for succeeding year, new inventory should be adjusted upward to new standard.

Material in Process

28. Raw material in process should be viewed in its constituent elements in the same manner as actual raw material in stores not yet put into process and priced on same basis as stores, viz., cost or market whichever lower, in the same manner indicated above under raw materials.

29. In such event where standard cost system is used, raw material in process should be treated in the same manner as answered above under raw material.

30. Raw material put into process loses its character as such and adjustment to market price should be based on the finished product which it will eventually represent and not the raw material prices.

31. Recognizing that raw material price structure would necessitate reduction in raw materials in process if viewed as raw materials but that finished product market prices are above cost, it is not necessary to adjust inventory cost arrived at through normal and proper functioning of cost system.

Standard Cost

32. Where substantial debit or credit price or usage variations occurred during the period the inventory was built up, it is not necessary to adjust price to reflect actual cost of raw material in process.

33. Such cost must be adjusted to show the effect of variations.

34. Where new standard is to be made effective at beginning of succeeding year, inventory should be valued at new standard and not at old.

Factory Burden in Process

35. Overhead on product in process should be priced at actual reflected on books through normal functioning of cost system.

36. It should be adjusted to closing month's actual rate of overhead.

37. It should be priced at predetermined rate set at beginning of the accounting period.

38. It should be set at new rate based on review of year's operations.
39. Cost of carrying wholly idle and unused buildings, floors, etc., may be included in overhead and represented in inventory pricing.
40. Cost of carrying unused time of only part-time departments, machines, etc., may be included in overhead pricing.

Standard Cost

41. Overhead in process should be based on current year's standard and not on new and lower standard set for succeeding year.
42. Rate (price) must be adjusted for inventory pricing purposes upward or downward to include effect of variations (carried direct to profit and loss) during period product in inventory was in process.
43. Only credit variations need be considered in adjusting price; debit variations may be disregarded.

Market Price—Work in Process

44. When it appears that work in process when finished will cost substantially more than selling price of finished goods, work in process inventory should be reduced by some amount to effect an equivalent reduction to market value of the goods in process.
45. If so, it is sufficient to reduce inventory by the percentage of reduction occasioned in pricing the finished goods inventory and reducing that inventory to market.
46. Or, because such work in process cannot be sold until finished, provision must also be made and charged to profit and loss for a further loss to market which will occur on that part of the cost not yet incurred but which must be incurred to make the goods marketable.

Finished Goods

As to Cost

Cost price is that which is taken from perpetual inventory record cards:

47. Priced on an average basis.
48. Priced on a "first-in, first-out" basis.
49. Priced at the cost of last lot purchased.
50. It is the current month's cost (i.e., current replacement cost).
51. Where new raw material contracts at lower price, decrease in wage rates, etc., become effective at the beginning of the succeeding year, finished goods prices (deemed less than market) should be adjusted downward to include the effect of new lower costs, to state such inventory at the new anticipated cost.

As to Market Value

52. The lowest market price even though quoted to a few favored large quantity customers must be used.
53. Though lower prices may be offered to a favored few, the fair average price offered to the trade generally is the proper price.
54. Where quantity discounts are offered to trade, rebated at the end of the year, market price should be adjusted to allow for expected rebates.
55. "Market price" is not the offered price to customers but must be reduced further by proper allowance for selling, delivery, etc., expenses, to constitute "market price for inventory purposes."
56. It must be further reduced by an allowance for administration expenses.
57. "Cost or market, whichever is lower" means that as to individual items, those which cost less than market are not adjusted while those which cost more than market are written down to market.
58. "Cost or market, whichever is lower" means that individual items are separately priced both at cost and at market and if a grand total at cost is in excess of the grand total at market, the inventory is reduced by this difference, i.e., both increases and decreases at market are considered and netted to constitute the proper write-down to market.

APPLICATION OF THE COST OR MARKET RULE TO A WOOLEN COMPANY *

By Clarence B. Nickerson

I T IS THE purpose of this article to describe and comment upon certain inventory problems and practices of an actual company to which we shall assign the fictitious name, Davis Textiles, Inc. No attempt is made to discuss the various bases of valuation and their respective merits, since a brief treatment would not do justice to such a subject. The subject of the present paper might be stated in the form of a question. Given cost or market, whichever is the lower, as the basis of valuation, what problems arise in a specific company in establishing cost and market for its inventories?

Though the practices of this woolen company serve as a specific example, many of the matters considered are equally applicable to other manufacturing enterprises.

Inventory Classes

Davis Textiles, Inc., classified its inventories, with the exception of supplies, under four general headings, namely: top, yarn, grey cloth and finished goods. These groupings had been selected because they represented the four stages in which the bulk of the inventory was to be found at the close of an accounting period, which in this company was a quarter of a year.

The amount of top on hand was subject to considerable variation, depending upon the rate at which the mill was operating and prospective market conditions. The amount of yarn and grey cloth on hand was small compared to the annual output, since most of the manufacturing was to order. Occasionally, however, when conditions seemed to warrant it, standard types of both yarn and grey cloth were produced for stock. The finished goods inventory was always very small and practically all of it was covered by orders. Usually it consisted of goods held awaiting the completion of the quantity ordered or pending shipping instructions.

At the close of an accounting period there was always some

* From the *Bulletin* of April 15, 1937.

material actually in process between these stages. This was the smallest, and at the same time the most troublesome part of the entire inventory. In the first place it was difficult, if not impossible, to tell accurately how much material there actually was in process. Secondly, since the company did not keep complete lot cost records, it was impossible to tell how much of the outlay for labor and overhead of a department should be allocated to work in process remaining within it at the close of a period.

This second problem might have been met by making elaborate cost studies, setting up standard costs, making arbitrary allocations, or by combinations of these methods. It had been decided, however, that no such allocation was worth the effort. First, the work actually in process was only a minor part of the inventory. Second, the greater part of the cost was for raw material which could be priced with reasonable accuracy. Third, any allocation was arbitrary at best, delayed inventory computation, and took time away from other and more productive work.

Thus the company adopted the fiction, so far as pricing was concerned, that at the close of a period there was no work actually in process, except at these four stages, and that all of the inventory was definitely in the form of top, yarn, grey cloth or finished goods.

Establishing the Cost of the Inventory

Wool top was purchased by the company on a bone dry basis plus 15 per cent moisture regain, which was standard practice in the trade. At the time of purchase the vendor tested the wool top to determine the actual moisture content. The actual weight of the lot of wool top being purchased was then reduced to its weight on a bone dry basis, to which was added the standard 15 per cent regain to arrive at the billed weight. The following is a typical invoice:

HIGGINS AND PERRIN

Wool Merchants and Top Makers

To Davis Textiles, Inc.   Dec. 8, 19—

25 Bags	62 S	Tops	Lot 5637
Wgt.	Tare	Net	
6,613 lbs.	198 lbs.	6,415 lbs.	
Less: 13/20%	Ave.		
Moisture Content		847	
		5,568	
Add 15% Regain		835	

6,403 lbs. Net at $1.05 = $6,723.15

Upon receipt of the wool the company tested it for moisture content but rarely found it necessary to put in a claim for adjustment.

In addition to entries in the books of account and on perpetual inventory cards the purchases of wool top were listed on quarterly sheets, a separate sheeting being kept for each grade. The columnar headings for a typical sheet with details taken from the invoice above would appear as follows:

Date	Purchased From	Vo. No.	Lot No.	Pounds	Price	Amount
Dec. 8	Higgins and Perrin		5637	6403	$1.05	$6,723.15

After taking the physical inventory, as described above, the detailed inventory sheets were combined and condensed to facilitate pricing. The final inventory sheets showed the total pounds of each grade of wool top in storage, the total pounds of each type or grade of yarn, and the total yards of each type or grade of grey cloth and finished goods.

In order to establish the cost per pound for each grade of tops in the inventory, the entire inventory was converted to pounds of tops by grades. The quarterly purchase sheet (illustrated above) for a given grade was then subjected to a backing up process. Starting with the latest purchase on the sheet, the quantities were added until the total agreed with the total quantity of that grade in the inventory. In other words, it was assumed that the material on hand in all stages had come from the most recent purchases, or conversely that the oldest material on hand was the first to be used in production. After locating the quantity on the purchase sheet, the amounts paid for the separate lots making up that quantity were added to find its cost. The cost was then divided by the quantity to arrive at an average cost per pound for the given grade. These average costs per pound for the various grades were used in pricing the inventory on a cost basis.

Establishing the Cost of the Wool Top Inventory

As indicated at the outset the wool top inventory included not only tops in storage but also material in process up to the point where it became yarn. This inventory was priced by applying the unit cost, developed as stated above, to the quantities of the various grades on hand.

The matter of moisture content made possible a slight error here since the quantities established by the physical inventory represented the actual weight at the time of purchase, less the tare, whereas the weights recorded on the purchase sheets were the billed weights. Thus, if the 25 bags of tops shown in the invoice above had still been on hand at inventory time, they would have been listed on the physical inventory sheets at a total of 6,415 pounds when, as a matter of fact, the price paid and the average cost per pound developed from the purchase sheet assumed the quantity to be on a bone dry basis plus 15 per cent moisture regain. The moisture content, however, varied with each lot purchased and tended to average around a 15 per cent regain. Consequently the error, if one existed, was believed by the management to be negligible.

Establishing the Cost of the Yarn Inventory

In pricing the yarn inventory, which included yarn on the looms as well as yarn in storage, the cost per pound for each grade was established by taking the cost per pound for the grade of tops used, as developed above, allowing a certain amount for waste and adding a standard processing cost.[1] In other words, the entire cost of material, labor and overhead was established per pound for each grade of yarn. These unit costs were then applied to the quantities shown by grades on the physical inventory sheets. The sum of the extensions gave the total amount of the yarn inventory in dollars on a cost basis.

Establishing the Cost of the Grey Cloth and Finished Goods

In pricing the grey cloth inventory, which included grey cloth in the finishing processes, the cost of material per yard for each grade was established by applying the cost per pound for the grade or grades of top used to the standard quantity or quantities of tops per yard. The standard quantity was set high enough to allow for the normal waste. A standard processing cost was added to the cost of material to arrive at a total cost per yard. These unit costs were then applied to the quantities shown by grades on the physical inventory sheets. The sum of the extensions gave the total amount of the grey cloth inventory in dollars on a cost basis.

[1] Further consideration of processing costs is presented later.

The procedure for establishing the cost of the finished goods inventory was the same as that for the grey cloth inventory.

Commentary on Establishing the Cost of Material in Inventories

To avoid spoilage and to have inventories consisting of fresh stock, it is common procedure to draw upon the oldest stock on hand in meeting production requirements. For various reasons this procedure is not always followed, particularly when the raw material is durable in nature, and is frequently violated by reason of accident or convenience at the time material is withdrawn. Nevertheless, there is a tendency to use up old stores first and in recognition of this practice many companies price their closing inventories at cost by working back from the most recent purchases. This was the method used by Davis Textiles, Inc., though no distinction was made between the various stages in which the inventory was located. That is, an average cost per pound for each grade was developed from the most recent invoices, and these unit costs were applied to the various grades throughout the inventory. If the first-in, first-out method had been followed closely, the wool top in storage would have been priced from the latest purchases, the yarn inventory from purchases further back, etc. However, this extra trouble and expense would have been unwarranted, since the main point was to separate the cost into that part which remained in the inventory as a whole and that part which had entered the cost of goods sold.

In some companies, where complete cost systems are in use and perpetual inventory records are kept in dollars as well as in quantities, withdrawals of material for production are priced on a first-in, first-out basis. In others the withdrawals are priced on an average cost basis. The weighted average cost for an item is computed by adding the purchases to the beginning inventory and dividing the total dollars by the total quantity. This weighted average cost is always used in pricing the closing inventory. There is considerable merit to the weighted average cost method, since it eliminates much of the detailed pricing, spreads the effect of price fluctuations, and is likely to be more satisfactory from an operating viewpoint, where costs on the average are of greater importance than are the costs of particular lots.

A third possibility is to maintain the identity of the material so that it can be priced at inventory time by reference to specific invoices, entries in the purchase record or entries in the inventory cards. However, the trouble and expense of identifying and pricing specific lots of material is usually prohibitive and other methods are ordinarily as satisfactory for all practical purposes.

It is often impossible to identify specific lots of material once they have entered the storeroom. In many other instances the material loses its identity upon entering production. In some industries it is desirable to follow specific lots through production to check the yield as a guide in future purchasing. This identification can be used for inventory pricing purposes but in many instances is applied only to trial runs or to a small part of the total inventory.

Treatment of Material in Process Between Inventory Stages

It was stated at the outset that inventories were classified under the four headings: top, yarn, grey cloth and finished goods.

The wool top inventory, then, included not only bales of tops but also all top in process up to the point where it became yarn. Thus at the close of a quarterly period all work in process in the spinning department, including the preparatory processes as well as the actual spinning, was priced for inventory purposes on the basis of its wool content.

Likewise the yarn inventory included not only yarn in storage but also yarn in process for warp and all material on the looms; warp, filling and partially completed pieces of cloth. That is, all work in process in the weaving room at the time of taking inventory was priced as so much yarn.

The grey cloth inventory, in turn, included not only grey cloth in storage but also cloth in process in the burling and mending department, in the dye house and in the finishing room. That is, all of the cloth in process in the finishing stages at the time of taking inventory was priced as though it were merely grey cloth.

This policy purposely omitted the difficult task of pricing the departmental labor and overhead expended upon work remaining in process within a department at the close of a period. It resulted in understating, to some extent, the inventory of goods in process. Under normal conditions, however, the amount in process was approximately the same at the close of each similar period, with the result that about the same float or hidden reserve existed from year to year.

The cost of goods sold tended to be unchanged by this policy except for: (1) the initial period during which the policy was adopted, (2) abrupt changes in costs, and (3) a marked abnormal or subnormal quantity in process at the time of taking inventory. The quarterly reports were affected more than the annual reports. For the first year the cost of goods sold was overstated to the extent that the inventories were understated. Each year thereafter benefited from starting with understated goods in process, but at the close of the year the ending inventories in process were also understated, leaving the cost of goods sold for the year approximately the same as it would be without such understatement of inventories.

Furthermore, the amount in process at the time of the preparation of the annual reports was only a small per cent of the annual production, and since this material was only partially worked upon the amount of labor cost and manufacturing expense affected was an even smaller percentage.

In some industries where the manufacturing time within any one department is short, it is often possible at inventory time to clean up all of the work on hand within a department before taking the inventory. All of the accumulated costs of a department can then be charged to the units completed by it. This does not mean that the entire production schedule should be upset to accomplish this, but there are many instances where this can be done with little, if any, friction.

A practice which is common in the shoe industry during the annual or semi-annual inventory period is to stop production by departments in rotation. This enables each department to complete the bulk of its work on hand before its inventory is taken, and reduces the number of items to be counted and priced. Only one or a few departments are idle at a time and the counting is done by experienced and responsible persons rather than by drafted clerks. Careful records are kept of goods entering production during the inventory period so that inventory figures can be brought up to the date of the balance sheet.

Establishing the Cost of Labor and Overhead in Inventories

As just indicated, the company did not compute the departmental cost of labor and burden expended upon goods actually in process within a department at the close of a period. It was necessary, however, to establish the cost of labor and overhead in the inventories classified as yarn, grey cloth and finished goods.

The company did not keep complete cost records to show the accumulated labor and overhead costs on these items of work in process and finished goods. It was therefore necessary to make estimates or computations so that a fair amount for these costs might be included in the inventory figures. For this purpose the company made use of standard unit processing costs for the various grades and types of yarn, grey cloth and finished goods. These were based, in turn, upon standard labor and overhead rates for the various operations. These standard unit processing costs had been developed primarily for use on cost estimates in connection with pricing and budgeting, but they could readily be adapted to the costing of inventories.

Thus the costs established for inventory purposes, as far as labor and overhead were concerned, were standard costs not actual costs. It should be understood, however, that these standard costs were constantly subject to revision in line with changes in wage levels, overhead expenditures and production processes, and when further test runs showed that it was desirable to change them.

They were subject to revision at longer intervals in line with changes in the management's concept of the company's normal volume of operation and significant changes in the component parts of the normal volume. An example of the latter might be an increase in the production of cloth for women's wear with a corresponding decrease in the production of cloth for men's wear.

The Use of Standard Costs for Inventory Valuation

With respect to overhead, it is the practice of many companies to make standard or normal overhead charges to goods in production and to carry overhead unabsorbed or over-absorbed directly to the cost of sales account or preferably to a separate account so that it will show up as a separate item in the profit and loss statement. So common is this practice that many people have come to think of actual cost as meaning actual material, actual labor and standard overhead.

When actual costs are used for overhead the actual cost per unit increases as production volume falls, which means that the stated value of the inventory on an actual cost basis increases with respect to the overhead element of cost as demand diminishes, and, though this is a statement of fact, it lacks the conservatism usually associated with inventory valuation.

A clearer picture of operations, as well as conservative valuation, is obtained if the overhead element of cost is priced at standard and the unabsorbed overhead shown as a separate item in the profit and loss statement.

The principal reason that standard costs for overhead are acceptable in inventory valuation is that many of the items of overhead are fixed and changes in the volume of operations have a marked effect on unit costs. The total direct labor, on the other hand, varies for the most part directly with volume. The only reasons for using standard labor costs in inventory valuation are (1) that the actual costs are not readily or economically obtainable and (2) that only efficient costs are to be allowed in the inventory. The first point is sufficient to justify the use of standard labor costs. The second point is not sufficient reason; for, if the standards are too idealistic, the inventories do not reflect representative costs, and, if the standards are reasonably attainable, high efficiency in some areas will tend to offset inefficiency in others, leaving actual costs satisfactory for all practical purposes.

Regarding raw material and the material cost in work in process and finished goods, it appears best to use actual costs rather than standard costs in establishing cost for valuation purposes. Practice varies in the treatment of standard material costs, the most significant difference being that in some companies raw materials are entered at standard cost at the time of purchase and the difference between actual cost and standard cost is carried to a purchase price variation account; whereas, in other companies raw materials are carried at actual cost and are charged into production at standard cost, the difference between actual cost and standard being carried to a price variation account or in some cases closed to the cost of goods sold account. The use of standard material costs for control purposes is commendable, but when used for inventory valuation they introduce fiction that distorts the balance sheet and net operating results, since such costs are relatively low when prices are high and relatively high when prices are low, unless they are changed so frequently as to become standard reproduction costs representing "market" rather than "cost."

With materials, marked changes in unit costs with changes in production volume are not found as in the unit cost of fixed over-head; hence this reason for the use of standard material costs does not exist. As to efficiency in the use of materials, standard waste allowances can be used with actual costs to avoid inflating inventories by inefficiencies.

Material, Labor and Overhead at "Market"

Davis Textiles, Inc. stated its inventories according to what it considered to be the lower of cost or market. We have discussed problems in determining cost and are now concerned with estab-lishing market values for inventories.

The company considered that reproduction cost, as of the date of the balance sheet, represented market in the case of raw mate-rial, and material in goods in process and finished goods. Exceptions to this were obsolete stock and seconds which are to be considered later.

The standard unit costs for labor previously described were con-sidered to represent the labor cost element at both normal volume and market. In other words, the standard costs were adjusted when cost studies showed them to be out of line and also when the wage scale changed, which occurred only infrequently. Thus the standard cost could be said to represent both cost and market.

Likewise, for the overhead component in goods in process and finished goods, standard cost is represented as market; in other words, current costs spread over a normal volume. In any event the standard cost was taken to represent the overhead element at both cost and market.

Commentary

Market, for raw material and for the raw material element in work in process, is generally understood to mean reproduction cost. Many of the problems faced in determining the amount of the in-ventory at cost are, therefore, to be met again in pricing it at market.

The labor element in work in process and in finished goods is commonly taken at actual cost or at standard cost, and is not adjusted to reproduction cost unless the wage scale in effect on the date of the balance sheet is markedly lower. If the inventories of work in process and finished goods are large in quantity and variety, the task of re-costing them by items on a reproduction basis is too expensive and time consuming. Under these conditions, if reproduction cost is desired the entire cost of labor in the inventories is reduced by a percentage calculated to bring it down to approximately that figure.

For the reasons given previously, it is common practice to use standard costs in pricing the overhead element of the inventory. For monthly statements these standard costs are not ordinarily adjusted to reflect current costs spread over the normal volume. By the close of the year in many companies, new standards have been developed for use during the new year and where this is the case the inventories should be adjusted, either in detail or approximately, to reflect the new standards if they are lower. When it is apparent that the old standards have been too high and new standards have not been set by the time the balance sheet is prepared, the overhead element in the inventories is commonly reduced by an amount calculated to bring it down approximately to the lower standards which could be established as "market."

Realization Value

In establishing a market value for finished goods it is necessary to consider not only reproduction cost but realization value as well. Theoretically, realization value should be determined by estimating the probable selling price of each item of finished goods inventory and subtracting from each the estimated selling expense. In practice, time is usually not available for such detailed computations since the financial statements must be prepared with a minimum of delay.

Leaving out of consideration obsolete goods, which should be accorded careful individual treatment, the following method is often used to arrive roughly at a realization value for the finished goods inventory. The profit and loss statements for the previous twelve months are combined to arrive at total sales, total cost of goods sold and total selling expenses for the twelve months. The total cost of goods sold and the total selling expenses are then subtracted from the total sales. General and administrative expenses are not included in this computation since they are more or less fixed and have no direct relationship to the sales, as is the case with the cost of goods sold and the selling expenses. If a loss is not shown at this point the assumption can be made tentatively, that when the finished goods now on hand are sold, enough will be realized to cover their cost and the cost of selling them.

Under these conditions the finished goods inventory will be valued at the lower of cost or reproduction cost, since the realization value is above both. If the subtraction of the cost of goods sold and selling expenses from sales results in a loss, the assumption can be made tentatively that when the finished goods now on hand are sold, the amount received will not be enough to cover their cost and the cost of selling them. Under these conditions the finished goods inventory will be valued at the lower of realization value or reproduction cost, either of which can be said to represent market. In order to establish the realization value of the finished goods inventory, the loss indicated above is divided by the cost of goods sold to develop the percentage of loss to the cost of goods sold. The finished goods inventory at cost is then reduced by this percentage to arrive at its realization value.

EXAMPLE

Sales	(For preceding 12 months)......		$1,200,000
Cost of Goods Sold	(For preceding 12 months)......	$1,000,000	
Selling Expense	(For preceding 12 months)......	300,000	1,300,000
Loss			$ 100,000

Loss, $100,000 ÷ Cost of Goods Sold, $1,000,000 = 10%

Current Finished Goods Inventory (at Cost)........	$150,000
	×.90
Current Finished Goods Inventory (Realization Value)	$135,000.00

Two Common Errors in Computing Realization Value

In computing the realization value of the finished goods inventory in this manner, two errors are commonly made. First, the percentage of loss is sometimes taken as the percentage of loss to sales. This is incorrect, for when the finished goods on hand are sold they will become part of the cost of goods sold; therefore, the percentage of loss should be taken as the percentage of loss to cost of goods sold. Second, the realization value is frequently computed as indicated above without adequate consideration of current conditions and prospects in the near future. In other words, it is assumed that the current inventory of finished goods will be sold under the same average conditions which existed during the past twelve months. This may be far from the truth, particularly for those industries in which the volume of production is subject to considerable fluctuation and for all industries during periods of markedly unsettled business conditions. The method indicated above is but a rough approximation which must be tempered or adjusted in the light of current conditions and estimates of the trend of sales and selling prices for the near future.

In companies such as Davis Textiles, Inc., where the finished goods inventory is not large, it should not be much of a task to compute its market value based on current, or most recent, selling prices. Past experience would indicate the average discounts taken and this could be used to arrive at the estimated net selling value of the current inventory. It would also be possible to determine from past experience the average percentage of selling expenses to net sales. This could then be increased or decreased in the light of current conditions and the resulting percentage could be used to arrive at the estimated net realization value of the inventory. General and administrative expenses not directly applicable to either production or sales should not be subtracted in arriving at the net realization value since, as stated previously, these expenses are more or less fixed and have no direct relationship to the sales.

It is occasionally apparent, from the current trend of finished goods prices, that by the time work in process has been completed it will be sold at a loss. Under these circumstances it is desirable to compute an estimated realization value for the inventory of work in process. This is commonly done in the same manner as indicated above for finished goods, except that it is necessary to increase the cost value of the inventory of work in process by the estimated additional cost to bring it to completion.

In establishing market value for raw material and the replacement cost of material in work in process and finished goods, the question often arises as to which of several alternative prices shall be taken. One point generally accepted is that market quotations at the date of the inventory should be used rather than the purchase price of the latest material purchased.

When published quotations are available representing the average prevailing prices derived from a sufficient number of transactions to make them representative, they should be used in preference to quotations from only one or a few sources of supply. The objection to the use of individual quotations as against published quotations is that a company may first decide whether to be conservative or not and then use whichever quotation will support its position. There are some occasions when trade is so dull that all quotations are meaningless except as matters of opinion. Under these conditions it is preferable to price the inventory at cost and to provide a reserve to care for possible inventory losses.

MISCELLANEOUS PROBLEMS IN INVENTORY VALUATION

Accounting for Cash Discounts

There has been considerable debate as to whether cash discounts should be deducted from the cost of material purchased or treated as financial income (by reason of the ability to finance the transaction within the time allowed). This matter will never be settled, but the writer joins with those who hold that the original price assumed liberality in the time of payment and exceeds the cash price by an amount calculated to cover interest and risk during the delay.[2] Under this concept the cash discount, if taken, should be deducted from the cost of the raw material; otherwise, this cost will include a charge for delay in payment—a service which was not made use of by the purchaser.

There are conditions, however, under which it is difficult or uneconomical to put this theory into practice. In many companies perpetual inventory records are maintained which include prices in addition to quantities, unit prices being taken from invoices. In such cases it is common practice, and sensible, to treat cash discounts as financial income rather than to re-compute unit prices. Better than this, the entire cash discount taken for a period can be shown in the operating statement as a deduction from purchases, and since the ending inventory will not include a deduction for cash discounts, for the reasons stated, the effect will be a reduction in the cost of goods sold to the full extent of the discount taken and a corresponding increase in the gross profit.

Allocating Storeroom Expense, Purchasing Department Expense, and the Cost of Accounting for Inventories

The purchase, storing and accounting of materials provide utilities which are, in the final analysis, part of the cost of the raw material.

[2] See *The Fundamentals of Accounting*, by William Morse Cole, page 132.

There is an objection, however, to writing up the stated inventory of raw material by converting such expenses into assets. Though the quantity of raw material on hand and the amount purchased are subject to considerable variation, the expenses of purchasing, storing, and accounting are practically the same from one period to another. In this sense they are expenses which can be attributed more closely to accounting periods than to specific lots of material. They can thus be more equitably treated as part of the general overhead rather than as charges to specific lots of material.

Interest on the Investment in Inventories

Many executives have expressed the opinion that there are too many other problems of greater practical significance to bother to account for interest on the investments in inventories. There are, however, two situations in which it is desirable to do this: first, for purposes of comparison when figures are being collected by a trade association or some other organization, and second, when inventories of raw material are kept some time for aging purposes. The latter is in a sense a production process, the expenses of which include interest on the investment. This is particularly applicable to inventories of tobacco. Here a company has the choice of buying raw material and aging it or of buying aged tobacco, the difference in cost representing for the most part carrying charges which include interest on the investment.

Technically the inclusion of interest involves a corresponding credit to some income account and it is this anticipation of profit that is objectionable.

Accounting for Freight-in

This is another item which is really a part of the cost of raw material, but the difficulties of allocation frequently result in treating it as an item of manufacturing expense without direct allocation. With respect to bulky goods the freight often constitutes a considerable element in the cost. Here the charges can be definitely allocated to specific lots and this is usually done. Under such conditions care should be taken, when determining the lower of cost or market at the close of a period, that the market value established shall take freight into consideration.

Accounting for Obsolete Stock and Seconds

When it is apparent that goods on hand have become obsolete, it is sound practice to write them down to an estimated conservative liquidation value. Frequently, however, a condition arises prior to definite obsolescence in which a change in the demand indicates that it will take longer than was originally anticipated to dispose of the inventory on hand of a particular product. If it is the policy of the company to liquidate such stock as soon as possible after this condition arises, even at a loss, then the entire quantity should be written down to the estimated liquidation value for balance sheet purposes prior to actual liquidation. It is a policy of some companies to hold such stocks, particularly if they are not extreme in style, until obsolescence has become more definite, in the hope of working off a good part of the inventory before that stage is reached. If this is the case, the company should make an estimate of the probable sales of this item for a reasonable period in the future and write off completely, or value at an extremely conservative amount, all inventory on hand in excess of this estimate. In other words, it is not necessary to write down the entire inventory of an item if part of it can be disposed of with certainty in the near future at a profit.

Seconds are commonly valued at the lower of cost or market, market being interpreted as the probable realization value. Where the quantity of seconds is small, in many companies no attempt is made to appraise each lot of seconds to determine its probable realization value; instead, a fixed percentage is subtracted from their value as firsts to arrive at what past experience has shown to be a conservative valuation. Some companies determine the probable realization value of seconds and deduct therefrom an amount sufficient so that upon their sale the same percentage of gross margin will be realized as would be the case if they were firsts.

Where a sure market exists for seconds at prices which can be estimated in advance with some degree of certainty, the first method indicated in the preceding paragraph is most acceptable. When the quantity of seconds is small an arbitrary valuation, provided it is conservative, is sufficient. The third method emphasizes the losses suffered through the production of seconds, and is useful where the quantity of seconds produced is high and a menace to profits. Under normal conditions, however, the production of some seconds is inevitable and this method causes the period in which the seconds were produced to suffer unduly. The first method makes the production period bear enough loss without charging against it a profit margin which never should be available on this type of production.

Accounting for Minor Materials and Parts Used in Production

When job or lot costs are kept the question is frequently raised as to the extent to which minor supplies used on jobs should be accounted for. For example, two material requisitions were lying side by side in the inventory control department of a large company. One requisition called for material amounting to over $1,000, while the other was a request for one-quarter of a gallon of gasoline at a few pennies. Accounting for each of these requisitions took the same amount of time. Considering the time spent in preparing, authorizing and pricing the requisition for gasoline as well as in recording the withdrawal on the perpetual inventory card and in making the charge to the job, the cost was more than the gasoline was worth. For the job as a whole, the cost of accounting for materials used is commonly but a small fraction of the total cost of the job, though the cost of accounting for a few of the minor materials or supplies used may be excessive.

The best way to handle such items appears to be to issue them in fair sized lots to foremen and hold them responsible for their proper use. For cost purposes, jobs can be charged in total for the amounts of these small items as called for on job specifications, with some allowance for waste. One company, in accounting for costs by jobs, charges five per cent in addition to the quantity of small parts called for by the specifications. This has proved ample to cover the waste on these items, which are easily damaged, dropped on the floor and swept out, or carried home in the pockets of the workmen.

Accounting for Goods Billed to Customers Before Completion

Not infrequently, textile companies receive orders to manufacture goods and hold them as grey cloth until the customers decide the manner in which they wish the goods to be finished. This is advantageous to the customer for it enables him to meet changes in demand more quickly and reduces the hazards of carrying a large finished goods inventory. It benefits the producer by reducing the need of a finished goods inventory; by reducing the cancellation of orders when styles change; and by facilitating a more even spread of production in economical lots. Orders are generally billed in the grey at finished goods prices and an adjustment is made for shrinkage, upon the completion and shipment of the goods.

With respect to inventory valuation, there is no objection to this practice provided: first, that material on hand already billed to customers is clearly marked and physically separated from other inventory; and second, that any liability on sales of this kind is set up in the books at the end of a period, both for balance sheet purposes and to prevent an overstatement of profit on these sales.

Conclusion

Problems in establishing cost and market involve a considerable area of both cost and financial accounting. This article has been largely a summary of certain problems and it is not the intention to further summarize at this point.

The present article has been an attempt to illustrate and comment upon certain of the problems indicated by Mr. Donaldson's article, "Cost or Market, Whichever is Lower." Regarding the general implications, it is to be expected that the many issues involved in determining cost and market lead to considerable variations in practice. This is not altogether to be condemned for there should be some room for the exercise of judgment in the light of particular circumstances. Nevertheless, greater uniformity would place published financial statements on a more comparable basis and to that extent would be an aid to investors and to management in comparing results with the results of others in the same industry. Likewise, uniformity of practice within an industry generally leads to a more intelligent understanding of costs, which is helpful to a particular company in controlling its operations and tends to strengthen the price structure since no producer is then unwittingly selling below cost. Greater uniformity can be brought about as business men read and discuss these matters and arrive at a better understanding of the principles involved. It will find expression in the development of uniform systems of accounting for particular industries, and has of course already done so in many industries. There should be less room for disagreement on concepts of cost and market between companies within an industry than between industries, and if rules of conduct are to be effective they should be developed within industries and form part of the uniform accounting system of an industry.

Because of the variation in practice in this area, it is not sufficient for a company to state in its balance sheet that "inventories have been valued at the lower of cost or market." Supplementary information should be given regarding the company's concepts of cost and market. At least it should be indicated whether cost is actual cost, standard cost, or part of each; and whether market is reproduction cost or estimated net realization value. In so far as possible a company should be consistent from year to year in its inventory practice. Any substantial change in policy should be clearly stated in the report accompanying the financial statements.

VALUATION OF FINISHED GOODS UNDER THE STANDARD COST PLAN *

By C. J. Wibbelsman

IN ORDER to show clearly the means by which standard costs may be used in arriving at the proper valuation of finished goods inventories, I am taking the liberty of referring to our own methods for an illustration. The company with which I am connected manufactures a long line of rubber goods. Our standard costs are segregated into the following cost elements:

> Direct Material
> Packaging Material
> Scrap Material
>
> Direct Labor
> Setup Labor
> Packaging Labor
> Scrap Labor
>
> Direct Burden
> Packaging Burden
> Scrap Burden
>
> Loss on Seconds
> Purchase, Receiving & Stores Expense (which incidentally is often absorbed as a part of direct material costs)
> Royalties
> Mold Depreciation

or a total of fourteen separate and distinct cost elements.

At first glance this may seem to many of you as excessive and unnecessary detail in the development of standard costs, but our present breakdown is the result of quite a few years of experience in the use of standards. As a matter of fact, we have gone from year to year into still finer segregations of cost elements and the results have proven this practice to be a profitable one, enabling us to realize substantial cost reductions. These reductions have been

---

* Part of an article from the *Bulletin* of September 15, 1936, under the title "Accounting for Control of Finished Goods."

realized through improved operating efficiencies, which can be traced directly to the cost data collected by actual experience with definitely segregated and limited cost factor fields.

For purposes of simplicity in presentation and, I hope, consequently, for a better understanding thereof, this illustration will be confined to an analysis of three of the cost elements outlined previously, namely direct material, direct labor and direct burden —the so-called "prime" cost factors.

Cost Entries Outlined

If you will refer to Exhibit 1, I believe it will be easier to follow, as I shall attempt to outline and explain the methods we use in arriving at our inventory valuation factors and in correctly stating cost of sales in our earnings statements.

Journal entries 1, 2 and 3 record the input of material, labor and burden to goods in process. In entry 1, goods in process is charged with the material delivered from raw materials stores. Such deliveries are priced at both average actual stores cost and at predetermined standard costs, the difference between these two amounts being charged or credited to a purchase variation account, depending upon whether average actual costs are greater or less than the predetermined standard costs.

Entering Material, Labor and Burden

With respect to material, predetermined standards are established once each year as of January 1, so that throughout the year we can secure a cumulative picture of the relationship of actual material costs to the established standards and the current trend of such actual costs.

In entry 2, goods in process is charged with the value of the work performed by direct labor, priced at standard cost, with the difference between the actual direct labor accrued payroll and the related standard being charged to labor effectiveness variations. This variation, incidentally, is seldom a credit if labor standards are tightly set.

In entry 3, goods in process is charged with an amount of burden (determined from budgets) equivalent to a percentage of the standard direct labor amount. The credit is to the actual burden accounts,

Exhibit 1

CONTROL AND VALUATION OF FINISHED GOODS: RELATIONSHIP TO STANDARD COSTS

Journal Entry No.	Title of Accounts	Dr.	Cr.	Basis
1.	Goods in Process	100,000		Deliveries to process at predetermined standard cost prices.
	Raw Materials Stores		90,000	Deliveries to process at average actual cost prices.
	Purchase Variation		10,000(a)	Difference.
2.	Goods in Process	40,000		Production by operation at predetermined standard cost rates.
	Labor Effectiveness Var.	2,000(b)		Difference.
	Accrued Wages		42,000	Actual accrued direct labor payroll.
3.	Goods in Process	60,000		Predetermined % absorption on standard labor in entry #2.
	Volume Variation	6,000(c)		Difference—segregated on basis of budgets showing absorption of fixed expenses at various rates of capacity.
	Expense Variation		3,000(d)	Accrued salaries and indirect wage payroll.
	Accrued Salaries and Wages.		20,000	Deliveries at average actual cost.
	Supplies Stores		15,000	Direct purchases and expense charges.
	Accounts Payable		14,000	Actual provision.
	Reserve for Depreciation		10,000	Actual accrual.
	Accrued Taxes		3,000	Actual write-off.
	Prepaid Insurance		1,000	
4.	Finished Goods	200,000(y)		Finished production priced at total standard cost for all cost elements combined.
	Goods in Process		200,000	Transfer to valuation account.
5.	Purchase Variation	10,000(a)		do
	Expense Variation	3,000(d)		do
	Labor Effectiveness Var.		2,000(b)	do
	Volume Variation		6,000(c)	do
	Inventory Valuation Account.		5,000(x)	Transfer from variation accounts.
6.	Cost of Sales	100,000(z)		Sales priced at total standard costs.
	Finished Goods		100,000	
7.	Inventory Valuation Accounts..	2,500		Ratio of x to y applied to z.
	Manufacturing Cost Penalties (P & L Acct.)		2,500	

with the difference being charged or credited to burden variations. In this entry we have segregated the burden variation into two kinds, volume variance and expense variance.

I shall not take the time to explain the means used in determining this segregation, as this would require lengthy and somewhat technical treatment. It is shown here merely to be noted in passing, as its use will be referred to in just a few moments.

Entering Finished Goods

Entry 4 records the relief of goods in process for the completed production delivered to the finished goods warehouse. The standard costs used herein are built up from manufacturing specifications, as prepared by the technical development department, with the specified materials and the specified direct labor being priced at the same standards as used in entries 1 and 2, and with burden allowed for at the same percentage on labor as used in entry 3.

Closing Variation Accounts

In entry 5 you will note that the offsetting items are cross-referenced with small letters. This was done to identify the items without a separate exhibit showing the individual "T" accounts. As you can see, this entry merely transfers the balances in the variation accounts to a single account which we have termed the "Inventory Valuation Account." Separate variation accounts are provided, however, for the reason that in actual practice we have found it necessary to keep these accounts segregated in order to obtain cumulative ratios of actual to standard costs of production for inventory valuation purposes, and for monthly comparisons for management purposes in analyzing the trends of efficiencies in manufacturing and changes in basic costs, such as increases in purchase prices of materials, changes in wage rates, etc.

Recording the Cost of Sales

Entry 6 is one with which, undoubtedly, all of you are familiar. The first part of this entry has been omitted, which if shown would read—

Accounts Receivable
Sales

Looking back at entries 1 to 4 inclusive, you will note that the illustration assumes no change in the inventory of goods in process, the input (entries 1, 2 and 3) and the outgo (entry 4) being equal. In entry 6 we have further assumed that but half of the production was sold, this being done to illustrate the function of the valuation account with respect to earnings, without cluttering up the picture with too many accounts and balances.

Adjusting Cost of Sales and Inventories to Actual

As a result of the above entries, we find that the standard cost of production was $200,000, that the combined variations totaled a credit of $5,000 or 2½ per cent of standards. In other words, actual cost was 97½ per cent of standard. Applying this valuation factor to the standard cost of sales, results in stating sales in our earnings statement, as well as the inventory in our balance sheet, at average actual cost. This adjustment of cost of sales and inventory values to actual cost is made through entry 7.

Variation for Annual Statement Purposes

The methods just outlined are felt to be satisfactory for purposes of monthly financial statements to management, but with respect to inventory values for purposes of annual published statements, a slight deviation in practice, but not in principle, is made.

The annual physical inventory in units is extended, in the same manner as is our monthly production, by standard costs according to the various cost elements. This calculation provides the total standard amount of finished goods inventories, segregated as to the amounts representing each cost element.

The several cost variation accounts are then reviewed, in order to determine the ratio of actual to standard cost for each element. In this analysis, we select the longest consecutive periods representing current cost conditions, whether such periods be a month, several months, or a year.

The ratios so determined are then applied to the total amounts of the several cost elements, as contained in the standard value of finished goods inventories, the resultant amount representing the current average actual cost of finished goods. For example, if the standard direct labor in an inventory of $500,000 amounted to

$100,000, and the current ratio of actual to standard direct labor costs was 105 per cent, the value of direct labor as contained in such inventory would then be stated as $105,000.

Market Value for Inventory Purposes

In spite of the elaborately outlined, and perhaps complicated, methods used in evaluating finished goods, we are still governed of course by the "lower of cost or market" principle in finally stating inventory values.

The determination of market for a manufacturing concern can be rather difficult and, I believe, requires consideration from two angles. Market has a different meaning for the manufacturer of a product, the selling price level of which is established by competition within the industry, as compared with the manufacturer of a product, the selling price level of which is established by the manufacturer himself on the basis of his cost.

With respect to the former, the inventory should be extended at the industry's current sales price level, and the market is then determined by deducting a percentage of gross profit from the amount at sales price levels, such percentage of course being based on prior years' experience along conservative lines. The market so determined then represents the maximum amount at which inventories can be valued by such manufacturers. The actual inventory value, determined in the manner previously outlined, is then compared with this maximum market, and the lower value of the two is used for financial purposes.

For the latter, there is in reality no market, except that price which the trade will bear, and while inventories can legitimately be adjusted to current actual cost, care should be taken to exclude cost variations due to low production volume, the volume variation item mentioned in the illustrative journal entries, or in other words, to follow generally a conservative policy.

These actual to standard cost ratios not only serve as inventory valuation factors, but also as important factors in estimating or determining costs for purposes of establishing selling prices. Here again, though, the volume variation factor must be given more than passing review, as the danger of "costing ourselves out of business" is ever present in these days of keen competition.

DISPOSITION OF VARIANCES FROM STANDARD *

By Clifford G. Wood

THE QUESTION which I am going to discuss, dealing as it does with variances from standard, presupposes a knowledge of the character and derivation of such variances and the procedure giving rise to them. Many who do not employ standard costs may not be entirely familiar with the principles involved. I shall therefore devote a few moments to a very brief outline of some of the basic principles.

Standard Costs and Variances

Standard costs have been defined by many writers on the subject, one definition being that they are "predetermined costs computed on the specifications of the product." Cost figures derived by accumulating actual material costs, actual direct labor costs, and an item of "normal" or "average" burden are often considered "standard costs." Such a system might be described as a "part-standard" cost system. A "full-standard" system implies the use of predetermined standards for all elements entering into the product —standards for material and for labor as well as for manufacturing burden. In this connection it should be noted that in establishing standards for material, for example, the elements of quantity and price would both have to be determined. Likewise, labor wage-rates as well as hours would be involved in the establishment of labor standards.

In the limited space available, I cannot attempt an explanation of the various bases upon which standards may be developed. Regardless, however, of what methods are used, certain differences between actual costs and standard costs will be encountered in practice. These differences are termed "variances." In a full-standard cost system the following variance accounts would be set up on the records:

* From the *Bulletin* of January 1, 1939.

As to Material:
Usage variance
Price variance

As to Labor:
Efficiency variance
Wage-rate variance

As to Manufacturing Burden:
Efficiency variance
Activity variance
Expense variance

Variances Explained

The variances with respect to material and labor are more or less self-explanatory. Burden variances may require some explanation for the benefit of those unaccustomed to their use. "Burden efficiency variance" measures the difference between the product of actual hours at the standard rate and the product of standard hours at the standard rate. "Burden activity variance" measures the difference between the budgeted burden at a certain percentage of plant capacity and the product of the actual hours times the standard rate. "Burden expense variance" measures the difference between actual burden and the budgeted burden at a certain percentage of plant capacity.

Not all concerns employing standard cost procedure use the seven variance accounts outlined above. Some use only three accounts, one each for the aggregate variation of the elements of material, labor and burden. Moreover, individual preferences or prejudices are evidenced by the treatment of standard costs on the records. In most cases, perhaps, the cost system is completely tied in with the general accounting records, but it is not unusual to find instances where so-called standard cost records are maintained apart from the general accounting records. These are utilized as a form of statistical record by means of which comparisons are made between actual results and hypothetical standard cost procedure.

I may, perhaps, have devoted more time than was necessary to outlining the foregoing principles. However, a discussion of the treatment of variances from standard would be somewhat meaningless to anyone not having at least a rudimentary conception of their nature. For the remainder of my discussion I am going to assume that we are dealing with an instance in which the cost system is tied in with the general records. For the most part, it will be immaterial whether extended variance analysis is in effect or whether only three variance accounts are employed.

Further Definition of Terms

Our question is: "Should variances from standard be absorbed in the period in which they occur or should they be absorbed in the period in which the product is sold?" This question contains several terms which should be defined before proceeding with the discussion. My opening statements were intended to define the terms "variance" and "standard," so far as such terms can be defined in a few words. With reference to "absorbing" variances, I have construed the word "absorbed" in this connection to mean taken through the profit and loss account. The term "period" may be considered as either a full accounting period of twelve months or an interim period of a month, or a quarter, or six months. For the purposes of my discussion, I have construed "period" to mean a complete accounting period of twelve months. In this connection, let me say that if, hereafter, I use the word "year" instead of "period" I am referring to a "natural business year," comprising twelve calendar months but not necessarily ending on December 31. We are discussing certain phases of operation under a full standard cost system, and any organization sufficiently progressive in its management to adopt standard cost accounting should not hesitate to adopt a natural business year.

Two Viewpoints on Nature of Standard Costs

The question under discussion is not new, nor is it one, I believe, upon which an overwhelming majority opinion can be obtained. Accountants, generally, appear to be divided into two groups over the question and their views are almost diametrically opposed. One group holds that costs can only be "actual" costs, and that, therefore, standards, no matter how useful from a statistical standpoint, should not be reflected in the general records. This group, however, will modify their beliefs to the extent of permitting the elimination from costs of variances due to idle plant capacity, but they feel that all other forms of variances are merely fictitious debits and credits which should be ignored in the general records. Another major group of accountants holds that standard costs are "true costs" and that any excess over standard costs is a waste, and, therefore, a proper profit and loss charge. Their contention is not so much that this excess over standard is not a *cost,* but that it is a *cost of waste or inefficiency* and should not be confused with *cost of goods or product.*

It should be obvious that the variance accounts at the end of any particular period may have either debit or credit balances. Moreover, not all of the variance accounts need have the same type of balance. Credit balances in variance accounts are less frequently encountered than debit balances, and it might be well, therefore, to dispose of this phase of the subject first before going on to a discussion of the treatment of the more common debit balances.

Disposition of Credit Variances

Credit balances in variance accounts may arise from improperly set standards or because the plant has worked an extra number of hours, or at a greater average percentage of capacity than normal, or perhaps through some unanticipated savings in expenses. If the standards were improperly set, or if the change in the percentage of plant capacity utilized is to continue, there can be no question but that the standard costs should be revised to reflect these new conditions, and the inventories and cost of goods sold restated upon the basis of the new standards. The necessary adjustments resulting from such a restatement would, of course, be charged to the variance accounts. These adjustments might completely eliminate the credit balances or there might remain a credit balance in some of the variance accounts. If we assume that the standards have been properly set, and that there still remains a credit balance in one or more of the variance accounts, these credit balances should be split into two parts. One part would represent the amount of the variance applicable to the product already sold, while the second part would represent the amount applicable to goods on hand. The scope of my topic does not permit any discussion of the methods by which such a segregation of the variance balances may be effected. We shall have to assume that the division has been made.

The portion of the credit balance applicable to goods already sold is, of course, a realized profit and may be taken into the profit and loss account. The portion of the credit balances applicable to goods on hand represents, however, an *unrealized profit* in the manufacture of the product. As such it has no place in the income account of the current period. The most conservative treatment of this item would be to apply it as an adjustment to inventory valuation, although some arguments are advanced for its treatment as a deferred credit to income. If applied to reduce inventories, such application may take the form of an adjustment of specific items or of a valuation reserve applied to reduce the total inventory. Generally speaking, the reserve method is preferable since, if the standards were properly set, as we have assumed, the unit values of the items in the inventory should not be disturbed.

Disposition of Debit Variance

We now come to the treatment of debit balances in the variance accounts. Here again I think it is safe to assume that we are speaking of an instance in which proper standard costs have been established. As a matter of fact, if the standards have not been properly established, they should be adjusted and the necessary adjustments carried through the variance accounts. In most cases debit balances would still remain. We will consider that we are working with debit balances under the assumption of properly set standards.

Debit balances in variance accounts are, generally speaking, due to waste, inefficiency or idle plant capacity. Arising from such causes, they are expenses. I may be challenged on this point by those who contend that these variances are costs. I will not dispute the use of the word "cost" instead of "expense," but I contend that they are *costs of waste and inefficiency* and not of the product. As costs of waste, they can have no relation to inventory value. They are a loss of the period in which they occur and should be borne in that period. As a matter of fact, the effect upon the profit and loss account over a long cycle will be the same. If the inventories at standard cost at the end of a certain period should be $1,000 and the variance accounts had aggregated debit balances of $100, it will readily be seen that the total profit and loss charge for this $100 item will be the same over a two-year period, whether written off in the current period or whether it finds its way through the cost of goods sold in the subsequent period. There is, moreover, no objection to deferring debit variances from month to month during the accounting year in order to equalize the monthly statements in a seasonal business. This procedure is quite frequently followed and has considerable merit. Because of the limited space available, this phase of the subject cannot be covered and I have restricted my discussion to the treatment of variances existing at the end of a full accounting period.

Nature of Variances Distinguished

I made a general statement to the effect that debit balances are usually the result of waste, inefficiency or idle plant capacity. Of the seven variance accounts which I mentioned in my opening statements, four of such seven contain items properly classified as waste, inefficiency or idle plant capacity. These variance accounts are material usage variance, labor efficiency variance, and burden efficiency and activity variances. Any debit balances in these accounts may properly be construed as the result of inefficiency, waste or idle plant capacity. It is difficult to see how any support could be brought to the contention that such items could increase the inventory valuation. They are expenses and should be borne in the period in which they occur. Argument can be advanced for a difference in the treatment of material price variance, labor wage-rate variance and burden expense variances, and these items are included by some accountants in the inventory on the theory that inventories must be at cost where cost does not exceed market values. This appears to be fallacious reasoning, for if a concern is operating under a full standard cost procedure, and if the standards are properly set, they are "true costs." As a practical matter, if the standards are well set, the debit balances of the last three variance accounts will be reduced to a minimum, and conservative accounting would dictate that they also be written off to profit and loss.

Alternative Treatment Not Approved

Up to this point I have expressed the opinion that debit variances should be absorbed into profit and loss in the period in which they occur while credit balances should be taken into profit and loss or deferred as a reduction of inventory value, depending upon whether the product to which the credit variance applied was sold or unsold at the end of the period. It might be well to mention a different treatment which is sometimes given these variances and to point out the possible errors into which one may be led. The alternative treatment involves the use of surplus reserves and may be briefly described as follows:

Credit variances applicable to product sold within the period are sometimes set up as direct credits to a reserve account instead of being passed through the income account; in other cases the reserve is set up out of surplus after the credit variances have gone through the income account and been closed to surplus. The expressed purpose of the reserve is to absorb charges for debit variances in subsequent periods in order to mitigate the effect on the income account of sharp fluctuations from standard costs. It will readily be seen that, if the reserve is established *from surplus* after having previously credited income with credit variances, the income account is materially distorted between periods since it receives the benefit of credit variances but no charge for debit variances. This distortion is avoided if credit variances are passed directly to the reserve account without being included as income. This latter procedure is followed by some organizations, but, generally speaking, it is preferable to carry both the credit and debit variances through the income account. If a surplus reserve is deemed advisable, it may be established out of surplus but care should be taken that it is not used to relieve the income account of charges which should properly be included therein.

Suggested Treatment Accords with Fundamental Accounting Principle

Most of the controversy with regard to the question under discussion arises between cost accountants and general or public accountants in the preparation of financial statements. I do not see that statements prepared for financial or credit purposes need differ in principle from those prepared for internal use. It has long been an axiom among accountants, particularly public accountants, that financial statements should provide for all losses but reflect no unrealized gains. I have set forth the opinion that credit variance balances applicable to goods on hand should be applied as a reduction of inventory valuation, while debit balances should be absorbed as an expense in the period in which they occur. Where this procedure is adopted, it seems that the axiom of providing for all losses but anticipating no gain has been well met, and that no conflict need arise between general and cost accountants.

In conclusion, I should like to emphasize that the statements and opinions I have expressed represent only my own views on the question involved and should not be construed as representations of the firm with which I am connected.

THE NORMAL STOCK METHOD OF INVENTORY VALUATION *

By H. T. Warshow

THIS PAPER will provide a specific explanation of the inventory valuation methods used by the National Lead Co., but will indirectly cover the first sentence of the program, which reads as follows: "The enormous shrinkages in inventory book values revealed by financial reports now being published emphasize the importance of adopting accounting methods which will tend to minimize the disastrous influence of value fluctuations." It is with this sentence in view that I have written this paper.

The high income and excess profits taxes brought about by the war have resulted in bringing into relief a great many problems in accounting which heretofore had either been entirely neglected or else had been restricted to discussion in purely academic circles.

Importance of Inventory Valuation in Profit Determination

The determining factor in the income of a business is the valuation of the assets and liabilities on hand at the end of the fiscal period as compared with those on hand at the beginning. The valuation of natural resources has given rise to many theories of depletion; the valuation of plant and equipment leads to the very important questions of depreciation, obsolescence and amortization. The valuation of accounts receivable has resulted in a great many tax rulings on bad debt reserves; and in the same way, valuation of stocks, bonds and other investments, prepaid expenses, etc., have had their own special rulings. Perhaps the most important of these problems is the valuation of merchandise inventory, since in a manufacturing or a selling organization, it is the determining factor in the amount of profits realized or losses sustained. The correctness or the superiority of a suggested method of valuation of inventory is determined by its suitability to the purposes for which the results are to be used.

Let us, accordingly, examine some of the current theories of

* From the 1922 Year Book.

242

inventory valuation before taking up in greater detail the method used by the National Lead Co., since the National Lead method is a combination of several prevailing methods.

METHOD 1.—The *prevailing market price* at the end of the fiscal period is used to value the entire inventory on hand.

This method, less the cost of marketing, has been allowed by the Bureau of Internal Revenue for the valuation of inventory for livestock raisers and other farmers. It is also pretty generally used by dealers in second-hand metals. While no specific ruling has been issued definitely permitting such use, it has been generally accepted by the Bureau.

METHOD 2.—The *straight cost method* of valuation. In this method the actual cost of the goods is used, based, however, upon the assumption that goods on hand are deemed to be the goods most recently purchased.

METHOD 3.—*Cost or market, whichever is lower.*

This method is also based upon the assumption that goods on hand are deemed to be the goods most recently purchased. The latter two methods are most generally accepted and are prescribed for general purposes by the Bureau of Internal Revenue.

METHOD 4.—*Average cost.*

There are a great many variations of this method of valuation.

(a) The *average cost of producing* all of the inventory products during the taxable year when the return is made, may be used to price the inventory. If a greater amount is on hand than was manufactured during the year, the difference is priced at the cost of manufacture during the previous year. This method was allowed by Treasury Decision 3024 for use by lumber manufacturers.

(b) *Monthly average cost.*

This method was used by the tobacco companies and disallowed by the Advisory Tax Board in 1919. Later, the decision was reversed and the method allowed by the Board of Review and Appeals. Briefly, the method is as follows: "Goods purchased during a month are added both as to quantity and cost to the quantity and cost balance of the previous month, and the average cost at the close of the month is computed by dividing the total quantity into the total money figures. This average is then applied to the quantity of materials used for manufacture during the month and the amount so computed is credited to the material account."

METHOD 5.—*Actual cost* based upon the assumption that the inventory is made up of the earliest rather than the latest purchases. In other words, the goods sold are assumed to be the latest purchased. This method is the nearest approach to the normal stock method used by the National Lead Co.

METHOD 6.—*Normal stock,* also known sometimes as the "base stock" or "minimum method."

Choosing a Method to Fit the Condition

No method of valuation of inventory has yet been devised which reflects in every respect the actual facts of a given situation. The cost or market basis, as it is generally used, is based upon the assumption that the goods on hand at the end of the fiscal period are made up of the latest purchases. This may be true in some cases, or as near an approximation of the truth as it is possible and practicable to obtain, but it certainly does not hold true for the plants of the National Lead Co., where at the bottom of piles of lead there are many pigs that may have been in the plant a great many years. As a matter of fact, whenever practicable, pigs of lead coming in are taken directly to the melting pot in order to avoid double handling. Although the assumption that the latest purchases are the first to be consumed, manufactured and sold, is just as much of a fiction as the opposite assumption, it approaches the actual state of the white lead industry much more closely.

The process of manufacture of white lead covers a period of five to six months and for that reason necessitates a constant and more or less uniform quantity of goods in process. It is obvious that were this quantity of goods in process sold, the company would be compelled to cease doing business at least for a period of six months until the supply of manufactured goods could be replenished. Theoretically, therefore, a certain portion of the inventory of the National Lead Co. is placed in the category of a piece of machinery which the company is compelled to keep on hand as long as it desires to continue the process of manufacture. This portion of the inventory is called the "normal stock." Normal stocks are provided for goods in process and manufactured products, as well as for the basic metals. The values, however, are all based upon the basic metals plus the cost of manufacture in each particular case.

Determining Normal Quantities

The amounts to be included in the normals were determined in the following manner: A study by qualified experts was made for each of the National Lead Co. plants as to the normal quantity of lead, tin, antimony, etc. (in every state of manufacture, from the raw metal to the finished product) necessary for the continuous operation of each plant. The opinion of the superintendent of the plant was given careful consideration in every case, and a decision was not made until all possible contingencies were properly considered. Some of the factors which enter into the determination of the normal stock are as follows:

1. The amount of metal normally in transit from the smelters to the plants.
2. The amount of raw metal which it is necessary to keep on hand in the factories to prevent a possible suspension of manufacture due to delays in transportation and other unforeseen difficulties.
3. The metal in process of manufacture, which in the case of white lead is a considerable amount, since the process extends over a period of five or six months.
4. The amount of manufactured products necessary to carry in stock at factories and warehouses in order to make prompt delivery upon short notice.

Valuation

The result is that 80 per cent of the total inventories of the National Lead Co. is included in normal stocks and is valued at the lowest prices reached by metals since the year 1913, which is $3.40 per hundred. These values were estimated by the management of the company in the year 1913 at the inauguration of this method, as the lowest that could reasonably be anticipated within the immediate future. Should the market prices, however, fall below these accepted values, the values of the normal stock would be adjusted to the lower existing level. Inasmuch as the purchases of raw material from month to month approximately equal the sales of metal in the form of manufactured products from month to month, we operate upon the assumption or fiction that the metal sold in the form of manufactured products during any given month was made out of the metal purchased during that month, and that the normal stock is never impaired.

This is true theoretically, but practically, however, it is not likely that a National Lead Co. salesman would refuse an order and give as an excuse that "it is against our principles to sell out of our normal stock." For practical purposes, therefore, we sell out of the normal stock whenever necessary, but the theory is maintained that the normal stock is still entirely on hand and that some portion of it has been temporarily borrowed and will have to be replaced at current market prices. For instance, let us take the extreme case of a normal stock of pig lead of 1,000,000 pounds at 4 cents per pound, giving a value of $40,000, of which there remains on hand at the end of the fiscal period only 800,000 pounds, 200,000 pounds having been borrowed and sold. Assuming that the market price has risen to 6 cents per pound, it will cost $12,000 to replace the 200,000 pounds borrowed, so that the present value of the inventory on hand is the difference between $40,000 and $12,000, or $28,000. The inventory will therefore appear as 800,000 pounds valued at $28,000.

In the event that there is an excess rather than a deficiency under the normal stock, the excess is valued at cost. This is arrived at by taking the purchases of the month, quantity and value, and either adding thereto the excess, quantity and value at the beginning of the period, or deducting therefrom the deficiency, quantity and value at the beginning of the period, whichever the case may be. You will note that this portion of the method resembles the monthly average cost method explained a little earlier in the paper under 4-b. It is obvious, therefore, that this method of valuation is really a cost basis, based upon the assumption that the normal stock was acquired in 1913 and valued at the prices current in that year, and that the excess which has been acquired since is valued at the purchase cost.

Examples

Examples with actual figures will make this explanation much simpler and clearer. As a matter of fact, the actual price used for valuing our normal stocks is 3.40 cents per pound. I shall, however, in these computations, for the purpose of simplicity, use 4 cents per pound.

EXAMPLES OF THE WAY INVENTORIES ARE FIGURED ACCORDING TO THE NORMAL STOCK METHOD SHOWING COST OF LEAD USED ON A DECLINING AND AN ADVANCING MARKET

DECLINING MARKET

Premise

Lead on hand at the beginning of the period...... $4.50 per hundred pounds
Cost of lead received during the period.......... 4.35 "   "   "
Replacement value of lead.................... 4.10 "   "   "

Example No. 1

Where there is an excess stock on hand at the beginning and end of the period.

On hand at the beginning of the period:

Normal, 100,000 lbs. at $4.00......... $4,000.00		
Excess, 100,000 lbs. at $4.50......... $4,500.00		
	200,000 lbs.	$ 8,500.00
Purchased	100,000 lbs.	4,350.00
Total	300,000 lbs.	$12,850.00

On hand at the end of the period:

Normal, 100,000 lbs. at $4.00......... $4,000.00		
Excess, 25,000 lbs. at $4.425........ 1,106.25		
	125,000 lbs.	5,106.25
Used	175,000 lbs.	$ 7,743.75

Average of lead used, 4.425.

Example No. 2

Where there is an excess stock on hand at the beginning of the period and a deficiency at the end.

On hand at the beginning of the period:

Normal, 100,000 lbs. at $4.00......... $4,000.00		
Excess, 100,000 lbs. at $4.50......... 4,500.00		
	200,000 lbs.	$ 8,500.00
Purchased	100,000 lbs.	4,350.00
Total	300,000 lbs.	$12,850.00

On hand at the end of the period:

Normal, 100,000 lbs. at $4.00....... $4,000.00		
Deficiency, 25,000 lbs. at $4.10....... 1,025.00		
	75,000 lbs.	2,975.00
Used	225,000 lbs.	$ 9,875.00

Average of lead used, 4.388.

Example No. 3
    Where there is a deficiency at the beginning of the period and an excess at the end of the period.
On hand at the beginning of the period:
    Normal,   100,000 lbs. at $4.00....... $4,000.00
    Deficiency, 25,000 lbs. at $4.50.......   1,125.00

	75,000 lbs.	$2,875.00
Purchased	100,000 lbs.	4,350.00
Total	175,000 lbs.	$7,225.00

On hand at the end of the period:
    Normal, 100,000 lbs. at $4.00......... $4,000.00
    Excess,   35,000 lbs. at $4.30......... 1,505.00

	135,000 lbs.	5,505.00
Used	40,000 lbs.	$1,720.00

Average of lead used, 4.30.

Example No. 4
    Where there is a deficiency at the beginning and end of the period.
On hand at the beginning of the period:
    Normal,   100,000 lbs. at $4.00....... $4,000.00
    Deficiency, 25,000 lbs. at $4.35.......   1,087.50

	75,000 lbs.	$2,912.50
Purchased	100,000 lbs.	4,350.00
Total	175,000 lbs.	$7,262.50

On hand at the end of the period:
    Normal,   100,000 lbs. at $4.00....... $4,000.00
    Deficiency, 25,000 lbs. at $4.10.......   1,025.00

	75,000 lbs.	2,975.00
Used	100,000 lbs.	$4,287.50

Average of lead used, 4.2875

ADVANCING MARKET

Premise
    Lead on hand at the beginning of the period...... $4.10 per hundred pounds
    Cost of lead received during period............. 4.35 "   "   "
    Replacement value of lead...................... 4.50 "   "   "

Example No. 5
    Where there is an excess stock on hand at the beginning and end of the period.
On hand at the beginning of the period:
    Normal, 100,000 lbs. at $4.00......... $4,000.00
    Excess, 100,000 lbs. at $4.10......... 4,100.00

	200,000 lbs.	$ 8,100.00
Purchased	100,000 lbs.	4,350.00
Total	300,000 lbs.	$12,450.00

On hand at the end of the period:
    Normal, 100,000 lbs. at $4.00......... $4,000.00
    Excess,   25,000 lbs. at $4.225....... 1,056.25

	125,000 lbs.	5,056.25
Used	175,000 lbs.	$ 7,393.75

Average of lead used, 4.225.

Example No. 6
    Where there is an excess stock on hand at the beginning of the period
and a deficiency at the end of the period.
    On hand at the beginning of the period:
    Normal, 100,000 lbs. at $4.00......... $4,000.00
    Excess, 100,000 lbs. at $4.10.........   4,100.00

                                            200,000 lbs. $ 8,100.00
    Purchased .... 100,000 lbs.   4,350.00

    Total .... 300,000 lbs. $12,450.00
    On hand at the end of the period:
    Normal,   100,000 lbs. at $4.00....... $4,000.00
    Deficiency, 25,000 lbs. at $4.50.......   1,125.00

                                             75,000 lbs.   2,875.00

    Used .... 225,000 lbs. $ 9,575.00
                    Average of lead used, 4.255.

Example No. 7
    Where there is a deficiency at the beginning of the period and an excess
at the end of the period.
    On hand at the beginning of the period:
    Normal,   100,000 lbs. at $4.00....... $4,000.00
    Deficiency, 25,000 lbs. at $4.35.......   1,087.50

                                             75,000 lbs. $2,912.50
    Purchased .... 100,000 lbs.   4,350.00

    Total .... 175,000 lbs. $7,262.50
    On hand at the end of the period:
    Normal, 100,000 lbs. at $4.00......... $4,000.00
    Excess, 35,000 lbs. at $4.35.........   1,522.50

                                             135,000 lbs.   5,522.50

    Used ....   40,000 lbs. $1,740.00
                    Average of lead used, 4.35.

Example No. 8
    Where there is a deficiency at the beginning and end of the period.
    On hand at the beginning of the period:
    Normal,   100,000 lbs. at $4.00....... $4,000.00
    Deficiency, 25,000 lbs. at $4.35.......   1,087.50

                                             75,000 lbs. $2,912.50
    Purchased .... 100,000 lbs.   4,350.00

    Total .... 175,000 lbs. $7,262.50
    On hand at the end of the period:
    Normal,   100,000 lbs. at $4.00....... $4,000.00
    Deficiency, 25,000 lbs. at $4.50.......   1,125.00

                                             75,000 lbs.   2,875.00

                                             100,000 lbs. $4,387.50
                    Average of lead used, 4.387.

Elimination of Book Profits and Losses

At the annual meeting of the American Economic Association in Pittsburgh last December, Mr. Dennison, the President of the Dennison Manufacturing Co., was one of the speakers. In discussing the method of business forecasting used by his company, he made a statement to this effect: "The best proof of the value of this forecasting method is the fact that our pockets are full of gold and our shelves are comparatively empty, so that we have very little merchandise which we are compelled to write down; whereas, the pockets of our competitors are quite empty and their shelves are quite full." This is the acid test of the success of the system. The same might be said for the method of valuation of inventory used by the National Lead Co. For instance, the market price of pig lead advanced from the low prices ruling in the years 1913 and 1914, which were 3.40 cents to 3.44 cents per pound, to 11 or 12 cents during the war years, and on December 31, 1920, it had receded to 4.75 cents per pound.

Inasmuch as we had never taken any book profits on this rise in price, we did not have to take any book losses. This illustrates very clearly that over a period of years, if the period is long enough, the result will be the same regardless of what method had been used in the interval. The ups and downs offset each other in the final calculation. However, since fiscal periods are comparatively short, limited to only one year, it behooves us to anticipate to as great an extent as possible this leveling process, and by some means such as a safe and conservative method of valuation of inventories, to do it from year to year and thus avoid taking book profits which cannot be realized and which are sure to be followed by book losses during a period of declining prices. Of course, facts cannot be changed by books.

Although the ultimate result over a long period of years is the same, it is nevertheless extremely important to prevent these large paper profits from appearing on the books and in published statements from year to year. For example, take the record of the National Lead Co. during the war years. Had the basis for the valuation of the merchandise inventory been cost or market, profits of seven to eight million dollars in excess of the figures published would have been shown, but these profits could not have been realized except by liquidating the business. Such a showing of profits, however, would have created an irresistible demand for extra cash or stock dividends; it would have justified extreme demands for increases in salaries as well as wages; in short, it would have promoted extravagance and waste. In the years 1919 and 1920, however, it would have been followed by an offsetting loss of practically the same amount, due to declining prices and perhaps resulting in inability to pay dividends and a possible impairment of credit. Inasmuch as this apparent profit was not taken into the books of the company, it was not necessary to take this offsetting and apparent loss. The result was that in 1920, the National Lead Co. was in the fortunate position of not being compelled to either lower the dividend rate or to decrease the salaries of any of its employees.

I desire to add, parenthetically, that credit for the installation of the normal stock system is due to my predecessor, the late Mr. Stratford A. Miller, at that time Assistant Secretary of the Company. Thanks to the business vision and sagacity of our President, Mr. E. J. Cornish, and his associates on the Board, this system has become the accepted policy of the Company.

Not Accepted for Tax Purposes

The normal stock method of valuation of inventory has proved to be a very large factor in leveling the gains and losses over a period of abnormal price conditions such as that which prevailed during the years 1916 to 1921. This result is obtained by offsetting undue inventory gains due to abnormal price conditions of one year against undue inventory losses under abnormal price conditions of another year.

This method has not been accepted for tax purposes by the Bureau of Internal Revenue or by the British Board of Inland Revenue. Briefly, the reason given is as follows: that it does not reflect the true taxable income for any one single year. In view of the fact that this method was used by such a small minority of taxpayers, "it would work an unjustifiable discrimination against the great majority of manufacturers and dealers who have not used it." The National Lead Co., however, is continuing to use the method both for its domestic and foreign corporations. At the end of the taxable year the inventories are revalued for tax purposes in accordance with the inventory regulations of the Bureau of Internal Revenue. This additional work is entirely warranted on account of the value of the normal stock method to the company.

When Is Adoption Warranted?

It is quite obvious that the normal stock method as described presents some striking differences in practice and results from the methods commonly used. The question naturally arises: Under what circumstances and conditions is the adoption of this method warranted? While it is difficult to formulate a comprehensive definition on this point, it may be pertinent to draw attention to the character of the white lead industry by way of illustration.

The manufacture of white lead is one of the oldest manufacturing industries that employ chemical processes requiring a prolonged period of time for completion. Pig lead is the preponderant element of cost in the manufacture of white lead. The proportion of pig lead consumed in the white lead industry, however, is small compared to the total production of pig lead, averaging not more than about 20 per cent. For this reason, the forces of supply and demand determining the market price of pig lead are beyond the control of the white lead industry. We have a situation, therefore, where the price of the most important raw material is determined by conditions foreign to the white lead industry. Moreover, the sources of supply are widely scattered. A political disturbance in Mexico, for instance, may cause a sudden rise in the price of pig lead. As there is a turnover of but twice a year, such variations afford no speculative opportunities, and those who expect to remain in the business and be successful must possess inherent and commercial conservatism.

In any business, therefore, which must hold itself responsive to serious fluctuations in the market prices of its basic elements, and which, because of natural obstacles to rapid readjustment, cannot readily protect itself, a reliable method of inventory valuation must be one that adapts itself sufficiently to current advances and declines in prices, but controls the major portion of its merchandise assets by stabilizing influences.

The normal stock method of inventory valuation fulfills this function. It may now be considered an integral part of the methods of the National Lead Co. and is but one manifestation of the conservative spirit that prevails in all of the activities and in the general business policy of the company. The present sound economic and financial condition of the National Lead Co., reflected by the unlimited credit at its disposal, by the highest market price its capital stock has ever reached, and by its reputation for stability and conservatism in the trade, is a vindication of this policy.

THE LAST-IN, FIRST-OUT INVENTORY VALUATION BASIS *

By Earl W. Graham

THE INVENTORY is one of the more important balance sheet items by reason of its effect on the net current asset ratio and because of its direct relation to the profit and loss for a given period. Preliminary to a discussion of inventory valuation it would be well to review the generally accepted principles pertaining thereto. For many years the basic rule has been valuation at "cost or market, whichever is lower." The inventory *should not be valued at more than its probable realization value,* which provides for taking into account all losses but anticipation of no profits. Slow-moving, obsolete and unsalable stocks should be written down to a price at which no loss should result in the succeeding period. Profits should not be taken on unsold inventory stocks. The inventory *at the beginning and end of the period* should be valued *on the same basis,* although at times it may be difficult to agree upon the true meaning of the words "same basis," due to fluctuating sales prices, costs and other factors. An inventory valuation method *should be well adapted to the industry in which it is used.* Undoubtedly, all of you agree with these valuation principles. However, I believe we should examine them closely.

Main Purpose of Inventory Valuation

The principle of providing for all losses but anticipating no profits indicates that the main purpose of valuing an inventory is the determination of income or losses for a given, limited and artificial period. Probably the traditional use in commercial pursuits of the year of twelve months was founded on the fact that our basic industry, agriculture, finds its natural fiscal period in the calendar year, by reason of the unvarying influences of the changing seasons, from planting time in the Spring to harvest time in the Autumn. Also it is true that at regular intervals rentals, taxes, interest and other

* From the *Bulletin* of March 1, 1937. Originally published under the title "Current Practices in Inventory Valuation."

recurring expenses must be met. Dividends or other profit distribution are usually declared at more or less regular intervals.

However, even a casual review of price ranges and production statistics in most industries indicates that the business cycle extends over a longer period than a year—in some instances five or more years; from periods of low prices and curtailed production through periods of expansion, increased production and high prices, and back again to periods of low prices and decreased production.

Many Interpretations of "Cost"

Let us consider briefly the meaning of the term "cost" as applied to the inventory, and the several interpretations which we find applied to it. All public accountants learn from their earliest experience that the meanings attached to the term "cost" as applied to the inventory by their several clients cover a wide range. A company may claim to value the inventory at "actual cost," which may or may not include the expense of avoidable and unnecessary waste, losses and mistakes. Full allowance may or may not be made for idle plant conditions or temporary non-operating intervals by treating such expense as "unabsorbed operating burden," separate from costs applied to the inventory. Then there is the use of standard costs in inventory valuation, predetermined upon the basis of normal, attainable operating performance, cumulative average costs, so-called closely estimated costs and other variations too numerous to mention. Every one of these methods has its effect upon the income account through the cost of sales group of accounts.

Further Explanation of "Cost or Market" Needed

Undoubtedly, you have known for years that these many interpretations are applied to the term. Consideration of this fact, however, causes us to wonder at the almost general acceptance, without question, of financial statements wherein the inventory valuation is stated as being upon the basis of cost or market, whichever is lower. To my mind, further explanation is necessary, that is, whether all individual material units comprising the inventory are below market value, or whether some are valued above market but the aggregate inventory value is below market.

Inventory on hand at any given time represents an uncompleted transaction and the estimates of profit on uncompleted transactions should be made on a very conservative basis. It is certain that the difference between such an estimate and the actual realized profit or loss will be reflected in succeeding periods. Of all the approximations which must be made at the close of an accounting period the most difficult and the one which has the most influence upon the accounting results is the determination of the value of the inventory.

Use of Market Value Sometimes Misstates Income

Many times we have seen losses taken upon the basis of adjustments of inventory values to market prices below cost, and in the ensuing year or two a return of the market prices to the level from which they dropped, with resultant distortions of profits as between the two or three years. I recall in my public accounting experience the close of the year 1920, or 1921, and the price slump of that year —a minor depression—the grave concern of company officials who had seen profits made during the first part of the year washed away by large inventory adjustments at the close of the year, and I recall also that at the close of the next succeeding year the price of those same commodities had increased to almost the previous year's high levels. Certainly the profit and loss results as shown upon this basis were erroneous.

Cost or Market Basis Not Always Logical

Thus it is seen that valuation upon the basis of cost or market, whichever is lower, while generally conservative, is not logical in all cases. It provides for losses on the basis of market value at inventory date which losses actually have not or may never be sustained, as the inventory may be sold in a succeeding period at more than its cost.

My remarks to this point may appear to be a direct frontal attack upon the basic rule of cost or market, whichever is lower. That, however, is not the case, and I hasten to correct that impression if you have gained it. I agree with the principle of providing for all losses and not anticipating profits, of writing down slow-moving

and obsolete materials to realizable values, and of consistency of
practice at the beginning and end of an accounting period and
throughout the existence of a business venture. I have endeavored
only to point out the principal shortcomings of the so-called basic
rule of valuation, cost or market, whichever is lower.

At times we dislike to change our minds about subjects which
we have grown up with and we hesitate to rearrange our ideas of
values, as we are inclined to feel that we came by our judgments
logically and even judicially, although we may recognize subsequently an overbalancing factor that tends to change the entire
situation.

Inadequacies of "Cost or Market" Basis Recognized

Recognizing these certain inadequacies of the principle of cost
or market, whichever is lower, and the divergencies in the application of the general principle in the petroleum industry, to a
large degree due to very appreciable fluctuations in the market value
of crude oil and its derivative products, the American Petroleum
Institute passed the following resolution on November 12, 1934:

> RESOLVED: That the uniform method of valuing petroleum inventories
> called the "last-in, first-out" system, as presented by the committee on
> uniform methods of oil accounting, is hereby accepted and recommended
> for adoption for the calendar year 1934 or as soon thereafter as prac-
> ticable, as a method of valuing petroleum inventories, to be used in con-
> junction with the general form of balance-sheet and text as approved
> December 9, 1926, as a system for keeping books and accounts and for
> making the report for all those engaged in the oil industry, it being under-
> stood this uniform method of valuing petroleum inventories, as well as
> the balance-sheet and text, is subject to such changes and improvements
> from time to time as the committee may deem necessary after approval
> by the board of directors.

In the remainder of this discussion I shall endeavor to explain
to you the basic principles of the last-in, first-out method of inventory valuation. To those who have read the "Report of the Special
Committee on Inventories of the American Institute of Accountants"
published in the August, 1936 issue of the *Journal of Accountancy*,
it will be noted I have drawn to a large extent upon that article in
explaining this method of valuation. I refer also to the "Uniform
System of Accounts for the Oil Industry—Revised to June 30,
1936," recently issued by the American Petroleum Institute.

It should be remarked that while I speak of the petroleum industry, it is only by reason of the fact that the American Petroleum Institute promulgated and recommended the last-in, first-out system of valuing inventories to its member companies, that most of the available reading matter upon this subject has been in that connection, and that I am associated with the petroleum industry. This method of valuation can be applied logically to other industries, and this brings me to the first point in the discussion of this method of valuation.

Quick Communication of Raw Material Price Changes to Products

You will recall that I mentioned at the outset that an inventory valuation method should be well adapted to the industry in which it is used. I refer to the characteristic of quick communication of price changes in raw material commodities to the derivative products. In the petroleum industry, price changes in the raw material, crude oil, exert practically a simultaneous and corresponding effect on the finished products, but such characteristic is not peculiar to the petroleum industry alone. In the base metal manufacturing trades, such as copper, pig iron, lead, spelter, and certain other industries, the same characteristic is evident. The cotton textile and grain milling industries are afforded a means of "price protection" by the futures traded in in those markets. Where price changes in the raw materials exert a corresponding influence on the derivative commodities, the margin of profit very frequently is conceived as representing the spread between current sales prices and the replacement cost of raw materials, rather than inventory costs. The difference between this concept of the profit margin, and that resulting from the use of inventory costs is, of course, more pronounced if the raw materials experience frequent and relatively substantial price fluctuations, as in the case of the petroleum industry. Thus while over a long period, such as a complete economic cycle, profits would aggregate substantially the same total by whichever method computed, the divergence in results from year to year might be considerable.

Methods of Costing Sales

Reviewing very briefly the most generally used methods of costing sales, we find they may be classified as:

(1) The first-in, first-out basis
(2) The last-in, first-out basis
(3) The basis of cumulatively averaged cost.

During periods of rising prices, inventories valued on the basis of first-in, first-out will aggregate a larger valuation than on the basis of last-in, first-out; conversely, in a period of falling prices, inventories valued on the basis of first-in, first-out will aggregate a lower valuation than upon the basis of last-in, first-out. The basis of cumulatively averaged cost takes the middle ground between these two bases. These remarks, of course, are without consideration of market value adjustments. The foregoing indicates that the second and third bases will result in a more conservative operating result than the first method in periods of rising prices. In other words, their effect upon the income accounts is a closer correlation of current sales prices and current purchase costs.

The matter at issue between the first-in, first-out, and the last-in, first-out bases resolves itself into this question:

> Should cost of sales be regarded as meaning "previously inventoried cost" or may it mean "current reproduction cost"?

To illustrate the different results under these two bases, I cite the example used by the Special Committee on Inventories of the American Institute of Accountants, as follows:

A wagon maker has a wagon in stock which cost him $50, the selling price of which is $65 to yield him his desired profit of $15 per wagon. Before he sells the wagon he learns from the concern supplying him with his material of a price increase, the result of which is to make the reproduction cost of his wagon $60. By reason of this knowledge the wagon maker "marks up" his wagon to $75, at which figure he sells it for cash and builds a new wagon costing him $60. The net change resulting from the whole transaction is that his till shows $15 more cash than he had before.

Now the advocate of "reproduction cost of sales" says to the wagon maker:

"The profit you made is $15, and the proper inventory price for the present wagon you have in stock is $50. That is the number of dollars of your capital invested in your stock-in-trade; the only change that you have effectively realized in that investment is the substitution of one wagon for another exactly like it—the same wagon, in fact, except only as regards physical identity."

On the other hand, the advocate of "first-in, first-out" says to the wagon maker:

"Your profit is $25, although you may have only $15 more in cash to show for it. The other $10 is contained in the increased cost and value of the new wagon—$60 as against the old one at $50. You must not fail to recognize and to give effect to the price level change."

Considering the other side of the problem, let us assume that after the above transaction the price level reverted to its original status, thus consummating the economic cycle; accordingly the wagon at present in stock, which actually had cost $60 to build (but was inventoried at either $50 or $60, according to the procedure followed) is sold for $65 and replaced in stock by one which cost $50 to build. Now, under either procedure the latest wagon will be inventoried at $50. The profit on the second transaction, however, will have been $15 according to the "reproduction cost of sales" advocate, or $5 according to the "first-in, first-out" advocate. The aggregate profit on the two transactions, of course, will be the same in either case, but the periodic distribution will differ.

Prime Purpose Is to Correlate Sales Revenues and Cost of Sales

The Board of Directors of the American Petroleum Institute has indicated that "the prime purpose of the last-in, first-out principle is to bring about in the determination of profits a substantial correlation between sales prices and those raw material prices which have been directly causative of such sales prices. In other words, the purpose is that the revenue from high sales prices be burdened with the high costs which brought about the high sales prices and not leave high-priced inventories to be absorbed in later periods by revenue at a lower price level. It appears to follow that, whereas the principle of cost or market, whichever is lower, accomplishes a conservative inventory valuation from a short-term viewpoint, the last-in, first-out method looks to the longer economic period and the eventual return to low prices after a high price level interim.

The last-in, first-out method as enunciated by the American Petroleum Institute does not require the inventory prices to be reduced to market prices where lower than the regular inventory value, presumably on the assumption that the inventory value adopted at the outset of the last-in, first-out method will be so conservative that the price level thus shown in the inventory will be lower than that which ordinary market fluctuations may be expected to reach. It also presumes that those occasions when market prices are below the inventory values are only temporary and unusual conditions from which a prompt recovery is looked for.

Importance of Values Adopted at the Outset

This method places the utmost importance on the inventory values adopted at the inauguration of the last-in, first-out method. If the market declines frequently to a value below the inventory value it must be assumed that too high a value was adopted at the outset, as frequent write-downs to market would defeat the prime objective of the last-in, first-out method, that is, to correlate sales revenues with the costs responsible for the prices reflected by such sales revenue. We would point out also that the last-in, first-out method assumes in determining the cost of sales that the goods delivered were those currently purchased.

An Illustration

These principles are shown in an example which I have prepared and are set forth in the exhibits which appear at the end of this article. Let us consider these for a moment. The first three exhibits were prepared as a comparison of valuation upon the last-in, first-out basis and the lower of cost or market basis.

In Exhibit 1 the quantities and prices upon which the figures in this example are based are given. Reference to the inventory prices as shown in the right-hand columns indicates that under the last-in, first-out method a high valuation of $1.025 per unit was reached at the end of the fifth year, which compares with $1.35 per unit under the lower of cost or market basis at the end of the third and fourth years. In respect of the fourth year, a write-down is indicated, under cost or market, from cost of $1.60 to market of $1.35 per unit.

In Exhibit 2 the closing inventory valuations have been calculated. Please note that for the first four years the quantity on hand decreased, and accordingly under the last-in, first-out method the unit price of $1.00 remained constant. Compare this with the unit price under the lower of cost or market method; in each of the first three years the unit price increased due to rising purchase costs. By reason of the adjustment to market in the fourth year the price held at $1.35 per unit.

With regard to the effect upon the income account as shown in Exhibit 3, it will be observed that the profits under the last-in, first-out method do not show the extreme fluctuations that they do under the lower of cost or market basis, which is entirely by reason of burdening the revenues at high price levels with the costs which cause the high prices; or, in other words, a determination of closing inventory values upon a "replacement cost basis."

Contrasted with "Base Stock" Method

The last-in, first-out principle has been likened to the "base stock" or "base inventory" method of valuation, the purpose of which likewise is to assure that the revenue produced from high sales prices is burdened with the costs which cause the high sales prices. The base stock method, however, approaches the problem by way of ascertaining a "normal" inventory stock and the "low price level" at which the stock is to be valued. If you will refer to Exhibit 4 you will find the "year-to-date" method adopted by the American Petroleum Institute. You will note that the quantity is basic for a one-year period only and that the inventory price is adjusted by averaging (1) the excess of the production and purchases over the sales volume, and (2) the volume on hand at the beginning of the year. Thus it is seen that in those years in which the quantity increases a new basic volume and price adheres. This differs from the base inventory method, as that method maintains a normal inventory stock and price for a longer period than one year.

Answer to Criticisms

Certain criticisms have been directed toward the last-in, first-out method of valuation. For instance, it has been remarked that during periods of declining market prices the inventories are overstated in the balance sheet, and that the profits are likewise overstated under this method. To provide for such contingency the American Petroleum Institute Committee has provided that, "where the market value of the inventory is less than that carried in the balance sheet, such condition should be shown in parentheses or as a footnote in such manner that the approximate difference can be ascertained either in dollars or as a percentage." As pointed out before, upon the inauguration of the last-in, first-out method, an inventory valuation should be adopted which will be lower than that which ordinary market fluctuations may be expected to reach.

Also, it has been said that this method does not follow the physical movement of the products. To some extent that is true, but in a large measure the physical movement of production in the petroleum industry is from the well to the refineries. Reserve stocks, of course, are utilized to whatever extent is required. In the earlier days business structures were simpler, whereas the more complex business relations and situations of today render identification of products and "identifiable costs" almost impossible and have caused nearly every large industry to resort to an arbitrary allocation.

It has been said that the valuation of the residual inventory has not been dealt with beyond requiring it to be at a "conservative or reasonable figure" and that consequently the valuation of the inventory as it appears in the financial statements of the various oil companies will reflect the particular valuation price level which each company may regard as "conservative or reasonable." It does not appear to me that this condition differs from the present situation with regard to the various companies in any industry. I commented on this earlier with regard to the different interpretations of costs, and although I did not dwell upon the interpretations which might be placed on market value, it is my experience that the range of conceptions thereof is equally wide.

Conclusions of the Special Committee

After a complete review of the subject matter pertaining to the last-in, first-out method of valuation and joint deliberation with the Sub-Committee of the American Petroleum Institute, the Special Committee on Inventories of the American Institute of Accountants summed up their conclusions as follows:

> The "last-in, first-out" method for the valuation of oil company inventories, as recommended by the American Petroleum Institute, constitutes an *acceptable accounting principle for those companies which, finding it adaptable to their needs and views as correctly reflecting their income, apply it consistently from year to year;* it is important, however, that full and clear disclosure in their published financial statements be made by the companies adopting it, both as to the fact of its adoption and the manner of its application, including information as to the period adopted for the unit of time within which the goods last in are to be deemed first out, that is, whether the fiscal year or a shorter or longer period.
>
> Since the method as outlined by the Committee of the American Petroleum Institute requires that the valuation to be placed upon the inventory be "conservative or reasonable" without, however, providing for a uniform standard or common basis in the determination of such valuations, it must be understood by readers of the financial statements of companies adopting the method that the inventory valuation of one such company is not to be regarded as comparable with that of another, except only in so far as the current replacement valuation arrived at under the method affords such a comparison.
>
> The foregoing conclusion of our Committee, however, does not preclude our viewing other methods as being either equally acceptable or preferable in the case of other companies where different conditions may prevail.

Exhibit 1

QUANTITIES AND PRICES ON WHICH FIGURES ARE BASED

	Units	Price	Inventory Price	
			Last-in, First-out	Cost/Market
First Year:				
Opening Inventory	1,000,000	$1.00	$1.00	$1.00
Sales	1,500,000	1.25		
Purchases	1,450,000	1.10		
Closing Inventory	950,000		1.00	1.10
Second Year:				
Sales	1,700,000	1.25		
Purchases	1,600,000	1.15		
Closing Inventory	850,000		1.00	1.15
Third Year:				
Sales	1,600,000	1.50		
Purchases	1,500,000	1.35		
Closing Inventory	750,000		1.00	1.35
Fourth Year:				
Sales	1,300,000	1.75		
Purchases	1,250,000	1.60		
Closing Inventory	700,000		1.00	1.35*
Fifth Year:				
Sales	1,100,000	1.35		
Purchases	1,200,000	1.20		
Closing Inventory	800,000		1.025	1.20*
Sixth Year:				
Sales	1,150,000	1.20		
Purchases	1,450,000	1.00		
Closing Inventory	1,100,000		1.0182	1.00
Seventh Year:				
Sales	1,650,000	1.10		
Purchases	1,750,000	.90		
Closing Inventory	1,200,000		1.0083	.90
Eighth Year:				
Sales	2,050,000	1.00		
Purchases	2,100,000	.80		
Closing Inventory	1,250,000		1.00	.80
Ninth Year:				
Sales	2,150,000	.95		
Purchases	2,000,000	.80		
Closing Inventory	1,100,000		1.00	.80
Tenth Year:				
Sales	1,800,000	1.15		
Purchases	1,700,000	1.00		
Closing Inventory	1,000,000		1.00	1.00

* Market.

Exhibit 2

CLOSING INVENTORIES

	Last-In, First-Out Basis—A. P. I. Method			Lower of Cost or Market Basis			Inventory Increase (+) or Decrease (−)	
	Units	Price	Amount	Units	Price	Amount	Normal	Lower of Cost or Market (+) or Cost (−)
First Year	950,000	$1.00	$ 950,000	950,000	$1.10	$1,045,000	$ 50,000−	$ 45,000+
Second Year	850,000	1.00	850,000	850,000	1.15	977,500	100,000−	67,500+
Third Year	750,000	1.00	750,000	750,000	1.35	1,012,500	100,000−	35,000+
Fourth Year	700,000	1.00	700,000	700,000	1.35*	945,000	50,000−	67,500−
Fifth Year	700,000	1.00	700,000	800,000	1.20*	960,000	0	0
	100,000	1.20	120,000	0	0	0		
	800,000	$1.025	$ 820,000	800,000	$1.20	$ 960,000	120,000+	15,000+
Sixth Year	800,000	$1.025	$ 820,000	1,100,000	$1.00	$1,100,000		
	300,000	1.00	300,000					
	1,100,000	$1.0182	$1,120,000				300,000+	140,000+
Seventh Year	1,100,000	$1.0182	$1,120,000	1,200,000	$ .90	$1,080,000		
	100,000	.90	90,000					
	1,200,000	$1.0083	$1,210,000				90,000+	20,000−
Eighth Year	1,200,000	$1.0083	$1,210,000	1,250,000	$ .80	$1,000,000		
	50,000	.80	40,000					
	1,250,000	$1.00	$1,250,000				40,000+	80,000−
Ninth Year	1,100,000	$1.00	$1,100,000	1,100,000	$ .80	$ 880,000	150,000−	120,000−
Tenth Year	1,000,000	1.00	1,000,000	1,000,000	1.00	1,000,000	100,000−	120,000+

* Market.

EXHIBIT 3

PROFIT AND LOSS STATEMENT

LAST-IN, FIRST-OUT BASIS—A.P.I. METHOD:	First Year	Second Year	Third Year	Fourth Year	Fifth Year	Sixth Year	Seventh Year	Eighth Year	Ninth Year	Tenth Year	Total
Sales	$1,875,000	$2,125,000	$2,400,000	$2,275,000	$1,485,000	$1,380,000	$1,815,000	$2,050,000	$2,042,500	$2,070,000	
Cost of Sales:											
Opening Inventory ..	$1,000,000	$ 950,000	$ 850,000	$ 750,000	$ 700,000	$ 820,000	$1,120,000	$1,210,000	$1,250,000	$1,100,000	
Purchases ..	1,595,000	1,840,000	2,025,000	2,000,000	1,440,000	1,450,000	1,575,000	1,680,000	1,600,000	1,700,000	
	$2,595,000	$2,790,000	$2,875,000	$2,750,000	$2,140,000	$2,270,000	$2,695,000	$2,890,000	$2,850,000	$2,800,000	
Less—Closing Inventory .	950,000	850,000	750,000	700,000	820,000	1,120,000	1,210,000	1,250,000	1,100,000	1,000,000	
Total Cost of Sales..	$1,645,000	$1,940,000	$2,125,000	$2,050,000	$1,320,000	$1,150,000	$1,485,000	$1,640,000	$1,750,000	$1,800,000	
Profit	$ 230,000	$ 185,000	$ 275,000	$ 225,000	$ 165,000	$ 230,000	$ 330,000	$ 410,000	$ 292,500	$ 270,000	$2,612,500
LOWER OF COST OR MARKET BASIS:											
Sales	$1,875,000	$2,125,000	$2,400,000	$2,275,000	$1,485,000	$1,380,000	$1,815,000	$2,050,000	$2,042,500	$2,070,000	
Cost of Sales:											
Opening Inventory ...	$1,000,000	$1,045,000	$ 997,500	$1,012,500	$ 945,000	$ 960,000	$1,100,000	$1,080,000	$1,000,000	$ 880,000	
Purchases ...	1,595,000	1,840,000	2,025,000	2,000,000	1,440,000	1,450,000	1,575,000	1,680,000	1,600,000	1,700,000	
	$2,595,000	$2,885,000	$3,002,500	$3,012,500	$2,385,000	$2,410,000	$2,675,000	$2,760,000	$2,600,000	$2,580,000	
Less—Closing Inventory .	1,045,000	977,500	1,012,500	945,000	960,000	1,100,000	1,080,000	1,000,000	880,000	1,000,000	
Total Cost of Sales..	$1,550,000	$1,907,500	$1,990,000	$2,067,500	$1,425,000	$1,310,000	$1,595,000	$1,760,000	$1,720,000	$1,580,000	
Profit	$ 325,000	$ 217,500	$ 410,000	$ 207,500	$ 60,000	$ 70,000	$ 220,000	$ 290,000	$ 322,500	$ 490,000	$2,612,500

EXHIBIT 4

EXAMPLE OF THE "LAST-IN, FIRST-OUT" UNIFORM METHOD OF VALUING PETROLEUM INVENTORIES

Approved by the American Petroleum Institute, Nov. 12, 1934

(When applied on a year-to-date basis)

1936	Opening Inventory	Production or Purchases	Cost of Sales	Closing Inventory
1. January	100 @ 10¢	200 @ 9¢	150 @ 9¢	100 @ 10¢ 50 @ 9¢
2. February	100 @ 10¢ 50 @ 9¢	200 @ 8¢	175 @ 8.07¢	100 @ 10¢ 75 @ 8.5¢
3. 2 Months		400 @ 8.5¢	325 @ 8.5¢	
4. March	100 @ 10¢ 75 @ 8.5¢	175 @ 7¢	275 @ 7.681¢	75 @ 10¢
5. 3 Months		575 @ 8.043¢	575 @ 8.043¢ 25 @ 10¢ } Avg. 8.125¢ 175 @ 7.086¢	
6. April	75 @ 10¢	225 @ 7.5¢	175 @ 7.086¢	100 @ 10¢ 25 @ 7.890¢
7. 4 Months		800 @ 7.890¢	775 @ 7.890¢	
8. May	100 @ 10¢ 25 @ 7.890¢	220 @ 9¢	240 @ 8.904¢	100 @ 10¢ 5 @ 8.130¢
9. 5 Months		1,020 @ 8.130¢	1,015 @ 8.130¢	
10. June	100 @ 10¢ 5 @ 8.130¢	215 @ 10.5¢	230 @ 10.426¢	90 @ 10¢
11. 6 Months		1,235 @ 8.543¢	1,235 @ 8.543¢ 10 @ 10¢ } Avg. 8.554¢	
12. July	90 @ 10¢	205 @ 11.5¢	225 @ 11.369¢	70 @ 10¢
13. 7 Months	70 @ 10¢	1,440 @ 8.964¢	1,440 @ 8.964¢ 30 @ 10¢ } Avg. 8.985¢	
14. August		210 @ 12.5¢	200 @ 12.625¢	70 @ 10¢
15. 8 Months	80 @ 10¢	1,650 @ 9.414¢	1,650 @ 9.414¢ 25 @ 10¢ } Avg. 9.412¢	80 @ 10¢
16. September		230 @ 13.5¢	215 @ 13.744¢	
17. 9 Months	95 @ 10¢	1,880 @ 9.914¢	1,880 @ 9.914¢ 5 @ 10¢ } Avg. 9.914¢	95 @ 10¢
18. October		235 @ 13¢	230 @ 13.065¢	
19. 10 Months	100 @ 10¢	2,115 @ 10.257¢	2,115 @ 10.257¢	100 @ 10¢
20. November		240 @ 12.5¢	235 @ 12.545¢	
21. 11 Months	100 @ 10¢ 5 @ 10.485¢	2,355 @ 10.485¢	2,350 @ 10.485¢	100 @ 10¢ 5 @ 10.485¢
22. December		250 @ 11.5¢	240 @ 11.553¢	100 @ 10¢ 5 @ 10.485¢
23. 12 Months		2,605 @ 10.076¢	2,590 @ 10.583¢	100 @ 10¢ 15 @ 10.583¢ } Avg. 10.076¢

1937 (New Opening Inventory) January 115 @ 10.076¢

Conclusion

The main point in this opinion would appear to be the matter of *consistent application* from year to year. Most accountants and business men recognize consistency and conservatism as paramount in good business. It occurs to me that the "cost hypothesis" which I have described, acting as a leveler of the peaks and valleys of industry's profits and losses, should recommend itself to the consideration of prudent management. We have just passed through the period after 1929 and witnessed the ills of boom profits followed by tremendous losses or meager profits. It would seem that a policy or method which would, at the least, alleviate a recurrence thereof should receive our earnest consideration. It is recognized that the last-in, first-out valuation method is not a panacea for business ills. It requires sound judgment in management and consistency of application, as do all valuation methods. It may have been reborn of the depression, but it is distinctly not new, and with relation to the petroleum industry was inaugurated during a low price era. It looks to the longer economic period—the return of normalcy after periods of fluctuating prices and operations. It is recommended for your consideration.

REGULATIONS RELATING TO ELECTIVE METHOD OF TAKING INVENTORIES

Regulations 103

Sec. 19.22(d)-1. *Inventories Under Elective Method.*—Any taxpayer permitted or required to take inventories pursuant to the provisions of section 22(c), and pursuant to the provisions of sections 19.22(c)-1 to 19.22(c)-8, inclusive, may elect with respect to those goods specified in his application and properly subject to inventory to compute his opening and closing inventories in accordance with the method provided by section 22(d), as amended. Under this elective inventory method, the taxpayer is permitted to treat those goods remaining on hand at the close of the taxable year as being:

First, those included in the opening inventory of the taxable year, in the order of acquisition and to the extent thereof, and

Second, those acquired during the taxable year.

This elective inventory method is not dependent upon the character of the business in which the taxpayer is engaged, or upon the identity or want of identity through commingling of any of the goods on hand, and may be adopted by the taxpayer as of the close of any taxable year beginning after December 31, 1938.

If the elective inventory method is used by a taxpayer who regularly and consistently, in a manner similar to hedging on a futures market, matches purchases with sales, then firm purchase and sales contracts (i.e., those not legally subject to cancellation by either party) entered into at fixed prices on or before the date of the inventory may be included in purchases or sales, as the case may be, for the purpose of determining the cost of goods sold and the resulting profit or loss, provided that this practice is regularly and consistently adhered to by the taxpayer and that, in the opinion of the Commissioner, income is clearly reflected thereby.

Sec. 19.22(d)-2. *Requirements Incident to Adoption and Use of Elective Method.*—The adoption and use of the elective inventory method is, by section 22(d) and regulations thereunder, made subject to the following requirements:

(1) The taxpayer shall file an application to use such method specifying with particularity the goods to which it is to be applied;

269

(2) The inventory shall be taken at cost regardless of market values;

(3) Goods of the specified type included in the opening inventory of the taxable year for which the method is first used shall be considered as having been acquired at the same time and at a unit cost equal to the actual cost of the aggregate divided by the number of units on hand, such actual cost of the aggregate being determined pursuant to the inventory method employed by the taxpayer under the regulations applicable to the preceding taxable year;

(4) Goods of the specified type on hand as of the close of the taxable year in excess of what were on hand as of the beginning of the taxable year shall be included in the closing inventory, regardless of identification with specific invoices, at costs determined as follows:

(a) By reference to the actual cost of the goods most recently purchased or produced;

(b) By reference to the actual cost of the goods purchased or produced during the taxable year in the order of acquisition;

(c) By application of an average unit cost equal to the aggregate cost of all the goods purchased or produced throughout the taxable year divided by the total number of units so purchased or produced, the goods reflected in such inventory increase being considered for the purchases of section 22(d) as having been acquired all at the same time; or

(d) Pursuant to any other proper method which, in the opinion of the Commissioner, clearly reflects income.

Whichever of the several methods of valuing the inventory increase is adopted by the taxpayer and approved by the Commissioner shall be consistently adhered to in all subsequent taxable years so long as the elective inventory method is used by the taxpayer;

EXAMPLE (1): Suppose that the taxpayer adopts the elective inventory method for the taxable year 1939 with an opening inventory of 10 units at 10 cents per unit, that it makes 1939 purchases of 10 units as follows:

January	1 @ 11 =	11
April	2 @ 12 =	24
July	3 @ 13 =	39
October	4 @ 14 =	56
Totals:	10	130

and that it has a 1939 closing inventory of 15 units. This closing inventory, depending upon the taxpayer's method of valuing inventory increases, will be computed as follows:

(a) Most recent purchases—

$$
\begin{array}{lcr}
10 @ 10 & = & 100 \\
4 @ 14 \text{ (October)} & = & 56 \\
1 @ 13 \text{ (July)} & = & 13 \\
\hline
\text{Totals: } 15 & & 169
\end{array}
$$

or

(b) In order of acquisition—

$$
\begin{array}{lcr}
10 @ 10 & = & 100 \\
1 @ 11 \text{ (January)} & = & 11 \\
2 @ 12 \text{ (April)} & = & 24 \\
2 @ 13 \text{ (July)} & = & 26 \\
\hline
\text{Totals: } 15 & & 161
\end{array}
$$

or

(c) At an annual average—

$$
\begin{array}{lcr}
10 @ 10 & = & 100 \\
5 @ 13 \ (130/10) & = & 65 \\
\hline
\text{Totals: } 15 & & 165
\end{array}
$$

EXAMPLE (2): Suppose, in addition to the facts stated in example (1), that there is a 1940 closing inventory of 13 units. This closing inventory, being determined wholly by reference to the opening inventory, and being taken in the order of acquisition, and depending upon the taxpayer's method of valuing its inventory increase for the preceding taxable year, will be computed as follows:

(a) In case the increase was taken as most recent purchases—

$$
\begin{array}{lcr}
10 @ 10 \text{ (from 1938)} & = & 100 \\
1 @ 13 \text{ (July, 1939)} & = & 13 \\
2 @ 14 \text{ (October, 1939)} & = & 28 \\
\hline
\text{Totals: } 13 & & 141
\end{array}
$$

or

(b) In case the increase was taken in order of acquisition—

$$
\begin{array}{lcr}
10 @ 10 \text{ (from 1938)} & = & 100 \\
1 @ 11 \text{ (January, 1939)} & = & 11 \\
2 @ 12 \text{ (April, 1939)} & = & 24 \\
\hline
\text{Totals: } 13 & & 135
\end{array}
$$

or

(c) In case increase was taken on basis of an average—

$$
\begin{array}{lcl}
10 @ 10 \text{ (from 1938)} & = & 100 \\
3 @ 13 \text{ (from 1939)} & = & 39 \\
\hline
\text{Totals: } 13 & & 139
\end{array}
$$

(5) The taxpayer shall establish to the satisfaction of the Commissioner that the taxpayer has not, in the taxable year for which the elective inventory method is first used or in any subsequent taxable year, used in determining income, profit, or loss, for credit purposes, or for the purpose of reports to shareholders, partners, or other proprietors, or to beneficiaries, any inventory method other than that referred to in section 19.22(d)-1 or at variance with the requirement referred to in paragraph (3) of this section, the taxpayer's use of market value in lieu of cost not being considered at variance with this requirement;

(6) Goods of the specified type on hand as of the close of the taxable year preceding the taxable year for which this inventory method is first used, whether such preceding taxable year began before or after December 31, 1938, shall be included in the taxpayer's inventory for such preceding taxable year at cost;

(7) The elective inventory method, once adopted by the taxpayer with the approval of the Commissioner, shall be adhered to in all subsequent taxable years unless—

(a) A change to a different method is approved by the Commissioner; or

(b) The Commissioner determines that the taxpayer has used in ascertaining income, profits, or loss, for credit purposes or for the purpose of reports to shareholders, partners, or other proprietors, or to beneficiaries, and for years subsequent to his adoption of the elective inventory method, an inventory method at variance with that referred to in section 19.22(d)-1 and requires of the taxpayer a change to a different method for such subsequent taxable year or any taxable year thereafter; and

(8) The taxpayer shall maintain such accounting records as will enable the Commissioner readily to verify the taxpayer's inventory computations as well as his compliance with these several requirements.

Sec. 19.22(d)-3. *Time and Manner of Making Election.*—The elective inventory method may be adopted and used only if the taxpayer files with his return for the taxable year as of the close of which the method is first to be used (or, if such return is filed prior to the ninetieth day after the approval of Treasury Decision 4959, approved December 28, 1939, then at any time prior to the expiration of such ninetieth day), in triplicate on Form 970 (revised), and pursuant to the instructions printed thereon and to the requirements of this section, a statement of his election to use such inventory method. Such statement shall be accompanied by an analysis of all inventories of the taxpayer as of the beginning and as of the end of the taxable year for which the elective method is proposed first to be used, and also as of the beginning of the preceding taxable year. In the case of a manufacturer, this analysis shall show in detail the manner in which costs are computed with respect to raw materials, goods in process, and finished goods, segregating the products (whether in process or finished goods) into natural groups on the basis of either (1) similarity in factory processes through which they pass, or (2) similarity of raw materials used, or (3) similarity in style, shape, or use of finished products. Each group of products shall be clearly described.

The taxpayer shall submit for the consideration of the Commissioner in connection with the taxpayer's adoption or use of the elective inventory method such other detailed information with respect to his business or accounting system as may be at any time requested by the Commissioner.

As a condition to the taxpayer's use of the elective inventory method, the Commissioner may require that the method be used with respect to goods other than those specified in the taxpayer's statement of election if, in the opinion of the Commissioner, the use of such method with respect to such other goods is essential to a clear reflection of income.

Whether or not the taxpayer's application for the adoption and use of the elective inventory method should be approved, and whether or not such method, once adopted, may be continued, and the propriety of all computations incidental to the use of such method will be determined by the Commissioner in connection with the examination of the taxpayer's returns.

Sec. 19.22(d)-4. *Adjustments to be Made by Taxpayer.*—A taxpayer may not change to the elective method of taking inventories unless, at the time he files his application for the adoption of such method, he agrees to such adjustments incident to the change to or from such method, or incident to the use of such method, in the inventories of prior taxable years or otherwise, as the Commissioner upon the examination of the taxpayer's returns may deem necessary in order that the true income of the taxpayer will be clearly reflected for the years involved.

Sec. 19.22(d)-5. *Revocation of Election.*—An election made to adopt and use the elective inventory method is irrevocable, and the method once adopted shall be used in all subsequent taxable years, unless the use of another method be required by the Commissioner, or authorized by him pursuant to a written application therefor filed with him as provided in section 19.41-2.

Sec. 19.22(d)-6. *Change from Elective Inventory Method.*—If the taxpayer is granted permission by the Commissioner to discontinue the use of the elective method of taking inventories, and thereafter to pursue some other method, or if the taxpayer is required by the Commissioner to discontinue the use of the elective method by reason of the taxpayer's failure to conform to the requirements detailed in section 19.22(d)-2, the inventory of the specified goods for the first taxable year affected by the change and for each taxable year thereafter shall be taken—

(a) In conformity with the method used by the taxpayer under section 22(c) in inventorying goods not included in his elective inventory computations; or

(b) If the elective inventory method was used by the taxpayer with respect to all of his goods subject to inventory, then in conformity with the inventory method used by the taxpayer prior to his adoption of the elective inventory method; or

(c) If the taxpayer had not used inventories prior to his adoption of the elective inventory method and had no goods currently subject to inventory by a method other than the elective method, then in conformity with such inventory method as may be selected by the taxpayer and approved by the Commissioner as resulting in a clear reflection of income; or

(d) In any event, in conformity with any inventory method to which the taxpayer may change pursuant to application approved by the Commissioner.

INVENTORY RESERVE PLANS *

By Wyman P. Fiske

A. Introduction

Importance of Prices as Profit Factor

Price fluctuations are familiar to business men, all of whom recognize price oscillations as a profit factor, serving at times to expand profits, and at other times constituting a source of major loss. Nevertheless, the large part which prices play as a factor in total profits is not as widely recognized as it should be, for the simple reason that the amount of profit which can be directly traced to price changes is not usually determined by business men.

Two illustrations, one from the packing industry and the other from the manufacture of farm machinery, will show the possible magnitude of price gains and losses in relation to total profits. The packing industry obviously is one operating under conditions of extreme and rapid price changes. Packing companies have therefore been forced to give particular consideration to the problems arising from price changes. In 1934, Swift & Company felt it necessary to set aside $6,500,000, out of a net income of $11,-400,000, as an appropriation to cover possible price declines. While there was no definite statement that this was exactly the amount of the price gain, there was the implication that it was at least an approximation of this type of profit. The amount set aside was almost 60 per cent of the total net income for the year. A further appropriation of $6,000,000, or 45 per cent of the net income for the year, was felt necessary in 1935.

The International Harvester Company offers the other example. Price problems have long been a factor affecting its accounting policy. Although its methods have changed, some sort of inventory reserve plan has been in use for twenty years. In 1934, it reported a net income of $3,948,600, after including as a deduction, "Provision for Inventory Reserve—$3,500,000." Thus its reported profit

* From the *Bulletin* of July 15, 1938.

for the year was only one-half of that which would have been reported under more conventional techniques. An additional $5,000,000 was set up in 1935.

Financial Effect

The significance of price changes is to be found not only in their effect upon profits but also in their financial effect. This phase is well described in the 1935 Yearbook of Swift & Company (covering the period from October 28, 1933 to October 27, 1934), where it is stated by the President:

> I wish particularly to stress the point that profits on inventory, due to rising prices, disappear quickly when prices fall. Experience has shown that they can go as unexpectedly as they come. During the period they stand on our books, they provide no additional cash for the payment of dividends, for the maintenance of property, or for plant extensions. On the asset side of our balance sheet, they are in the inventory account in the form of higher-valued products. While it is true that inventories are constantly being sold and cash is realized, the cash so obtained must be reinvested in new inventories at the higher level of prices if our trade is to be taken care of.
>
> We are, of course, glad to have inventory profits; in fact, we must have them in a period of rising prices if our working capital is to be preserved. But inventory profits are really capital gains, part of which should remain in the business as insurance against losses resulting from falling prices. Had the financial and business community given proper recognition years ago to the real nature of inventory profits and the distinction between such profits and cash profits, all of us would be better off to-day.
>
> What we need and are seeking most of all is cash profits, profits that can be paid out in dividends or reinvested in the business as occasion requires.

It thus appears that the volume of price profits must be recognized in determining sound dividend policy and in working capital financing. Specific financial effects are well illustrated by the experience of the Firestone Tire & Rubber Company in the 1920's. During a portion of this period, the British Rubber Restriction Act was in force with a marked effect on prices and financial problems. To quote from the 1925 annual report:

> The operation of the British Rubber Restriction Act has reduced the world's working supply of rubber far below the normal requirements of the industry. This has caused an increase in the price of rubber during the year, ranging from a low of 36 cents to a high of $1.23, with the present price around $1.00 per pound. Due to this increased cost of crude rubber and the rapidly expanding business of your Company, your Directors deemed it advisable to provide further working capital and during the past month have issued an additional $10,000,000 of the authorized 7 per cent Preferred Stock. Before this financing, the Company again closed its fiscal year with no bank indebtedness.

And from the 1926 report:

> At our last Annual Meeting I advised you that during the year rubber
> had ranged in price from a low of 36 cents to a high of $1.23 and that the
> price on that date was around $1.00 per lb. The operation of the British
> Rubber Restriction Act gave 100 per cent releases on February 1st this year
> and rubber again dropped to 36 cents per lb. (Rubber is now selling
> around 37 cents per lb.). It is necessary for your company to have pur-
> chases in the East, afloat, and stock in Akron equal to four months' con-
> sumption, and as we use approximately 10,000,000 lbs. per month, it is very
> evident that these wide fluctuations in price made it a difficult year for
> large manufacturers.

The question mark attachable to the validity of surplus under such
conditions hardly need be mentioned.

Effect Under Graduated Undistributed Profits Tax

Further proof of the significance of price profits may be found
in a consideration of the undistributed profits tax which was in
force for a time during the middle thirties. Price profits are not
a safe basis for dividends. Yet if dividends were not declared the
profits as reported were subject to a graduated tax which, under
the 1936 law, reached a rate as high as 27 per cent. Thus, under
the undistributed profits tax (or under any sharply graduated tax)
currently accepted bases of valuing inventory had the effect of
increasing substantially the tax bill of those businesses which suffered from extreme price fluctuations. This condition alone was
enough to warrant a serious study of the situation with a view to
elimination of this inequity between concerns differently affected
by price changes and led to the adoption, and recognition by the
income tax law, of the so-called last-in, first-out method of inventory
valuation.

B. Types of Inventory Reserve Plans

A Number of Alternatives Possible

Several approaches to a solution of the problems raised by the
price phenomenon have been attempted and may be found reflected
in published corporate reports. The title of this paper was selected
with the definite intention of including all varieties of plans rather

than of confining the discussion to some of the more widely publicized plans. All inventory reserve plans have as their objective the determination and reporting of accounting facts necessary in a sound approach to solving the business and investment problems raised by price fluctuations.

One group of procedures is based upon an underlying philosophy that profits should be so defined as to exclude price gains. Such companies usually report their net income exclusive of both price profits and price losses. A second group of companies recognizes the financial aspects of the problem but seeks a solution through a method which still permits of the inclusion of price gains and losses in reported net income. Although arguments may be advanced in favor of both, the concept of profits held by the first group (excluding price gains and losses from income) has been widely attacked and has only a narrow acceptance. Unfortunately, all proposals for inventory reserves tend to be grouped together, with the result that the objection to this profits concept has tarred all with the brush of radicalism. Perhaps, too, the plans have suffered from their support by individuals who advocate various degrees of stabilized accounting.

Another classification of the plans is possible: those which attempt to meet the problem through use of appropriated surplus reserves set up on the liability side of the balance sheet; and those which value inventories on bases other than the conventional cost or market, whichever is lower. Wide differences in balance sheet presentation of the information exist, with bad effects on comparability and analytical use.

Illustrative Cases

A few illustrations of various types of plans will demonstrate the contrasting effects. As an example of a company using a surplus reserve to meet the price problem, The Goodyear Tire & Rubber Company may be cited. On its balance sheet of December 31, 1925, there appeared a special raw material reserve amounting to $7,500,-000. (See Appendix, page 293.) In regard to this new surplus reserve, the following was included in the text of the annual report.

> We have already reported to you that your Board of Directors appropriated $3,000,000 out of the first six months' earnings as a "Special Raw Material Reserve" to partially provide against a possible decline in crude rubber values. While our rubber inventories and commitments at cost were

substantially under market values on December 31, 1925, the market continues to fluctuate violently on levels that are abnormally high and economically unsound. In the belief that considerable shrinkage in values is still possible and that should this materialize abruptly the Company should be prepared to meet the emergency if and when it occurs, your directors have increased the Special Raw Material Reserve to a total of $7,500,000. This entire amount has been appropriated out of and is shown as a deduction from 1925 earnings.

The subsequent history of this reserve shows charges to it in 1926 (see Appendix, page 294) and 1928, and an addition to it in 1927. Beginning with 1928 the reserve was merged with the Reserve for Contingencies and so lost its separate identity. Among other companies which have included a reserve on the liability side of the balance sheet can be mentioned the American Smelting and Refining Company, the Plymouth Cordage Company, and the Endicott Johnson Corporation.

The group of companies which have met the situation by revaluation of the inventory on a basis other than cost or market, whichever is lower, have accomplished the result in at least two different ways. The United States Steel Corporation and the International Harvester Company have at various times set up special inventory reserves which have been deducted from the inventory on the asset side, thus bringing the value of the inventory below a cost or market, whichever is lower, basis. An explanation of the use and effect of the reserve plan used by the International Harvester Company was included in the 1932 report as follows:

> The deficit for the year made it necessary to transfer $10,000,000 from general reserves to surplus. These reserves, on which we also drew heavily in 1931, were established from earnings of prior years as a blanket protection against market declines in inventories throughout the world, decline in dollar exchange value of current assets in foreign countries, and other unforeseen contingencies. Years of experience have shown that a world-wide business such as ours is subject to many contingencies and losses not predictable as to time, place, nature or extent. This policy of providing general blanket reserves has seemed to the management the best protection against such contingencies, and we are fortunate in having them available at this time; they are necessary insurance, operating for the benefit of both stockholders and customers and should be renewed when earnings again permit. The balance of these blanket reserves not yet used is $15,000,000. This has been applied in the balance sheet as a deduction from inventories, such inventories having been valued at cost or market, whichever was lower. How much of these reserves may be required to meet further declines in prices and foreign exchange rates depends, of course, on the economic conditions prevailing during the next few years.

A further deduction from this reserve was made in 1933 and additions were resumed in 1934 and 1935. During and following the

war period, the United States Steel Corporation used a similar
reserve which equalled the excess over values at the close of 1915.
The U. S. Steel plan differs from that of the Harvester Company in
that it appears to reflect a more definite attempt to maintain a reserve
sufficient to absorb losses down to a specific price level.

The plan which has had the greatest publicity, namely the so-called
Base Stock or Normal Stock Principle, is a further illustration of
a policy involving a revaluation of inventories.   Under this plan a
minimum or normal stock is carried at an unchanging price regardless of actual price fluctuations.   In periods of rising prices this
portion of the inventory is always valued at the lower prices in
force before the price rise started; the higher the level which prices
actually reach, the greater will be the divergence between reported
inventory value and cost (which under rising prices will be less
than market).

Since the plan, as ordinarily operated, follows the principle that
income should exclude price gains and losses, reported net income
also varies from the conventional figure as prices fluctuate.   Computations by T. H. Sanders [1] show that this effect in the case of the
National Lead Company has reached an amount as high as $5,600,000
and has resulted in showing a profit of $3,500,000 when conventional
methods would have produced a loss of $2,100,000.   In spite of,
or rather because of, this effect, the Lead Company has been using
the plan for over twenty years.

A final type of plan is somewhat different in its procedure from
any of the others previously cited, although it likewise results in
unorthodox inventory values.   This is the so-called last-in, first-out
basis of pricing goods into process and into cost of sale.   Instead
of charging goods into process at the price of the oldest units in
the lot, the price is that of the newest units of the lot.   As a result,
charges to process tend on the whole to approximate replacement
costs, and the inventory contains the oldest units as far as price
is concerned.   If this plan is started when prices are low, its effect
is to keep inventory values at approximately those low levels,
while sales are costed substantially on a replacement basis.   This
plan has received recent publicity through its recommendation to
the petroleum industry by the Petroleum Institute.   In its final
effects it does not differ greatly from the base stock plan.   It is

[1] *Journal of Accountancy,* December, 1926.   "Some Variations in Inventory
Valuations," p. 432.

permissible under certain conditions for tax reporting, a recognition which has never been accorded to the base stock method.

C. Choice of Policy

There is, then, a considerable array of alternatives from which to choose if the price risk in any industry is great and if the company wishes specifically to recognize price changes in its accounts. Thus consideration of the relative advantages and disadvantages of the different approaches is necessary if a logical selection is to be made. Many factors are involved, among which are tax effects, the effect upon annual profit figures and upon surplus, the effect upon the balance sheet, the effects upon stockholders and public relations, and cost and ease of operation. Because of its current interest, tax aspects provide a good starting point for discussion.

Tax Aspects

The tax history of inventory reserve plans has been most uneven. Until 1938 income tax regulations did not permit the use of the normal stock basis, or of the last-in first-out basis, and any plan which involved a surplus reserve set up by an appropriation of income obviously was (and still is) useless as a means of reducing income taxes. In 1938 the new tax law permitted the use of the last-in first-out basis in the tanning and non-ferrous industries for tax purposes. In subsequent years the law was liberalized to permit the use of the same plan by a wider group of companies, under rather strict regulations. Even today the base stock method is not recognized as a permissible basis for tax reporting. Except under a graduated tax the Government has a real advantage taxwise in permitting the use of such plans, since the effect is to increase taxable net income in years of bad business when taxes fall off and tax revenue is most needed. The graduation feature, however, results in actual loss of tax revenue, since the Government loses high bracket income in good years and gains low bracket income in bad years.

From the company point of view price profits do not provide the cash needed to pay taxes. Indeed there are times when high price profits produce some financial stress not only by tying up the gains in inventory but also by requiring increased capital in the higher-priced accounts receivable.

The proposal has been made that the tax problem can be met by successful group action to reinstate the carry-over feature. The carry-over provision would undoubtedly ameliorate the situation but it fails in two important respects. It has always been for a limited period only, and there is more than a chance that the period will expire before profits have made up the losses suffered, resulting in a definite tax loss. Further, the provision is absolutely no protection against progressive rate features in excess profits and undistributed earnings taxes. Sound finance requires that distributions in years of high profits recognize the inevitability of future losses; progressive rates on undistributed earnings result in rank discrimination against businesses operating soundly under conditions of high inventory risks.

Effects on Profit and Loss Statement

The effects of the several plans on profit and loss statements are quite different and fall into three groups. One group, which includes the base stock approach and the last-in, first-out basis, directly affects the costs of sales, decreasing gross profit and net income in years of increasing prices with a reverse effect in years of declining prices. Price gains and losses are excluded from profits. No indication of the amount of the effect on the profit and loss statement will appear unless specially computed and segregated. National Lead Company is the best example.

A second group includes the plans followed by the Goodyear Tire & Rubber Company (see Appendix, pp. 293 and 294) and the International Harvester Company (see Appendix, p. 292) and shows the addition to a surplus reserve as a deduction on the profit and loss statement, before arriving at net income. In these cases the amounts of additions to the reserve appear upon the face of the statement for those who care to see them. Charge-offs against the reserve will not appear unless specially segregated, since their effect is to reduce cost of sales. Net income is shown after provision for price profit. This effect is clearly shown in the reports of The Goodyear Tire & Rubber Company for 1925 and 1926 (see Appendix, pp. 293 and 294).

A final group sets up the reserve as a direct surplus appropriation. Under this approach, net income in years of rising prices will include price profits, but, in years in which inventory losses are charged against the reserve, net income will be increased by such use of the reserve. Thus the effect is to increase income in bad years but not to reduce it in good years. The method is objectionable for these reasons. Consistency in reporting net income, either as including price gains and losses or as excluding price gains and losses, would seem to be a minimum requirement. Further, since those who use any inventory reserve plans are still in the minority, it would appear desirable that disclosure of the amounts involved should be made. While this is not ordinarily done under the base stock approach, it can be and is done by some companies. The condensed profit and loss and operating surplus account of the Plymouth Cordage Company for the year ended September 30, 1936 (see Appendix, p. 289) shows operating profits based upon inventories taken at the lower of cost or market, and then shows as a deduction the additions to the reserve [2] revaluing the normal inventory and restating the operating profits excluding price gains. In this way both figures are indicated and analysis and comparison are possible. A similar treatment is used by Endicott Johnson Corporation (see Appendix, p. 295).

Effects on Balance Sheet

The balance sheet effects also differ considerably. Under the plan followed by the National Lead Company, the single inventory figure reflects two valuation bases. Minimum or normal quantities are valued at a minimum or base price, and the excess over normal is valued at cost or market, whichever is lower. The result is an inventory markedly different from current general practice. Since the prices used to value the minimum stock are set very low, the effect is to decrease apparent working capital in years of higher prices. Also, balance sheet comparisons with companies using other plans become extremely difficult. Balance sheet ratios are affected; in particular, the inventory turnover ratio loses most of its significance. The plans followed by the United States Steel Corporation and the International Harvester Company are thus better than that of the National Lead Company for, even though the inventory is

[2] This company has since adopted the last-in, first-out basis.

similarly valued on the balance sheet at prices less than cost or market, whichever is lower, the amount of the reserve is disclosed in the annual report. In the case of the United States Steel Corporation, the disclosure was to be found in the tabulation of the inventory. In the case of the International Harvester Company, the amount of the reserve is indicated in the text portion of the annual report. Both treatments make it possible to recast the figures for purposes of comparison and to determine working capital at current price levels.

Best of all the plans from the balance sheet point of view would appear to be those followed by the American Smelting and Refining Company, by the Plymouth Cordage Company, and by the Endicott Johnson Corporation. These companies value inventories in the current asset section at cost or market, whichever is lower, but set up, on the liability side of the balance sheet, a reserve to revalue the inventory down to the desired levels. This procedure provides full disclosure, makes the balance sheet directly comparable with balance sheets of other companies, and states working capital at current prices. At the same time, it provides the management with all necessary information for sound financial policy.

Stockholders and Public Relations

In a discussion with one controller, concerning the desirability of adopting some sort of an inventory reserve plan, it was brought out that the stock of the company in question was being used by investors as a hedge against inflation. Hence any plan which would conceal price profits and show inventories valued at other than cost or market, whichever was lower, would be a positive disadvantage in investment analysis. This situation illustrates the need of considering stockholder and public relations. Mere provision for the information requirements of management is not enough. Complete disclosure of accounting policies and significant figures is essential where unusual methods of accounting are followed. The importance of disclosure was well stated by the Committee on Co-operation with Stock Exchanges of the American Institute of Accountants, as follows:

> Most investors realize today that balance sheet and income accounts are largely the reflection of individual judgments, and that their value is therefore to a large extent dependent on the competence and honesty of the

persons exercising the necessary judgment. The importance of method, and particularly of consistency of method from year to year, is by no means equally understood.

In considering ways of improving the existing situation two alternatives suggest themselves . . .

The more practicable alternative would be to leave every corporation free to choose its own methods of accounting within the very broad limits to which reference has been made, but require disclosure of the methods employed and consistency in their application from year to year . . .

Within quite wide limits it is relatively unimportant to the investor what precise rules or conventions are adopted by a corporation in reporting its earnings if he knows what method is being followed, and is assured that it is followed consistently from year to year.

Full disclosure enables the competent analyst to rearrange and adapt the statements to fit his particular needs. Where accounting policy affects comparability because of departures from general practices, it is the responsibility of the company adopting the new policy or procedure to provide a basis for comparison; this is a part of its obligation to its stockholders and to the public.

Possible Effect Upon Credit

A further possible difficulty where disclosure is not made as to the basis for valuation is the effect upon the credit of the company. There is a positive disadvantage in any accounting policy which precludes comparison of resulting statements with those of like enterprises. Bankers, credit men and investors are rightfully suspicious of departures from widely accepted accounting practice. Analysis is made more difficult, and generally used standards are useless. Unless confidence in the management can overcome the handicap, or unless the company gains the advantages of a "mystery stock," the effect upon credit may be unsatisfactory even though the plan followed is essentially super-conservative. The only way that this objection can be overcome is likewise by a frank disclosure of policies and discussion of the reasons for the adoption of the change.

Inventory reserve and basic inventory plans affect the statements in various manners. The least drastic effect from the point of view of analysis is that of inventory reserve plans using a simple surplus reserve on the liability side of the balance sheet. The most drastic effect appears to be that caused by a treatment under the basic inventory type of plan which shows the basic or normal portion of the inventory among the fixed assets valued at a nominal price, with the excess over normal (or the speculative portion) among the current assets value at cost or market, whichever is lower. In this case working capital is sharply reduced because of the elimination of the major portion of the inventory from current assets. The widely used current ratio is distorted, and figures as to inventory turnover are seriously warped. Unless an industry as a whole adopts such a plan, comparison is almost impossible and, even if adoption is industry-wide, the analyst will need to reconsider his techniques and standards.

Cost and Technical Difficulties

Finally, the cost and ease of operating the several plans must be considered. Of course, the least effect upon routine accounting procedure will be found where the principle of last-in, first-out is adopted and carried through the cost records. Most companies which have found an inventory reserve plan desirable have been able to overcome this difficulty comparatively easily. Under the base stock approach it is entirely possible to use the first-in, first-out basis in the cost records and then to make the adjustment from this ordinary method of accounting to the base stock method at the end of the period. One company in particular is determining its figures upon three bases. It shows its profit on the basis of cost or market, whichever is lower, on a replacement basis, and on the base stock approach. This particular company, in the metal business, finds the computations necessary to obtain all three profit figures comparatively simple.

D. CONCLUSION

The profit effects of price trends are becoming rather widely recognized. To the extent that sales prices tend to be based on replacement costs of material, regardless of actual historical costs, profits and losses include an element representing the difference between cost and replacement values of inventories under ordinary methods of accounting for cost of goods sold. In those industries which have relatively long processing cycles and suffer extreme fluctuations in basic raw material prices, the effect is tremendous and results in extraordinary swings in profit amounts. On rising markets profits skyrocket and on declining markets profits toboggan to equally great deficits. There is produced as a consequence a series of financial and administrative problems that demand serious attention. Dividend policy in good times must recognize and estimate the probabilities of future inventory losses. Inventory control must seek to maximize the profits and minimize the losses by alternate increases and liquidation of quantities. Taxes, under plans which do not permit carry-overs of losses, which include progressive rates on higher profit brackets, or which tax undistributed earnings at progressive rates, will result in substantial discriminations against industries of the types suggested.

The importance of the problems presented merits careful consideration of all proposals claiming to eliminate any or all the difficulties. Many have been made, varying from the use of adequate surplus reserves to the determination of profits on radically different bases of costing the goods sold. Most of them have had adherents with the courage to undertake their use, in some cases in very large and prominent companies.

It would appear desirable that some recognition of the price factor be given in the financial statement prepared for stockholders. How this should be done would appear to be considerably less important than the fact that it must be done somehow. Prices have already risen considerably from the lows of 1933 and, if economic conditions follow their normal course, are likely to rise still further. There is talk of inflation in the air.

As to how it should be done, if the tax feature could be neglected, my own conclusions would approve the plans followed by the American Smelting and Refining Company, by the Plymouth Cordage Company, and by the Endicott Johnson Corporation. These companies use the normal stock approach and separate inventory quantities into two parts, a minimum and an excess or speculative portion. The excess over normal is valued at cost or market, whichever is lower; price gains and losses arising from this portion of the inventory are included in annual profits exactly as they are by companies entirely avoiding the question. The minimum quantities are also included in inventory at cost or market, whichever is lower, but a reserve is maintained at the amount of the difference between current values and base values. This reserve is shown on the balance sheet on the liability side; it is not deducted from the inventory as in the case of the National Lead Company. There is thus a full disclosure of policy and amounts and a maximum comparability with statements of companies not following the same method.

Unfortunately the tax factor does not apply alike to all methods. Most are not permitted for tax reporting; only one—the last-in, first-out—has internal revenue sanction. This fact alone gives the last-in, first-out approach a great advantage and has led to fairly wide adoption. Some companies have changed over from other plans which they really like better to this approved plan in order to get the tax advantage. It does not appear that under the last-in, first-out plan it is necessary on the balance sheet to fail to disclose the current market value of the inventory. Both this value and the value as determined by operation of the method may be shown, thus avoiding one of the objections to the plan.

Inventory reserve plans have suffered from the taint of unorthodoxy. However, contrary to general opinion, they are used in a considerable number of large and important companies in statements which have been certified by reputable accounting firms. In a period of rising prices their use should be extended. It is not nearly so important which treatment is selected as it is that there be wider acknowledgment of the need for doing something.

APPENDIX

PLYMOUTH CORDAGE COMPANY
BALANCE SHEET, SEPTEMBER 30, 1936
ASSETS

Cash items and Securities	$ 3,385,317.01
Receivables—net	779,449.00
Merchandise and Supplies—At cost or market, whichever lower	5,191,457.34
TOTAL CURRENT ASSETS	$ 9,356,223.35
Deferred Charges	175,605.22
Loans to Employees	48,406.91
Miscellaneous Securities and Stock of Subsidiaries	480,330.79
Fixed Assets—less reserves	3,611,884.36
	$13,672,450.63

LIABILITIES

TOTAL CURRENT LIABILITIES	$ 484,506.93
Pension and Insurance Fund—Employees	53,849.49
Reserve Revaluing Normal Inventory	1,098,800.00
Capital Stock—Less in Treasury	6,891,580.00
Capital Surplus	1,029,290.16
Operating Surplus	4,114,424.05
	$13,672,450.63

CONDENSED PROFIT AND LOSS AND OPERATING SURPLUS ACCOUNT

Operating Profit—After regular charge for Depreciation of Plant and with Inventories taken at the lower of Cost or Market		$ 1,151,877.48
Deduct—Addition to Reserve Revaluing Normal Inventories		426,178.00
		$ 725,699.48
Miscellaneous Profit and Loss and Surplus Items		
Add Other Income	$104,133.36	
Deduct—Reserve for Taxes, adjustment of prior taxes, and miscellaneous surplus items........	186,529.68	82,396.32
		$ 643,303.16
Deduct—Advances and stock written off		177,372.17
Net Addition to Operating Surplus before Dividends		$ 465,930.99
Dividends Declared		379,085.58
Net Addition to Operating Surplus for the Year		$ 86,845.41
Operating Surplus Beginning of Year		4,027,578.64
Operating Surplus End of Year		$ 4,114,424.05

APPENDIX

PLYMOUTH CORDAGE COMPANY (Continued)

In the Annual Report of September 30, 1936, the Treasurer includes a paragraph as follows:

Inventory Reserve

We have spoken of an inventory reserve in previous reports, pointing out that losses in value of inventory investment appear inevitable on the next down-swing of prices and that the provision of a reasonable reserve supplies a cushion which will absorb at least a part of these unavoidable losses. Continued study of this subject leads us to the belief that our aim should be to maintain a reserve sufficient to revalue down to previously experienced low levels such amount of inventory as may be required to operate the business at a volume reasonably to be expected. Because of selling customers of the trade, and the fact that our raw materials come from great distances, the amount of inventory so required is in the aggregate fairly large, both in physical volume and in value, with of course correspondingly large losses in value in case of price decline.

Regardless of the probability at any time of a decline in price, this normal inventory so required is just as necessary to continued operation as buildings and machinery, and shrinkage in its value appears to be inescapable. Therefore, as we see it, to the extent that it is possible, these losses should be anticipated as circumstances permit and, as explained last year, current profit or loss presented only after the revaluation of this normal inventory.

Investment in inventory in excess of the normal required represents a market operation which may or may not be profitable, and the results therefrom should be reflected in the current figures.

Possibly we should point out that the new Federal tax on undistributed net income may present a real problem in maintaining the reserve we have been discussing, as that law does not recognize (by relieving such reserves from tax) the necessity or desirability of providing this protection. For a business like ours, requiring a considerable inventory investment with accompanying and unavoidable fluctuations in value, this will be of particular moment. This new law which taxes undistributed net income does not apply to our fiscal year just closed.

APPENDIX

SWIFT AND COMPANY

Included among Current Assets in the Consolidated Balance Sheet of October 26, 1935, were the following items:

INVENTORIES—Products where cost was not ascertainable, were valued at approximate market prices, allowing for estimated selling expenses; other products and ingredients and supplies at the lower of cost or market—

Product	$92,405,143.93
Ingredients and Supplies	5,578,276.38
	$97,983,420.31

Included among "Reserves" on the liability side of the same balance sheet was the following:

Reserve for Inventory Price Decline	$16,767,000.00

CONSOLIDATED INCOME STATEMENT AND SURPLUS ACCOUNT
for the Period from October 27, 1934 to October 26, 1935

Sales less Cost of Goods Sold	$34,918,623.65
Other Operating Expenses	13,464,312.83
Operating Income	$21,454,310.82
Other Income	1,186,759.00
	$22,641,069.82
Interest Charges	2,479,976.55
	$20,161,093.27
Provision for Income Tax	2,509,641.32
	$17,651,451.95
Special Deductions:	
Writing off Unamortized Discount and Intangible Assets	2,884,149.56
Balance for Year	$14,767,302.39
Appropriation for Inventory Price Decline	6,000,000.00
Balance to Surplus Account	$ 8,767,302.39

INTERNATIONAL HARVESTER COMPANY

Included among the Current Assets on the Consolidated Balance Sheet, December 31, 1935, were the following items:

INVENTORIES:

Raw Materials, Work in Process, Finished Products, etc., at lower of cost or market	$111,743,686.32
Deduct: Inventory Reserve	13,500,000.00
	$ 98,243,686.32

INCOME ACCOUNT FOR 1935

Sales		$217,583,447.31
Deduct:		
Cost of Goods Sold, Selling, Operating, Administrative Expenses, etc.	$188,012,498.89	
Ore and Coal Depletion	850,535.80	
Plant Depreciation	7,842,363.91	
Addition to Inventory Reserve	5,000,000.00	
Reserve against Foreign Losses	4,000,000.00	
		205,705,398.60
Net Operating Income		$ 11,878,048.71
Add: Other Income		7,740,189.32
Profit for Year 1935		$ 19,618,238.03

APPENDIX

THE GOODYEAR TIRE AND RUBBER COMPANY

Included as a Current Asset on the Consolidated Balance Sheet, December 31, 1925, was the following item:

Inventories, at cost or market, whichever is lower.... $15,883,470.47

Included on the Liability side of the same balance sheet under Reserves was the following item:

Special raw material reserve .... $ 7,500,000.00

PROFIT AND LOSS AND SURPLUS ACCOUNT
for the Year Ending December 31, 1925

Total Net Sales	$205,999,829.57
Net Sales of Akron	$169,470,112.10
Deduct: Manufacturing cost, selling, admin. and general expense and provision for Fed. income taxes	151,822,651.09
	$ 17,647,461.01
Add: Surplus net operating profits of subsidiary companies and foreign branches, and other income	8,637,211.03
Total Earnings before Interest and Other Charges	$ 26,284,672.04
Deduct: Interest charges	3,970,199.39
	$ 22,314,472.65
Deduct: Other Charges (proportion of discount on funded debt, etc., loss on properties liquidated)	1,308,573.81
Total Profits for Year	$ 21,005,898.84
Deduct: Special raw material reserve	7,500,000.00
Balance carried to Surplus account	$ 13,505,898.84
Add: Surplus December 31, 1924	22,798,576.51
	$ 36,304,475.35
Deduct: Dividends	5,655,156.00
Surplus at December 31, 1925	$ 30,649,319.35

THE GOODYEAR TIRE AND RUBBER COMPANY

Included under Current Assets on the Consolidated Balance Sheet, December 31, 1926, was the following item:

Inventories, at cost or market, whichever is lower.... $ 67,915,299.69

Included on the Liability side of the same balance sheet under Reserves was the following item:

Special raw material reserve .... $ 2,750,000.00

CONSOLIDATED PROFIT AND LOSS AND SURPLUS ACCOUNT
for the Year Ending December 31, 1926

Net Sales	$230,161,356.57
Deduct—Manufacturing cost and charges (including depreciation), selling, administrative and general expenses, and provision for Federal income taxes (*after charging excess cost of rubber and cotton to the net amount of $5,250,000 to special raw material reserve previously created therefor*)	215,240,427.87
	$ 14,920,928.70
Add—Other Income	1,517,961.78
Total Profits before Interest and Other Charges	$ 16,438,890.48
Deduct—Interest and other charges	6,336,297.14
Total Profits for Year	$ 10,102,593.34
Deduct—Profits of subsidiary companies applicable to stocks not held by The Goodyear Tire & Rubber Company	1,303,454.62
	$ 8,799,138.72
Add—Surplus December 31, 1925	30,649,319.35
	$ 39,448,458.07
Deduct—Dividends paid by The Goodyear Tire & Rubber Co.	8,743,444.00
Surplus at December 31, 1926	$ 30,705,014.07

APPENDIX

ENDICOTT JOHNSON CORPORATION

Excerpts from the November 30, 1936 Annual Report of the Endicott
Johnson Corporation:

1. FROM THE STATEMENT OF EARNED SURPLUS FOR THE YEAR
   Deductions
   Appropriation for reserve at December 1, 1935, in order to give effect to
   the normal stock method of inventory valuation $1,048,600
2. FROM THE STATEMENT OF PROFIT AND LOSS FOR THE YEAR
   Cost of Goods Sold (material, labor, direct and indirect manufacturing expense) including $111,286 transferred to reserve in order to give effect for
   the year to the normal stock method of inventory valuation.....$52,125,759
3. FROM THE BALANCE SHEET, NOVEMBER 30, 1936

Asset side

Current Assets
Inventories, on the basis of cost or market whichever is lower (See Note
(1), and reserve per contra):

Finished Footwear	$10,356,211	
Footwear in Process	924,207	
Raw Materials on hand and in transit	6,075,632	
Miscellaneous Supplies	915,840	$18,271,890

Liability side

Reserves
Reserve for reduction of normal inventories to fixed prices......$1,159,886
  (See Note (1))

Footnotes
NOTE (1): The inventories of the Corporation treated as normal and the
fixed prices to which they are reduced are as follows:

Fixed Prices

Hide value in (a) raw hides and hides in process
  (26,000,000 lbs.); (b) own upper leather
  (5,500,000 lbs.); (c) own sole leather
  (1,600,000 lbs.); and (d) upper leather in footwear
  (12,000,000 lbs.) .... 7 cents per lb.
Purchased upper leather (1,000,000 feet) .... 13 cents per ft.
Rubber, crude and in footwear (2,000,000 lbs.) ...... 5 cents per lb.

Inventories in excess of these normals remain on the basis of cost or market,
whichever is lower.

INVENTORY VALUATION—THE USE OF PRICE ADJUSTMENT ACCOUNTS TO SEGREGATE INVENTORY LOSSES AND GAINS *

By Clarence B. Nickerson

WITHIN recent years considerable interest has developed in problems of inventory valuation. In part this is due to a more widespread appreciation of the inherent difficulties in valuation and of the significant effects that differences in inventory valuation can have on stated assets and stated profits. However, it is probable that rising prices, with their concomitant inventory profits, and income tax considerations have been the major causes of this revival of interest.

There has been much discussion of the normal stock, last-in, first-out and inventory reserve methods and several companies have fairly recently joined the ranks with those who have used such methods for many years.

Suggested Method Compared with "Ideal" Standard Costs

In addition to the tax considerations there appears to be a growing conviction that during the upswing of prices and prosperity there should be in some manner a clarification of the sources of stated profits and provision for expected inventory losses. In this connection, it is of some interest to study methods used in Europe during the periods of inflation following the World War when companies wished to have a clearer understanding of the nature and sources of their profits. It is the purpose of this article to describe and comment upon one such method which involves the use of what amounts to "ideal" standard costs as practiced in the U. S. A., assuming that the standard costs are adjusted at frequent intervals in line with current costs. The method differs from our practice to some extent in technique, but the major difference lies in the treatment of the price adjustments or variations between actual and standard costs. In our country it appears to be common practice to close such variations to the cost of goods sold account

* From the *Bulletin* of October 1, 1937.

at the end of an accounting period and not to show them at all in the published financial statements. Under the method to be described it appeared to be common practice to carry forward from one accounting period to another the balances in the adjustment accounts with the result that credit balances were built up as prices rose, representing the reservation of inventory gains, and these were used to absorb losses as prices fell, leaving the stated profits or losses as clear of inflationary profits and losses as was practicable.

The use of replacement costs is one of the most important features of the method. Raw material enters production not at actual cost but at replacement cost. Goods completed are entered in the finished goods account at their replacement cost as of the time of completion. The cost of goods sold is taken to be their replacement cost as of the time of sale. Assuming that finished goods prices bear some relation to replacement costs, the resulting gross profit is considered to be the manufacturing gross profit. Losses and gains from price fluctuations are segregated in special accounts.

Recording Raw Material Entering Process

Material is entered in the raw material account at actual cost including freight and a charge for material overhead (purchasing, accounting and storing). It is credited out for production at its average cost and a corresponding debit is made to a raw material price fluctuations account. At the same time it is entered in a work-in-process account at its replacement cost, including a percentage for freight and material overhead, and a corresponding credit is made to the raw material price fluctuation account. This price fluctuation account thus absorbs the difference between the average cost of the material and its replacement cost at the time it enters production. Though the use of replacement cost is a fundamental concept, as a practical matter minor fluctuations in the market are ignored. A list of standard prices is prepared for all materials corresponding to the frequently adjusted or "ideal" standard costs used in the United States. This list is in effect a list of current market prices standardized to the extent of avoiding minor fluctuations of the market. When market prices have deviated sufficiently from the standard prices a new list of standard prices has to be made which subsequently is followed until it is time to make a new list of standard prices again.

In addition to raw material at replacement cost the work-in-process account is charged for actual labor expended, and either actual overhead or overhead absorbed through standard burden rates, depending upon the cost accounting system in use.

Accounting for Goods Completed

Goods completed are credited out of the work-in-process account at an amount determined by the cost accounting records which represents a proper share of the material, labor and overhead charged to that account. A corresponding debit is made to a work-in-process price fluctuations account. At the same time they are entered in a finished goods account at their replacement cost as of the time of completion and a corresponding credit is made to the work-in-process price fluctuations account. This price fluctuation account thus absorbs the difference between the costs charged to goods during their production and their replacement cost at the time of completion. Practice varies as to whether replacement cost is computed at this point for material alone or for all of the elements of cost, that is, for material, labor and overhead. In either case, use is made of lists of standard prices as described for raw material above.

Accounting for Cost of Sales

Goods sold are credited out of finished goods at the same price at which they entered that account. A corresponding debit is made to a finished goods price fluctuations account. They are entered in a cost of goods sold account at their replacement cost as of the time of sale and a corresponding credit is made to the finished goods price fluctuations account. This fluctuation account thus absorbs the difference between the cost of the goods as determined at the time of their completion and their replacement cost at the time of sale.

Practice likewise varies here as to whether replacement cost is computed for material alone or for material, labor and overhead. In some cases replacement cost is figured at this point for material, labor and overhead even though computed for material alone at the time goods enter the finished goods account.

Treatment of Balances of Price Adjustment Accounts

The information received regarding the method did not indicate a uniform treatment of the balances remaining in the price adjustment accounts. It appears to be left to the discretion of the management as to whether they are to remain in the books or be closed entirely or in part to the profit and loss account. It is known that in one company balances were allowed to accumulate in these accounts when prices were rising, which enabled them to absorb losses when prices fell without bringing either the gains or the losses into the stated profits.

Since the method requires the use of additional accounts and the calculation of replacement cost for goods in their various stages, it would appear to be more costly to operate than ordinary methods. The only information received on this point is that in one company the method was adopted without any increase in the personnel.

Possible Simplification

The method could be simplified and used in connection with the valuation of inventories at the lower of cost or market. The following suggestions indicate how this could be done.

Only one price fluctuation account need be used, namely, that for finished goods. Inventories of raw material, work-in-process and finished goods should be valued at the lower of cost or market at the close of the period and the adjustments, if any, necessary to bring them from cost to market should be carried directly to the profit and loss account. Raw material used should be transferred to the work-in-process account at actual cost (the actual cost for any material on hand at the beginning of the period being the lower of cost or market at that time).

So too, goods completed should be transferred from work-in-process to the finished goods account at actual cost. The actual cost of goods should then be transferred from the finished goods account to the finished goods price fluctuations account. The latter account should then be credited for the replacement cost of the goods sold, and the cost of goods sold account should be debited for the same amount.[1] The balance in the finished goods price fluctuations account should then be closed to the profit and loss account. The exact method of closing the cost of goods sold and sales accounts will depend upon the particular practice of the given company; suffice it to state here that eventually the gross margin based on reproduction cost will be brought into the profit and loss account.

---

[1] Replacement cost is meant here to consist of the replacement cost of material, the actual cost of labor, and burden absorbed.

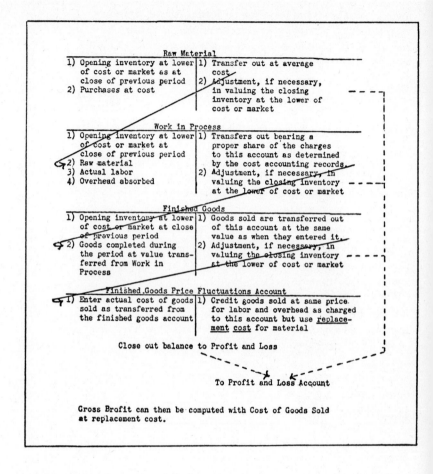

Method Illustrated

This method would have substantially the same advantage as the method described in the case and would be much simpler to operate. Typical accounts and pro forma profit and loss statements are presented above and on the opposite page.

These profit and loss statements are over-simplified but they do indicate that under the proposal the reader would be given a more definite picture of the nature and sources of the net operating profit. Essentially the proposal is simply an adaptation of standard costs

A.   CONDENSED PRO FORMA PROFIT AND LOSS STATEMENT
                UNDER CONDITIONS OF RISING PRICES
          (*Assuming actual cost of goods sold to be* $335,000)

Net Sales		$500,000
Cost of Goods Sold (Material at replacement cost).......		350,000
Gross Profit		$150,000
Administrative Expense	$25,000	
Selling Expense	70,000	95,000
		$ 55,000
Burden Over Absorbed		5,000
Profit from Rising Prices (representing inventory profit as measured by the difference between the actual cost and replacement cost of material in goods sold)......		15,000
Net Operating Profit		$ 75,000

B. Under present practice a condensed statement for the same period would appear as follows (Cost of Goods Sold being at actual cost less burden over-absorbed):

Net Sales		$500,000
Cost of Goods Sold		330,000
Gross Profit		$170,000
Administrative Expense	$25,000	
Selling Expense	70,000	95,000
Net Operating Profit		$ 75,000

C.   CONDENSED PRO FORMA PROFIT AND LOSS STATEMENT
                UNDER CONDITIONS OF FALLING PRICES
          (*Assuming actual cost of goods sold to be* $350,000)

Net Sales		$500,000
Cost of Goods Sold (Material at replacement cost).......		335,000
Gross Profit		$165,000
Administrative Expense	$25,000	
Selling Expense	70,000	95,000
		$ 70,000
Burden Un-absorbed	$ 5,000	
Loss from Falling Prices (representing inventory loss as measured by the difference between the actual cost and replacement cost of material in goods sold)..........	15,000	
Inventory Adjustment (representing the loss taken by writing down inventories on hand to replacement cost)	5,000	25,000
Net Operating Profit		$ 45,000

D. Under present practice a condensed statement for the same period would appear as follows (cost of goods sold being the actual cost of $350,000; plus the inventory write-down of $5,000 under valuation at the lower of cost or market; plus the burden unabsorbed of $5,000):

Net Sales		$500,000
Cost of Goods Sold		360,000
Gross Profit		$140,000
Administrative Expense	$25,000	
Selling Expense	70,000	95,000
Net Operating Profit		$ 45,000

carried into the financial records and statements. Having established the amount of the inventory gain, and given full disclosure to this important item, all or such part of it as the management deemed advisable, could be reserved to cover inventory losses realized in the future and given equally full disclosure. As far as net profits available for dividends or justifiably subject to taxation are concerned, the result could be just the same as under the normal stock method and the last-in, first-out method. The method would differ from these methods, however, in that the reserve would be stated instead of hidden; the inventories would be carried at their debt paying ability (cost or market, whichever is lower) rather than in large part at low fixed prices; and full disclosure would be given to inventory gains and losses instead of eliminating from the financial statements the price gains and losses on the normal stock.

Conclusion

The methods illustrated are not panaceas, but they have been presented in the hope that they may stimulate further thought and discussion on the problems of inventory valuation. The technique is not of paramount importance. Regardless of any given method of accounting the growing recognition of the ephemeral character of inventory profits and the desire to make provision for inventory losses are healthy signs. Certainly traditional practice can be improved, first, by the clarification of stated profit so that among other things stockholders and management will know to what extent the profit has been affected by inventory gains and losses, and second, by more careful consideration and provision of inventory reserves during periods of rising prices to protect surplus from the inevitable losses when prices fall.

Traditional practice has been based on a short-run view of profits and has been dominated by balance sheet considerations. The normal stock method involves a long range viewpoint of profit and in its extreme form makes the balance sheet subservient to the statement of profit and loss. Some companies have adopted methods which improve traditional practice and include certain of the desirable features of the normal stock method. The extension of standard costs to the financial records and statements along the lines suggested in the present article offers possibilities in this direction.

PART III

INVENTORY TAKING

METHODS OF PLANNING AND TAKING
INVENTORIES *

By Samuel J. Broad

TAKING the inventory is one of the necessary evils of corporate and business procedure. It disorganizes the routine, it adds to the expenses and, when it is all over, the enterprise is no better off financially than it was before.

In the cases in which there is an investment by stockholders or creditors who have no part in management, it is, however, one of the responsibilities of management periodically to make an accounting for its stewardship, to report to the investors how the business stands and what progress it has made during the period.

Importance of Inventory to Profit Determination

The inventory is recognized today as an important element in such an accounting by an industrial or trading enterprise. It is of much greater importance relatively in determining the net income for the year than it is in determining the balance sheet position. An error of 5 per cent in the total of the inventory may not be of major importance in reference to the current position or the net worth of an enterprise, but when we come to the income account, such an error may easily result in cutting the profits in half or in doubling them. This will readily be seen if we bear in mind that the amount of the inventory is, in effect, a credit to, or an addition to, the net income for the year and that when we are dealing with the net income we are usually dealing with a figure very much smaller than the figures which appear on the balance sheet. The relative importance of a discrepancy is thus very greatly increased.

The value of an investment in an enterprise today is measured to a large extent by what the enterprise will earn over a period of years. An enterprise which cannot earn money has little value other than what can be realized in liquidation; whereas, one which

* A part of an address by Mr. Broad delivered before the New York Chapter in 1940. The balance of Mr. Broad's address will be found in the section on Inventory Valuation, starting on page 184.

makes profits may have a value substantially greater than that reflected by its balance sheet. It has been stated that "a fair determination of income for successive accounting periods is ordinarily the most important single purpose of the general accounting report of a corporation." In view of its effect on the income, the importance of a carefully taken and reasonably accurate inventory cannot be over-emphasized.

Physical and Perpetual Inventories

Generally speaking, there are two methods of determining the amount of the inventory: one is to rely entirely upon a physical inventory taken periodically; the other method, which is being used increasingly in well organized enterprises, especially the larger ones, is to determine the inventory by means of book records which are currently maintained and show under various classifications the amount of inventory which should be present in the absence of errors and irregularities—in other words, perpetual inventory records. However, perpetual inventory records, due to the possibility of errors and irregularities, require confirmation from time to time by comparison, in whole or in part, with actual stock on hand. It is considered good practice today, where reliance is placed primarily upon perpetual inventory records, to confirm their reliability and accuracy by making a comparison of book records with stock on hand for all portions of the inventory at least once a year. This does not necessarily mean that the physical inventory should be taken all as of one date. For years past some concerns have made it their practice to "stagger" the comparison in such a manner that certain items are checked from month to month or from quarter to quarter throughout the year, the whole inventory being covered at least once during a twelve-month cycle. The adoption of such a practice is, I believe, becoming more common and it is one which should be encouraged, even in the case of those organizations which desire, in addition, to take a complete inventory at a specified date. It adds to the measure of reliance which may be placed on book inventories at interim dates and reduces year-end adjustments to a minimum.

A continuous check of this type soon develops a pattern or measure of approximately what differences may be expected. An effort is usually made to determine the cause of major discrepancies; experience has shown that sometimes the records are at fault and sometimes the physical count. If experience shows, generally speaking, that divergences are small and that the perpetual inventory records are substantially accurate, I think one is justified in regarding the book inventory as being the primary inventory and in regarding the taking of a physical inventory largely as a procedure to be undertaken for the purpose of checking, supporting and periodically adjusting the book inventory. Where we have a carefully kept and controlled perpetual inventory maintained by employees who otherwise have no interest in the operations of the business—an inventory the accuracy of which is periodically being substantiated by other employees who undertake the stocktaking—we have two strong links in the chain of evidence. If the links are strongly welded by adequate control and efficient methods, they give strong support to the credibility and substantial accuracy of the inventory reported.

Increased Attention to Verification in Recent Years

It is said that there is nothing new under the sun. I think this applies to a large extent to inventory procedures. This does not mean that old methods cannot be, or are not being, improved. There is a constant development and improvement in methods of application, and a continually increasing adoption of improved methods throughout business as a whole.

But while there may not, perhaps, have been much change in method, there has, during the last two or three years, been a change in the points of emphasis on particular features of the work. Some things which were considered desirable procedure are now considered essentials. A desire for additional safeguards to ensure that a careful and honest inventory has been taken has increased the emphasis on control over the various procedures, and on the relative independence and disinterestedness of those who may undertake the various operations. Methods of internal check and control which have heretofore been emphasized to a greater extent in connection with transactions involving the handling of cash have been applied more extensively to operations affecting the control and the taking of inventories.

Organization

Inventory-taking is a tedious and often thankless task. It requires good organization to keep to a minimum disturbance of plant operations with its attendant loss of production, and to avoid duplication of effort, delays due to bottlenecks, and disorganization.

A cardinal feature of adequately planned and controlled inventory-taking is complete written instructions. These will vary so widely in content and phraseology that a pro-forma set would be of limited usefulness. It will be more helpful to outline instead the topics which should be covered, to serve as a sort of check list with which any particular draft of instructions may be compared. The wording and the precise arrangements must be such as to fit each individual case.

The personnel for the taking of the inventory should be thoroughly organized. Individual persons should be appointed for specific duties in prescribed areas. This should be arranged so that, (1) there shall be no division of responsibility and each person shall know to whom he is to report, and (2) no one shall be placed in sole charge of reporting the inventory of stock normally in his custody during the regular operations of the business; for instance, a stock room clerk responsible for certain materials should not be in a position to report, without independent check, the physical count of his own stock.

Plans should be worked out to have available a sufficient number of men to complete the physical count at all locations within approximately the same time, usually one day. The men should be divided into squads of two or more, and there should be separate squads for (1) counting, and (2) checking counts. The provision for checking counts may be either such as to completely duplicate the initial count or such as to confine the recounts to tests of selected items.

Whether the initial count is completely duplicated or tested is ordinarily determined by the conditions. In the case of valuable merchandise, a complete duplicate count is probably desirable. But where the inventory is made up of a great number of comparatively small items, a test may be all that is required and if the test proves that the work has been carefully performed, it may be unnecessary to go further.

In addition, in an extensive inventory one or more squads of men should be available as mobile squads who can be sent to assist in spots where unforeseen difficulties have arisen or where the progress of the count is falling behind schedule.

A time table, either formal or informal, should be worked out according to which the progress of the count is expected to proceed. The time table should set deadlines for the completion of the respective parts of the program, and the turning in of lists, schedules, reports or tags.

Use of Tags

Usually the count will be taken by means of tags to be affixed to each lot of goods. Due to ease of use in checking and assembling, this method is usually more efficient and flexible than the use of sheets or lists, although not invariably so. It is important that all tags and sheets be serially numbered in advance and be issued in blocks for use under control by number so that all shall be accounted for. It is preferable that the tags be uniform in size to facilitate handling. Sometimes tags are used of a size and type which can be adapted later for tabulating purposes.

It is also preferable that differently colored tags be used for the various classifications of the inventory, namely, raw materials, parts, finished products, work-in-process, supplies, etc. Where stock is slow-moving so that articles on hand at the end of one year may still be on hand at the end of the next, it may be well to change colors from year to year. The classification of the inventory should include provision for goods which are not to be included in the inventory, when this condition exists, in order that there shall be no exception to the general rule that everything must be counted. Sometimes a different color is also used for slow-moving stock and, if so, it should be determined in advance who is to be responsible for deciding what stock is to be so classified.

Another advantage of the use of tags over sheets or lists is that a perforated portion of the tag is usually left attached to the stock on which the more important information, such as description and quantity, is also shown. It has sometimes been found effective to have the foreman of each department, after the completion of the inventory, make a tour of his department and undertake a visual check for substantial errors in quantities and descriptions. The

attaching of tags also permits a final quick review after completion
to assure, first, that all stock has been tagged and thus included in
the inventory, and, second, that no stock other than inventoriable
items has been included.

Other Considerations

The inventory instructions should be planned and written far
enough in advance so that sufficient preparation can be made for
instructing the personnel and for obtaining the necessary supplies.
The length of time in advance will be determined by the requirements. It should be sufficient to enable the holding of a meeting
or two of those who will be in charge of the work, so as to guard
against misunderstanding, duplication of effort or division of responsibility, and so as to promote the highest possible degree of
co-operation, upon which will depend the smoothness and accuracy
with which the inventory is taken.

It is part of good organization to require each individual to take
responsibility for the work which he has performed and also to
provide for means of checking him up if necessary. Thus, it is
desirable that each individual undertaking a particular operation,
such as listing or checking or pricing, should signify his responsibility by initialing for the work he has done.

Frequently it is possible to prepare in advance the writing of the
descriptive legend which must appear on the tags. For example,
in the case of a stockroom for parts or finished products, it is known
that at least one tag will be required for each kind of article; hence
it is possible to prepare tags in advance from stock records in
readiness for the insertion of quantity, etc. The same can be done
for work in process by adopting the practice some time in advance
of including among the tickets which usually accompany an order
through the shop, a suitable inventory tag available for use wherever
the order may be at the time of the physical count. Any tags returned because the job is finished before the date of the inventory
can, of course, be voided.

Inventory Cut-Off

A vitally important part of the inventory procedure is to provide
for proper co-ordination of the inventory with the books of account.

Half a dozen purchase invoices covering goods included in the inventory, if unentered, may make more difference in the final result than all the errors which are likely to creep into the actual stock-taking. Thus, it is customary for the receipt and movement of goods to cease during the inventory-taking and for a sharp cut-off to be made so that all goods received before the effective time of taking the inventory are included in the inventory and the liability set up, and so that all goods received subsequently are excluded. The same precautions are necessary with reference to sales shipments, returned goods received, purchases to be returned and inter-departmental or inter-plant transfers. The same need for proper co-ordination with the records applies to the stock records with which the inventory is to be compared. The usual procedures in this respect are so well understood that I need do no more than stress their relative importance. In the added stress now being placed on the actual counting, weighing or measuring of quantities, it would be unfortunate if we minimized the importance of these accounting requirements.

Determination of Prices

Where there is an extensive inventory, the determination of prices also requires advance planning and preparation. To the extent practicable, price lists, quotation sheets and cost figures should be prepared and supplied to those who are responsible for inserting the prices and to those who are responsible for checking prices thus inserted.

Here again the use of tags, particularly tabulating cards, may speed up the work as they make possible an arrangement or sorting of the cards by articles, groups of articles or departments.

PLANNING FOR THE PHYSICAL INVENTORY *

By Stanley G. H. Fitch

BECAUSE of the extra and overtime work involved and the necessary interruption of regular factory and office routine, inventories have always been regarded with mingled feelings of dread and dismay by the bookkeeping department, the storeskeepers, the factory accountants, and others concerned in the work of taking, pricing and figuring. With the more general use of perpetual inventory records, the disruption in business routine arising from annual or periodical physical inventories has to some extent been relieved. However, at some time or other, in practically every industrial and mercantile business, an actual count of stock must be made. Consequently, it behooves us as interested parties to consider carefully whatever steps may be taken to facilitate inventory taking, thereby saving time, eliminating interruptions in business routine, and enhancing the value of the inventory record by virtue of speed and accuracy in completing the job.

In theory the problem of taking inventory may be regarded as the same in every business. Practically every business has a problem of its own, arising from the nature of the merchandise or materials handled. It is difficult, therefore, to treat the subject before us in general terms. Accordingly, as a typical case, a large machinery manufacturing plant, operating its own foundry in which many of the ordinary inventory problems are met, has been selected as a basis for discussion. Reference will be made also to other industries, such as soap manufacturing, tanning, shoe manufacturing, cotton textiles and the department store, all of which present questions peculiar to their own inventory taking.

This paper will not take up a discussion of the problem of inventory pricing. It is intended here to outline the procedure for obtaining an accurate physical count or measurement which may be used for subsequent valuation.

* From the *Bulletin* of January 15, 1927.

When to Take Inventory

Annual inventories are generally taken as of the close of a fiscal year. Similar inventories are frequently taken semi-annually, quarterly or monthly. The annual inventory, however, is usually more thorough and accurate than other periodical inventories because upon it rests in large measure the accuracy of the annual profit and loss statement and the balance sheet. It is an axiom that the close of a fiscal year should coincide with the completion of the annual cycle. At such times stocks should be at the lowest levels consistent with sound business judgment, so that the task of taking inventory may be reduced to the minimum.

Avoidance of Plant Shut-Downs

In order to obtain an accurate count of stock, it is sometimes regarded as necessary to shut down the plant for a period of from a day to a week or more. Except in the case of a seasonal business in which an annual shutdown results from lack of orders, such a procedure should be avoided, if possible, because of the interruption in output and the dissatisfaction felt by the employees at an enforced lay-off. Frequently a Sunday and a holiday can be utilized to eliminate or minimize a shutdown.

If it is essential to complete a large inventory in a limited time, a considerable number of people must be assigned for that purpose. It is, however, often difficult to find enough people acquainted with the nature and location of the stock to do an intelligent job. Accordingly, if the time factor may be disregarded, the stock-taking period may conveniently cover from two or three days to a month prior to the actual inventory date, as more fully described later in this paper.

Physical Inventory Facilitated by Perpetual Inventory Records

Where perpetual inventory records are in use it is customary throughout the year to make systematic counts of stock on hand and comparisons with inventory balances as to quantities, followed by necessary adjustments for errors found. The proof of total values shown by the perpetual inventory records with the inventory controlling accounts, however, is usually made only at the close of the fiscal year when a complete physical inventory is taken. Further checks upon perpetual inventory balances are made when the various materials or lots become exhausted or reach their stock minimum or order points. Consequently, the annual inventory under such conditions becomes a repetition of routine procedure; unusual discrepancies in stock should be rare; and the inventory should approach the goal of absolute accuracy always sought, but practically never reached.

Storeroom House Cleaning

The orderly arrangement of materials and supplies in the storeroom, warehouse or yard will greatly facilitate the inventory taking. The inevitable accumulation of scrap or waste should, if possible, be sold except in cases where such material is to be put into process again, as in the case of cast iron scrap which should be collected from the machine shop and delivered to the iron foundry where it comprises one of the items of raw material. Parts known to be obsolete or unsalable should be scrapped and removed from the storeroom for final disposition.

Boxes, kegs, bags, bales, or other original packages should be stacked in rows or piles so that by counting the number of units in the width, depth and height of the pile the total can be obtained by quick multiplication, thus avoiding a laborious count of every package.

Materials received shortly before the actual counting of stock begins should be held in a separate part of the receiving room and should not be mingled with the materials in the storeroom. Such materials should be listed separately for inclusion in the inventory.

Inventories of bulk materials stored out of doors, such as coal, coke, sand and pig and scrap iron, are based on surveys and measurements and the quantities so ascertained should be compared with perpetual inventory balances. If such materials are stored so that the piles can be identified with specific carloads, the preliminary work can include the complete checking of the quantities, subject only to adjustments to actual inventory date. The inventory of lumber can be quickly taken if the lumber is piled in tiers and a tally kept of the board feet in each tier, and the tiers numbered or otherwise marked for identification and record on the perpetual inventory. It is then necessary only to check off the unbroken tiers and to tally the lumber in the partly used tiers. If conditions permit, each carload should be piled separately and identified in the perpetual inventory.

Other time-saving short cuts for stock taking might be cited, but the foregoing are sufficient to emphasize the importance of orderly arrangement as a preliminary to the actual counting, weighing or measuring of the materials.

Schedules and Instructions for Physical Inventory

The custody and physical control of inventories is usually vested in the chief operating official (e.g., works manager or superintendent) with a general storeskeeper directly in charge. The accounting control is exercised by the chief accounting official (e.g., chief accountant or controller). Obviously, plans for inventory taking should be worked out by those officials in co-operation, since they both have a stake in proving the correctness of the inventory total. A plan of the plant should be made, if not already available, showing the location of every department where inventory is to be taken. For this purpose an elaborate plan is not needed; a rough diagram will do for practical purposes. A schedule should then be prepared showing the departments, the nature and extent of the stock in each (e.g., in the storeroom, the approximate number of items carried in stock), the number of people to be assigned to take each departmental inventory, the estimated number of days allowed for the job, and the date on which the actual counting in each department is to begin. It may be remarked in passing that a record should be kept of the time required for inventorying each department and a later comparison made with the scheduled estimates. Discrepancies might indicate excessive time consumed due to poor arrangement of stores or work in process, which should be reported for improvement before the next inventory date.

Supplementing and accompanying the inventory schedule should be found inventory instructions from the controller or works manager, embodying general directions governing the use of inventory sheets and inventory tags or cards, and specific directions for inventorying and reporting upon certain materials which require special consideration, such as obsolete or slow-moving materials, repair parts carried for discontinued lines, excessive stocks of materials, materials held on consignment, etc. The inventory instructions may properly invite recommendations for changes in maximum and minimum stores quantities, based on experience as recorded on the bin cards or perpetual inventory records or on changes in design of product. In other words, inventory time provides an opportunity to study and improve methods of keeping, handling and accounting for materials, supplies, work in process and finished product; and this can readily be done without waste or duplication of effort, if advance notice is given that information along that line will be wanted after the actual taking and listing of the inventory has been completed.

Inventory Tags and Inventory Sheets Prepared in Advance

Inventory tags or cards, serially numbered, should be prepared as far in advance as possible for all items in the inventory, showing bin number, piece number, if any, and description of material or part. If the actual count is to be made in advance of the inventory date, provision should be made on the tag for recording the quantity counted and subsequent receipts and deliveries to inventory date. All tags issued should be charged to the respective departments and any unused tags should be returned.

TAKING THE INVENTORY

The actual counting, weighing or measuring of the materials and supplies, work in process and finished product on hand in the various storerooms and manufacturing departments should be started according to the inventory schedule. As the work progresses the quantities should be recorded on the inventory tags which should be attached to each bin or lot. Each section of the storeroom, shop or warehouse should be carefully surveyed before leaving the work to make sure that every item or lot has been properly tagged.

Inventory sheets should be prepared in advance for all regular stock material, showing location, bin number, piece number and brief description, so that when the inventory is listed only the quantities remain to be recorded. The listing of the inventory is usually done by stock-takers working in pairs, which may comprise one man from the stores department and one from the accounting department. The latter will usually test the quantities as the listing proceeds, and lift the tags as he calls the quantities to his partner who records them on the inventory sheets previously prepared. The tags subsequently should be compared with the perpetual inventory records and any differences in the balances should be promptly investigated and adjusted. Such a check will disclose errors in physical count or discrepancies in the perpetual inventory record arising from unrecorded receipts and deliveries or careless clerical work. If no tests of the count are required the listing can proceed more rapidly. In fact, it may be found convenient to lift the tags without listing where the material is located and to transfer that work to the office. Both tags and inventory sheets should be planned to facilitate tabulation of inventory items according to the three basic calculations, i.e., raw materials, work in process and finished product, with further subdivision according to established accounting control.

If the conditions under which the inventory is to be taken require a complete check, either by the company's internal auditor or by an independent firm of accountants or engineers, the inventory tags should carry a coupon numbered like the tag on which the description and quantity should also be recorded. After completion of the count and the testing thereof, the coupons should be lifted by the representative of the auditor while the tags should be used by the stores department as already described for writing up the inventory. After pricing and figuring, the inventory sheets should be turned over to the auditors for comparison with the tag stubs as a precaution against the inclusion of quantities other than those shown by actual count.

Work in Process

The inventory of work in process presents some difficulties not encountered with raw materials and finished product. If the plant is to be shut down for inventory, it will be possible to complete many, if not all, of the small parts on orders in process and transfer them to the assembly floors or storeroom. Otherwise, many hundreds or thousands of unfinished machine parts will have to be counted and listed in a partly finished condition, with an accurate description of the extent of the work thereon. Where the manufacturing operations are effectively controlled by production orders, the orders in process should be listed by the cost department and used as a basis for the identification and checking of the work in process.

In the average foundry the work in process will give little trouble. After the day's heat has been poured there will remain little in process except in the case of moulds for very large castings requiring more than one day for completion. These may be inventoried as work in process on the basis of actual moulding labor and overhead expense applicable thereto. Castings in the cleaning room may be taken as finished castings with an allowance for cost of cleaning.

As already stated, the metal-working foundry and industries were selected as presenting many of the typical inventory problems found in various industries. A few illustrations from other industries, such as soap manufacturing, tanning, shoe manufacturing, textile manufacturing and the department store, will now be given, as they present further specific inventory questions which should be considered.

Specific Illustrations

Soap Manufacturing

In soap manufacturing, which may be taken as typical of the group of chemical industries, bulk raw materials comprising fats and oils are stored in large tanks. To inventory such materials it is necessary only to record the tank levels and to translate the figures into quantities by the use of constants.

Soap in process is found chiefly in kettles, storage tanks and mixers. In order to obtain results approaching uniformity, it is necessary to take the contents of soap kettles after boiling and settling for a stated time. At the same time a sample of the kettle stock is drawn and submitted to the laboratory for analysis as to soap content and the percentage reported is used in computing the quantity of soap in the kettle.

As it is not practicable to inventory all kettles at the same time, care must be used in taking the soap in the storage tanks and mixers not to duplicate any soap already inventoried as in process in the kettles. This can usually be accomplished by following the accounts for the respective kettles stocked.

Tanning—Upper Leather

At the time of purchase hides are identified by lot numbers which are recorded in an inventory record or lot book showing the weights and numbers of hides billed. Hides are received in bundles, two or three per bundle, but the bundles are not usually broken until the hides are put into process. At that time they are counted and checked with the number shown by the lot book. Up to that point the units are weight and quantity. The *hides* are then cut down the back and become *sides* and the lot number is stamped on each side. The sides are then put into soak and during the subsequent processes of unhairing, splitting, tanning, etc., the *side* remains the unit of count. When the tanning processes are completed the unit of measurement for the leather becomes the square foot.

If the inventory is to be taken without shutting down, the sides in process present a difficult problem. The soaking process takes from two days in the paddle wheels—sulphide process—to six days in the pits—lime process—and obviously the sides could not well be withdrawn for counting and put back in the pits. All lots put into soak to remain there over the inventory date should be counted and recorded for inventory and any sides taken out of soak should be counted and checked for inventory at that point. In inventorying sides in subsequent stages of the tanning process, care should be taken to see that no duplication results from counting a second time, sides that have already been taken and included in the inventory earlier in the tanning process.

The tanned sides, i.e. leather, will be found stacked on trucks, horses and racks. Wherever possible the leather should be sorted and piled by lot numbers, as that preliminary work will greatly facilitate the counting and listing. Numerous lots are put through together, however, so that as a practical matter the sorting by lot numbers may not be possible. Furthermore, some difficulty in identifying the skins always arises from loss of lot numbers in buffing, tacking and staking, and there is an actual loss of sides in liming, etc., so that it rarely is possible to tie up the inventory count with the balances called for by the lot book. With allowance for losses, gained by experience, variations should not be large.

Shoe Manufacturing

Shoe factory inventories are usually taken at the end of a seasonal run, either spring or fall, or both, when it may be convenient to shut down. Under such conditions there will be no work in process, as all orders will have been completed prior to shutting down. Raw materials, supplies and finished goods can readily be taken in the usual procedure. When a shutdown is undesirable, owing to manufacturing activity, an accurate inventory can be taken provided an adequate force is used and plans are laid in advance for avoidance of delay in the work. In each of the manufacturing departments, viz., cutting, stitching, lasting, making, finishing and packing, a day or two before inventory date all materials, findings and supplies should be arranged conveniently for quick counting, the quantities listed on inventory slips and any changes noted up to the close of business on the inventory date. Shoes in process should be listed in each department according to tag number with a description of the stage of manufacture reached, as this provides a basis for subsequent pricing according to cost sheets for the respective styles of shoes.

Under conditions where a partial shutdown is permissible, a third method of inventory is sometimes used. After the cutting room has completed the work on the last day-sheet for the old run, it will shut down for a day or two. The stitching room will follow suit after completing the work on all the old run orders received from the cutting room. This procedure will be followed in successive departments until, say, two or three weeks after the cutting room shutdown, all old run shoes will have been completed and either inventoried as finished goods or accounted for as sales as of the close of the old run. In the meantime, the cutting room will have started up again and the new run goods will be coming through the factory, but behind the last of the old run. In order to make a correct accounting for inventory under this method, all labor and expense accrued against the old run goods subsequent to the closing date must be taken up as a liability as of that date and must be accounted for separately from similar expenditures on the new run shoes.

Cotton Mill

The inventory of raw materials and finished product in a textile mill presents no unusual features. With respect to work in process, however, it is advisable, wherever possible, to close down the mill at inventory time, as it is very difficult to take an accurate process inventory while the materials are constantly moving from one department to another.

Employees charged with the responsibility of taking the inventory should be instructed in advance to leave the materials in their respective departments in as orderly a manner as possible at the time of closing for inventory purposes and should be cautioned against moving material from one department to another after the work of taking the inventory has started and remains in progress. Piece goods in finished goods department should be arranged in orderly fashion on tables and racks.

Departmental tests to establish unit weights may be made in advance of the inventory taking, as, for example, in the card room, the average weight of laps and of sliver in cans; in the speeding department, the average weight of roving on bobbins; in the spining department, the average weight of yarn on bobbins; in the spooling department, the average weight of yarn on spools. Such data, ascertained in advance, will facilitate the completion of the inventory when the actual count and weight of materials in process is taken.

In the spinning department, in taking the actual count of bobbins in creels, the bobbin capacity of the spinning frames is used, the bobbins being regarded as half full; and similarly for yarn on bobbins, the spindle capacity of the frames is used, the bobbins again being regarded as half full.

On the looms in the weave room will be found both process material and cloth, i.e., filling yarn and warp beams on one side and cloth on the other. The filling at the looms may be ascertained from the number of looms in operation, the average number of bobbins per loom and the weight of filling yarn per bobbin.

When warp beams are set in looms they are considered as being in the weaving process. A beam consists of a certain number of cuts, each cut representing a fixed yardage and having a standard weight per cut which varies with the kind of fabric. Each beam has a ticket attached showing the quality, yardage, cuts, etc. A strip of tickets for the operator is attached to the loom, each ticket representing one cut of material. As each cut is taken from the loom in the form of cloth a ticket is torn from the strip and sent to the weave room office by the operator. The clerk in the weave room office posts it up against the particular loom on the weave room sheets and deducts it from the original number of cuts charged against the loom when the warp was put on. These sheets will show at all times the number of cuts in process. However, the cuts in process are not all in warp, as almost invariably each loom will have some cloth on it (i.e., it has passed the weaving operation); and, inasmuch as the cloth has both warp and yarn filler, it has to be deducted from the warp cuts remaining in process and valued as cloth in looms. An estimate of one-third cut per loom is made for cloth. The warp inventory in process should be verified by checking from the weavers' tickets—attached to looms—to the weave room sheets in support of the number of cuts shown to be in process by this record.

In the weave room all quantities are expressed in pounds. Upon leaving the weave room the material is converted into yards.

Department Store

Owing to the variety of merchandise carried by a department store, its inventory involves an extraordinary amount of detailed work and presents some problems peculiar to the retail business. The procedure in taking a department store inventory is substantially as follows:

About four weeks before the inventory date, detailed written instructions as to the methods to be employed in counting, weighing or measuring merchandise are transmitted to the heads of the various departments and in turn are transmitted to the salespeople. All stock sheets and final inventory sheets are issued from the controller's or auditor's office as needed and charged to the various departments. All have to be accounted for whether used or not.

Upon receipt of the instructions, the work of counting, measuring and marking commences and continues until completed. This work is done by the salespeople in their own departments during the periods of the day when business is slack and, if necessary, after business hours, so that all of this work is completed at least one day before listing.

During the two or three days prior to the listing of the inventory on the final inventory sheets, the merchandise is listed on serially numbered stock sheets. A stock sheet is placed in each subdivision of every fixture and the contents of the respective subdivisions listed thereon. On the date the inventory is taken, the entries on the stock sheets are transcribed on the final sheets by the salespeople in each department. The items listed on the final inventory sheets are then checked by salespeople from other departments or by non-selling employees. Merchandise in the stock rooms and warehouses is usually listed in the same manner as merchandise on display in the selling departments.

The method of classifying merchandise by age, i. e., by seasons in which purchases were made, depends upon the system in force in this respect. Some stores assign a letter to each season, and this letter appears on the original tags or tickets attached to the articles in the marking rooms. When the merchandise is listed the season letter appears against each item, so that it is possible to classify the merchandise by seasons and determine the amount of slow-moving stock on hand in each department. Other stores use different colored final inventory sheets for listing the merchandise by age.

Care should be taken in checking furniture and other large articles to see that items sold and charged to customers, but undelivered, are not included in the inventory. The sold items are usually tagged with a special colored tag and can be readily identified, but items are also sold from floor samples and delivered from the reserve stock in the warehouse, and this is where errors may occur.

With regard to departments rented to outsiders, no action need be taken in respect to the inventory, as the store is not interested.

It is a policy of department stores nowadays to send electrical appliances and other merchandise to customers' homes on approval. Such articles remain the property of the store and should be included in the inventory, and can be verified by reference to the memo sales slips in the controller's office.

For some time before the inventory date, all merchandise received, except special orders and merchandise for special sales, etc., remains in the receiving room or marking rooms and is not considered as part of the inventory; nor is the liability therefor included as accounts payable. This is done primarily to enable the various departments, store and office, to bring all work up to date, and also to keep the inventory as low as possible, thereby reducing clerical work thereon.

Department stores, as a general rule, now value their merchandise inventories by the "retail method," a method which is recognized as sound and conservative for balance sheet purposes and is accepted by the United States Treasury Department as a basis for determining taxable income. It is therefore important to note that simultaneously with the listing of the articles they must be valued at the current retail price in order that a comparison may be made of physical and book inventories by departments to determine overages and shortages in merchandise.

UNIFORM PROCEDURE FOR PHYSICAL
INVENTORY TAKING*

By George V. Fortune

UNIFORMITY in the system and method by which an accounting problem is approached is one of the keys with which to obtain accuracy and speed in its solution. Industrial accountants and cost accountants often exert much wasted energy by failure to acquaint themselves with all the facts. They fail both to "make the plan" and "work the plan," and at the same time prepare the plan and the work so that the most inexperienced individual can follow it without excessive lost motion.

This paper deals with a plan for taking physical inventories, put into effect over a year ago. Because of its uniformity it has weathered three physical inventory periods to the satisfaction of top management, plant managers, plant accountants, cost accountants, and last but not least, the public accountants who physically inspect inventories and take an active part in the actual count.

The company whose procedure for taking physical inventories is reported here operates ten plants and has five subsidiary companies. Accounting control is vested in the treasurer of the corporation, with the systems and methods division operating as a staff function responsible to the treasurer. In conjunction with their other duties, internal field auditors police the carrying out of the prescribed systems and methods in co-operation with the systems department. The setup of productive facilities is such that the finished product of one plant may be the raw material of another.

Management's Responsibility

In the "Report of the Special Committee on Auditing Procedure" approved by the council of the American Institute of Accountants, May 9, 1939, the following statements appear:

Management itself has the direct responsibility for the maintenance of an adequate and effective system of accounts, for the proper recording of transactions in the books of account and for the safeguarding of the assets of a concern.

---

* A previously unpublished article.

Your committee is of the opinion that recognition should be given to the widespread demand for an extension of auditing procedure with regard to inventories and receivables. However, it should be noted that additional expense to business will be involved in the added procedures, and business concerns which do not have them undertaken must recognize the necessity of disclosure of their omission.

Canvass for yourself, if you will, and determine to what extent management and industrial accountants have given thought to the system, method and cost of taking adequate physical inventories prior to and even subsequent to this statement by a committee of the American Institute.

A simple questionnaire, embracing the following points, sent to operating plants within an industrial manufacturing concern will develop, it is safe to say, considerable evidence of lack of uniformity in method and procedure followed:

1. Methods employed for segregation of material prior to inventory.
2. Individuals having jurisdiction over actual physical count.
3. Résumé of methods used for listing inventoried material.
4. Résumé of basis used for determining quantities.
5. Résumé of methods used for control and accounting for materials issued during inventory period.
6. Résumé of methods used for control of materials in transit.
7. Résumé of methods used for:
    (a) Recording undistributed paid transportation charges.
    (b) Attesting to correctness of inventory.
    (c) Pricing inventories.
    (d) Adjusting inventories.
8. Disposition of inventory work sheets, cards, tally sheets, etc.
9. Résumé of method used for preparation of final inventory.
10. Copies of forms, work sheets, card or tally sheets used.

The standard practice instructions for the taking of the physical inventory presented on the following pages shows how one company has endeavored to overcome this lack of uniformity and provide for a standard procedure in all of its plants and subsidiaries.

STANDARD PRACTICE INSTRUCTIONS FOR PHYSICAL INVENTORY TAKING

1. Effective immediately, the following procedure shall govern inventorying at all plants and warehouses.

2. All classes of material and supplies—raw, in process, finished, second-hand and scrap—shall be inventoried as of .... All plant operations shall shut down from the beginning to the completion of the physical count and check.

3. *Inventory Assignments*

(a) Inventories shall be taken with assistance of operating and stores departments, under the immediate jurisdiction of plant managers and of accounting department representatives as designated by the treasurer.

(b) Inventory schedules for each plant and warehouse shall be prepared by the accounting department representatives, after consultation with operating and stores department officials and representatives, to show the following information:

| Division | Location or Department | Stock | To Be Taken By | | Starting Point | Date |
			Accounting Dept. Representative	Operating or Stores Dept. Representative		

(c) These schedules shall be approved by the operating executive of each plant and warehouse and shall be submitted on or before .... to the treasurer. Copies of approved inventory schedules shall be distributed to operating, stores and accounting department representatives or employees affected.

4. *Representation by Public Accountants*

The public accountants for the company will, at their discretion, have present at each location during the taking of the inventory a representative whose duty it will be to satisfy himself that inventory methods and procedure meet their requirements from an audit standpoint.

5. *Segregation of Material Prior to Inventory*

(a) To facilitate counting, weighing and measuring, arrangements shall be made with officials in charge to have material and supplies in process and finished goods at storerooms and at other points assembled and segregated by classes and kinds, and to have scrap material, rejected material, inferior material, etc., collected and stored at concentration points and surplus stocks returned to storerooms, wherever possible, not later than ....

(b) Prior to inventory, accounting department representatives in charge shall inspect stocks of material at all points under their jurisdiction. If material has not been properly arranged, they shall take the matter up personally with officials in charge and see to it that prompt remedial action is taken.

6. *Restriction of Material Issued During Inventory*

Under no circumstances without written approval of the plant manager shall materials of any description be drawn upon during the inventory period.

7. *Forms*

(a) Forms specified below shall be used in inventorying stock:

Form 1—"Inventory Ticket"—A separate color will be used for each inventory classification.

Form 2—"Aluminum Receiving Record."

Form 3—"Lead Record Card."

Form 4—"Tin Record Card."

Form 5—"Tally Sheet," for accumulating quantities of materials.

Form 6—"Inventory," for transcribing final inventory.

Form 7—"Recapitulation of Inventories by Account Classification."

(b) To expedite the work, Form 1 shall be prenumbered and quantities of prenumbered forms shall be allotted to each plant. Each plant must account for all numbered forms allotted to it and shall prepare Form 1 *in advance wherever possible and practical* for each item, class or sub-class of material and securely attach them to the material, arranged in order of physical location of the stock. *No quantities are to be shown until the date of physical count.*

(c) In cases where Forms 2, 3 and 4 are used to identify material or for physical inventory count, weight, etc., they shall be securely fastened to and supported by Form 1.

(d) In cases where Form 5 is used to accumulate quantities, the ticket number to be shown in the space marked "Ticket No." shall be the Form 1 number assigned to each lot that is accumulated on Form 5. In such cases, one controlling Form 1 shall be securely fastened and faced with the

ATTACH THIS END TO MATERIAL INVENTORIED

P. O. No._____

№ 10767

QUANTITY_____

ANNUAL INVENTORY 1940

IN PROCESS

P. O. No._____ № 10767

NAME OF ARTICLE

STOCK No.

SIZE	YIELD	GAUGE

DEPARTMENT				
QUANTITY	DO NOT WRITE BELOW THIS LINE			
		UNIT COST		INVENTORY
		PER		
INVENTORIED BY				
CHECKED BY				
EXTENDED BY				
EXTENSIONS CHECKED BY				
	ANNUAL INVENTORY 1940			

FORM 1

```
ALUMINUM RECEIVING RECORD

Tally No._____         Load No._____

Bundles}  In Load_____         Wt. (Lbs.)_____
Pigs    }
                                             Date
Car Int. & No._____    Rec'd_____

Shipper_____    Ex._____
                                   Date
Purity_____    Used_____
                                   Used
Furnace No._____    By_____
```

FORM 2

```
CAR TALLY SHEET NO._____

Lead Record Card No._____

Pigs in Pile_____ Lbs._____

Car No._____ Initial_____

Invoice_____ Received_____

Date Used_____ Furnace No._____

By Whom Used_____

              Stock Clerk_____
```

FORM 3

```
STRAITS
Tin Record Card No._____

Pigs in Pile_____ Lbs._____

Car No._____ Initial_____

Invoice_____ Received_____

Date Used_____ Furnace No._____

By Whom Used_____

              Stock Clerk_____
```

FORM 4

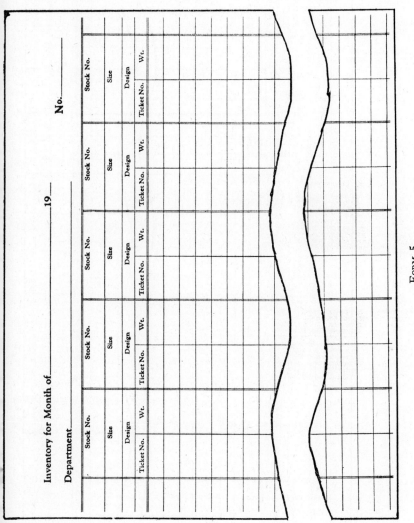

FORM 5

STOCK NO.	DESCRIPTION	SIZE	UNIT OF MEASURE	QUANTITY	VALUE		√
					UNIT PRICE	AMOUNT	

INVENTORY

SHEET NO.

PLANT   DEPT.   DATE   PAGE NO.

CLASSIFICATION   ACCOUNT NO.

CALLED BY   COUNT CHECKED BY

                   EXTENSIONS MADE BY   EXTENSIONS CHECKED BY

PRICE BY

19

FORM 6

RECAPITULATION OF INVENTORIES
by ACCOUNT CLASSIFICATION

PAGE NO. ....

PLANT _____ DEPARTMENT _____ DATE _____ 19__

Covering Detailed Work Sheets Identified As: _____

Account No.	Classification or Description	BOOK INVENTORY		PHYSICAL INVENTORY		OVER		SHORT	
		QUANTITY	VALUE	QUANTITY	VALUE	QUANTITY	VALUE	QUANTITY	VALUE

FORM 7

tally sheet to facilitate the pricing or further accumulation of accumulated quantities.

(e) In cases where it is impractical to price and transcribe to Form 6 each inventory ticket (as in process and finished goods), such inventory ticket shall serve as "physical count tickets" only. The quantities thereon shall be accumulated on Form 6 or appropriate work sheets designed by each plant in order to accommodate and accumulate the necessary breakdown for each item of material, labor, overhead, supplies, etc., into its respective element.

8. *Separate Inventories of Each Stock*

(a) Separate inventories shall be taken at each plant and warehouse of material in each department and at each point, except as may be specifically excluded upon the authority of the treasurer.

(b) Each inventory shall be subdivided to show account classification control pursuant to the uniform inventory account classification adopted and by:

> Raw Material
> In Process
> Finished
> Rejected Material
> Inferior Material
> Scrap Material

9. *Inventory Crews*

(a) Each inventory crew under the supervision of an accounting department representative shall be responsible for numbered copies of Form 1 issued to it and shall, upon actual count, measurement or weight of material, record such physical inventory of quantities on Form 1 in the space marked "Quantity." The individual making the count shall initial in the space "Inventoried by."

(b) A recheck of the physical count shall be made by an individual other than the person making the original count, and if the count is found to be correct he shall initial in the space "Checked by."

(c) *Inventory crews shall be diligent to properly mark inventory tickets for rejected, inferior or scrap material.*

(d) The tag part of Form 1 shall remain securely attached to the material inventoried, the lower section detached, all numbers shall be accounted for and shall be delivered to the accounting department for listing and pricing. To prevent duplications or omissions, those taking stock shall make certain that the tag of Form 1 is securely attached to the material after the lower section of the card has been removed.

(e) Material shall be described in accordance with trade names or specifications under which purchased or manufactured.

(f) The accounting department representative in charge will review the material after physical count has been completed. All articles of material not bearing the tag part of Form 1 will be checked to disclose omissions, if any.

10. *Basis for Determining Quantities*

(a) Quantities of material and supplies shall be determined by actual count, measured or weighed.

(b) Quantities and kinds of scrap material shall be weighed and agreed upon after inspection by representatives of accounting, operating and stores departments.

(c) Large storage piles of materials shall be cross-sectioned and cubic contents and tonnage computed by representatives of the engineering departments or competent authority.

(d) Care shall be exercised to avoid overlooking material, especially in out-of-the-way places.

(e) In cases where it is impractical to inventory finished goods, using Form 1, the following procedure shall govern:

The physical inventory of finished goods shall be checked with the shipping memorandums and case tickets on file in the finished goods or shipping department storerooms, and upon satisfactory proof that all items have been accounted for, such shipping memorandums shall serve as the record of quantities on hand.

11. *Undistributed Paid Transportation Charges*

All paid freight and express bills on hand shall be distributed wherever possible. Undistributed paid freight and express bills on hand shall be listed, and, if affecting inventories, shall be included in the inventory as "Undistributed Freight Charges." Undistributed freight and express for other than inventoried materials shall be included in an account "Undistributed Freight and Express."

12. *Material in Transit*

(a) All supplier's invoices and shipping notices dated on or prior to the date of inventory for which no material received record has been made shall be listed on a statement of "Materials in Transit" and entry recorded in account "Material in Transit."

(b) Inter-plant transfers of materials in transit shall be included in the inventory since the inter-plant billing of such material is entered by the shipping plant as of the month in which the material is actually shipped. *Accounting department representatives shall furnish each other with information covering shipments in transit from one operating plant division or department to another.*

13. *Certifying to Correctness of Inventory*

Each accounting department representative having jurisdiction over inventories shall certify to the correctness of the work and each employee engaged in counting and listing the material on hand shall execute the following certificate:

"We hereby certify that on ...., 194.., we did inventory and record the materials and supplies, then on hand at .... plant and located in the following departments:

(DEPARTMENT)	(RAW MATERIAL)	(IN PROCESS)	(FINISHED)	(MISCELLANEOUS)

That the sheets or cards hereto attached and hereby made a part of this certificate to the best of our knowledge and belief, do reflect the true record of the materials inventoried at the points or places and on the date or dates aforesaid.

Signatures of inventory crews $\left\{ \rule{0pt}{60pt} \right.$ _____

_____

_____

_____

_____

_____

Certified Correct:

_____

Accounting Department Representative
Crew Supervisor

14. *Pricing Inventories*

(a) All material inventoried shall be priced in accordance with values as reflected by the cost methods employed at the various locations, some of which are as follows:

RAW MATERIAL:

At market prices published by purchasing department, if less than cost.

At average book value.

At standard costs where standards are used.

At last invoice value.

At actual delivered prices.

IN PROCESS MATERIAL:

Material—At values prescribed above, or standard.

Labor—At standard costs to stage of last operation.

At predetermined costs to stage of last operation.

At piece work costs to stage of last operation.

At actual costs to stage of last operation.

Overhead—At standard costs to stage of last operation.

At predetermined costs to stage of last operation.

At actual costs to stage of last operation.

FINISHED STOCK:

Prevailing basis for computing cost of sales.

REJECTED OR INFERIOR MATERIAL:

At standard value or book value, whichever is lower.

SCRAP MATERIAL:

Aluminum Scrap—At prescribed standard cost values.

Other Scrap—At determined scrap values.

15. *Listing Inventoried Material*

(a) Where pricing is done on Form 1, all material so priced will be listed on Form 6 "Inventory" according to:

Plant
Department
Classification
Account No.

The listing to be transcribed from Form 1 shall be:

Ticket No.
Stock No.
Description
Size
Unit of Measure
Quantity
Unit Price
Amount

(b) In cases where Form 1 is used as a physical count ticket only, the quantities thereon shall be listed on Form 6 or on appropriate work sheets designed by each plant (see paragraph 7), and such listings shall be priced as prescribed in paragraph 14 according to breakdown for each item of material, labor, overhead, supplies, etc.

(c) The listings as prescribed in paragraph (a) and (b) above shall be carried by totals according to account classification to a work sheet "Recapitulation of Inventories by Account Classification," Form 7. The listings shall be supported by detailed working papers and shall be recapitulated according to:

> Account Number
> Classification or description of material
> Book Inventory—Quantity
>   Value
> Physical Inventory—Quantity
>   Value
> Over—Quantity
>   Value
> Short—Quantity
>   Value

16. *Adjusting Inventories*

The following inventory adjustments shall be made and complete details recorded:

(a) ADJUSTMENT FOR "OVER OR SHORT"

The book inventory for quantities and values shall be posted to the appropriate column on Form 7 according to account classification. Material inventoried shall be compared by account classification with book record by quantities and value to determine quantities and value over or short. If an overage or shortage exists, the item or items shall be rechecked wherever possible, and if correct the quantity and value over or short will be inserted in the appropriate column.

(b) ADJUSTMENT TO MARKET IF LOWER THAN COST

In cases where market value for materials inventoried are lower than cost, the market value used for pricing the physical inventory will be inserted in the "Value" column of Form 6, prefixed by the red letter "M" thus:

	Unit	Value	Amount
	Price		
(M)	1.25		

and extended to the "Amount" column at the market price.

(c) OTHER ADJUSTMENTS

1. (Charges in Transit) The value of material on hand or issued and charged out, for which suppliers' invoices *have not* been taken into account shall be adjusted by appropriate entry to inventory accounts and the liability recorded through the account for "Unaudited Vouchers." Beginning on the 20th of the inventory month, a statement shall be prepared of such material and shall be posted currently until the inventory is completed.

2. Add the amount of inter-plant invoices for which no material has been received. (See Paragraph 12, Material in Transit).

3. Add the value of "Undistributed Freight Charges" affecting material inventories (See Paragraph 11, Undistributed Paid Transportation Charges).

17. *Comparing Current Inventory with Previous Inventory*

Items of material in the previous inventory shall be compared with similar items in the current inventory. If no quantities of material listed in the preceding year appear in the current inventory, investigation shall be made to determine whether the stock was overlooked or included under another description.

18. *Disposition of Inventory Work Sheets, Inventory Tickets, Tallies, Cards, Etc.*

Inventory work sheets, tickets, tallies, cards, etc., shall be retained by the accounting department representatives of the company and that representative will be responsible for them.

19. *Recapitulation of Inventory and Final Summary*

From work sheet "Recapitulation of Inventories by Account Classifications" prescribed in Paragraph 15 (c), the final recapitulation and summary shall be transcribed by typewriter on Form 7. Original and five copies shall be made.

20. *Indexing Inventory Sheets*

Completed inventories shall be arranged and sheets numbered consecutively in order of the "Uniform Inventory Control" chart of accounts.

21. *Adjusting Ledger Balances to Inventory Values*

(a) No adjustment of differences between inventory and book balances as of the close of the inventory month shall be made until authorized by the treasurer.

(b) Unless instructions are issued to the contrary, all authorized adjustments shall be made in accounts for the year in which the inventories are taken.

(c) Differences in each stock maintained for special purposes, such as "Project Authorizations," shall be adjusted through the account or appropriation involved.

(d) Differences in raw material, in process, finished, rejected, inferior and scrap stocks shall be adjusted through the appropriate inventory adjustment accounts, namely:

ADJUSTMENT OF BOOK INVENTORY TO PHYSICAL AT COST

Inventory Adjustment at Cost—Material

Inventory Adjustment at Cost—Direct Labor and Manufacturing Expenses

Inventory Adjustment at Market—Material

and other specific inventory adjustment accounts, except in cases where specific "Reserve for Inventory Adjustment" has been provided, in which case adjustment shall be made through such reserve.

22. *Auditing Inventories*

Upon completion of inventories at plants, mathematical computations will be audited, and important items sight-checked by qualified employees as to reasonableness of quantities, unit values, extensions and footings. Irregularities shall be investigated, corrections made, and final differences in each general stock determined.

23. *Authority for Adjustment of Differences*

(a) Differences between final inventory values and book balances as of the close of the inventory month, by classes of material and by "Inventory Adjustment Accounts" affected, with explanations and recommendations as to dispositions, shall be reported to the treasurer. On receipt of authority for adjustment from the treasurer, accounting representatives shall make adjustments as prescribed in accounts for the year in which the inventories are taken.

(b) Unusual differences in final inventory figures compared

with book inventory balances, shall be investigated and fully explained by letter to the treasurer.

24. *Disposition of Inventories*

Inventory Form 7 shall be distributed as follows:

Original—To support plant voucher for inventory adjustments.

Copy—Filed with treasurer.

Copy—Sent to accounting representative in charge of inventory.

Copy—Sent to plant manager.

Copy—Sent to public accountants to support their working papers.

Copy—For plant office general use.

25. *Cost of Inventories*

Each plant shall issue a "Work Order" covering the inventory taking to which shall be charged all expense in connection with inventories. The costs shall be borne by the respective plants and shall be taken up in operating expenses for the month in which incurred.

PART IV

INVENTORY PRACTICE

PRACTICE IN ACCOUNTING FOR RAW MATERIALS *

Compiled by
The Research and Technical Service Department,
National Association of Cost Accountants

PART I—VALUATION OF RAW MATERIALS

THIS PAPER is a report of the findings in a questionnaire study carried on by the Research and Service Department at National Headquarters under the direction of Harry E. Howell, National Director in charge of Research. The data which are summarized here were obtained from members' replies to the questionnaire shown on page 346. Ten copies of this questionnaire were sent to each chapter secretary and distributed by the secretaries to a selected list of the members of such chapters. Over two hundred members returned filled-in questionnaires to National Headquarters, but because a few of those related to non-manufacturing companies, only 197 replies are included in the present report. The number of replies received, the care with which they were filled out and the additional explanatory comments on many of the questionnaires is an indication of the spirit of co-operation which prevails in the Association.

Charging Purchases to the Raw Material Account

The replies to the first question can be summarized as follows:

BASIS FOR CHARGING PURCHASES TO RAW MATERIAL ACCOUNT

	No. of Co's.	Per Cent of Total
1. At invoice price	177	89.9
2. At standard cost	17	8.6
3. At both actual and standard cost (basic standard cost) ..	3	1.5
Total reporting	197	100.0

It should be noted that the above is no indication of the extent to which standard costs are used by manufacturing concerns, since

* From the *Bulletin* of March 15, 1937.

345

THE VALUATION OF RAW MATERIAL INVENTORIES
N. A. C. A. Research Study
(Check the correct answers)

1. Do you charge purchases to the raw material account at:
   A. Invoice price ( )
   B. Standard cost ( )
   C. Some other base (Please explain)....................... ( )
   ....
   ....

2. Do you include in the inventory value of raw materials:
   A. Freight and cartage in ( )
   B. Purchasing department expense ( )
   C. Receiving and storing expense ( )
   D. Any other costs (Please list)........................... ( )
   ....
   ....

3. What portion of your inventory of raw materials is controlled through perpetual inventory records?................................%

4a Do you check your perpetual inventory records by physical count and measurement throughout the year?   Yes ( )
                                                                No ( )

4b If the answer to (a) is "yes," do you find a complete annual or semi-annual physical inventory necessary?   Yes ( )
                                                                No ( )

5. Do you charge raw material into process:
   A. On a first-in, first-out cost basis ( )
   B. On an average cost basis ( )
   C. On a standard cost basis ( )
   D. On a last-in, first-out basis ( )
   E. On some other basis (Please explain).................... ( )
   ....
   ....

6. For balance sheet purposes, do you value your raw material at:
   A. Cost or market, whichever is lower ( )
   B. Standard cost ( )
   C. Retail method ( )
   D. Base or normal stock method ( )
   E. Some other base (Please explain)....................... ( )
   ....
   ....

7. Do you make use of an inventory reserve for valuing raw materials on the balance sheet? Yes ( )
                                                No ( )
   A. Please state purpose of this reserve:.....................
   ....
   ....
   B. What account is charged when reserve is set up?
   ....
                                    Name ....
                                    Company ....
                                    Industry ....

under many standard cost setups materials are recorded at invoice price when received, but charged to process at standard when issued. It is interesting to note that 9 of the 17 companies which entered purchases at standard report the use of standard costs in valuing the raw materials for balance sheet purposes. In only two cases is there any indication that the standard cost valuations are reduced to market when the standard is higher than market.

Ten of the 20 companies which enter raw material at standard or at both standard and actual report the use of inventory reserves for valuing raw materials on the balance sheet, but in only three cases is there an indication that the purpose of this reserve is to reduce standard costs to the lower of cost or market, when such figures are lower than standards.

Other Costs Included in the Inventory Value of Raw Materials

The replies to the second question brought a mild surprise by indicating that a large majority of the reporting companies include inward freight and cartage as an element of raw material costs. On the other hand, other costs such as purchasing, receiving and storing are not recorded as raw material costs in the great majority of cases. The figures are shown below:

OTHER COSTS INCLUDED IN THE INVENTORY VALUE OF RAW MATERIALS

Item	No. of Companies Including	Per Cent of Total Companies Reporting
Freight and cartage in	180	91.4%
Receiving and storing expense	25	12.8
Purchasing Department expense	7	3.6
Unloading expense	4	2.0
Interest on borrowed capital	2	1.0
Allowance for shrinkage	2	1.0
Container cost	1	.5
Sampling and laboratory expense	1	.5

Perpetual Inventory Records

The extent to which raw materials are controlled by perpetual inventory records is evidenced by the answers to the third question, which can be summarized as follows:

USE OF PERPETUAL INVENTORY RECORDS

Per Cent of Raw Material Controlled	No. of Companies	Per Cent of Total
100%	133	67.5%
90–99%	24	12.2
50–89%	16	8.1
Under 50%	11	5.6
Not used	13	6.6
Totals	197	100.0%

Under a perpetual inventory system it is usually considered desirable to frequently check the goods actually on hand with corresponding stores records and then to adjust inventories for discrepancies. It has often been stated that where this is regularly done the taking of a physical inventory at the end of the accounting period is unnecessary. Questions 4a and 4b were designed to determine the extent of current practice in this respect. It is apparent from the answers to a supplementary questionnaire which will be referred to later that question 4a was not clearly stated and was misunderstood by some members who thought that the taking of monthly, quarterly, or semi-annual physical inventories and the checking of such inventories against the book records justified a "yes" answer to this question.

Since this question was intended to determine the proportion of companies which carried on a continuous checking of their raw material records, it is likely that the results obtained from this question are distorted and they will not be reported here, except to state that a great majority of the companies included in this study report that a continuous check of the raw material records is carried on. Undoubtedly a substantial majority would have made this reply if the question had been more accurately stated.

Are Physical Inventories Necessary?

When raw materials on hand are controlled by perpetual inventory records and these records are checked throughout the period by comparison with the actual quantities on hand, is it necessary to take a complete physical inventory at the end of the accounting period? Question 4b was designed to throw some light on this question and the information obtained is most interesting. In order to make analysis possible it was found necessary to classify the replies received into seven groups as shown below:

PHYSICAL INVENTORIES UNDER A PERPETUAL INVENTORY SYSTEM

Group	Portion of Raw Materials Controlled by Stores Records	Is a Continuous Check Made?	Do you find a Physical Inventory Necessary?	No. of Companies
1	100%	Yes	No	43
2	Less than 100%	Yes	No	12
3	100%	Yes	Yes	65
4	100%	Partial	Yes	6
5	Less than 100%	Yes	Yes	38
6	100%	No	Yes	19
7	Less than 100%	No	Yes	14
				197

The figures for the first three groups are the most significant. It is logical that the companies in Group 4 should find physical inventories necessary, since only a partial check of inventory records is carried on during the period. In the case of the companies in Group 5, the fact that the entire raw material inventory is not controlled by stores records probably explains the necessity for physical inventories, although it would be interesting to know whether in these cases a complete physical inventory is necessary. Since the companies in Groups 6 and 7 report no inventory checking during the period, the reason why physical inventories are necessary is obvious.

The information secured from the companies in Groups 1, 2 and 3 is conflicting. If 43 companies with 100 per cent of raw materials controlled through inventory records and 12 companies with partial control find that a continuing check against these records throughout the accounting period makes physical inventories unnecessary, why should 65 other companies with 100 per cent control and a continuous testing throughout the period find physical inventories necessary? This is the question which was propounded to the 65 members whose replies placed them in Group 3 above. The results of this supplementary questionnaire are presented in the second part of this report. In addition to the information given there, some of the comments relating to question 4b of the first questionnaire are quoted below:

Personal opinion is that periodic checks are more accurate and that with them annual inventories could and should be abolished.

Physical inventory not needed, but one is taken as a safety measure, not because of variations.

Book inventory used, as same is adjusted for discrepancies developed by perpetual check monthly.

Physical inventory not necessary, but we take one annually.

Physical inventory taken *at present*.

A physical inventory is not necessary but we take one annually for policy and audit reasons.

Bases Used in Charging Raw Material into Process

In charging raw material into work in process the methods used by the reporting companies were as follows:

METHODS USED IN CHARGING RAW MATERIAL INTO PROCESS

Method	No. of Companies	Per Cent of Total
Average cost basis	95	45.4
First-in, first-out basis	57	27.3
Standard cost basis	42	20.1
Actual cost basis	9	4.3
Last-in, first-out basis	5	2.4
Highest cost first	1	.5
	209	100.0

In replying to this question, 10 members reported using two or more methods, and 2 members failed to answer the question. In the above tabulation each method reported is counted, which explains why the total number of answers to this question are in excess of the number of companies reporting.

It is interesting to note that the use of the last-in, first-out method is reported by a manufacturer of heavy machinery (for part of inventory only), by a manufacturer of business machines, by an oil company, by a manufacturer of electrical equipment, and by a fabricator of base and precious metals. There were not a sufficient number of such industries included in this study to give any indication of the extent to which this plan has been adopted by oil companies, tanneries, metal refineries and similar industries.

Valuation of Raw Materials for Balance Sheet Purposes

As was to be expected, the vast majority of companies were reported as valuing their raw material inventories at cost or market, whichever is lower, for balance sheet purposes. The chief interest in the tabulation which follows is in the nature of the exceptions from this recognized rule.

BALANCE SHEET VALUATION OF RAW MATERIALS

Basis	No. of Companies	Per Cent of Total
Cost or market, whichever is lower....	172	87.3
Standard cost	9	4.6
Actual cost	6	3.1
Basic or normal value.................	4	2.0
Average cost	4	2.0
Miscellaneous	2	1.0
	197	100.0

The basic or normal stock method is reported in use by a manufacturer of industrial instruments, a copper and brass fabricator, a cotton textile company and a metal fabricator. The manufacturer of industrial instruments reports using this basis for the valuation of the entire raw material inventory. The copper and brass company uses it for copper and zinc only, but values "copper and zinc in the *entire* inventory at 5 cents delivered and 3 cents St. Louis, respectively." The cotton textile company uses the basic figure "provided it is not too much higher than market and depending on the market trend since closing date." This company uses an inventory valuation reserve upon occasions. The metal fabricator reports that "normal stocks are valued at the base price, and the inventory in excess of normal at cost or market, whichever is lower." This company uses an inventory valuation reserve "to maintain a normal stock at a normal price and to provide for abnormal fluctuations in market prices."

Use of Raw Material Inventory Valuation Reserves

Of the 197 companies covered in this study, 46 reported the use of raw material inventory valuation reserves. The various purposes for which reserves were provided is shown in the tabulation on page 353. The number of purposes listed is in excess of the number of companies reporting because some companies use such reserves for more than one purpose. A summary of the accounts which are charged at the time the reserves are set up is also shown.

It is rather surprising that the use of a reserve to reduce the inventory from cost to market is not more general when we consider that the majority of reporting companies carry their raw material accounts at cost, but use the cost or market basis for balance sheet purposes. When one recalls that perpetual inventory systems are in use in most of the reporting companies, one wonders how the inventories can be reduced from cost to market without throwing the raw material account out of agreement with the stores records unless an inventory reserve is used. The same question arises in connection with companies using standard or basic values which are reduced to market when lower. It would seem that in all such cases the use of inventory valuation reserves would be useful.

Undoubtedly, the presence of perpetual inventory systems accounts for the use of inventory reserves by the companies who use such reserves to provide for shrinkage, obsolescence, and losses from slow-moving stock. Where these losses have been definitely determined and related to specific raw materials, the revised valuations can be entered in both the raw material account and the subsidiary stock records, but where the losses are estimated or not directly related to specific raw materials, the reduction in inventory valuation cannot be made in the raw material account without throwing it out of agreement with the stores records. A reserve seems indicated in these cases. The same is true if these are estimated future losses from obsolescence or from anticipated price declines.

To summarize, the most usual purposes for which valuation reserves are applied against raw material inventories are:

1. To reduce cost value, standard value, or normal value of inventory to market, when lower.
2. To recognize losses due to shrinkage, obsolescence and slow-moving stock, which losses have not been related to specific raw materials.
3. In anticipation of future losses due to the above causes or to price declines.

It is apparent from the tabulation on page 353 that there is little agreement on the proper treatment of the charge at the time an inventory valuation reserve is set up. Cost of sales is charged to reduce the inventory from cost to market, to take care of losses due to shrinkage, obsolescence and slow-moving stock, and to make adjustments for the difference between the book inventory and the physical inventory. Manufacturing cost, and thus the inventory, is

INVENTORY RESERVES—PURPOSES AND ACCOUNTS CHARGED

Purpose	No. of Co's.	Accounts Charged when Reserve Set Up			
		Cost of Sales	Mfg. Cost	Profit and Loss	Unclassified Charges
To reduce cost to market	9	2	1	1	Other income and expense Inventory adjustments Inventory shrinkage adjustment Loss on adjustment of R.M. Inv. to market value Not answered
To reduce standard to market	3				Variation in raw material cost Allowance for contingency Price variances
To reduce normal stock to market	2			2	Inventory reserve(?)
To allow for shrinkage	9	3	3		Inventory adjustment Work in process
To provide for obsolescence	14	4	4	1	Obsolescence Other deductions Provision for loss on obsolete material Inventory adjustment Inventory shrinkage adjustments
To write down slow-moving stock	4	1	1	1	Not answered
To guard against losses from price declines	3			1	Capital account (Single proprietorship)
To adjust for difference between book and physical inventory	3	1		2	
To give a conservative valuation	2			1	Surplus
For tax purposes	1			1	
When market factors make hedge insecure	1				Deducted from final inventory value(?)
Totals	51	11	10	10	

charged for all of these purposes except the last, and, in addition, to provide against losses from price declines. And profit and loss is charged for all of the same purposes as the other two.

Apparently there is need for some agreement on principles here. The following is suggested as a possible test:

1. Is the provision being made for a loss or for an expense which can be capitalized in inventory? Unless the cost represents a proper addition to the valuation of goods in process and finished goods, it should not be charged to manufacturing cost.
2. Is the provision a responsibility of the manufacturing division or of the general administration? If a responsibility of the manufacturing division, a charge to cost of sales would seem to be justified; if a responsibility of the general administration, a charge against profit and loss is in order.

Some of the comments made by members in replying to this question are interesting. One member in reporting that a reserve was used to reduce the inventory from cost to market reported that "such a reserve is not shown on the balance sheet but is carried as contra account in the inventory accounts." Another member reports that in order to provide for slow-moving materials the "inventories are aged monthly and reserve set up."

The most conservative practice noticed is a case where a 15 per cent reserve is applied against all inventories. This reserve is "created by a direct charge to profits and built up by a policy of overcosting by increasing cost of sales billed."

An interesting procedure is reported by a company which carries its raw materials at standard cost on its books, but uses cost or market, whichever is lower, for balance sheet purposes. The reserve is used in this case "to bring standard to cost or market and to forecast profits during the year." The procedure followed by the company is illustrated by the following entries:

At time of purchase:		
Inventory at Standard	$10.00	
Purchases		$8.00
Cost/Market Reserve		2.00
At time of sale:		
Cost of Sales at Standard	10.00	
Inventory at Standard		10.00
Cost/Market Variance	2.00	
Price Variance		2.00

In this case the Cost/Market Reserve always reflects the balance of the price variance in inventory.

Inventory Practice in Specific Industries

One often hears the statement that cost accounting practice varies widely because of the differing requirements of various industries. Had it been possible, it would have been interesting to determine the extent to which the variations in practice which were noted in this study were due to the differing requirements of the industries represented. Because of the large number of industries included in the present study, the representation of each industry was not sufficiently large to make possible any accurate analysis of this sort. However, it is interesting to note certain variations in practice between the manufacturers of machinery and the iron and steel companies which are represented. These two groups were selected for study because they are the two groups with the largest representation.

Of the 36 reporting companies in the machinery manufacturing industry, 5 entered purchases in the raw materials account at standard, while 6 used standard costs in pricing material charged to process. Of the 34 iron and steel companies studied, 3 entered purchases in the raw material account at standard, while 7 used standard costs in pricing material charged to process. Stated on a percentage basis in comparison with all companies reporting, this shows:

PERCENTAGE OF COMPANIES USING STANDARD COST

	All Companies	Machinery Manufacturers	Iron and Steel Companies
In entering purchases	8.6%	13.9%	9%
In charging material to process	20.1	14.3	20

If the samples studied can be taken as representative, the above would seem to indicate that, while standard costs are not used as generally in the machinery manufacturing companies as in manufacturing companies as a whole, the practice of entering purchases at standard is more common in machinery manufacturing companies.

It would seem also that companies manufacturing machinery are more successful than the average in doing away with physical inventories under perpetual inventory system. Eighteen out of 36, or 50 per cent, of the machinery manufacturing companies reported that physical inventories were unnecessary, compared with 27.9 per cent of the 197 companies from all types of manufacturing companies reporting them unnecessary.

Another interesting comparison relates to the prevalence of the first-in, first-out method as compared with the average cost method in charging material to process in the industries studied. The percentage figures follow:

USE OF FIRST-IN, FIRST-OUT AND AVERAGE COST BASIS COMPARED

	All Companies	Machinery Manufacturers	Iron and Steel Companies
First-in, first-out basis	27.3%	45%	17%
Average cost basis	45.4	33.3	60

This would seem to indicate that the first-in, first-out method is more popular in the machinery manufacturing industries than in industry in general, while the use of average cost as a basis for charging material into process is more generally favored by iron and steel companies.

PART II—THE NEED FOR PHYSICAL INVENTORIES

As stated in Part I of this report, 65 of the 197 members whose replies are included in this study reported that they considered physical inventories necessary where perpetual inventory records covering 100 per cent of their raw materials were in use and were proved regularly by actual count and measurement. These replies contrasted with the replies of 43 members with perpetual inventory records for 100 per cent of their raw materials and 12 members with similar records for less than 100 per cent who considered a physical inventory unnecessary. In an effort to obtain more light on this subject and to determine the reasons for this difference of opinions the questionnaire shown on page 357 was sent to each of the 65 members who had stated that they considered physical inventories necessary. Replies were received from 50 of this group.

The information obtained was so varied that it has been found impossible to express the findings quantitatively. Moreover, the individual comments obtained by this questionnaire are so interesting and informative that it was thought desirable to present them

THE NECESSITY FOR PHYSICAL INVENTORIES UNDER A PERPETUAL INVENTORY SYSTEM

SUPPLEMENT TO N. A. C. A. STUDY OF RAW MATERIAL VALUATION

Note that reference is to *Raw Materials* only

1. On an average, how many times per year do you check the quantity of each item of raw material on hand against the book records?...................

   Any comments ....

   ....

2. Why do you consider that a complete physical inventory is necessary when you have a 100% book inventory for raw materials which is regularly proved by count and measurement?

   A. Auditors require .... ( )
   B. Management desires .... ( )
   C. Interim check not sufficiently complete.................... ( )
   D. Interim check not often enough........................... ( )
   E. Shrinkages need to be determined to inventory date........ ( )
   F. Accurate perpetual records not possible because of method
      of issue .... ( )
   G. Other reasons (Please explain).......................... ( )

   ....
   ....
   ....
   ....

                              Name ....
                              Company ....
                              Chapter ....

in detail. The replies are summarized here in four groups. In the first group are the replies of members who report that the first questionnaire was incorrectly answered and that physical inventories are not taken. The replies in the second group are from members who considered the taking of a monthly, quarterly, semi-annual or annual inventory as a regular check on perpetual records but indicated that there was no checking of book records between physical inventory dates. In the third group are replies from four members who do not consider physical inventories necessary but now take them. The elimination of these three groups leaves 31 replies from members with companies which carry on a continuing check but find physical inventories necessary. There may be some questions in the case of some of these companies as to whether the checking as reported is adequate. The reasons given by these members for the taking of physical inventories are given in tabular form and followed by some rather interesting comments made by the co-operating members. The replies to questions 1 and 2 of the above questionnaire are summarized by groups on the following pages.

No Complete Physical Inventory Taken—Group I

Reply No. 53:

1. Raw material inventories are written up from cards, using the figures shown by these records at the end of the fiscal year.
2. *Comment:* It now appears that our previous report was in error.

Reply No. 58:

1. We have checkers checking various items of the raw material all the time. When a certain stock of raw material gets down to a low point where it will not necessitate so much labor to get an actual count, we take that count and adjust our perpetual inventory accordingly.
2. *Comment:* All of our raw stocks are checked some time just prior to listing the actual inventory. At the time of listing the inventory we do not go out into the factory and warehouse and count the raw materials that we have on hand. We simply take them from our perpetual inventory records which are checked continuously.

   I see no reason why it would be necessary in our case to go into the plant on December 31 or January 1, as the case may be, and take an actual count of every item of raw material for inventory purposes, as we are quite satisfied that the inventory as represented by our books is substantially right at all times.

Reply No. 114:

1. Some once a year only, and others each month.
2. *Comment:* Some misunderstanding here as we regard at least one physical check to be needed, but all items do not need to be checked at the same time.

Reply No. 148:

1. This depends on how fast or slow moving the different inventories are. Some are checked once a year and others as many

as six times.   We usually check when we reach minimum quantities.

2. *Comment:* We do not close down at the end for a complete physical inventory but instead concentrate on checking most of our slow-moving inventory during the last quarter of the year.   Our card records at December 31 are taken as our physical.

Reply No. 181:

1. Major items are checked monthly, other items checked when stock is replenished.   Smaller items are checked at inventory time.
2. *Reasons physical inventory considered necessary:*
   a. Interim check not sufficiently complete.
   b. Items that are checked monthly are automatically a part of the physical inventory on the last check of the year.

Book Records Checked Only at Time Physical Inventory Taken—Group II

Reply No. 3:

1. We do not check throughout the year.
2. *Reasons physical inventory considered necessary:*
   a. Interim check not sufficiently complete.
   b. Shrinkage needs to be determined to inventory date.
   c. Accurate perpetual records not possible because of method of issue.
   d. Lack of clerical help and production records makes it necessary to take physical.

Reply No. 32:

1. Four times each year we find it advisable to take a *physical* inventory.   In case of any difference between our book records and the physical inventory, we can adjust more readily.
2. *Reasons physical inventory considered necessary:*
   a. Auditors require.
   b. Shrinkages need to be determined to inventory date.

Reply No. 100:

1. Once each year.
2. *Reasons physical inventory considered necessary:*
   a. Auditors require.
   b. Management desires.
   c. Book inventory for raw materials is adjusted only annually by complete physical inventory. Our stock control records do not tie in with our general ledger controls.

Reply No. 116:

1. Each six months. (Reply to first questionnaire indicates a semi-annual physical inventory taken.)
2. *Reasons physical inventory considered necessary:*
   a. Management desires.
   b. Shrinkages need to be determined to inventory date.

Reply No. 126:

1. On May 31 and October 31.
2. *Reasons physical inventory considered necessary:*
   a. Management requires.
   b. Shrinkages need to be determined to inventory date.
   c. Physical inventories needed in order to verify as closely as possible the actual to book records for insurance valuation report—a condition in fertilizer manufacture.

Reply No. 127:

1. We do it just twice a year and then by physical inventory.
2. *Reasons physical inventory considered necessary:*
   a. Our chief inventory items are gold, silver and platinum.
   b. Our standards must include shrinkage and refining losses.
   c. All concerned therefore desire a complete physical check of book inventories twice a year.

Reply No. 169:

1. No regular check.
2. *Reasons physical inventory considered necessary:*
   a. Management desires.
   b. Interim check not often enough.

Reply No. 177:

1. At the *end* of each quarter.
2. *Reason physical inventory considered necessary:*
   a. Management desires.

Reply No. 189:

1. Monthly.
2. *Reasons physical inventory considered necessary:*
   a. Interim check not sufficiently complete.
   b. Accurate perpetual records not possible because of method of issue.
   c. Persons who handle raw materials are not accurate in record-keeping, although sufficiently so if checked monthly by *physical inventories.*

Reply No. 192:

1. Once each year.
2. *Comment:* Our system does not call for periodical counts. Inventory is taken only once a year.

"Possibly Physical Inventory not Necessary"—Group III

Reply No. 30:

1. Once each year.
2. *Reasons physical inventory considered necessary:*
   a. Interim check not sufficiently complete.
   b. Where a quantity of material is carried constantly it is sometimes difficult to secure interim check. If interim check was available once or twice a year on all articles, I would waive all requirements as to annual inventory.

Reply No. 138:

1. Twice a year.
2. *Reasons physical inventory considered necessary:*
   a. Management desires.
   b. We don't expect to have a fire, yet we continue carrying insurance. Don't know of any better way to explain rea-

sons for physical inventories in our case. (In replying to first questionnaire asking whether physical inventories were considered necessary this member replied, "No, but we take one anyway.")

Reply No. 139:

1. Our setup is comparatively new, but we expect to check each item at least once, perhaps oftener.
2. *Comment:* Here again the newness of our system requires a physical inventory to prove and sell it. We definitely expect to discontinue complete physical inventories in the near future.

Reply No. 145:

1. At least four times per year.
2. *Reason physical inventory considered necessary:*
   a. We take physical inventories for policy reasons, even though we make test counts continuously during the year. In my opinion the physical inventory at the end of the year is not necessary, but inasmuch as the management desires to have it done, I have never seriously contested this point. Possibly when the results of your investigation are published, I will be able to secure authority to discontinue the annual physical inventory.

SUMMARY OF REPLIES REGARDING NECESSITY FOR PHYSICAL INVENTORIES—GROUP IV

Reply No.	Average Number of Times Checked Per Year		Reasons Physical Inventories Considered Necessary						
	No. of Times	Comment References	Auditors Require	Management Desires	Check Not Complete Enough	Check Not Often Enough	Shrinkage to Inventory Date Needed	Method of Issue Prevents Accurate Records	Comment References
18	2			x			x	x	
41	12			x				x	
49	4		x				x		1
52	2		x				x		
64	3				x				2
66	12								3
69	1 or 2		x	x					4
71	6			x	x		x		5
77	2			x					6
79		A	x						
82		B	x						
88		C	x		x		x	x	7
89		D	x		x		x	x	8
111	2							x	
117	2							x	
119	1	E	x	x	x		x	x	9
120	12							x	
121	2			x					
128	1		x	x					10
135	1		x	x					11
155	2		x	x				x	
159	2		x	x		x			
160	12	F		x	x		x		12
163	2	G		x					13
167				x					
168				x		x			14
179		H	x	x			x		
185	4	I	x	x			x	x	15
193	1		x						16
197	1						x		17
199			x	x			x		18
Totals from 31 replies			16	18	6	2	12	10	

Comments on Average Number of Times Checked Per Year

Comment A—Varies from every few days for some items to once each month for others. Depends on the rapidity of turnover and volume of materials.

Comment B—Our products are so varied that it is impossible to set any definite time. For instance, oil would be gauged when the tank is almost empty and with 500 tanks of different capacities the checking is a continuous one. Other products are checked once a month and still others three or four times a year, depending upon the products.

Comment C—Barley and malt checked monthly; hops checked every other month.

Comment D—Whenever an item gets to a low point there is a physical check.

Comment E—Rough measurements monthly; weigh-up annually.

Comment F—There is a more or less continuous check. Also, a physical check on slow-moving lots is made twice a year. We have very few adjustments to make.

Comment G—Whenever we run out or the supply gets low enough so that it is easy to count or weigh.

Comment H—We check the general ledger once a year by a physical inventory, at which time weights and values are adjusted. No quantities are carried in the general ledger. Stock records of quantities are checked probably 10 to 20 times a year.

Comment I—In some cases, stocks are very low at close of month and are physically checked to prevent errors.

Comments on Need for Physical Inventories

Comment 1—Due to diversity of goods manufactured we have thousands of classes of raw materials, each of which is checked according to specific requirements.

Comment 2—It is difficult to obtain accurate records from shop personnel. Therefore, it is necessary to make frequent checks.

Comment 3—Human errors make absolutely accurate perpetual inventory impossible.

Comment 4—Interim check not sufficiently complete, as we do not check inactive items regularly.

Comment 5—Some items are sold on theoretical weight and *you cannot roll steel* to exact weight. Inventories are in tons. Bookkeeping errors are corrected in this way. Errors of opinion on which inventory a particular sale refers to are corrected.

Comment 6—Our inventory is made up of a large number of similar materials and the turnover is around fifteen times. However, there are some slow-moving items of special character which may be lost sight of, and frequent substitution makes a physical count advisable.

Comment 7—Nature of raw material does not allow accurate measurement except at certain times.

Comment 8—There are varying weights in sizes of coils of wire rods. It is too expensive to weigh each batch, so they are charged out at average weight per coil. When the stock reaches a low point a check is made.

Comment 9—Book inventories cover only total quantities of each grain. Estimates by rough measurement are made each month to determine proportion of each grade and to check general accuracy of book records, but ordinarily adjustments are made only once a year when complete physical weigh-up is made.

Comment 10—We know that no system, no matter how perfect, can eliminate all errors because of the human element involved, and we want our records to be kept accurate to the point of perfection. The inventory can be taken in the space of a few hours by three men, and the cost is negligible.

Comment 11—To check accuracy of book inventory record.

Comment 12—Inventory should be as of a certain date. It should be counted and checked to obviate book inventory errors. Check book inventory to physical count.

Comment 13—We feel that men are more careful if you have an annual check-up and tell clerks where their figures are not up to standard.

Comment 14—Prevent inventory losses.

Comment 15—Material is costed from stock at a current market valuation. A physical inventory is required to adjust the perpetual inventory to cost or market, whichever is lower.

Comment 16—A perpetual record cannot be sound unless checked often, as a clerk may issue a substitute and not change requisition, thereby posting to incorrect card.

Comment 17—Our materials are subject to deterioration. Ink, once the can is opened, surface-dries like paint, causing minor loss. Paper is subject to dust, moisture, etc. Acids like ink evaporate when once opened. Deposit calls for actual stock put in. Issue calls for actual stock taken out. Physical check-up accounts for these minor losses.

Comment 18—Due to special sizes and lots.

Summary

As a result of the information obtained from the answers to the first questionnaire and the replies above, it is possible to make certain generalizations regarding the need for physical inventories. It may be necessary to take a physical inventory of raw materials under the following circumstances:

1. *Where the auditors require or the management desires that physical inventories be taken.* In general, public accountants and corporation officials are more reluctant to discontinue physical inventories than are industrial accountants who are more familiar

with the operations of their perpetual inventory systems and more likely to appreciate the lack of necessity for a physical inventory. Here is an opportunity for the industrial accountant who is operating a good perpetual inventory system to sell his company officials and auditors on the possibility of savings arising from the elimination of physical inventories.

2. *Where the unit of measuring raw materials at the time of receipt differs from the unit of measurement at the time of issuance.* In some industries certain types of raw materials are purchased by the ton and issued by the foot or by the unit. Since a ton of a certain raw material will not always contain the same number of units, it is natural that the stock records will not be completely accurate, and in many cases a physical count at the end of the accounting period is desirable.

3. *Where the raw material is subject to shrinkage or loss while in storage.* In such cases it would seem desirable that such raw materials be physically inventoried at the balance sheet date in order that all shrinkages to that date may be accounted for. However, in some cases it is possible from experience to determine rates of shrinkage and apply these rates to the last physical measurement which was made, without a great sacrifice in accuracy.

4. *Where the raw material is of a type which makes it expensive to make accurate periodic checks.* Thus a flour mill, a manufacturer of stock feed, or a brewery will have difficulty in measuring accurately the quantity of grains in elevators throughout the accounting period because of varying moisture content, settling and other factors. In such a case estimates may be made throughout the accounting period and more accurate measurement applied only at the close of the period.

5. *Where the perpetual inventory records are not checked throughout the accounting period by physical count and measurement.* This is the procedure followed by the companies whose replies are listed in the second section above. In these companies stock records are checked only at the time physical inventories are taken; in other words, quarterly, semi-annual, or annual inventories take the place of continuous check throughout the accounting period. It is obvious that in such cases physical inventories are necessary, otherwise there would be no check on the accuracy of the book records.

6. *Where the perpetual inventory system is not accurate.* No system can be absolutely accurate, but a good perpetual inventory system will usually give as accurate results as can be obtained from a physical inventory. If checks of the stock records indicate frequent and appreciable differences between the inventory figures and the quantities actually on hand due to errors in keeping the records, reporting receipts, and issuances of raw material and in the measurement of raw material issued, a physical inventory at the end of the accounting period would seem to be necessary to discover all discrepancies which have occurred since the last time that each type of raw material was checked.

In contrast to the above, it would seem that a physical inventory is not likely to be necessary in the following cases:

1. *Where a portion of the raw material usually made up of slow moving items is not controlled by the stock records or where stock records are kept for such slow moving items but are not checked regularly throughout the accounting period.* In such a case it would not appear necessary to take a complete physical inventory but only to physically inventory at the end of the period the items not controlled or not checked regularly. The perpetual inventory records can then be used for that portion of the inventory which is adequately controlled and periodically checked to the book records. This is the procedure described previously in Reply No. 148. Of course, this can only be done if it is possible to accurately eliminate the portion of the inventory which is under control and be certain of including all raw material items in the physical count which are not so controlled.

2. *Where the reason for taking a physical inventory is that the human element makes accurate stock records impossible.* It is obvious that the human element is as important in the taking of a physical inventory as in keeping stock records and periodically checking them. In fact, the necessity for taking a physical inventory in a short period of time requiring the use of inexperienced help is likely to cause errors due to the human element more frequently in the taking of a physical inventory than in the keeping of perpetual records.

Apparently the number of times during the year that the inventory records are checked is not an important element in determining whether or not a physical inventory is necessary at the end of the accounting period. Only two members in replying to the questionnaire indicated that physical inventories were necessary because the interim check was not made often enough. In one of these cases the stock records were checked only once during the year, while in the other case they were checked twelve times during the year. Apparently the amount of checking which is required will vary according to the type of raw material and the accuracy with which the perpetual inventory records are kept. A company which assembles machinery from purchased parts can control these parts more accurately through stock records than can a chemical plant or a flour mill where the raw material is not divided into definite measurable units and where shrinkage is likely to occur. A lax system of reporting receipts and issuances of raw materials or of measuring raw materials when received and issued, will require more frequent checking of inventory records to eliminate the necessity for a physical inventory than would be necessary where a more accurate system of perpetual inventory prevails.

FINISHED GOODS INVENTORY PRACTICE *

Compiled by
The Research and Technical Service Department,
National Association of Cost Accountants

T HIS study of finished goods inventory practice can be roughly divided into two parts: (1) valuation and (2) verification and control. Included under the head of valuation are such questions as the type of cost system used, the treatment of variances from standard costs, the valuation base used for balance sheet purposes, the disposition of under- and over-absorbed balances and similar problems. Included under the second head are the questions relating to perpetual inventories, the staggered count, physical inventories and co-operation with external auditors. Also included is a summary of the answers to three supplementary questions dealing with the last-in, first-out basis of inventory valuation.

This report summarizes the practices of 325 industrial companies, representing a wide variety of industries. While small as well as large companies are included in this group, the majority of the companies would be classified as large or medium sized.

Proportion of Sales from Inventory

As a means of indicating the importance of finished goods inventories in each company, members were asked to report the per cent of total sales filled from (1) finished goods inventories and (2) current production, i.e., not filled from stock but manufactured to customers' orders. A few members had difficulty in interpreting the reference to sales filled from current production and did not answer this question.

Of the 304 companies represented by replies to this question, 80 manufacture exclusively for stock and 14 exclusively on customers' orders with no finished goods inventories, while the remaining 210 companies manufacture both for stock and on order in varying proportions as follows:

* From Section III of the *Bulletin* for March 15, 1940.

Companies

From 60 to 99 per cent for stock........................ 67
From 20 to 59 per cent for stock........................ 64
Some manufacture for stock, but less than 20 per cent.... 79

210

These proportions should not be taken as representative of industry as a whole, because the sample is too small and because it is probable that members employed with companies manufacturing wholly or largely on order would not be as likely to reply to the questionnaire as those with companies manufacturing largely for stock, due to the absence or small importance of finished goods inventories in their companies.

Method of Cost Accounting Used

As a first step in indicating the methods used in valuing finished goods inventories, members were asked to state the method of cost accounting used by their companies. A summary of the answers follows:

METHOD OF COST ACCOUNTING USED

Companies

Job costs 66
Process costs 67
Ideal or current standard costs........................ 103
Basic or measure standard costs........................ 21
Various combinations of job, process and standard costs 44
Unclassified 18
No answer to this question............................ 6

325

If the companies using two or more methods are counted once for each method used, the figures are changed to the following:

METHOD OF COST ACCOUNTING USED EITHER EXCLUSIVELY OR IN PART

Companies

Job costs 96
Process costs 90
Ideal or current standard costs........................ 131
Basic or measure standard costs........................ 29
Unclassified 18
No answer to this question............................ 6

Total 370

The methods used by 18 of the companies are listed in the above tabulation as "unclassified." The descriptions given in the questionnaire replies of the methods used by these companies are listed below:

Predetermined
Average costs
Average actual monthly
Average cost of merchandise
Actual cost, accrual basis
Actual costs for the month
Article cost based on past experience
Progressive standard cost
Formula cost plus average expenses
Do not try to cost each product
Continuous mass production actual cost
Standard costs, but not carried through ledgers
Opening inventory, plus purchases, less closing inventory
Job costs, but one division uses metal shipped costed at per pound actual
Actual prime cost with standard burden for 85% of production; job cost for special jobs
We have departmental costs in detail and use unit averages
Current reproductive costs, not incorporated with accounting
Standard conversion costs with either actual material costs or last-in material costs

Answers to Questions 1 and 2 Combined

In view of the statements in cost accounting text books regarding the adaptability or non-adaptability of standard costs and process costs to companies manufacturing for stock as compared with those manufacturing on order, it is interesting to combine the answers to questions 1 and 2. In the following tabulation the 304 companies which replied to question 1 are divided into two groups, (1) those manufacturing primarily for stock, and (2) those manufacturing largely on order, and the per cent of the total of each group using each type of cost plan is indicated:

COST METHOD USED BY TWO CLASSES OF COMPANIES

Cost Method Used	Per cent of 152 companies with 50% or more of production for stock	Per cent of 152 companies with less than 50% production for stock
Job costs	7.9	32.9
Process costs	24.4	17.8
Ideal or current standard costs	38.8	23.0
Basic or measure standard costs	5.9	7.9
Combinations	15.8	11.8
Unclassified	5.9	4.6
No answer	1.3	2.0
	100.0	100.0

The interesting feature of these figures is not that standard and process costs are used more widely in companies producing primarily for stock than in companies producing largely on order, but that the companies producing most of their goods on order use standard and process cost methods as widely as they do. Six of the 14 companies which indicate that they produce only on order report the use of standard costs, four using the ideal and two the basic plan.

Inventory Pricing Methods

It seems desirable, in reporting methods of these companies in pricing their finished goods inventories at the end of the fiscal period, to present the data separately for two groups as follows:

1. Companies using the ideal or current standard cost system.
2. Companies using actual costs.

Companies using the basic standard cost plan are included in the second group, because the use of this costing method results in obtaining finished goods inventories valued at average actual costs. The distinction which it seems well to make for our present purpose is between those companies whose cost system results in inventories valued at a predetermined or standard cost and those companies whose cost system results in inventories valued at so-called "actual" costs.

Inventory Pricing Practice Under Standard Costs

The basis for pricing finished goods inventories used by the 131 companies which reported the use of ideal standard costs either in whole or in part is shown in the following tabulation:

METHODS OF VALUING FINISHED GOODS INVENTORIES
COMPANIES USING IDEAL STANDARD COSTS

Method	Standard Costs Used for All Costing No. of Companies	Standard Costs Used in Conjunction with Some Other Method No. of Companies	Combined No. of Companies
At cost or market, whichever lower....	41	14	55
At new standards, applicable to the coming year	24	8	32
At cost, as provided by cost system used	20	5	25
At new standards, adjusted by reserve to lower of cost or market	2	—	2
Unclassified	12	1	13
No finished goods inventory	4	—	4
Totals	103	28	131

Included as unclassified in the above tabulation are thirteen companies which report the following inventory valuation bases:

Current standards, adjusted by the proration of purchase price variance.
Current standard costs, with raw material component reduced to lower of cost or market (2 companies).
Labor and burden at new standards, material at lower of cost or market.
Standard costs, adjusted if necessary.
Old or new standards, whichever seems closest to "lower of cost or market" idea.
Standard costs at time of manufacture, less depreciation.
Current standards may be 10 seconds or 10 years old.
Standard costs based on selected 10 years average experience.
Actual costs or standards, whichever lower.
Cost or market, except for certain items which are carried at fixed prices below cost or market.
Cost or market or new standards.
List, less lowest discount, less 40 per cent to bring average costs.

Use of Old or New Standards for Balance Sheet Valuation

The interesting and rather surprising feature of this tabulation is the number of companies which value their closing inventories at either the current year's standard costs or at the standards applicable to the year ahead, or, stated differently, the number of companies which apparently do not adjust their finished goods values to an "actual" cost or market basis. Twenty-five of the companies report that finished goods are valued "at cost, as provided by the cost system used," which in these cases is the ideal standard cost system. Since the answers to another question to be reported later indicate that variances from standard costs are usually not applied as adjustments of inventories, it would appear that these companies use the standard costs of the period when goods were manufactured as the basis of valuation for the final inventory. It would be interesting to know how these companies justify this practice in periods of falling prices when market is lower than the standards used. Of these 25 companies, 5 use some other cost method in conjunction with cost standards, so that in these cases the comments apply only to that portion of the inventory which was originally costed at standard.

An additional 32 companies value their final inventories at the new standards established for the coming year. In the case of the 8 companies using standard costs in conjunction with some other cost plan, it is assumed that such standards apply to goods manufactured for stock and therefore included in final inventories, while the other cost method reported (usually job costs) is used for goods manufactured for customers' orders. Probably in most of these 32 companies these new standards represent the market level at the year-end, or approximate such market. This raises an interesting question in those cases where the market values (and new standards) are higher than the standards of the previous year, resulting in a write-up of inventory values as calculated under the old standards.

Obviously this method of valuation would be difficult to justify except in those cases where the actual costs for the current period exceeded the old standards, resulting in debit variances sufficiently large to give actual costs equal to or in excess of the new standards. It will be noticed that two other companies reported the use of new standards for the valuation of the final inventory, but with the adjustment of the resulting value to the lower of cost or market by the use of a reserve. This would appear to be the preferable procedure in cases where the new standards are higher than those used during the current year.

Midway between the position of the companies which value their inventories at current or new standards and those which use a cost or market basis are the first four companies in the unclassified group. These companies use either current or new standards as a valuation base, but either adjust the material component to actual cost or the lower of cost or market.

Valuation at Cost or Market by Companies Using Standard Costs

The majority of the companies using standard costs report that inventories are valued at cost or market, whichever is the lower. It is not possible from the answers of these 55 companies to know definitely whether this means valuation at the lower of "standard cost or market" or at the lower of "actual cost or market," but there are indications that possibly in the majority of cases "standard cost or market" is meant. Seven of the companies so specify, while no company in this group definitely specifies that "actual cost or market" is used. In addition, the methods reported for the disposition of variances from standard would indicate that few companies adjust their finished goods inventories for these variances in order to arrive at actual costs.

To summarize, it would appear that the majority of companies using standard costs value their finished goods inventories at the end of the fiscal year at either standard cost (current year's or new year's) or at the lower of standard cost or market. Apparently so-called "actual" costs are not generally used for the valuation of finished goods inventories by companies using standard costs.

Valuation Practice in Companies Using Actual Costs

Turning now to the companies which do not use ideal or current standard costs, we find the practice in valuing finished goods inventory at the end of the fiscal year to be as follows:

METHODS OF VALUING FINISHED GOODS INVENTORIES
COMPANIES NOT USING IDEAL STANDARD COSTS

	Companies
At cost or market, whichever lower	84
At cost, as provided by cost system used	75
At cost, with raw material component reduced to the lower of cost or market	4
Unclassified	12
No answer	2
No finished goods inventories	10
Replies inconsistent	7
	194

The companies which are listed above as making inconsistent replies are companies which reported that inventories were valued at new standards, whereas their replies to an earlier question reported the use of some method of costing other than ideal standards. The companies listed above as unclassified reported the following method for valuing the finished goods inventory:

Annual nominal standards (Basic standard used).
Cost for machines, cost or market for tools.
Average cost for the year.
Actual cost less overhead eliminations.
Last-in, first-out basis.
At average cost for last three months. No grade costs used.
Material and burden written down by per cent of average for the year.
Sales price less average mark-up.
Arbitrary figure, well below market, consistently followed.
Selling price less provision for selling, delivery and administrative costs.
Approximate selling price less obsolescence, less fixed percentage for selling, administrative expenses and profit.
At current reproduction costs of labor and material, with burden at actual, partially adjusted to activity.

It is rather surprising to find such a relatively large percentage of companies valuing finished goods inventories at cost, with almost as many companies using this basis as use the lower of cost or market. In contrast with these figures, an earlier questionnaire study showed 172 out of 197 companies using the lower of cost or market basis for the valuation of raw material. Undoubtedly the fact that it is more difficult to arrive at a market price for finished goods than it is for raw materials, explains but does not justify the practice of less frequently valuing finished goods at market than is the case with raw materials.

Disposition of Variances from Standard Costs

Reference has been made previously to the indication of valuation methods provided by the disposition made of variances from standard costs. In Table 1 is summarized the practices of 131 companies using ideal standard costs in whole or part in disposing of standard cost variances at the end of the month and at the end of the year. These answers apply to all variances other than over- and under-absorbed burden balances.

At first glance it appears rather surprising that 34 of the questionnaires should have contained no statement as to end-of-year treatment of variances and that 11 should have contained no answer to end-of-month treatment. It will be noticed, however, that only two companies failed to report either end-of-year or end-of-month treatment. Why should so many companies report on either end-of-year or end-of-month treatment, but not on both? It seems possible that in the 34 cases where end-of-year treatment was not reported, the question was interpreted as applying to disposition of the variance in the accounts. Under such an interpretation a company closing its books monthly would have no end-of-year treatment to report, unless the variances were carried forward monthly as deferred items. In the same way, it is possible that the 11 companies failing to report end-of-month treatment closed their books only at the end of the year.

Less Common Methods of Disposing of Variances

One frequently hears the argument that, while standard costs are proper and desirable for control purposes, they are not true costs

TABLE 1

DISPOSITION OF VARIANCES FROM STANDARD COSTS AT END OF MONTH AND END OF YEAR SHOWING NUMBER OF COMPANIES USING EACH METHOD

Methods of Disposing of Variances from Standard Costs Other Than Over- and Under-absorbed Burden	End of Year Treatment	End of Month Treatment					
		Carried Forward to Next Period	Included in Cost of Goods Sold	Shown as Addition to Cost of Goods Sold	Treated as Profit and Loss Charge	Unclassified	No Answer
Totals..........	131	15	23	32	45	5	11
1. Variances included in cost of goods sold	44	9	14	5	10	2	4
2. Variances shown separately as part of cost of goods sold	26	4	—	17	—	2	3
3. Variances treated as profit and loss charge below gross profit figure	22	1	—	—	20	—	1
4. Unclassified	5	—	—	1	2	1	1
5. No answer to this question.	34	1	9	9	13	0	2

and any variance from standard should be prorated at the end of the period between inventories and cost of goods sold in such a way as to give actual costs. Apparently this concept of standard cost has not been accepted to any extent in practice, since only 2 of the 131 companies report making any adjustment of inventories for variances from standard. One of these companies states that, "all variances are taken up in inventory and charged net to cost of sales as the goods are sold." The other states that "variances are treated as profit and loss charges at the end of each month, but as adjustments of inventory values at the end of the year."

In Table 1 these two companies are listed as unclassified with respect to end-of-year treatment. The other three companies included in this group report the following methods of disposing of variances from standard:

Labor and overhead variances included monthly in cost of sales, material variances charged to profit and loss annually as an inventory adjustment.

Variances treated at the end of year as charges or credit to a reserve, created either from over-absorbed burden or by a charge to profit and loss.

Variances not calculated. Costs not tied in with general ledger accounts.

Four of the five companies listed as unclassified, so far as end-of-month treatment of variances is concerned, report the use of two methods each. Two companies state that variances are shown separately as additions to cost of goods sold and/or carried forward to the next period. One company reports that variances are partially included in cost of goods sold and partially carried forward to the next period, while the fourth company treats variances either as amounts to be included in cost of goods sold or shown separately as additions to that figure.

More Common Methods of Disposing of Variances

Having discussed the more unusual practices and the incomplete replies, let us consider the more usual practices which are indicated in Table 1 opposite, to the left of the heavy lines. Of the 92 companies whose end-of-year treatment of variances is included in the group, 70 treat such variances as either a part of, or an addition to, the cost of goods sold, while 22 companies treat them as charges to profit and loss below the gross profit figure. In developing the questionnaire it was thought desirable to distinguish between amounts *included in* cost of goods sold and amounts shown separately as *additions to* cost of goods sold, since this would indicate whether or not the information on variances was presented as such on the face of the profit and loss statement.

The differences shown by this tabulation in the treatment of variances at the end of the month and at the end of the year is interesting. The most general end-of-year treatment is to include variance in cost of goods sold, while the most general end-of-month treatment is to charge profit and loss for the variance. It will be noticed that of the 22 companies which charge variances to profit and loss at the end of the year, 20 follow the same practices at the end of the month while, in contrast, of the 44 companies which include variances in cost of goods sold at the end of the year, only 14 follow this practice at the end of the month.

Probably the differences exhibited by these figures are due largely to the difference in the use made of monthly and annual statements. Monthly statements are prepared for use within the business and designed to give management the essential information. Accordingly, we find it most usual practice in monthly statements to treat variances as separate items of cost of goods sold or profit and loss, rather than to bury them in the cost of goods sold figure. Annual statements, on the other hand, are prepared for the information of stockholders (present and prospective), bankers and others not engaged in the management of the business to whom the variances would not be essential information. Thus, the inclusion of variances in a single cost-of-goods-sold figure is the most common practice for year-end statements.

It is also significant that, while 15 of the 131 companies carry standard cost variances forward from one month to the next, no companies reported the practice of carrying the variances forward from one year to another.

Classification of Companies with Respect to Treatment of Over- and Under-Absorbed Balances

In accumulating and organizing the data on over- and under-absorbed burden for this report, various methods of presenting the data in tabular form have been considered. In addition to reporting the number of companies using each method of disposing of over-absorbed and under-absorbed burden at the end of the month and end of the year, it was considered desirable to compare end-of-month with end-of-year practice with respect to over-absorbed burden with practice with respect to under-absorbed burden. As a result, the 325 companies have been grouped under the four following heads:

1. Those companies whose treatment of over-absorbed burden is similar to their treatment of under-absorbed burden and whose end-of-month treatment (where reported) is similar to their end-of-year treatment (where reported). This group of 159 companies is further divided into three sub-groups as follows:
   a. Companies reporting same end-of-month and end-of-year treatment. Total, 85 companies.
   b. Companies reporting end-of-month treatment only. Total, 53 companies.
   c. Companies reporting end-of-year treatment only. Total, 21 companies.
2. Those companies whose treatment of over-absorbed burden is similar to their treatment of under-absorbed burden, but whose end-of-month treatment differs from their end-of-year treatment. Total, 46 companies.
3. Those companies which do not treat over-absorbed burden in the same way as under-absorbed burden, and in addition use different treatment at the end of the month and at the end of the year. Total, 37 companies.
4. Those companies which failed to answer the two questions dealing with over- and under-absorbed burden. Total, 83 companies.

Practice in Disposing of Over- and Under-Absorbed Burden

The totals for these four groups are summarized at the bottom of Table 2, which provides a summary of the methods followed by companies in the first group in disposing of over- and under-absorbed balances. The probable reason for some companies reporting on end-of-month treatment only or on end-of-year treatment only was discussed in connection with standard cost variances.

Table 3 deals with companies of the second group, which accord the same treatment to over-absorbed and to under-absorbed burden, but use a different method of disposing of balances at the end of the year from that used at the end of the month. It will be noticed that while 18 companies carry over- or under-absorbed balances forward from one month to another, no company makes a carry-over

TABLE 2

DISPOSITION OF OVER- AND UNDER-ABSORBED BURDEN

COMPANIES GIVING SIMILAR TREATMENT TO OVER- AND UNDER-ABSORBED BURDEN AND SAME END-OF-YEAR AND END-OF-MONTH TREATMENT

Methods of Disposing of Over- and Under-absorbed Burden:	Number of Companies			
	Companies Reporting Same Treatment at End of Year and End of Month	Companies Reporting End-of-Month Treatment Only	Companies Reporting End-of-Year Treatment Only	Totals
1. Balance over-absorbed treated as reserve; balance under-absorbed charged against reserve or carried forward..	4	5	—	9
2. Balance over-absorbed credited to cost of goods sold; balance under-absorbed debited to cost of goods sold.....	19	10	16	45
3. Balance over-absorbed shown separately as deduction from cost of goods sold; balance under-absorbed shown separately as addition to cost of goods sold...........	31	16	4	51
4. Balance over-absorbed treated as other income below gross profit; balance under-absorbed treated as charge to profit and loss below gross profit............	30	20	1	51
5. Balance over- or under-absorbed divided pro-rata between inventories and cost of goods sold...........	1	2	0	3
Totals	85	53	21	159

Companies whose end-of-month treatment differs from end-of-year treatment (Table 3)		46
Companies whose practice varies in both respects (Table 4)		37
Companies providing no answers with respect to either over- or under-absorbed burden		83
Total		325

TABLE 3

DISPOSITION OF OVER- AND UNDER-ABSORBED BURDEN

COMPANIES GIVING SIMILAR TREATMENT TO OVER- AND UNDER-ABSORBED BURDEN
END-OF-MONTH TREATMENT DIFFERING FROM END-OF-YEAR TREATMENT

| | | Number of Companies | | | | |
| | | | End of Month Treatment | | | |
Method of Disposing of Over- and Under-absorbed Burden:	End-of-Year Treatment	Balance Carried Forward or Charged Against Reserve	Balance Shown as Addition to or Deduction from Cost of Goods Sold	Balance Treated as Profit and Loss Charge or Credit	Unclassified
1. Balance over-absorbed credited to cost of goods sold; balance under-absorbed debited to cost of goods sold..........	31	7	6	16	2
2. Balance over-absorbed shown as separate deduction from cost of goods sold; balance under-absorbed shown as separate addition to cost of goods sold.......	8	7	—	1	—
3. Balance over-absorbed treated as other income below gross profit figure; balance under-absorbed treated as charge to profit and loss below gross profit figure.......	3	2	—	—	1
4. Balance over- or under-absorbed divided pro-rata between inventories and cost of goods sold.......	4	2	1	1	—
Totals.......	46	18	7	18	3

at the end of the year. Of interest also is the fact that of 18 companies which treat burden balances as profit and loss items on a monthly basis, 16 charge or credit such balances to cost of goods sold at the end of the year. No doubt this is explained by the difference between internal and external statements referred to previously.

The 37 companies which reported methods of handling over-absorbed burden which differed from their methods of handling under-absorbed burden and whose end-of-year treatment differed from their end-of-month treatment represent such a diversity of practice that it is only possible to report on the distribution of practice under each of the four heads. This is done in Table 4. It is interesting to note that while 13 companies treat an over-absorbed balance as a reserve to be carried forward from one month to another, no companies carry such a reserve beyond the year-end; and while 15 companies treat an under-absorbed balance at the end of the month as an amount to be carried forward or charged against a reserve created by previous over-absorption, only one company follows this practice at the year-end. Of interest, also, are the figures showing 12 companies prorating over-absorbed balances between inventories and cost of goods sold at the end of the year, but only one company making such a proration of under-absorbed burden. Notice also the smaller number making the proration monthly compared with those making it annually.

Some Generalization

Table 5 is a summary of the three previous tables. From it the following generalizations are possible:

1. The most general practice is to debit or credit over- and under-absorbed burden to cost of goods sold, or to show it as additions or deductions from cost of goods sold. Such balances are treated as cost of goods sold items in about twice as many companies as they are treated as profit and loss items. In addition, cost of goods sold is more likely to be charged or credited for end-of-year balances than for end-of-month balances.

2. As is to be expected, inventories are more frequently adjusted by the proration of over-absorbed burden to inventories than by the proration of under-absorbed burden, and this adjustment of inventories is made more often at the end of the year than

TABLE 4

DISPOSITION OF OVER- AND UNDER-ABSORBED BURDEN
BY COMPANIES WHOSE PRACTICE VARIES
SHOWING NUMBER OF COMPANIES USING EACH METHOD

Method of Disposing of Over- and Under-absorbed Burden:	Over-absorbed Burden		Under-absorbed Burden	
	End-of-Year Treatment	End-of-Month Treatment	End-of-Year Treatment	End-of-Month Treatment
1. Balance over-absorbed treated as a reserve; balance under-absorbed charged against reserve or carried forward	—	13	1	15
2. Balance over-absorbed credited to cost of goods sold; balance under-absorbed debited to cost of goods sold	5	3	12	4
3. Balance over-absorbed shown separately as deduction from cost of goods sold; balance under-absorbed shown separately as addition to cost of goods sold	4	4	7	4
4. Balance over-absorbed treated as other income below gross profit; balance under-absorbed charged to profit and loss below gross profit	3	3	5	4
5. Balance over- or under-absorbed divided pro-rata between inventories and cost of goods sold	12	6	1	—
6. Unclassified	13	8	11	10
Totals	37	37	37	37

TABLE 5

SUMMARY OF METHODS OF DISPOSING OF OVER- AND UNDER-ABSORBED BURDEN
SHOWING NUMBER OF COMPANIES USING EACH METHOD

Method of Disposing of Over- and Under-absorbed Burden:	Over-absorbed Burden		Under-absorbed Burden	
	End-of-Year Treatment	End-of-Month Treatment	End-of-Year Treatment	End-of-Month Treatment
1. Balance over-absorbed treated as a reserve; balance under-absorbed charged against reserve or carried forward	9	35	10	37
2. Balance over-absorbed credited to cost of goods sold; balance under-absorbed debited to cost of goods sold	65	38	72	39
3. Balance over-absorbed shown separately as deduction from costs of goods sold; balance under-absorbed shown separately as addition to cost of goods sold..	59	46	62	46
4. Balance over-absorbed treated as other income below gross profit; balance under-absorbed charged to profit and loss below gross profit	57	52	58	53
5. Balance over- or under-absorbed divided pro-rata between inventories and cost of goods sold	19	7	8	1
6. Unclassified	—	3	—	3
Totals	209	181	210	179

at the end of the month. However, it is interesting to note
that some companies do make this proration monthly (especially
for over-absorbed balances), but rather surprising that such a
relatively small number (19) treat over-absorbed burden as an
adjustment of year-end inventories.

3. Some companies attempt to carry the theory of normal overhead to its logical conclusion, as witnessed by the 9 companies
which treat year-end over-absorbed balances as reserves to
absorb future under-absorption, and by the 10 companies which
either charge year-end under-absorbed balances against such
reserves or carry them forward to the next period. The fact
that the latter group should be the larger is rather surprising.
Naturally, a considerably larger group carry month-end balances
forward.

Normal Burden Rates in Process Industries

Of the 325 companies, 83 failed to answer the two questions relating to over- and under-absorbed burden. Naturally some of those
failing to reply did so because their companies use actual rather than
predetermined burden rates and thus have no burden balances to
dispose of at the end of the month and end of the year. But in a
previous study dealing with methods of overhead accounting, only
8.5 per cent of the companies reported using actual burden rates,
whereas the 83 companies failing to answer the question represent
25.5 per cent of all companies included in this study.

In an effort to locate the reason for the lack of answers to these
two questions, the questionnaires of these 83 companies were grouped
by types of cost systems used with the following result:

COMPANIES CLASSIFIED BY TYPE OF COST SYSTEM

Cost System Used	Companies
Process Costs	45
Job Costs	13
Combinations	6
Basic Standard Costs	4
Ideal Standard Costs	3
Unclassified	12
Total	83

It will be noticed that over half of the companies in this group
operate process cost systems. In addition, 10 of the 12 companies
listed as unclassified are really of the process type of manufacture.

But without considering these ten companies, 54.2 per cent of the companies in this group use process costs, compared with 20.6 per cent of the entire group of 325 companies using this method of costing.

The industries most commonly represented in this group are breweries, oil companies, chemical companies, paper companies, textile companies and manufacturers of dairy products. In these and similar industries using process costs, the costs are usually calculated and burden applied at the end of the process period, which is normally one month in length. Naturally, predetermined burden rates are not needed for the calculation of current costs when they are calculated only at the end of the month, at which time the actual burden amount is available. However, it does seem just as logical in this case as under any other type of cost system to apply overhead on the basis of normal capacity, which would result in over- or under-applied balances even though the costs are not calculated until the end of the month. Apparently some companies do use normal burden rates in connection with a process cost system, as 22 of the 67 companies using this plan reported the methods used in disposing of over- and under-absorbed burden.

Disposition of Difference Between Inventory Records and Actual Count

Under a plan of perpetual inventories it is customary to carry on during the period a staggered count of goods actually on hand for comparison with the book records. Members were asked to report what disposition was made of any discrepancies revealed by the staggered count. Eliminating 14 companies which do not have finished goods inventories, 41 who either do not have perpetual inventory records or for some other reason failed to answer the question with respect to them, and 5 companies which failed to answer the present question, we have 265 companies reporting their practices as indicated at the top of page 389.

Listed as unclassified in the above tabulation are five companies which replied as follows:

 Reviewed monthly and errors corrected.
 Reviewed daily and errors corrected.
 Perpetual records not tied in. No adjustment necessary.
 Not handled accountingwise.
 Correction automatically reflected in profit and loss.

Companies

Treated as part of cost of goods sold................... 110
Treated as separate item added to cost of goods sold.... 36
Treated as a separate profit and loss item.............. 51
Charged against a reserve previously created............ 36
Not adjusted currently; adjusted at time physical inven-
    tory is taken at the end of the year............... 10
Combination or alternative treatment................... 7
Treated as an adjustment of production................ 3
Charged to factory overhead 3
No differences 3
Charged to selling expense........................... 1
Unclassified 5

                                                    265

The three companies which report no differences have the following to say:

In ten years no discrepancies.
Never have such an item.
There can be no discrepancy because of the nature of the item.

The seven companies which reported either alternative or combination treatments gave the following answers:

Treated as part of cost of goods sold if in factory stock, as selling expense
if in field stock.
Small differences treated as part of cost of goods sold, major differences
as profit and loss charges.
Treated as part of cost of goods sold on internal statements; as separate
addition to cost of goods sold on external statements.
Treated as separate addition to cost of goods sold and/or charged to a
reserve previously created.
Treated as part of cost of goods sold and/or charged to profit and loss.
Treated as part of cost of goods sold and/or charged to reserve previously
created (2 companies).

Disposition of Year-End Inventory Write-Downs

The valuation of the finished goods inventory at the end of the year on any base other than the costs recorded in the account during the year will result in an inventory write-down. This write-down may be due to pricing at market values which are below costs, to valuation at new standards which are lower than old standards, to shortages which are revealed by the taking of a physical inventory or by decline in inventory value due to obsolescence or any damage to stock which reduces its value. The treatment accorded such write-downs by our 325 companies is shown in the following tabulations:

DISPOSITION OF INVENTORY WRITE-DOWNS AT THE END OF THE YEAR

	Companies
Treated as addition to cost of goods sold	137
Treated as separate profit and loss item	93
Treated as a charge to a reserve previously created	53
Practice varies	10
No answer	18
No finished goods inventory	14
	325

The 10 companies who report that their practice varies, indicated that the following dispositions were made:

Treated as cost of goods sold on published statements, as profit and loss on internal statements.

Usually treated as part of cost of goods sold; but as a profit and loss charge in unusual cases.

Usually treated as part of cost of goods sold, but occasionally as a profit and loss charge.

Treated as a part of cost of goods sold and/or charged against reserve previously created.

Treated as a profit and loss charge and/or charged against reserve previously created.

Reserve charged to extent thereof; balance treated as part of cost of goods sold.

Reserve charged if in existence, otherwise treated as profit and loss charge.

Treated as profit and loss charge if small; large write-downs charged against surplus.

Use of Reserves to Absorb Write-Downs

In the two previous sections reference was made to the practice of charging inventory write-downs and differences between book records and an actual count to a reserve previously created. Thirty-six companies report that differences between inventory records and an actual count are charged to such a reserve, while 53 companies report the use of a reserve to absorb inventory write-downs at the end of the fiscal year. Of these companies, 29 make use of such a reserve for both of these purposes, while 24 use it for annual write-downs only, and 7 only for absorbing discrepancies revealed by the staggered count. In a separate question members were asked to report the charge made in setting up a reserve for these purposes. The following tabulation shows the practices followed:

METHOD OF PROVIDING RESERVE FOR YEAR-END INVENTORY
WRITE-DOWNS AND ABSORPTION OF SHORTAGES
REVEALED BY STAGGERED COUNT

	Reserve Used for Annual Inventory Write-down	Reserve Used to Absorb Short-ages Revealed by Staggered Count	Reserve Used for Both Purposes	Total
By charge to cost of goods sold	4	3	9	16
By charge to profit and loss	8	—	5	13
By charge back to burden or operating cost	1	1	8	10
No answer to this question	11	3	7	21
Totals	24	7	29	60

The practice of making the charge to burden or operating cost at the time the reserve is set up is interesting, but raises the question of whether the types of losses which later will be charged against the reserve created in this way are logically burden elements or manufacturing costs, and therefore proper additions to the cost value of inventories. One wonders if these same companies would feel justified in charging inventory write-downs at the end of the year and differences revealed by a staggered count during the year directly to burden or manufacturing cost. That it is done is revealed by the tabulation on page 389 which shows 3 companies adjusting production and 3 companies charging factory overhead for differences revealed by the staggered count.

In reply to a question as to whether the reserves created in this way were used for any other purpose, a few companies replied that they were used for absorbing obsolescence, shrinkages in inventories and items of this sort, which normally will be revealed by the staggered count or the physical inventory.

Basis for Classifying Products as Slow-Moving

In the valuation of finished goods an important factor is the proper valuation of goods which are slow-moving or obsolete. Members were asked in two questions to state any rules followed by their companies in determining when a product is slow-moving or when it is obsolete. Naturally a great variety of methods were mentioned, although in a majority of cases it was stated that there was no definite rule. The methods mentioned for the location of slow-moving stock can largely be included in four groups, as follows:

1. The rate at which the product is sold is used in determining whether or not it is slow-moving. Some members report that in their companies this is determined by reference to the sales records for the past period, while others state that a comparison is made between current sales and sales of prior periods. In other cases, the fact that no sales of a product have been made for a certain period of time is used as a basis for classifying it as slow-moving. In a number of companies the perpetual inventory records are used in determining whether a product is slow-moving. In such cases a comparison can be made between the sales per unit of time and the quantity of stock on hand.

2. The age of the inventory item is a guide to whether or not it is to be classed as slow-moving in a number of companies. The use of stock record cards of a different color each year, serial numbers and other evidences of age makes it possible to segregate the over-age items. Naturally, the age limit varies greatly from one industry to another, the higher limit applying to companies making parts which may be called for until all the units of the product on which they are used as replacements have been retired, while the lower limit applies to goods which are more or less perishable. One member connected with a company manufacturing parts as well as finished products reported that parts sales continued for 15 to 20 years after a model was discontinued, but that the parts in stock were written off entirely at the end of 5 years.

3. In some companies products are considered slow-moving when they are excluded from the regular line. Reference is made to removal from price lists and catalogues, changes in design and comparisons of year-end inventory with latest specifications.

4. In some cases the quantity of a product on hand is used to determine whether or not it is slow-moving in whole or part, usually by comparison with the sales requirements as shown by recent sales reports.

A few other methods of determining when products were slow-moving were mentioned, among the more interesting being a monthly check of actual sales with budgeted sales, and the practice of treating a product as slow-moving when its sales price is reduced in order to move it.

Basis for Classifying Stock as Obsolete

The methods reported for determining when a product is obsolete would indicate that in very few cases is there a clear-cut distinction between slow-moving and obsolete products. All of the methods mentioned above for determining when a product is slow-moving were also reported as used for determining when a product is obsolete. However, the third method mentioned above, i.e., the exclusion of a product from the regular line, was probably the most common method reported for locating obsolete products, and this method was much more frequently mentioned in connection with obsolete products than for slow-moving products. The discontinuance of a product, a change in design, and removal from the price list or catalogue are the most frequent statements of how this method is applied. In a smaller number of cases the age of the product or the lack of sales for a specified period of time was stated to be the method used as the basis for selecting obsolete products.

Basis for Valuing Slow-Moving and Obsolete Stock

Relatively few companies have any predetermined base or rule for the valuation of goods classified as slow-moving or obsolete. The most common reply to the question of how slow-moving stock is valued was that it is carried at cost until judged obsolete. Some companies consign to slow-moving stock a valuation set at some fixed per cent of cost, while others use forecasted selling prices less selling expenses as a guide to valuation. Where some stock is considered slow-moving because of an excess supply on hand, the excess quantity may be carried at no value. However, few companies follow the practice of writing down slow-moving stock to either scrap value or no value.

In the case of obsolete stock the general practice is to write down such stock to scrap or salvage value, or to write it off entirely where the product cannot be reprocessed or has no salvage value. At the time of the write-down there is normally a physical transfer of the obsolete goods to a reclaim or salvage department.

Individual or Committee Responsible for
Classification and Valuation

In many companies the classification of stock as slow-moving or obsolete and the valuation of such stock is left to some individual in the organization or to a committee of two or more officials or department heads. Members were asked, where this condition applied in their company, to give the title or position of the individual or the make-up of the group. In 78 cases a single individual was named, in 61 a two-man committee, in 41 a three-man committee, and in 20 cases a committee of four or more individuals. Naturally, there was a great variation in the titles used, so that in the following list of the individual or departments having sole responsibility for the location and valuation of slow-moving and obsolete stock only the main functional groups are indicated.

INDIVIDUALS OR DEPARTMENTS HAVING RESPONSIBILITY FOR DETERMINING
EXISTENCE AND VALUE OF SLOW-MOVING AND OBSOLETE STOCK

Accounting (Controller, Accounting Department, Cost Department)	20
Executive (President, General Manager, Vice-President, etc.)	19
Sales or Merchandising (including managers of sales branches)	17
Factory (Production Manager, Plant Manager)	11
Financial (Treasurer, Assistant Treasurer)	7
Engineering	2
Stores	2
	78

In companies where two individuals or two departments share the duty of determining and valuing slow-moving and obsolete stock, the accounting and sales departments are most often mentioned, with a combination of these two departments being the most general method followed. Of secondary popularity was the co-operation of the accounting and executive departments, with the accounting and stores department in third place.

The Use of Perpetual Inventory Records
for Finished Goods

The remaining questions deal largely with the control and verification of inventory quantities. Control is usually based on some system of perpetual inventory records and members were asked in the first question of this group to report the per cent of their finished goods inventories controlled through perpetual inventory records. In the following the replies have been classified into groups based on the per cent of inventories controlled.

PER CENT OF FINISHED GOODS INVENTORY CONTROLLED
BY PERPETUAL INVENTORY RECORDS

	No. of Companies	Per Cent
100% Controlled	228	70.1
Partially controlled	42	12.9
No book records	35	10.8
No finished goods	14	4.3
No answer to this question	6	1.9
	325	100.0

The accuracy and value of a perpetual inventory system is to a considerable extent dependent on some plan for checking the book records with the actual quantities on hand. This is often called the "continuous check" or "staggered count." The following tabulation summarizes the replies to a question on the average number of times per year each finished goods item is checked by the 270 companies using perpetual inventory records for finished goods.

AVERAGE FREQUENCY OF CHECK OF RECORDS BY STAGGERED COUNT

No. of Times per Year	No. of Companies
Once	83
Twice	56
Three times	14
Four times	26
Five to eight times	8
Twelve times	36
Daily	5
Varies from 1 to 2 to 10 to 12 times	16
Unclassified	16
No answer to this question	10
Total	270

Frequency of Physical Inventories

An interesting question, where a 100 per cent perpetual inventory is kept and where the book records are checked frequently by a staggered count, is the necessity of a physical inventory at the end of the year. In 1937, in a study of raw material inventory practice, it was found that 55 out of 197 reporting companies, or 28 per cent, considered physical inventories unnecessary under an adequate system of perpetual inventory records proved through continuous count. The percentage is not so high in the case of finished goods as shown by the following tabulation:

FREQUENCY OF TAKING PHYSICAL INVENTORIES

	No. of Companies	Per Cent
Never depend on current checking of perpetual inventory records for accurate figures	51	15.7
Annually	155	47.7
Semi-annually	41	12.6
Quarterly	12	3.7
Monthly	30	9.2
Unclassified	22	6.8
No physical inventories	14	4.3
Totals	325	100.0

Date of Taking Final Physical Inventory

There has been apparent recently a trend toward the practice of taking the final physical inventory a month or more prior to the end of the fiscal year. This is possible, however, only when an adequate book inventory makes possible the audit of inventory changes between the date of the final inventory and the balance sheet date. Of the 222 companies who replied to a question on the date of taking the physical inventory, 150 stated that the finished goods inventory was taken as of the end of the fiscal year, 64 reported taking the inventory a month or more prior to the balance sheet date, and 8 reported that practices in recent years had varied.

Co-operation with External Auditors

As a final question, three methods of co-operating with external auditors in the verification of inventories were listed and members were requested to indicate which of these methods were followed and to report any other method of co-operating followed by their companies. Of the 325 companies, 87 reported that it was their practice to arrange for representatives of the auditors to participate in some of the detailed checking of perpetual records during the year (the staggered count), 123 reported that they arranged for representatives of the auditors to participate in the taking of the annual physical inventory, and 207 reported that they preserved all working papers showing discrepancies between stock records and physical counts and disposition of these adjustmetns for audit by the external accountants. It is believed that these practices are growing.

Among the most important of the other methods of co-operating with auditors mentioned on the questionnaire was the practice of having the external auditor review and approve all inventory procedures, and the employment of engineers where materials are in stock piles or bins and the quantities are based on estimates. Naturally many companies referred to the making of spot checks by auditors, the test-checking of inventory sheets, and in a few cases to the provision of inventory certificates by management.

BIBLIOGRAPHY

INVENTORY CONTROL

Heckert, J. Brooks. "Accounting Systems: Design and Installation." Ronald Press, 1936. Chapter 21, *"Inventory Control and Material Cost Procedure."* pp. 294-321.

Metropolitan Life Insurance Company. "Inventory Control Methods." Policyholders Service Bureau, 1941.

Neuner, John B. "Costing Accounting." Business Publications, Inc., 1938. Chapter 9, *"Inventory Records."* pp. 151-181.

Newlove, George H., and Gardner, S. Paul. "Elementary Cost Accounting." D. C. Heath & Co., 1941. Chapter 14, *"Inventory Difficulties and Complexities."* pp. 370-404.

Articles and Other Publications

Beaudry, D. Phillip, Jr. *The Supply Inventory and Its Control.* N.A.C.A. Bulletin. August 1, 1941.

Davis, Ralph C. *Effect of "Dead Time" on Inventory in Process.* Society for the Advancement of Management Journal. May, 1936, pp. 71-74.

Dutton, H. P. *Inventory Control.* Supplement to Factory Management & Maintenance. August, 1935.

French, R. G. *Inventory Control for 45,000 Items Stocked in 22 Branches.* American Business. April, 1940, pp. 22-24, 51.

Lewis, H. I. *Inventory Control for Reduced Overhead.* "Quality and Inventory Control." Production Series # 114. American Management Association. 1939, pp. 23-28.

Madison, William J. *Accounting for Material Costs.* 1937 Year Book— National Association of Cost Accountants. pp. 76-85.

Midworth, C. A. *Practical Methods of Eliminating Old Stock from Merchandise Inventories.* Balance Sheet. December, 1937, pp. 14-17.

Peck, Sam A. *Inventory Control.* Society for the Advancement of Management Journal. March, 1938, pp. 68-71.

Porteus, Kenneth. *Factory Orders and Inventory Records: A Case History of Their Mechanical Preparation.* Factory Management & Maintenance. September, 1937, pp. 60-80.

Poulton, P. K., and Goldsmith, P. H. *Budgeting Inventories and Stabilizing Employment.* Factory Management & Maintenance. December, 1939, pp. 52-55.

Ruxton, R. G. *Investigation of Inventory Differences.* Balance Sheet, September, 1938, pp. 16-20.

Schmalz, Carl N. *The Problem of Merchandise Control in A Department Store.* N.A.C.A. Bulletin. August 15, 1941.

BIBLIOGRAPHY 399

Thompson, Kenneth W. *Accounting Control in A Chain of 4,000 Grocery Stores.* N.A.C.A. Bulletin. August 1, 1935.
Urich, John E. *Accounting for Productive Materials.* N.A.C.A. Bulletin. January 1, 1936.
Warner, Sydney W. *Production and Inventory Control.* N.A.C.A. Bulletin, September 15, 1940.
Whitmore, Eugene. *Appleton Electric Licks A Tough Inventory Problem.* American Business. October, 1939, pp. 18-20.
Wylie, Harry L. *"Stop-Loss" Inventory Methods.* American Business. May, 1939, pp. 30-32.
———*Systems to Simplify Inventory Accounting.* American Business. March, 1939, pp. 26-27, 49.
Zinck, W. C. *Low Inventories Because——.* Factory Management & Maintenance. July, 1938, pp. 65-66, 128, 130.

INVENTORY VALUATION

Cotter, Arundel. *"Fool's Profits."* Barron's Publishing Co., 1940.
Gilman, Stephen. *"Accounting Concepts of Profit."* Ronald Press Co., 1939. pp. 357-473.
National Industrial Conference Board. "Prevailing Practices in Inventory Valuation." Studies in Administrative Control No. 1. February, 1938.
Specthrie, Samuel Waldo. "Mathematics for the Accountant." Ronald Press, 1940. Lecture 12.—*"Mathematics of Inventories."* pp. 141-159.

ARTICLES AND OTHER PUBLICATIONS

American Institute of Accountants, Special Committee on Inventories. *Valuation of Inventories.* Journal of Accountancy. August, 1936, pp. 122-132. January, 1938, pp. 29-32.
———Committee on Federal Taxation. *Last-in, First-out Inventory Method.* Journal of Accountancy. November, 1938. pp. 310-314.
———*Inventories.* Journal of Accountancy. October, 1940, pp. 324-335.
———*Inventories—A Preliminary Statement of the Research Department.* Journal of Accountancy. June 1940, pp. 438-439.
———*Inventories.* Research Department. Journal of Accountancy. April, 1941, pp. 294-303.
———Round Table. *What Is the Lower of Cost or Market.* Fiftieth Anniversary Celebration. 1937, pp. 335-362.
Arthur, Henry B. *Something Business Can Do About Depressions.* Journal of Accountancy. January, 1939, pp. 7-14.
Crandell, J. Chester. *Principles Related to Inventory Valuation.* Papers on Accounting Principles and Procedure. American Institute of Accountants. 1938, pp. 21-25.
Crocheron, Clarence. *Inventory Valuation From An Appraisal Viewpoint.* New York Certified Public Accountant. February, 1940, pp. 266-269.

Davis, Albion R. *Inventory Valuation and Business Profits: The Case For A "Stabilized" Basis.* N.A.C.A. Bulletin. December 1, 1937 (o.p.).

Ellis, Cecil A. *The Financial Consequence of Stores Accounting.* Canadian Chartered Accountant. August, 1940, pp. 77-85.

Ferrie, G. C. *A Preliminary Examination of Some Methods Used for Valuing Inventories.* Canadian Chartered Accountant. March, 1940, pp. 143-159.

Harvey, John L. *Some Observations on Accounting Practice with Special Reference To Inventory Valuation.* Journal of Accountancy. December, 1937, pp. 440-451.

Kassander, Arno R. *The Last-in, First-out Inventory Method.* New York Certified Public Accountant. February, 1940, pp. 259-265.

Kracke, Edward A. *Inventories and Taxes.* Journal of Accountancy. December, 1939, pp. 369-376.

—— *Inventories: From Fetish to Creed.* The Accounting Review. June, 1941, pp. 175-182.

—— *Inventories—Past, Present and Future.* Journal of Accountancy. June, 1941, pp. 486-492.

Littleton, A. C. *A Geneology for "Cost or Market."* Accounting Review. June, 1941, pp. 161-167.

—— *Inventory Variations.* Journal of Accountancy. July, 1941, pp. 7-16.

May, George O. *Valuation or Historical Cost: Some Recent Developments.* Journal of Accountancy. January, 1940, pp. 14-21.

New York State Society of C.P.A.'s, Committee on Inventory Methods. *Summary of Discussion* by Maurice Peloubet. New York Certified Public Accountant. July, 1938, pp. 40-47.

Nickerson, Clarence B. *Inventory Reserves as an Element of Inventory Policy.* Accounting Review. December, 1937, pp. 345-54.

Paton, William A. *Last-in, First-out.* Journal of Accountancy. May, 1940, pp. 354-360.

Pelej, Joseph. *Valuation of Flour Mill Inventories.* Journal of Accountancy. July, 1939, pp. 35-47.

Peloubet, Maurice. *Inventories and the Auditor.* Journal of Accountancy. July, 1939, pp. 8-16.

—— *Last-in, First-out Once More.* Journal of Accountancy. June, 1940, pp. 446-450.

—— *Present Day Problems in Inventory Valuation.* 1936 Year Book—National Association of Cost Accountants. pp. 164-187.

—— *Problems of Present-Day Inventory Valuation.* N.A.C.A. Bulletin. March 1, 1937.

Rappaport, Percy. *Some Observations on the Valuation of Inventories on the "Last-in, First-out" Method from the Standpoint of the Petroleum Industry.* New York Certified Public Accountant. April, 1940, pp. 397-404.

Reitell, Charles. *Last-in, First-out.* Factory Management & Maintenance. May, 1940, pp. 55-56, 144.

Renner, Robert R. *The Last-in, First-out Method.* Cost and Management. February, 1941, pp. 400-405.
—— *The Normal Base Stock Method.* N.A.C.A. Bulletin. October 1, 1940.
Rolnik, Max. *Some Tax Problems in Inventorying Under the Last-in, First-out Method.* New York Certified Public Accountant. December, 1939, pp. 140-145.
Staub, Walter A. *Physical Tests of Inventory Quantities.* American Institute of Accountants. "Papers on Auditing Procedure and Other Subjects." 1939. pp. 59-90.
Sweet, Homer N. *Inventory Valuation and Business Profits: The Case for A "Cost or Market" Basis.* N.A.C.A. Bulletin. December 1, 1937 (o.p.).
Walker, Ross G. *Base-Stock Principles in Income Accounting.* Harvard Business Review. Autumn, 1936, pp. 76-94.
—— *Income Accounting and Base-Stock Inventory.* Credit and Financial Management. May, 1938, pp. 14-17; June, 1938, pp. 14-16.
—— *Some Financial Questions in Inventory Valuation.* 1936 Year Book—National Association of Cost Accountants. pp. 212-216.
Wilson, George A. *Further Consideration of the Last-in, First-out Basis of Inventory Valuation.* N.A.C.A. Bulletin. September 1, 1939.

INVENTORY TAKING AND VERIFICATION

ARTICLES AND OTHER PUBLICATIONS

American Institute of Accountants, Committee on Auditing Procedure. *Clients' Written Representations Regarding Inventories, Liabilities, and Other Matters.* Journal of Accountancy. March, 1941, pp. 221-228.
Armstrong, A. B. *Taking A Physical Inventory In Chain Stores.* Balance Sheet. April, 1938, pp. 9-12.
Broad, Samuel J. *Extensions of Auditing Procedure to Meet New Demands.* American Institute of Accountants. "Papers on Auditing Procedure and Other Accounting Subjects." 1939, pp. 41-47.
Granger, Marshall. *Auditing Inventory Pricing.* New York Certified Public Accountant. February, 1940, pp. 270-274.
Inventory Methods, *Corroboration of Inventory Quantities by Physical Tests.* New York Certified Public Accountant. April, 1940, pp. 417-431.
Knapp, Carl T. *Taking and Tabulating Inventory in the Specialty Store.* Balance Sheet. January, 1938, pp. 15-16.
Munoz, G. C. *A Plan for Making An Annual Physical Inventory.* Executive Service Bulletin. August, 1940, pp. 3-4.

INVENTORY—GENERAL

Alford, L. P., Editor. "Cost and Production Handbook." Ronald Press, 1934. Sec. 9—*"Inventory Control and Storekeeping."* pp. 445-514.

Foulke, Roy A. "Behind the Scenes of Business." Dun and Bradstreet, Inc., 1937. Chapter 3——"*Three Important Inventory Ratios.*" pp. 59-87.

———"*They Said It With Inventories,*" Supplement No. 2 to the 1937 Edition of "Behind the Scenes of Business." Dun and Bradstreet, Inc., 1939.

Kilduff, Frederic W. "Inventory Practice and Material Control." McGraw-Hill, 1925.

Articles and Other Publications

Arthur, Henry B. *Inventory Profits in the Business Cycle.* American Economic Review. March, 1938, pp. 27-40.

Ellis, Cecil A. *The Control and Valuation of Stores.* Canadian Chartered Accountant. December, 1937, pp. 425-442.

Inventories and Profits (Editorial). Journal of Accountancy. June, 1938, pp. 460-462.

Mitchell, Walter, Jr. *Collection and Interpretation of Inventory Data.* Journal of the American Statistical Association. June, 1939, pp. 283-290.

Testimony of Expert Witnesses at S.E.C. Hearings. Journal of Accountancy. April, 1939, pp. 199-220; May, 1939, pp. 279-297; June, 1939, pp. 350-363.

Thorp, Willard, and Russell, Helen B. *Inventories During the World War.* Dun's Review. February, 1940, pp. 17-22.

INDEX

403

eBay® Business
ALL-IN-ONE DESK REFERENCE
FOR
DUMMIES®